Box 6

Intimate Strangers

RICHARD SCHICKEL

Intimate Strangers

THE CULTURE OF CELEBRITY

DOUBLEDAY & COMPANY, INC.
GARDEN CITY, NEW YORK
1985

ISBN 0-385-12336-1
Library of Congress Catalog Card Number 78-1246
Copyright © 1985 by Gideon Productions Inc.
All Rights Reserved
Printed in the United States of America

Library of Congress Cataloging in Publication Data

Schickel, Richard.
  Intimate strangers.

  1. United States—Popular culture—History—20th
century. 2. Fame—Social aspects—United States.
I. Title.
E169.12.S33   1985   306'.4

FOR CAROL

INTRODUCTION

The Peach Basket

Todd Andrews, protagonist and narrator of John Barth's lovely first novel, *The Floating Opera,* spent much of his time working on "An Inquiry" into the causes and circumstances of his father's suicide. His method of research consisted of making notes on relevant material and tossing them into three peach baskets and a cardboard carton he kept handy for that purpose. The difference between the way he worked on his inquiry into the great eschatological question and the way I've worked on my inquiry into the somewhat lighter question of celebrity and how it works pretty much comes down to file style. I began using manila folders and ended by transferring their contents to plastic dairy crates. I also suspect my cartons contained more clippings from newspapers and magazines than Todd's did, since my subject, inevitably, is more public than his was.

Still, our approach to our subjects was as similar as our methodologies were. We both came at them as ordinarily intelligent, ordinarily well-read men of middle age drawn to our topics almost against our will and with no desire to hurry to or through final composition of our inquiries. The action of *The Floating Opera* takes place on a day seven years after Todd began his inquiry; this book appears eight years after I contracted to write it and well over a decade after I began thinking about it.

That process began in the early seventies when David Bazelon, the late Leslie Farber, and I conceived the notion of collaborating on a book about the power of celebrity and how it works—on those who have it, on those who want it, and on a society like ours, which places a large and thoughtless value on it. David is a reformed lawyer, a social commentator, and now a professor at the State University of New York at Buffalo. Les was a psychiatrist whose collections of essays on the workings of the will constitute a distinguished contribution to the understanding of contemporary reality—and an intellectual legacy that grows in value with the passing years. I was then what I remain; a film critic with more than a passing interest in the history of that medium as well as in the other institutions that shape our popular culture, two of which—journalism and television—I have worked in for many years. We thought that by bringing our differing but complementary talents and interests to bear on this subject we might make a good book. I think we would have. But after exchanging many ideas we found ourselves defeated by the practicalities of collaboration, especially since we were all leading busy lives, full of distractions.

What remained from that period was my habit of collecting material on our subject, the habit of thinking about it at odd moments and then jotting down some of the ideas that occurred to me. When I had enough of them I mentioned my interest in celebrity to Sam Vaughan of Doubleday, who then contracted for this book.

My notion, unchanged from the beginning, was to do what a critical essayist does, not what a reporter does, and not what a sociologist or psychologist does, namely, to comment personally on a number of phenomena that are apparent to any fairly thoughtful and decently informed individual, and to make some connections between these phenomena that have previously been overlooked. I hoped, and still hope, that I could transfer a discussion that has up to now been held on a very casual basis to a somewhat more intense plane. Or, to put it simply, to stir things up a bit.

The more I worked, the more it seemed to me that perhaps the least profitable way of studying celebrity was through the lives of people who have acquired it as an unearned increment of success deserved or undeserved. It is much more interesting, and much more difficult, to consider it in another way, as the principle source of motive power in putting across ideas of every kind—social, political, aesthetic, moral. Famous people are used as symbols for these ideas, or become famous for being symbols of them. From this it follows that various institutions have found it convenient to play up and play off these figures— and not just for something as simple as advertising a product. They are turned into representations for much more inchoate longings; they are used to simplify complex matters of the mind and spirit; they are used to subvert rationalism in politics, in every realm of public life; and, most important, they are both deliberately and accidentally employed to enhance in the individual audience member a confusion of the realms (between public life and private life, between those matters of the mind that are best approached objectively and those that are best approached subjectively), matters that are already confused enough by the inherent tendencies of modern communications technology.

The result of all this is a corruption of that process of rational communication on which a democratic political system and reasonable social order must be based. Indeed, I have come to believe that those appalling acts of irrationality that have so shocked and disturbed us in the last two decades—the assassinations and the attempted assassinations of public figures—are far from being aberrations, given the workings of the celebrity system in our time; I have come to believe that they are, instead, the logical end products of that system and that those who perpetrate these dreadful acts may have a clearer perception of certain aspects of our shared reality than it is comfortable for the rest of us to acknowledge.

Such, at any rate, are some of the conclusions that finally arose over the years that were consumed by the actual writing of this book. I arrived at these conclusions reluctantly, and in some cases only after putting up a determined resistance to them. I cannot offer as much statistical evidence as a social scientist might; and I do not buttress my arguments with as many quotations from expert witnesses as a reportorial journalist might. Neither mode has ever had much appeal for me in any case, for it seems to me that both make use of tools too clumsy to capture the elusive quality of contemporary reality. Rather, I have chosen the mode that long ago chose me, that of the essayist, whose task, confronting any complicated object, is to invent a response of comparable complexity. Like any critic he must trust that what he sacrifices in "objectivity" (an illusory goal at best in this context) he may gain in finding some more interesting or more provocative level of insight. Like any responsible critic I want to start arguments, not end them, and ask of the reader only that he accord me earnestness in my effort. Nothing put forth in this volume was arrived at easily, for it seems to me that I virtually had to invent my subject as a coherent whole before I could start inventing an answering coherence of response.

But a subject it surely is. And perhaps merely by treating it as such, instead of as a minor adjunct of other subjects—politics, the arts, criminal psychopathy—merely by bringing together in one place a set of reflections on the many and disparate ramifications of celebrity everywhere we look in our culture, this book will perform its largest service. Once we begin to see that it has a power over us almost as transcendent as our sexual or monetary desires, we can begin, as individuals, to gain a better purchase on contemporary reality—and on our endlessly distracted, distractable selves. By ranging far and wide, by insisting on connections that I believe have not been generally noticed before, I hope to isolate celebrity for what it is: a—possibly *the* —most vital shaping (that is to say, distorting) force in our society.

Having said that, however, I must point out, in all objectivity, that like most works of social commentary this is a single-issue book. It therefore must not be imagined that I imagine we would magically achieve the good society merely by carefully addressing the issue it explores. Even if we achieved some kind of reform in the way we think about celebrity and the celebrated, there would remain all the other inequities and failings that plague us in our times.

I wish to acknowledge my indebtedness to several writers whose works have most influenced this one. I found as I explored my subject that though many had something to say that was useful in passing (and I hope all of them have been adequately acknowledged in the text), a handful had a shaping influence on my approach to my material. Most prominent among them are Jacques Ellul, Murray Kempton, and Garry Wills, who most deeply informed my chapter on politics; my colleague Robert Hughes, whose essays on art delight me in their expression almost as much as they startle and inform; Norman Mailer, whose analyses of the celebrity factor in almost every walk of American public life form the beginnings (and sometimes the end) of everyone's understanding of the subject; and George W. S. Trow whose remarkable book *Within the Context of No Context* illuminates this entire darkling plain. I must also thank the aforementioned Sam Vaughan for the witty tact with which he hectors writers about missed deadlines—and for being publishing's last gentleman. Sally Arteseros edited the manuscript with a deftness, grace, and conscientiousness that is especially to be treasured in an age when something called word processing seems to have replaced that antique art. Closer to my heart, I must once again acknowledge the love and patience of Carol Rubinstein, without whom nothing worthwhile is possible, with whom everything at least seems worth a try.

RICHARD SCHICKEL
New York City

ONE

Magic Bullets

It all coalesces in one malign, near-murderous moment.

The movie star president moves past the small crowd in the manner a half century of public life has bred into his bones—briskly, but with an unhurried air. The point is to seem at ease, in control, but to present the gawkers with no openings for intrusion, importunity, ugliness. One believes all the ex-presidents (and candidates) when they say that the fear of physical harm is not lively in them. But one also knows what they know: that the world is full of crazies, who will tear at your clothes, tear at your spirit, given half a chance.

There is one of them here today, one of the stock figures in the continuing drama of our national life. He is that lonely wanderer on the fringes of our consciousness, the kind of man we all brush past in our passages through the putrefying light of late night airports and bus stations and instinctively avoid, there being something in the self-absorbed intensity of his manner, some terrible onanistic privacy about him, that repels. In a matter of hours the details about this latest watcher in the shadows will have been filled in. They are the now familiar clichés—the cheap rooms, the junk food diet, the drifting path through life that leaves most people groping for any memory of him at all, with a few remembering an ordinary childhood, a few more recalling a passing distaste for him as an adult. His search for connections is thwarted by imbalances so palpable that even that legion of the damned, the American Nazi Party, rejected him.

But this time there is a difference in the portrait. It seems that John

W. Hinckley, Jr., had a focus not just for his hatreds, but for his frustrated impulse to love. He has been writing to an actress, a young woman of gift and seeming sobriety, who has become a freshman at Yale. At first she tosses his letters aside, as do all pretty women who appear in public, since they are constantly burdened by dismal missives of this kind. It is reported, in fact, that Jodie Foster, the recipient of Hinckley's unwanted attentions, received three thousand letters a month, and she is not truly a major star. Like her peers, she must know—and must try to ignore—the fact that she is constantly recruited, unwillingly, to work in degrading roles in the private cinemas of the male mind. It is best not to think about all that.

But a couple weeks before John W. Hinckley, Jr., made his attempt on the life of President Reagan there was, apparently, a sudden increase in the volume of mail from him to Miss Foster. This came soon after his visits to New Haven, when he took to delivering his letters personally, by slipping them under her door, and she became alarmed enough to turn some of the correspondence over to a school official, who gave them to the local police, who . . . did what with them?

No matter. What is known is that the movie running inside the would-be assassin's head was a distorted version of an actual film in which Jodie Foster had appeared, a blend of politics, sex, violence, and vengeance. It was the none too subtly ironic point of *Taxi Driver* to have the media as represented in that film misunderstand psychopathic behavior as a heroic act. Thus a lunatic originally bent on assassinating a politician is instead acclaimed for saving an adolescent (Miss Foster) from child prostitution, in the process winning her grateful love. Or, to put it another way: "Jody, I'm asking you please to look into your heart and at least give me the chance with this historic deed to gain your respect and love." Which is how John Hinckley put it to her in the letter discovered in his hotel room after he had fired the shots that would make him at least temporarily famous. People said they sounded like a car backfiring. People always say the shots sound like a car backfiring, even though cars don't backfire much anymore. But the witnesses know what they're supposed to say. They have read the accounts of previous shootings, and from them have gained a sense of the ritual's form and their proper place in the stylization the media imposes on these events.

Anyway, witnesses have nothing very useful to tell us about incidents of this kind. The invisible paths of the bullets trace connections equally invisible—connections that exist only in the mind of the man who pulls the trigger. It is only when the victim feels the pain—and then the rest of us do—that we begin to see, yet again, that invisible connections have real consequences.

In the aftermath of this episode, which, it need hardly be pointed out, is not without precedent in recent years, there were the predictable calls for legislation to control handguns—lack of which is a form of madness outside the scope of this book—and the usual observations about the role of television in particular, and the media in general, in encouraging emulative behavior in the psychopathic.

There is something in that, obviously. One is always struck, after the deed is done, by the wildly parodistic version of celebrity treatment that is accorded the criminal who has assaulted a well-known person. He gets a police escort and a motorcade whenever he emerges in public. He gets to make his well-guarded passages through crowds of the curious. He gets to feel the flashing lights of the photographers turned on him, hear the shouted questions of the reporters. For the first time in his hitherto anonymous life people will be curious about his history, his thoughts. In due course, his ravings may find their way into print. Or he will have his story told by a famous novelist.

But there is more to these murderous assaults on public figures than a desire to gun one's way to the top—though that explanation may, in fact, do for certain acts of terrorism in which, whatever political blather may surround them, the prime motive seems to be a desire to command media attention for some harebrained cause for a while. No, it seems to me that we are dealing, in recent years, with something more complex than the desperate, clutching reach of the psychopathic loner to assert his demented claim on those five minutes of celebrity that Andy Warhol once so famously predicted everyone would soon enjoy almost as a democratic right. It would be consoling if the matter were as simple as that, easier for us to understand and to process emotionally.

But just as the treatment of the criminal after his attack on a well-known individual parodies the privileges his victim enjoyed before he was struck down, so—I have come to believe—the criminal act itself parodies, with a dreadful viciousness, a very common relationship between the unfamous and the famous.

This new relation is based on an illusion of intimacy, which is, in turn, the creation of the ever tightening, ever more finely spun media mesh. These days, it seems to catch everyone up in an ensnarement that is not less powerful for being insidiously subliminal in its workings. In effect, it cancels the traditional etiquette that formerly governed not merely relationships between the powerful and the powerless, the known and the unknown, but, at the simplest level, the politesse that formerly pertained between strangers.

Most of us retain, in most of our private and professional dealings with people we don't actually know, a sense of their otherness, a decent wariness that protects both ourselves and the stranger from intrusion. But that shyness, if the term may be permitted, is not operative when we are dealing with celebrities. Thanks to television and the rest of the media we *know* them, or think we do. To a greater or lesser degree, we have internalized them, unconsciously made them a part of our consciousness, just as if they were, in fact, friends.

In its most benign form this new intimacy permits the suburban housewife to refer to the talk show hosts who relieve the isolation and boredom of her mornings or afternoons on a casual, first-name basis—Merv and Phil, Mike and Dick. They are, in a way, the modern icemen who cometh electronically. And it is always startling to hear one of these women holding forth on the latest doings and sayings of her daytime visitors. She gives the impression of having just returned from a tour of the Bel Air circuit with them, and in a way she has. For the audience picks up out of the air, as it were, the kind of chat you might actually overhear at an oversubscribed cocktail party full of well-known people—people with whom you might become tongue-tied if you were actually introduced to them, but to whom you also might unobtrusively sidle up in the hope of overhearing their conversation.

Some among us, however, are not tongue-tied. The people who make bold to address the celebrated when they venture forth into the ordinary world have, some of them, the good grace to be embarrassed when they approach their favorites but many are not in the least so. One is often struck, observing these meetings, by the palpable air of aggressiveness the unknown individual brings to them, a strange resentment that goes beyond simple envy and bespeaks, I think, a confusion of realms.

Some part of these people has been in intimate contact with the well-known individual for years. Secrets, hopes, and dreams have not exactly been shared with the celebrity, but he is somehow bound up in them. Another part of the approaching stranger's mind is, of course, aware that he is totally unknown to the celebrity. And he resents that unyielding fact. A chip grows on the shoulder. An undercurrent of anger is felt.

The situation is like an encounter with the old school chum or army buddy who has moved on up the social or professional ladder. The individual who "knew him when" is not entirely certain he will be recognized. As a result, he often does present himself badly, thus reinforcing the possibility that his worst fears about the encounter will turn into a self-fulfilling prophecy. In the encounter with the celebrity the working out of that worst-case scenario is virtually inevitable.

The celebrity, on his part—at least early in his fame—is puzzled by these encounters. The literature is full of variations on this theme: "They all know me; I don't know any of them." With experience of public life, the ability to maintain distance is developed. The rules of stardom were once summarized quite neatly by a lady who retired happily from the game, Esther Williams, of all people: "Walk fast. Don't stop and shake hands. You touch them, they don't touch you." You also learn to avoid eye contact, and that if you must give an autograph a simple hasty signature will suffice—no need to add some personal touch. Ideally the autograph should be granted indifferently, while you continue to carry on a conversation with someone else— which is one of the many uses of an entourage. When photographers are present, an almost imperceptible slowing of the pace, a quick, smiling glance in their direction will oblige them without putting the celebrity into the vulnerable full-stop position, where the goons can surround him.

All of this—common sense in action—naturally increases the resentment of the fan. Regal graciousness is not the response you want from old, good friends. What you want is to be able to tell them what they mean, have meant, to you, how they have inspired and consoled you, and, in turn, how sympathetic you have felt when you've heard about their troubles. A distant smile is not a sufficient response to intimacies of this character. The worst fears of rejection surface. And are expressed as democratic resentment: "Who does she think she is, anyway?" or, "Boy, does he think he's hot stuff." The formerly balanced equation between love and loathing tips.

But still we are in the realm of civility here. A case of the sulks, an awful feeling of embarrassment may follow one of these disappointing celebrity contacts. But not overt violence. Violence is the province of the psychopath, a last despairing attempt to get the loved object to acknowledge the lunatic's fantasy of intimacy as a reality. As in the case of John W. Hinckley, Jr. How could he accept that his all-consuming passion for Jodie Foster was purely a construct of his fevered imagination? It preoccupied so many of his hours, burned up so much of his psychic energy—impossible to believe that all that pain and longing were based on mere fantasy.

His unmailed letter makes all that clear. He had been skulking around New Haven, slipped those notes under Jodie Foster's door, had even apparently managed to reach her once or twice by telephone, and then felt "very good about the fact that you at least know my name and know how I feel about you." Hanging out around her dorm he had, he said, "come to realize that I'm the topic of more than a little conversation, however full of ridicule it may be." Acknowledgment! He had received acknowledgment! However reluctantly, distantly, derisively, she had become aware of his singular existence separated him from the crowd, took him into her consciousness. All unknowing, she had, in her way, violated Esther Williams's rules. John Hinckley had achieved more than most fans ever achieve. He boasted in bars about his relationship with her.

There remained only the problem of completing the connection. This was more than merely a matter of tightening his ties with Foster. Like any other lover, he wanted the whole world to see that there was a reality behind the dream, that it was not just the figment of his imagination. In other words, a still larger acknowledgment was required. Given the strained and distant relationship between John Hinckley, Jr., who was a loser, and John Hinckley, Sr., his father, who was a winner, and given the fact that, by common consent, the President of the United States is supposed to be everyone's ultimate father figure, everyone's ultimate winner, it is likely that two psychodramas became entangled at the point at which young Hinckley began to consider the ways and means of making visible—and historically indissoluble—the imaginary linkage between him and his beloved. And, of course, the politically powerful have traditionally exercised a terrible hold on the deranged psyche; one imagines more than one political assassin of the past has acted out in a need to symbolically murder his father. What is new in the matter of Hinckley vs. Reagan is the fact that the would-be assassin acted, it would seem, not so much as a performer in a drama that is explicable in coldly comforting Freudian terms, but out of a need to impress a famous woman who had not the slightest clue that she was his "lover." And then, of course, there is the fact that there was that movie plot to guide him in his planning.

We are dealing here with something unprecedented prior to recent years, the most appalling working out, acting out, of the habit of false intimacy with well-known people into which so many of us have fallen of late. John W. Hinckley, Jr., is assuredly a psychopath, and there is a difference of degree, therefore perhaps in kind, between his behavior and that of a middle-aged, middle-class woman first-naming talk show hosts in the beauty parlor, but there is an obvious analogy between the two types of self-deceptions, or, if you will, self-creations, and it grows increasingly clear that we live now in an age rife with such falsities.

Of self-creation, in our time, there is no end. In the final analysis, that is what this book is all about. But after the allusion to false intimacy here at the beginning, one other form of self-creation must also be mentioned, if only because it, too, must have been operative in the paradigmatic case of John W. Hinckley, Jr. That form resists characterization in a phrase but involves the ordinarily powerless person recasting life itself as a film and placing himself in the role of director, violently taking charge of formless existence and shaping it to his liking—every man his own *auteur,* the multitalented director-writer-star of his own drama. Surely after all those bus stations and airports, all those pawnshops and motels, John Hinckley had a need to exercise a creative role of this kind. That would show them!

It is as Brian De Palma, a movie director much criticized for the "violence" of his films, puts it: "I think there are a lot of psychopaths out there watching television—I don't think they're watching my movies particularly—and when they see someone like Gary Gilmore [the murderer turned into a celebrity by his refusal to fight the death penalty, and turned into something better than that, an existential hero, by Norman Mailer's book about him] giving press conferences they say, 'Hey, what am I doing in this motel room when I could be out there killing people, writing books, and being a celebrity.' "

In this connection one thinks of Theodore Robert Bundy, one of the most prolific mass murderers in American history, the killer-rapist of thirty-six women, and a man so outwardly charming that when the judge finally sentenced him to death he did so with visible regret—he spoke of the waste of talent Bundy represented and told him he would have made a good lawyer welcome to practice before the court then condemning him had circumstances been different. "Take care of yourself, young man, I say that to you sincerely," quoth the judge.

Interestingly, Bundy did not seem to care, at that point, whether he lived or died. Indeed, it seems he could have avoided the death sentence—*had he chosen to.* He could have copped a plea and received a seventy-five-year jail sentence rather than the electric chair. The trouble was, that did not fit his scenario. He wanted to have a full trial in which, acting as his own lawyer, he could play big scenes, which turned out to be dramatically satisfying (witness the way he won the judge) but which, in the end, led him to death row. A psychiatrist who examined him speculated that he killed to be caught, so he could stand in the spotlight the ensuing trial would focus on him, grab his moment on the evening news. "Mr. Bundy is the producer of a play which attempts to show that various authority figures can be manipulated, set against each other . . . Mr. Bundy does not have the capacity to recognize that the price for this 'thriller' might be his own life."

One wonders if anyone engaged in violent criminal activity involving any sort of premeditation fails to include in his calculations, these days, a Bundy-like contemplation of how the drama will eventually play in the media. And one is utterly certain that this ultimate dramatic effect has become a prime consideration—if not actually a motive—in planning almost all crimes of political violence, or to be more nearly accurate, violence to which political justification can be attached.

All of this—not to forget the basic theme of the chapter—naturally includes a great deal of false, violently enforced intimacy. It is a cliché of forensic psychiatry, not to mention common sense, that murder is the most intimate of acts, a dreadful forcing of attentions on the victim, who, in the kind of crime we are discussing here, is truly an innocent bystander, someone who just happens to find himself (or in Bundy's case, herself) in the path of the criminal's whirlwind dramaturgy. Hijacking and kidnapping, those favorite terrorist activities, also obviously involve a forced intimacy between perpetrator and victims. Again we see this terrible clutching at connection, a connection that the involvement of the media helps the madman to seal—not only between himself and the victim, but between himself and the previously indifferent world.

It's all television's fault. That sentence should probably be in quotation marks, since virtually everyone says it or thinks it when the talk turns not merely to celebrity, but to all the vast and radical changes that have afflicted our culture—perhaps, more properly, our ways of perceiving the cultural enterprise—in the last two or three decades.

Everyone speaks vaguely of the power of the medium, since it is self-evident that anything that can command so much of a nation's time, and is in itself such a potent economic entity, must be having a profound effect on all of us. Yet reading a compendium of research on this matter *(Televison and Human Behavior)*, one is struck by study after study indicating that most of us most of the time attend television in such a state of distracted stupefaction that it has, for instance, only the most marginal effect on political contests and is mostly useful in keeping those already committed to a candidate happy with their choice rather than in encouraging people to switch from one side to the other. Same way with the products it advertises. Mostly television keeps people content with the floor wax they're already using. Nor does it seem to encourage much in the way of emulative behavior. Most of the concern that television violence may breed real-life violence appears to be misplaced, in that there is no authenticated record of anyone watching a crime show and then going out and duplicating it on the street, unless, possibly, the viewer is for some reason already in a state of seething rage. In that case he may take a poke at his wife if she happens to cross his path during the commercial break. It is said, as well, that most criminal psychopaths watch very little TV. Why should they? Nothing fictional on television can compare, in emotional intensity, to the drama enacted before his mind's eye. What they do watch is what TV is pleased to call "actuality"—the drama into which the dimmest of them can imagine violently inserting himself.

But it must be doing something to us, this demanding, overgrown Venus's-flytrap that we have planted in the corner of the living room. And, of course, it is. The problem is that it has worked on us slowly, undramatically, in ways that are not measurable through conventional social science techniques. A subjective medium, it can be approached only subjectively. For the purposes of this book it seems to me to have one truly irresistible power arising out of its insinuating effect.

The power derives from television's ability to create the illusion of intimacy that we have been discussing here. It is the primary force in breaking down the barriers that formerly existed between the well-known and the unknown. This, of course, has something to do with the way it brings famous folk into our living room in psychically manageable size. By that I mean that we see them not from the alienating distance of the stage or lecture hall, which is where we were forced to view them in the preelectronic age, nor are they projected for us on very large screens, as they are in the movies, where scale helps to keep us humble before the image. The characterizations they offer in films, as they move through a fictionalized story, constantly remind us that these shadows are not necessarily what they seem to be, however "real" their art (and that of their fellow craftsmen) makes them appear to be. Beyond that, movies remain something of an occasion. We have to go out of our houses and sit in the darkness of the theater to watch them. It is not impossible to confuse what we see on the large screen with our daily reality, but it is fairly difficult to do so.

That much is obvious, perhaps. But there is more to the way television works on us than these matters of location and scale. There are within the conventions of the medium certain disorientating forces at work. Not long ago, when he retired as head of the photo archive he founded, Otto Bettmann voiced his dismay with the conventions of still picture taking in this century. In the nineteenth century, he noted, most people were photographed in a context, and pictures offered a multidimensional sense of an individual's place as well as his person. In the twentieth century the close-up has virtually replaced the medium and the long shot in portraiture. "Freudian," Bettmann calls close-up photography, though perhaps "pseudo-Freudian" would be closer to the mark. In any event, the close-up not merely encourages a sense of intimacy, but more than that, invites us to read character into the face, to formulate, from the lines and wrinkles therein, an impression easily mistaken for a detailed, knowledgeable portrait of the star. And television is, par excellence, a close-up medium, particularly in the reality shows.

It is interesting, in this connection, to observe that those performers who make important careers in the other media, who become "stars" capable of drawing paying customers into movies or the theater, are almost never drawn from television's dramatic and comedy series where, of course, the players are always situated in a more or less well-detailed fictional setting. Some actors, if their series runs long enough, become very familiar to us and receive our affectionate—if slightly distant—regard. But the stars this medium has created, the ones who command our greatest interest, are, for the most part, performers who appear as themselves, or as what we are gratified to think of as themselves. Johnny Carson is the most obvious example of this phenomenon, but one cannot forget that just by sitting there and reading the news Walter Cronkite became, according to the polls, the most trusted man in America. But the paradigm is, perhaps, Burt Reynolds. He had had a couple of television series, some starring roles in some forgettable movies, but was, in the mid-sixties, just another pretty face. Then he went on the talk shows and by frankly kidding himself and his image—a process notably aided by posing for a parodistic nude photo in *Cosmopolitan*—turned himself into a beloved figure through what amounted to an artful bit of naturalistic acting, a presentation of a partial self that was both vulnerable and believable. Something similar happened to James Garner, a reliable and well-liked light leading man in films and television for many years, when he started doing his Polaroid commercials. In these most mini of mini-dramas, a woman who was not his wife (Mariette Hartley) played his wife, and their affectionately querulous exchanges actually made TV audiences feel they were catching the star appealingly off guard, that they were getting to know him in the same way they had got to know Old Burt in his seemingly unguarded conversations with Johnny.

But note: none of the people just mentioned appears before us in anything that can be described as a normal or natural setting. Carson's —anyone's—talk show proceeds in a context that resembles nothing so much as the VIP lounge in an airport. That is to say, it seems to have a vague, historical relationship to the furnishings and ambience of a living room, but we are ever aware that it is not something most of us could settle into very comfortably for any length of time. It would take a heap a livin'—not to mention a heap of imagination—for that to happen. The newspeople come to us from settings that imply a beehive of journalistic enterprise, but bear roughly the same relationship to a genuine newspaper city room that Carson's set does to a living room. Both have been sterilized and departicularized. As for the Garner commercials, there were hints of a backyard, dining room, hallways, all with homey trappings in them, but only hints. Based on the clues we could pick up—a palm frond slightly out of focus in the corner of a shot, for instance—the Garner-Hartley manse was suburbia generalized, but done so in a manner as blandly impersonal as Carson's "living room."

That is just the point. The close-ups and the lack of a realistic, individuated setting in television are precisely what permit these crea-

tures of the electronic limbo—that nowhere that is anywhere and everywhere—to work so powerfully on us. Since they are rootless, unat-
tached to any recognizable place, we are able, if we like, to relocate
them anywhere that suits the purpose of our fantasies.

If we want to, we are able, over months and years of study in
television's clean rooms, to learn these faces as we learn those of our
best friends and relatives. Their tics and blinks and glances, we come
to know them so well. The secret thoughts and emotions they seem to
reveal through their unconscious gestures—we can read them at a
glance. (How cleverly Johnny, for example, without our ever being
overtly rude to him, lets us share his sense that a guest is bombing.)
Indeed, the absence of distracting setting helps to throw everything
into high relief: that cockeyed grin—so ingenuous; that modest downward glance—so appealing; that suddenly beaming smile—so open.
And there is nothing present to betray the performer—no personal
note in the setting that bespeaks an excess of intellect or ego or obsession that would counter or undermine the image that accretes over the
months and years of studying the close-up, which being performers (a
fact easily forgotten amid the studied informality of actuality television) they are trained to control.

Yes, it is true, no one can project a personality totally foreign to his
nature. But yes, that projection can be no more than a remembrance
of things past when you have become rich and alienated from your
roots and contemptuous of an audience that, you have come to understand, is so easily lulled and gulled by your little show. But keeps
coming up to you anyway, when you venture off the stage, innocently
expecting you to be the you it thinks it knows so well. No wonder the
relationship between the modern performer and his following is so
volatile, so marked by paranoia. The star has a secret—lots of them,
actually. And the crowd suspects he might have. And so must test
him, by offering precisely the friendliness he appears to invite. It is a
wonder this relationship is not marked by more violence, or anyway
by more of the terrible misunderstandings to which John W. Hinckley,
Jr., found himself prey.

"To photograph is to appropriate the thing photographed," Susan
Sontag remarks. And "There is an aggression implicit in every use of
the camera." Yes. And though television does not freeze moments
forever, as still photography does, it has an appropriative and aggres-

sive function. This is not serious for those who appear only occasionally on the tube. Their brief moments of exposure evaporate into the air, lost in the media hum of the age. But for those who must put themselves constantly at the mercy of the cathode ray, it is a problem. They are, after all, volunteers for this duty; no one is forcing them to undertake it. Therefore people think they must like it, need it. And some do, of course.

But like it or hate it, their lives in the public eye implicitly encourage appropriation and aggression. Even victims—people thrust into the news because they happened briefly to get in the way of history or of some lunatic convinced that he was history—are forced to endure this final victimization (which is akin to the often discussed second humiliation, at the hands of hospital personnel, police, and the legal machine, that a rape victim is forced to endure when she seeks redress). When the American hostages were finally returned from Iran, a State Department spokesman was quoted in the press as saying that they "would be free either to cooperate with news organizations and *become celebrities* or to withdraw quickly into private life" (emphasis added). Most chose the latter course after submitting to the orgy of welcome that was staged mainly for the benefit of the press. In a way, it was a well-managed business, a quick, healthy venting of built-up media steam. But surely there was no choice in this matter for this put-upon group. There really never is.

Be that as it may, since television has breached the walls of polite convention that formerly separated performer and audience, the well-known and the unknown, everyone now jostles rudely and noisily to exploit the opening in the defenses. They all pour through it, wave upon wave of journalists and pseudojournalists. They are, of course, abetted by modern technology. The jet plane, for example, can whisk the paparazzi to the most isolated of retreats. The telephoto lens permits the lurking photographer to sneak up on the famous, while the motor-driven shutter allows him to squeeze off many shots quickly—assuring him of at least one salable snap before the security men move in or the celebrated person pulls himself together and assumes his public face and posture. Lightweight film and tape cameras add to the mobility of the paid gawkers surrounding the famous.

In recent years, as a result of these "advances," we have been treated to glimpses, through a lens blurrily, of the contours of many famous breasts. Or to put the point as precisely as possible, we have been made privy to the breasts, et cetera, of many women whose fame does not rest on the display of their physical charms. For example, a former First Lady, the Princess of Monaco, even, for heaven's sake, that aged recluse, Greta Garbo. This is not to mention the many well-known actresses whose unit publicists did not control the output of their stillsman as carefully as they promised they would (or didn't notice the grip with a camera up on the grid). Outtakes of similarly unprotected moments, caught by the motion picture camera, somehow make their way from the trim barrel in the editing room to the pages of the less respectable skin books as well. From time to time the newsstands indeed offer one-shot magazines bearing some such title as *Celebrity Skin* (which at least meets the truth-in-advertising standard). What price the frisson provided by the forbidden or the unlikely? A suggestion: a sizable proportion of the male population is constantly being reduced to the status of the preadolescent, peering through the keyhole as his sister takes a bath. And that says nothing about legitimate feminine outrage over this exploitation.

But if the whole world went around swathed in the robes of Araby, the ubiquitous cameraman would still find a way to catch the famous engaged in some unflattering—or anyway, all too human—pose or activity. And the person with the notebook would be there to overhear their mots and squabbles, or to somehow persuade one of their intimates to discuss the state of their marriages or their affairs. For far more important than the technological developments that make the task of these professional voyeurs easier is the fact that, under the impress of television, there is now a powerful drive among all news-gathering organizations to obtain intimate behind-the-scenes, unofficial material. It's all a matter of competition.

It may have begun with Edward R. Murrow, when he successfully bifurcated into what the estimable Michael Arlen reminds us the equally estimable John Lardner called "the higher Murrow" (he who conducted *CBS Reports)* and "the lower Murrow" (he who conducted *Person to Person)*. In the latter enterprise, he presented his fellow newsmen with the example of a man who desperately did not wish to be stopped at the door of the Journalist's Club ("Sorry, Mr. Murrow, but the ethics committee met while you were out of town; I have to ask you for your membership card") just because he trafficked in electronic gossip. One recalls how Murrow congealed with embarrassment as famous people ushered his cameras through their homes, his attempts at light badinage as awkward as a headmaster trying to tell a risqué story at an alumni smoker. But, of course, that awkwardness, that discomfited air, doubtless sincere in Murrow's case, could be used as a *technique* by others. That is to say, if you gave the impression of embarrassment, even if you weren't, you could impart to intrusion and gossip the same respectable air that Murrow gave it with his gingerliness. The trick was to look like a serious fellow unbending, just a becoming tad, showing his human side. It was rather endearing.

The downward path from Murrow to Barbara Walters, who asks fanzine questions with the same stern inquisitor's tone that other reporters bring to the investigation of high crimes and misdemeanors, has taken some years to map out, but it is trod now not just by the wayward individual, but by institutions. Indeed, the old-fashioned gossip columnist, once the member of a powerful if entirely unrespectable clan, is virtually defunct. The august network news departments are the managers of the most important daily purveyors of chat— "Today" and "Good Morning, America." CBS News invented the "magazine" format, and if the celebrity interview is a staple part of the "60 Minutes" formula, it is something more than that over at competing "20/20." In print, the gossip sections of the newsmagazines grow in space (and in the deployment of color pictures). *People* is a huge success, and it has spawned its imitators. *The Star* and the *National Enquirer* abide, with their quack diets, miracle cures for common diseases, and astrological frissons, promising readers the same beauty and freedom from life's ordinary ills that their pieces about famous people seem to imply that the favored enjoy.

Meantime, in the newspapers, the number of interviews and profiles continues to rise, particularly in the style and arts sections which almost all dailies with any pretense to stature have added in recent years. As for the magazines that aspire to the same middle-class audience, content analyses reveal that the sort of people they profile has changed radically over the last half century or so. Where once the balance was tipped in favor of politicians, inventors, and entrepreneurs (when our most profound interest was in the process of acquiring wealth), it began swinging over to entertainers in the late twenties and early thirties. After World War II established new levels of mass prosperity, that trend was enhanced, for "celebrity" in the modern sense of the term is, among other things, a function of prosperity. Having learned from those the popular culture featured in its earlier incarnations how to make it, we now seek to discover, among other things, how to spend it. That is to say, we look to the mass media for glimpses of the good life, for models of public display, on the off chance that our prosperity might correlate somehow with at least local fame. Even if it doesn't, it's nice to know how an admired figure decorates her house, or herself, or for that matter, her poodle. Doing nicely, thank you, many of us can at least emulate the trappings of fame.

But we digress. The point to bear in mind is that gossip and news have very largely been desegregated in recent times. It was never easy to draw a firm line between them, but at least in the old days, the hard-core gossipists, purveying the latest chat from New York, Hollywood, and Washington, were set off typographically in the newspaper: one could not mistake Walter Winchell's "pillar" for Walter Lippmann's; the latter wrote in whole sentences, each thought separated by a single period instead of by three of them. And besides, Walter and Hedda and Louella—that crowd—were always presented rather sheepishly, if at all, in journals of any aspiration to quality, typically tucked around the movie ads—they lived in the slums, as it were.

They have gone away now. And their heirs and successors do not have the power the legends once had to command public morality for or against errant subjects or, for that matter, to command an exclusive. In an age when everyone deals in gossip—and calls it "the new journalism" or "investigative reporting"—no single journalist (if even that modest term is not too dignified for this discussion) can claim to exclusively possess a secret long enough for it to convey any power to him. Besides, the same impulses—those of a ferret—can be more profitably, and more stylishly, put to use in the newer forms, where, for example, participants in a large event are asked to comment on what their thoughts were as it unfolded and even what they think the thoughts of others caught up with them in, say, the Vietnam tragedy or the Watergate scandal might have been. And if memory is imprecise or absent, the journalist can always make it up. No footnotes asked. Gossip is still gossip (and still nobody's business) but you can hit the bestseller charts with *All the President's Men* and win prizes, too. It reads like literature, or serious history, and you don't have to feel like a second-class citizen when you write it.

But—to call it by its rightful name—this higher gossip also heightens our sense of false intimacy with celebrated people. Beyond that, it further blurs the line between fantasy and reality, a line that is essential if we are to keep our bearings in a complex world. We really have no guarantee, beyond the reporter's word of honor, that these recollections and speculations about the thought processes of people in crisis, or just people at the top, are not made up. It seems significant that for the first time in the history of those awards a Pulitzer Prize had to be withdrawn in 1981 when the piece for which it was given turned out to be at least in part a semifiction (but no more so, actually, than a lot of other contemporary journalism). Again, if one were to seek the source of this impulse to combine sources, to put into quotation marks what must be at best recollections of conversations, to impute interior monologues to people who surely cannot remember any better than the rest of us what they must have been thinking in some historic moment, it must again be identified a competitive one. Television shares with the movies the ability to "photograph thought" (the phrase is D. W. Griffith's). Or nonthought, as Roger Mudd's celebrated interview with Teddy Kennedy showed—a few simple questions, rather diffidently put, demonstrated that the would-be candidate was not a very coherent critic of his opponent, was an inarticulate advocate of his own positions—and, after all those years, still hadn't got his story straight on Chappaquiddick. That single hour of television may well have cost him a presidential nomination.

In effect, the new print journalism strives—strains—to achieve a similar effect, often at the expense of the traditional standards of the craft, that is, by employing the techniques of fiction to enliven allegedly factual material and to give it a knowing tone. As for investigative journalism, much of what it perforce reports as fact is, especially in the story's early stages of development, rumor and supposition, and it depends for its effectiveness on the accretion of detail that will induce what the novelist must induce, the willing suspension of disbelief. Thus, when Woodward and Bernstein report, at the end of their second book on Watergate, a loopy Nixon wandering the midnight corridors of the White House, talking to the portraits on the wall, or requiring his Secretary of State to drop to his knees and join him in prayer, we believe principally because throughout the work of these authors we are presented with hundreds of neutral, prosaic details that lend spurious credibility to the notion of a presidential paranoid running amuck. (If they have the furniture of the room right, then they must have the furniture of the mind right, too.)

Perhaps this was a true portrayal—the evidence of our own eyes, witnessing his mad television appearances, did nothing to contradict that vision of Richard Nixon. But how can we ever know for certain?

For the evidence on which the portrait is constructed is by its nature tainted. That is, it is provided by witnesses who have their own interests to protect or advance, perhaps their own grievances to redress. And just because Nixon became the dark star of our time and place, the symbol of the American Dream's downside, it is unwise to ignore the fact that what was done to him can as well be done to more palatable figures. When Carl Bernstein, co-author of *All the President's Men,* joined with a new collaborator to write a keyhole view of the Supreme Court *(The Brethren),* it was evident that much of the reporting was based on the gossip of the justices' law clerks, and hence bound to be spiteful stuff, since, just as no man is a hero to his valet, no judge can cut a very grand figure to the bright and ambitious young person who does his fetching and carrying.

But the point is not to once again observe that changing journalistic standards create changing journalistic problems (and there were plenty with the old ones of impersonality and objectivity). The point to ponder is, finally, not only how our new journalism, both print and video, changes our perception of prominent people who function as symbolic leaders, but how the quality of those symbols, the very way they function, has changed.

"No one governs," says Joseph Heller, the novelist. "Everyone performs." "The White House is now entirely a TV performance," says the McLuhanite anthropologist Edmund Carpenter, and his exaggeration is only slight.

To a degree, politics has always been a performance. It attracts people whose egos ache for instant gratification very much in the manner of actors, that is to say, people who require the balm of immediate applause. But until recently there was a separation between public man and private man, an understanding on everyone's part that so long as the politician did not number corruption among his personal habits, what he did or did not do when he was outside the public eye was pretty much his own business. Of course, word leaked out about a president's reading habits (or lack of them), culinary preferences, hobbies, vacation resorts, what-have-you. But little enough was made of all this. Roosevelt, for instance, was able to carry on an affair with his sometime secretary for many of his presidential years without anyone knowing. Nowadays, we know when a president's hemorrhoids are acting up—and "Saturday Night Live" does skits about this undignified affliction.

But ours is not to sympathize unduly with the modern politician, any more than we need sympathize unduly with the beleaguered movie star. The price one pays, in terms of violated privacy, when one enters upon either of these trades has been so well established, for so long, that it is virtually a condition of employment. If you don't like it, you don't have to sign on. No, the matter is more serious than personal inconvenience. In the realm of governance, we are now ever at risk of control by a new kind of charismatic leader. As Richard Sennett, whose work in this field is seminal, points out, such a leader need not be a demagogue, someone who uses his power to foment violence. As he observes in *The Fall of Public Man,* beginning sometime in the nineteenth century we began focusing on what the public personality felt, rather than on what he did, so "If a person could reveal himself in public and yet control the process of self-disclosure, he was exciting." This "psychic striptease" is in itself arousing, even though nothing very clear is revealed. The point is merely to render us passive at the performance, and thus malleable.

The consequences are, perhaps, obvious. At the simplest level the politician works a shell game. He dines with an ordinary worker at the very moment he enacts a law that is against the best interests of the very person with whom he is breaking bread, but we are so engaged by this demonstration of homeyness that we pay scant heed to the consequences of the new law. Or—Sennett's example again—the politician plays golf with a beloved comedian and distracts the old folks, whose own sedate golf games are jeopardized by a cut he is about to make in the social security program.

But beyond this kind of issue-oriented deception, there are other, larger forces constantly working in modern politics. For example, personality is used to defuse and deflect ideological complexities, thereby permitting the political process to proceed smoothly, that is to say, mindlessly, with everyone clinging to the center, and the candidates differentiating themselves one from the other by personality rather than by resorting to inconvenient principle. The trick, as Sennett sees it, is for the candidate to hide the "misfortune" of ideological commitment by focusing his audience's attention on his human impulses and offering a vision of controlled spontaneity, so that he appears to be acting out of an understandable personal need or desire, rather than out of devotion to some abstract, possibly incomprehensible, therefore disturbing belief. "Narcotic charisma," Sennett memorably calls this disguise of intellectual process as emotional commitment.

The road to this pass stretches further back in history than is readily apparent, but there is no question that television, and the media forced now to compete with it on its own "personalistic" terms, greatly accelerated our arrival there. As Sennett observes, we tend to watch and hear the politician in isolation, in our houses, away from the hurly-burly of political tours and meetings of the pretelevision age, where the potential for inconvenient outbursts and questions was always there, where the very formality of the occasion (and the distance of speaker from audience) tended to throw attention on issues rather than on personality. Moreover, TV insists that the leader speak to us softly, informally, as equals, and this treatment "becomes the means of avoiding ideological questions, and leads to a focus of the politician's person, the perception of his motives being something which everyone can appreciate and share."

This is clearly a complex subject and one to which we shall return, but a couple of consequences are worth pointing out now. The first is the breakdown of traditional party loyalties. Every poll in recent years has recorded the decline in these allegiances, and a different kind of sampling—the relentless polling of the citizenry's attitudes by candidates who now spend 60 to 70 percent of their campaign budgets on television—makes them instantly susceptible, instantly responsive, to every moody twitch of their constituencies. This encourages them, of course, to trim principles on the spot and forces even those who would prefer not to, to cut themselves free of those slow-moving institutions the parties, which, as journalist Lance Morrow has written, "served to organize possibilities, to discipline people and ideas into workable forms."

Morrow adds, "When practically every politician is a free agent, there is a tendency toward the anarchic, which may be a perfect political reflection of this narcissistic age." And, sadly, the press itself does almost nothing to discourage this trend. Quite the opposite, it goes with the flow. A recent Brookings Institution report on the Washington press corps, for example, shows that the journalistic enterprise in the capital has expanded along with the size of the government, and that though reporters are often dissatisfied with the emphasis on breaking news, and would, they insist, write longer, more reflective pieces if only their editors wanted them, most of them, when queried, said that if they were given more time they would use it "simply to do more interviews." In other words, they would continue to emphasize personality at the expense of ideas.

Moreover, though they all acknowledge that coverage of the federal regulatory agencies, those bureaucracies that make most of the decisions that most directly affect the quality of the individual's life, is inadequate, most of the press corps do not want to take on the assignment. In the words of the report, written by Stephen Hess, "heavy reliance on documents makes the beat 'dull,' 'boring,' 'drudgery'— words that are repeated over and over." No less than their readers do the reporters want to personify events and ideas, to find the individual who can conveniently symbolize an issue and thereby render it quickly and easily comprehensible. The same process, of course, proceeds elsewhere in the society, notably in the realm of culture and the arts, but it is obviously further advanced in politics, and, equally obviously, has the most dangerous potential consequences for society here.

🖐 🖐

Dangerous consequences! We so quickly circle back upon ourselves! For if politics has become personality, if the drive of the politician today must be to emphasize his commonality, his close personal identification with his constituency, and if this identification is achieved through a constant demonstration, before the cameras and the reporters, of his "human interest," then it stands to reason that in some cases the identification will work all too well. Mark David Chapman, who killed John Lennon, had identified so well with his victim that he apparently became convinced that he, Chapman, was Lennon, and Lennon was an imposter, a usurper of his life. He may have thought other famous people had done the same. He had a hit list of them. Johnny Carson was on it.

John W. Hinckley, Jr., had not gone quite that far. He had merely misidentified himself as a movie star's potential lover, a man in need of a deed to suitably impress her. But who can doubt also that this personally agreeable President, so warm and jokey and friendly, did not remind him all too well of some benign-appearing, yet disapproving, perhaps emotionally unreachable, perhaps frustratingly inimitable, authority figure in his own life. After all, both his father and his President were self-made men, men who had mastered the great American art of creating out of the common clay of themselves, enviable careers. The rest of the Hinckley family knew the family of George Bush, Reagan's Vice President. They moved near the top—

and their second son drifted along the bottom, lost in his own thoughts, tangled in them really, so tangled that he could no longer sort out real intimacies (or lack of them) from false ones.

And so the shots were fired. And five hours later, when the Secret Service was interrogating him, John Hinckley had a question of his own for the agents: "Is it on TV?" he eagerly asked. For the social commentator his act makes a catchy lead, and in its aftermath the victim becomes, if anything, still more human, less ideologically distanced than ever by his somewhat novel beliefs. His jokes, his good spirits during the days of his recuperation warmed us all. The political pundits counted this near tragedy as a plus for his program, his good recovery coupled with his repeated demonstrations of an attractive élan helped to disarm both critics and suspicions about some of the programs he was peddling.

We have come a very long way in a very short time, from the politics, the culture, into which most of us were born. We have come a very long way in a very short time from our former social contract to our present existential improvisations. We have come a very long way in a very short time to our present isolation, subjectivity, and desperate hope that the cult of personality may substitute for a sense of organization, purpose, and stability in our society. How we made the journey, what we have found, and how—inadequately—we are coping with it is what this book is about.

TWO

Where We Came In

First basic assumption: there was no such thing as celebrity prior to the beginning of the twentieth century. In fact, even though well-known people in the second and third decades of this century began to behave in a manner that we would now identify as celebrity-like, the term itself did not come into common currency until very recently. Forty years ago, when I was growing up, the word "celebrity" was almost never used in print, in conversation, in any sort of discourse, civilized or casual. Most of the people one read about in the papers, or heard about on the air, or who were the subject of magazine profiles, were "successful" or "famous." Sometimes they were both, but not necessarily. And if they were both, it was understood that there was a logical progression to their achievements. First, one did well in one's craft or business or profession—something that set one apart. Thereafter, one might or might not become famous, a condition one might or might not enjoy, but which assuredly one could regulate, so that it did not become a nuisance, or worse, actually begin to distort one's personality, interfere with the discharge of one's duties, or render one tiresome to others.

Occasionally, to be sure, a suspicious character appeared in the public eye, generally an actor or an actress, sometimes a pop musician or an overheralded rookie sports star—a "phenom" as the type was referred to in the latter realm—who did not seem to have endured the seasonings of arduous apprenticeship, that compound of false hope, wrong turns, and brief disappointments, which, in the traditional scheme of things, serve as earnests of good and sober intent. One tended to regard these figures with a certain reserve, to withhold admiration and affection until they had proved themselves.

Then again, one occasionally heard of untoward or excessive behavior, mob psychosis of one sort or another, being visited on a well-known personage. In 1942, for instance, scenes of adolescent rapture in near-riotous eruption attended the appearances of Frank Sinatra at New York's Paramount Theatre, and they were widely reported and commented upon in the press—often accompanied by gloomy interpretations of what they might portend for the future of civilization. As we will shortly have reason to reflect upon, occurrences of this sort were hardly unknown in human history. And, of course, the next decades would witness many more of them.

But these were, and continue to be, isolated outbursts of teen madness—something to do with hormones probably. They have very little to tell us about the more subtle and permanent power of celebrity, as we now define it, to cloud men's minds and to change our traditional modes of apprehending the world and responding to the world. For the moment it is important only to note that until very recently our relationship with the celebrated was as simple as it is now complex, and that our words of choice in referring to the well-known—"fame," "famous," "famed"—which derive from the Latin *fama*, meaning "manifest deeds," still meant, as late as the 1940s, something like what it had meant down through the millennia of Western civilization; it was the by-product of concrete, commonly agreed upon, perhaps even measurable, achievement. And it continued to carry, as it did in its original usage, the implication that the ability to perform such deeds, to attain such achievements, was connected to the concept of "virtù," meaning that nothing of great moment was likely to be accomplished by individuals who did not carry within themselves a singular prowess —a moral quality if nothing else—which probably began as a gift of God, but which was certainly developed as a result of stern self-discipline, pursued—often—without hope of worldly reward. That, naturally, was sometimes thrust upon the successful individual, along with fame. But it was to be accepted modestly, and some portion of the receipts of success was expected to be returned to the giving world in the form of good works or, at the very least, in a manner that was democratically self-deprecating, lacking in public pomp.

Yes, there had once been royalty, and rulers from the beginning of history had occasionally showed themselves to their public who, assuming their kingdoms were at the time peaceable, responded with awe and fervor to these brief glimpses of the mighty. And, yes, in more modern but still simple times, well-known people who were not to manor or manner born, but who had captured the hearts and minds of the populace, were received in the kingly style. Before Sinatra at the Paramount there had been, of course, Lisztomania in Europe. And well-favored actresses had had their carriages pulled through the streets by smitten young men. From time to time a traveling divine, a touring actor, a campaigning politician would sweep some crowd away by the power of their performance. The frenzy they occasionally elicited during the romantic nineteenth century, when it first occurred to the masses that a touch of talent might be the visible manifestation of a touch by God, that people might rule in the realms of art and rhetoric as their majesties did in the political realm—that is, by divine right—would seem entirely familiar to a modern rock star.

But the tone of the relationship between the admired and their admirers was quite different from that with which we are familiar today. It was not based on an imagined intimacy fostered by the media. On the contrary, it was based on a palpable reality, namely, the vast gulf that ordinarily separated the favored from the ill-favored, or the merely unfavored.

Given the state of communications and transportation throughout most of the nineteenth century, there was no way to regularly and conveniently bridge the distance between the prominent minority and the anonymous mass. Telegraphy communicated words, but not voices or images. Trains could, and did, inch their way across the country, but even actors who spent most of their lives on tour did not reach more than a tiny portion of their potential public in the course of a year, which is why, for instance, *The Count of Monte Cristo* or *Sherlock Holmes* could serve as exclusive vehicles for actors like James O'Neill and William Gillette, whose careers stretched on into our century. Reputations grew, as it were, by rumor, and by the time you got to see one of these stars you were acutely conscious that you had been given, literally, a once (or, at most, twice) in a lifetime opportunity to enter into the admired presence. It is no wonder that the reception for performers of this type was likely to be more impassioned than those we are now accustomed to. The audience was being presented with an opportunity to express the pent-up longings of the

years in these encounters, and so their gratitude was likely to be tu-
multuous—as was their disappointment if the star failed to live up to
expectations. The now vanished tradition of the rotten vegetable
hurled at the stage is very much a thing of this former historical
moment.

It was all very primitive, a historical curiosity as we look back on it.
Except that the mention of rock stars at the beginning of this section
was not idle, for in their world this model is still operative. Yes, of
course, their records circulate in the millions and are instantly available to all and sundry. But a recording is an abstraction, an offering of
but one aspect—albeit the most significant aspect—of the sacred presence. It is especially so considering the electronic wizardry that nowadays goes into making a disk—all that overdubbing and what-not—
enhancing, amplifying, and to a degree distorting the original performance.

When they are not recording, pop stars hold themselves very scarce.
They grant few print interviews and are almost never seen on the talk
shows or in films—other than videos, those carefully produced, tanta-
lizingly brief glimpses of them. They are not even observed very often
in public, at premieres or parties, or just dining out. Movie stars are, in
that sense, much more accessible as a rule. Indeed, most pop stars are
positively reclusive in their private lives, seem to have little to do with
their musical peers, even have less to do with their celebrity equals
from other realms, a pattern that is not at all similar to that of actors,
for example, or politicians, who, in the modern world, are constantly
trying to rub up against one another.

This reclusiveness, of course, adds to the sense of mystery surrounding the musicians. Just what goes on behind the high walls of their
isolated estates? Who are those anonymous women who are invited to
join the bands there? Rumors of outlawry abound. Or, if not outlawry,
then licentiousness. One thinks of life in a decadent court.

One also thinks, ironically, of life in a modern court. Royalty famously has no function anymore except the symbolic one. Especially
in the grandest of democratic monarchies, the United Kingdom, the
royals are supposed to exemplify the best, or anyway the most commonly held, values of their subjects—in this case that vague congeries
of niceties known as "middle-class values." In particular they are expected to be cheerfully dutiful as they go about their stupefying
rounds—opening agricultural fairs, visiting day care centers, paddling
about in the remnants of empire, neither patronizing nor anthropolog-

ical about the strange native ceremonies staged for their benefit. They cannot go into a studio and record their public appearances. Thus, wherever they go—including into attempted seclusion at one of their several castles—they cannot escape the prying camera eye. Which becomes particularly avid when, as it must to all bourgeois families, trouble comes—auntie has an indiscreet affair, the younger son hangs about with loose women, the daughter behaves in spoiled and sullen fashion. Even joy has its downside, as when the son and heir takes a bride or becomes a father, and finds himself, with his lady, fiendishly hounded by the press. Even when nothing much is going on in the family—perhaps especially at those times—the idle journalistic mind becomes a devil's workshop of rumor, innuendo, and loony speculation. By the winter of 1983 the House of Windsor—a royal wedding and a royal accouchement having whipped public interest in their doings to unprecedented heights, and the press into paroxysms of effort to keep a best-selling story alive—was begging for mercy.

Only a little of that quality, quite strained at that, was forthcoming. And it was wrapped in a bunting of hypocrisy. For what everyone was dealing with was an irony that dared not speak its name. That was that the royals, in their total functionlessness, had become the purest of celebrity phenomena. A rock star, by contrast, has infinitely more real work to do, and can claim its demands—composing his songs and recording them, or making his video on a closed set, or simply resting from the obvious rigors of a tour—as plausible reasons for demanding a surcease from his public importunings. In that sense he is like royalty in former times, when the duties of statecraft could always be invoked against public display. Modern royalty has no such excuse available. On the contrary, their only job is to disport themselves agreeably before their subjects, and anything short of illness which denies the public or its tribunes access to them can be—and usually is —seen as bad sportsmanship if not bone laziness or worse.

What a role reversal is here! The ultimate democratization of public life—the commoner treated as ruler, the ruler treated as exploitable commoner.

This is not to say that ordinary folks treat royalty casually when the latter may be encountered in the flesh. One need only join a street-corner crowd in London anticipating the passage of Her Majesty's limousine to sense the hum of anticipatory excitement the possibility of even so brief and distant an encounter generates. But it is not exactly like being witness to The Jackson Farewell Tour either. For by maintaining the traditional royal distance from their panting adolescent fans (and, most important, rigidly controlling press access to the sacred presence), the pop stars increase, of course, the emotional resonance of their very occasional tours—usually undertaken no more often than once every two or three years—and turn them into events of major significance for their devotees.

But, curiously, these too hold frustrations for their fans. For the groups cannot play in intimate surroundings. Their homes away from homes are huge arenas, where it is impossible to come close to the idols. The sound is deafening and, in its way, distancing—a wall of noise. Pot, or whatever other drugs are brought into the hall by the crowd, which is essentially unpoliceable, also has its distancing effect. So there is proximity but no intimacy, and, in the end, the occasion seems perversely designed to frustrate the very emotional connection which its anticipation seems to promise. They are—the Stones, the Dead, the Who, the Whoever—so near and yet still so far. No wonder these encounters sometimes turn deadly.

Not too long ago, when much of the adult culture was determined to romanticize the youth culture, these rock frenzies seemed more significant than they presently do. Now they begin to seem isolated phenomena and, seen in perspective, a stirring of antique—not to say almost irrelevantly primitive—emotions. They represent a curious eddy in a historic tide that has run for most of this century in quite another direction.

Second basic assumption: the history of celebrity and the history of communications technology over the last century are very closely linked. To put the matter simply, each new development in the latter field, aimed in its developers' minds toward speeding, multiplying, and generally easing the flow of information, thus serving the generally held democratic ideal of building an ever better informed populace, had, to a degree, the opposite effect.

Over a century's span, the proliferation of informaton has had two main consequences. It has first of all created a need for simplifying symbols—usually people, sometimes objects—that crystallize and personify an issue, an ideal, a longing. Ever more briefly as the flood of information, of competing stimuli, continues to mount, these figures help us to resolve ambivalence and ambiguity not only about the issues of the day, but about our own more private needs and desires. At the same time, each new development in communications has increased our illusion of intimacy with the celebrated. Not only do we think we know them, we think we know what makes them tick, which makes us want to tick as they do.

As a result, they can sometimes sell us anything, given the right circumstances. But not always. Products, ideas, political candidates—these are tricky and unpredictable areas, where sometimes the celebrity is effective, sometimes not. So much depends on the zeitgeist of the moment they enter the field. But, over a longer period of time, celebrities can put over general styles, manners of being and behaving. There being a point at which manners become a form of moral action, the celebrities have become, in recent decades, the chief agents of moral change in the United States.

We have arrived at that point in slow, easy stages, not quite aware where the tides of history have been carrying us. It is only in retrospect—never in the euphoria of its introduction, not even at the moment when everyone becomes aware that it is the basis for a big business, and therefore wields some kind of power in the society—that we can see how a new device for disseminating information, or misinformation, has worked on us. And, in fact, none operates discretely; all function together to produce the image world in which we seek some reality in which we can comfortably live.

It was so from the beginning. And the beginning, so far as we are concerned, was the invention of the rotary printing press, which, of course, begat the mass circulation newspaper. By 1895, when William Randolph Hearst arrived in New York to challenge Joseph Pulitzer's *World* for dominance in this field, the latter's Sunday paper was selling a half-million copies, with the daily edition at about half that number, and the formula for success had been well established. It had been described by a San Francisco competitor of Hearst's *Examiner,* where the publisher had rehearsed his routine as a daily effort to place before readers "the startling, the amazing and the stupefying." But Hearst, like Pulitzer, and like all who have inherited their mantle, down to Rupert Murdoch and his New York *Post* of today, was not truly a newspaper man, not in the customary sense, anyway. As his biographer, W. A. Swanberg, acutely noted, Hearst "was an inventor, a producer, an arranger. The news that actually happened was too dull for him, and besides it was available to the other papers. He lived in a childlike dream world, imagining wonderful stories and then going out and creating them, so the line between fact and fancy was apt to be fuzzy."

As with Pulitzer, Hearst's typical news budget was a blend of crime, large-scale disasters, small-scale human tragedies, a modicum of national and international political news. His singular contribution to reshaping the presentation of the news was to take the basic Pulitzer trick, which was to find human symbols whose terror, anguish, or sudden good fortune, whatever, seemed to dramatically summarize some local event or social problem or tragedy, and to apply it on a national or international scale. If he could make a hero out of one of his intrepid reporters in so doing—have him risk life or, anyway, limb, in order to right what appeared to be a wrong while bringing back an exclusive—well and good, but it was not essential. What was vital was the symbol.

Before he discovered what he insisted was a cruel tyranny in the Spanish governance of its Cuban province, he was all for sending one of his New York *Journal* reporters out to abduct Captain Dreyfus from jail. But Cuba, where his people kept discovering what they claimed were unjustly incarcerated American male citizens and sexually abused maidens (none of the stories proved out later), was more convenient and more suitable to his purposes. A war, if one could be whipped up, was a much better, and longer-lasting, story than Dreyfus or anyone else he could think of. And—notoriously, of course—he got one after the *Maine* mysteriously blew up in the Havana harbor, another "atrocity" that could be laid to the Spanish.

In journalistic history the emphasis has always been on deploring Hearst's distortions and outright inventions, which is proper, but altogether too easy a place to let the matter rest. What has not been stressed is what the rest of the press learned from him, namely, that when great events or abstract issues were placed before the public, its mind was much more readily engaged, its emotions much more intensely involved, if those events and issues were concretized through personification. Reduced to the simple old city room formula "Names make news," that principle, formulated at the turn of the century, has been the great force guiding the development not just of newspapers, but of all communications in this century. It applies with equal force not just to lowly tabloids, but to august magazines, rich and proud television news divisions, and even to so grand an institution as the New York *Times.*

In Hearst's ascendant years, this was not yet a system, although it was the humble foundation for one. There were two obvious defects to the Hearst-Pulitzer manner of doing business. One was that the newspaper proprietors were dependent upon events over which they had no control to supply them with high definition, easily readable symbols of the current events. What did they do on a slow news day? And what if the symbolic creatures proved, on closer examination, to be unsavory or intractable to manipulation? To be sure, journalists could fictionalize, but there were always rivals about, waiting to expose their lies and shadings. To be sure, the public's memory for yesterday's sensation was a short one. But the will to believe the printed word, the will at any rate not to disbelieve it, would be steadily eroded if time after time stories proved to be false. Also, of course, it was expensive to keep sending reporters out to look for stories that could be huffed and puffed into banner headlines. Richard Harding Davis and Frederic Remington, both of whom had been extensively involved in Hearst's Cuban capers, did not come cheap.

And then there was the second factor, more speculative perhaps, yet instinctively hard to deny. That was that there was a certain practical limit on novelty. The mass public did not seem to like too much of it. Or rather seemed to prefer a blend of novel sensations with what might be termed long-running serials about particularly favored symbolic figures. It is not hard to understand this. The pace of life was quickening, the flow of information beginning to speed up while mobility both geographic and social was stepping up as well. People began to need familiar figures they could carry about in their minds as they moved out and moved up, a sort of portable community as it were, containing representations of good values, interesting traits, a certain amount of within-bounds attractiveness, glamour, even deviltry.

The traditional public professions could supply some of this. For example, politics. William Jennings Bryan may have been the first celebrity politician in the modern sense of the term. In part, this was due to his skills as a public speaker. Once he had achieved the Democratic nomination in 1896, thanks to his legendary "Cross of Gold" speech at the convention, "The Boy Orator of the Platte" sustained himself between his several unsuccessful subsequent tries for the presidency by touring the lecture circuit and reciting that speech, until the boy orator was, in fact, well along into middle age. But the tours kept him and his views constantly before press and public, and that, in turn, generated for him the first substantial amount of what can only be termed "fan mail" ever to descend on a politician. According to Dixon Wechter in *The Hero in America,* Bryan received innumerable requests for personal advice, loans, and even romantic dalliance, a burden the likes of William McKinley did not have to shoulder.

Similar celebrity accrued to Bryan's sometime rival Theodore Roosevelt. His autobiographical writings stressed an archetypal tale, the drama of a sickly, overprivileged youth choosing the strenuous life and turning himself into the robust and colorful explorer–hunter–crime fighter–trustbuster of his maturity. And the wonderfully lively, occasionally tragedy-tinged family he sired was almost as good copy as TR himself. To a very large degree these two men accomplished—one with good effect on his career, the other not—what most modern politicians aspire to do. They diverted attention away from issues that were often abstract and inexplicable—who, after all, could actually understand what the implications of the gold standard or a protective tariff meant to the average man?—and focused it on themselves, on the power of their own personalities.

Long before the word "media" achieved its present implications, these two politicians had stumbled upon the secret of media success and turned their lives into long-running dramas that kept them alive in the journalistic imagination, therefore the public imagination, between political seasons. And one imagines the press as more than a little grateful for this service, since there were not enough individuals of their sort, in any profession, to feed its needs and its readers' needs for readily apprehensible symbols who did not wear out their welcomes too quickly and who had the capacity to keep reinventing themselves by placing themselves in interesting new situations.

This was a shortage, not a dearth. In a great age of industrialization, inventors like Thomas Edison and, a little later, Henry Ford, tycoons like Carnegie and Rockefeller (with a little help from his pioneering PR man, Ivy Lee) helped. They had all been shaped from common clay and people could identify with their modest backgrounds and, for the most part, seemly manners. Plain people fantasize themselves capitalizing on their skills and insights as these men had. "It only takes one good idea . . ." runs one of the oldest bits of common wisdom, and these figures helped to keep that great democratic dream of success alive—until it could be reposed in other, more approachable hands.

Others, of course, were permitted entry into the charmed circle. A writer like Jack London, that tough romantic wanderer, whose life was more entertaining than any of his books, and whose heroic vision of nature (for which a softer, urbanizing culture found itself suddenly nostalgic) was a useful character to provide for popular reveries. Brave Sarah Bernhardt (at one time a particular Hearst favorite) with her humble beginnings, her triumph over physical adversity, her endless farewell tours (like Bryan's repeated tries for the presidency, her stubborn refusal to quit the stage became the suspenseful substance of her drama) became a sort of theatrical archetype in the popular mind, just as Enrico Caruso, the first hero of the phonograph, came to symbolize the flamboyance and danger of artistic achievement. There were others, of course.

Sports, interestingly, were not what they would become. Baseball was fresh out of the pastures, football was still a game for college boys, basketball an eccentricity, the modern Olympic Games in their infancy. The leading athletic figures tended still to lurk in the shadows of legend rather than to stand forth in the hot light of heroic celebrity. They awaited the so-called Golden Age of Sports in the 1920s, when a grander and more colorful style of sports writing would begin to appear in the newspapers, along with richer photographic evidence of the players' prowess.

To a degree what was true of sports was true of other domains as well. For example, society. It is true that the old penny press made occasional good sport of "the 400" (a term coined, of course, by a newspaperman) and counted on its generally envied and resented members to make occasional fools of themselves, but it was the tabloids that converted the comings and goings of its giddy heiresses and nitwit playboys into public figures. Same way with crime. It is certainly true that the Harry Thaw–Stanford White–Evelyn Nesbit triangle, combining as it did sex, madness, murder, money, the social register, and a bit of show business, was a paradigmatic case. But it required the combined efforts of the picture and tabloid press to make, at a slightly later date, a new crime of the century every week or two.

Still, during the period—roughly 1895–1920—when the first blocks of the modern celebrity system were sliding into place everything was improvisatory, primitive. Something more was needed, something that could, on a fairly regular basis, provide the public with a reliable supply of new sensations together with an equally steady, glamorous, and easy-to-follow real-life serial adventure. Something that could, as well, allow the press to return to a slightly more passive role in gathering and presenting the news of these creatures, not force it constantly to risk its reputation in prodigies of invention.

Luckily for the inky wretches, help was at hand, not merely in the daily effort to fill their pages, but in building the model that would, in time, serve the entire celebrity enterprise. One day everyone looked up and discovered that an institution known as Hollywood had been invented.

We speak, naturally, of Hollywood-the-state-of-mind, not Hollywood-the-geographical-entity, whose contribution of a euphonious name to a whole complex of activities and attitudes is not to be sneezed at, but is not to be lingered over either. That state of mind was created out of three basic elements: a technique, an economic necessity, and isolation. No one can say which of the three should take precedence in this process of psychic creation.

Technique. Until 1908, when a failed actor-playwright named D. W. Griffith was set to work directing one-reel films at the Biograph studios in New York, it could be said that movies—then, in the commercial sense, only twelve years old—were nothing more than a technology in search of a technique. In the years before Griffith, they had succeeded first as a novelty, then as a primitive means of telling simple stories in pictures. But they were not yet, in the way they looked or worked on people, movies. Not as we know them, that is. Their power was yet to be unleashed.

The problem was the camera. It was, for the most part, passive, sitting on its haunches at a distance from the action sufficient to include all the players in a scene, and to show each of them head-to-toe, at that. It is said that the early entrepreneurs of the movies feared a consumer revolt if only half the cast or half an actor were shown in a shot. It is also said that they required straight-line action, and resisted the idea of cutting back and forth between two pieces of action proceeding simultaneously in different places; they feared confusing the audience. Whether that is true or not, the fact remains that despite an occasional close-up and an occasional simple attempt at crosscutting, most movies were photographed as if the camera had been given a nice center seat in a theater, a few rows back from the stage, and told not to fidget. It is also true that the plays it was employed to record were far simpler structurally than the intricately designed, and spectacularly staged if otherwise simple-minded, melodramas then dominating the popular stage.

Probably Griffith began experimenting with the camera in order to find some sort of visual equivalent in a silent medium for the florid dialogue of the stage, which he loved, but both wrote and spoke quite badly indeed. Most of his many innovations, though of the highest importance to the history of the cinema, are of small concern in the history of celebrity, but what is of incalculable importance is the close-up. He began to use the device as a form of punctuation, a visual variant heightening the dramatic impact of certain moments in certain scenes. But it had, as he quickly saw, a more powerful potential.

Immediately, it relaxed the silent medium's dependency on the broad, highly unrealistic gestures of pantomime—about the only way of communicating emotion in long shot. By moving in closer, Griffith was able to catch a subtler play of emotions on his actors' faces, in their eyes. He knew what he was doing; he was, as he quickly began telling people, photographing thought. It was dramatically effective. And it was something more than that. It was an activity unprecedented in the history of any art, a breakthrough to a new level of intimacy—or, at least, the illusion thereof.

Looming over the audience, magnified, far larger than life, these movie players, these strangers, were seen with erotic narrowness and nearness. We do not see our closest friends so intimately, or the people who share our homes, or our lives, except perhaps in the act of making love.

There was still more to Griffith's innovation—and this neither he nor anyone else saw at the time. The close-up, even the medium shot, has the effect of isolating the actor in the sequence, separating him or her from the rest of the ensemble for close individual scrutiny by the audience. To some immeasurable degree, attention is directed away from the role being played, the overall story being told. It is focused instead on the reality of the individual playing the part. Inevitably one begins to wonder about him or her, what he or she is really like off the screen. This was peculiarly so in the early days of film, when short pictures, no more than two reels in length (and in Griffith's case for most of his time at Biograph, only one reel long), were made on a once-a-week basis. Week in, week out, the audience saw the same faces in a ceaseless variety of roles. In these circumstances, the constant was the face, and the enigma that nagged at the audience was the reality that lay beneath that essentially unknowable and anonymous—because unbilled—face.

Over time, this had two results. There was, of course, a hunger to know more about the real lives of these increasingly familiar icons. But, at first, such information was deliberately kept from the audience, and thereafter it was falsified—at first wildly, later in more persuasively fictive forms. If many people never fully believed what they read or heard about these creatures, still they went on attending the publicity. This was particularly so if it reinforced the fantasies they had concocted while sitting there alone in the dark, concocted out of the basic human need to give some sort of psychological substance to these images, to make some more active connection with these powerful and inevitably erotic shadows.

Beyond that, as these images reappeared each week, there began to develop what would eventually come to be the largest singularity of movie stardom—a singularity that has now been appropriated in all the other forms of public life—namely, that the individual works themselves, in this case, the films, began to be perceived (albeit unconsciously) not as ends in themselves, discrete creations, but as incidents in a larger and more compelling drama—the drama of the star's life and career, the shaping and reshaping of the image of him or her that we carry in our minds.

To be sure, this drama did not begin to gain momentum until the movie players had been granted identity. In the beginning, as everyone knows, films did not carry credits, and however familiar and even beloved some images became, they remained anonymous. The organs of gossip and publicity were not yet in place and functioning. But it required only a moment to get them going.

Economic Necessity. By 1910, Griffith's style was almost fully formed, and it was being imitated throughout the picture business. Ironically, however, he was laboring for a studio that was a member of the Motion Picture Patents Company, a trust of production companies that controlled the rights to the basic machinery for making and projecting film. The trust's owners and managers did not understand the immutable truth of the entertainment business, which is that though you can make money that is steady and nice out of technology, the big, if erratic, money is to be found in what we now call "software" or, in the movie business, "product." Their interest, as they saw it, lay in keeping the costs of these latter items as low as possible. Their own functionaries told them of the growing interest in the players who worked for them as reflected in mail coming to the studios, and they saw the potential value in publicizing them. But the trust was renting film at flat footage rates, taking no percentage of box office receipts. And it was paying just five to fifteen dollars for actors. If the more popular among them began to get an inflated sense of their worth, there was no telling where their salaries might go.

No such inhibitions were operative among the trust's competitors, independents who were cranking out film using bootleg equipment and, since their films tended to be livelier than anyone's but Griffith's, doing fairly well in the independent theaters. One such was Carl Laemmle, later to found Universal Pictures, who hired Florence Lawrence, "the Biograph Girl," but not a Griffith favorite, billed her under her own name and paid her a somewhat advanced salary. To publicize her, so the legend goes, he caused to have planted in a St. Louis newspaper a story that she had been killed in a trolley car accident. Immediately the story broke, he denounced it as a fake, the work of the despicable trust (trusts of all kinds were under attack in this populist era, and an underdog's sympathy attached to anyone who appeared as their victim or principled opponent). Laemmle also announced what appears to be the first public appearance in movie history, Miss Lawrence's visit to St. Louis, escorted by her leading man, King Baggott, thereby giving the lie to this heinous fraud. She appeared, and there occurred a prearranged tumult in which her dress was divested of frills by her relieved and allegedly adoring public. Who knows, maybe their enthusiasm was genuine. The cynicism now surrounding stardom and its ceremonies had not yet taken root, and perhaps the good and innocent citizens of that then remote metropolis were venting genuine relief at seeing this favorite in the healthy flesh.

No matter. The point was made. Within a matter of four years salaries for leading players rose from the $5- to $15-a-week level to $250 to $2,500 a week. Soon some of them would soar well beyond that. Suddenly, these salaries were in themselves news, as was the manner in which they were spent, the company the stars kept, the style in which they passed their days. It is perhaps no coincidence that the first fan magazine began publication within the year that Lawrence and Baggott made their visit to St. Louis. It was called *Photoplay,* a borrowed word coined by poet Vachel Lindsay, who was also the first serious artist to make public his passion for the movies. It is certainly no coincidence that that publication carried, from the first, a gossip column which bore the subtitle, "Facts and Near-Facts About the

Great and Near-Great of Filmland," which had the virtue, at least, of honesty.

Isolation. What is a coincidence is that many of the film magazine's articles, also from the start, emanated from Hollywood. Shooting on the West Coast had begun around this time in part because the independents hoped to avoid entanglement with the trust companies, based in the East, who were not above sending out goon squads to interfere with independent companies working on location. That, anyway, is the story. It seems more likely that the steady supply of winter sunshine in Los Angeles, which ensured a steady flow of films for the weekly programs they promised exhibitors, was more significant to the calculations of the independents.

Agnes de Mille, daughter of one director, niece of another more famous one, once recalled in a television documentary that the railroad right of way, as one neared Los Angeles in those days, was alive with flowers. It seemed, she implied, that one's way to the Magic City was carpeted in natural glory. There was, of course, a prosaic explanation: as they neared their destination, passengers tended to throw out the bouquets that eastern well-wishers had given them, and it was the seeds of these flowers that had rooted along the tracks. Still, symbolically it made for an apt entrance, for to eastern (or middle western) eyes, Los Angeles was an Eden, especially around its fringes, where the studios were and the picture people congregated. After the spring rains, Miss de Mille recalled, "in the grass would be tangled the lupins, the poppies, the brodiaea, all of them exquisite, and all of them just blooming wild and in the gutter. You gathered them by the armful."

Hard now to imagine, after the movies themselves have given us a less attractive vision of Los Angeles, after we have seen it ourselves thanks to the jets and cheap tickets thereon, just how exotic all this was, and how open it was—the country still fresh, not yet (and never to be) locked within the rigid grid pattern that prevailed back East, nor within the rigid social grid of the older America either. One of the things that had weighed with the picture makers when they chose to settle here (and other places, like Florida and even Cuba, had been tried by some of them) was that mountains, sea, desert, and an urban area all coexisted within an hour of each other in Los Angeles, guaranteeing them a variety of backgrounds for their little dramas. But those varied ecologies also had social implications and encouraged a wild variety of architectural fantasies. And, of course, lifestyles to match.

"We were a bunch of kids, having fun," the silent star Viola Dana told Kevin Brownlow, the film historian. That "the movies" (as the locals called the newcomers) were so youthful, so pretty, so unformed, and suddenly, so overpaid by a business that had as yet established few rules and no traditions, also helped set a tone that was not so much licentious, as the sterner moralists quickly came to believe, but giddy. And in American life, entirely without precedent. Adela Rogers St. Johns, the Hearst reporter who worked for *Photoplay* as its first Hollywood correspondent, was to tell Brownlow, "Everybody had an excitement about the whole thing that I've never seen before. None of us knew even vaguely what we were doing . . . but it was great . . . right in the middle of this goldfish bowl, with everybody beginning to look at us."

"Los Angeles," Reyner Banham, the English architectural critic, would later write, in what may be the best L.A. one-liner of them all, "is the Middle West raised to flashpoint." By which he meant that, from the start, climate and topography encouraged immigrants to shake free of their inhibitions and repressions, to act out their fantasies. Here they were free to re-create themselves as they pleased. Or to lend themselves to re-creation by directors, producers, writers, anyone who cared to have a go at them.

And in this, the folks they left behind indulged them. One must not emphasize too much the steady mutter of moral criticism directed at the movies and the movie makers by small-town, Methodist America. Or by Catholic priests either. People continued to go to the movies no matter what. And, if not fired up by the press, as they were in 1921–1922 by the Fatty Arbuckle case, they were rather tolerant, maybe even amused, by reports of gaudiness and excess so far away.

So far away! That was the thing. Hollywood in those days was as remote as the Klondike, and perhaps people thought of the movie business as a kind of gold strike and excused the excesses of the movie makers as they had those of the miners. If we had been so lucky would we have behaved any better? Probably not. And anyway, we would like to give it a try. The new celebrities had, just here, plugged into the most basic of American fantasies, the dream of reward without apparent effort, the dream of being uplifted overnight. No wonder there was a well of forgiveness, which over the years ahead would wash away many sins.

But there was more to it even than that. We dream, all of us, of the Edenic. Or as Milan Kundera, the great Czech writer, puts it, "People have always aspired to an idyll, a garden where nightingales sing, a realm of harmony where the world does not rise up as a stranger against man nor man against other men . . ." So, it seems, "The Coast" appeared to be. Not only were its citizens beautiful, but it appeared that they had created, or were in the process of creating, a community of the beautiful in a place that was beautiful, where the palm trees flourished, where you picked oranges from trees that grew in your own backyard under a sun that shone three hundred and fifty days out of the year—according to the chamber of commerce.

Such a community could not have been created elsewhere. There would have been no room for it back East—no room geographically, certainly no room psychically. It required space in which to flourish, and privacy, freedom from the rub of quotidian reality. When you are trying on airs the deflating cries of groundlings must not be heard. And the groundlings, for their part, must be spared the sight of your nakedness between costumes, or all their illusions will flee.

Thus was it established, the basic structure of our celebrity system —the community and the others, the favored and the unfavored. Mutual dependency was implicit. For a convention was quickly established to govern the relationship between the two groups. It held that the favored, should they step too far out of line, could have their favors stripped from them, be returned to shameful anonymity at any time. It also held that, America being the land of opportunity, the unfavored might at any time be lifted up and granted favor. In our popular mythology, the talent scout is the messenger of the inscrutable gods, rainmaker to a populace ever parched for fame. In actuality, neither sudden doom nor sudden ascension would happen very often, but the possibilities added spice to the drama. And symbolically, there was accuracy in the portrayal.

The brilliant German critic Walter Benjamin dates the beginning of the dream of discovery earlier and places it in a literary context. "For centuries," he wrote in 1936, "a small number of writers were confronted by many thousands of readers. This changed toward the end of the last century. With the increasing extension of the press, which kept placing new political, religious, scientific, professional and local organs before the readers, an increasing number of readers became writers—at first occasional ones. It began with the daily press opening to its readers space for 'letters to the editor.' And today there is hardly a gainfully employed European who could not, in principle, find an opportunity to publish somewhere or other comments on his work, grievances, documentary reports, or that sort of thing. Thus the distinction between author and public is about to lose its basic character . . . At any moment the reader is ready to turn into a writer." Or, one might add, a celebrity manqué.

What Benjamin's austere and learned intelligence would have made of people like Judith Kranz, or on a slightly higher level, Judith Guest, one can only imagine. But the fact is, it happens: a lady turns to her typewriter to relieve the boredom of marriage, children, and suburbia and, by spinning out her frustrations and fantasies, ends up with millions of dollars in royalties—and a story in *People* about her miraculous rise to fame and fortune.

Not being interested in such matters, Benjamin did not comment on the propensity of film to elevate similarly ordinary souls to stardom because they happened to fit the moment's notion of comeliness, whatever the state of their talent, though surely that possibility had been well established by the time he wrote. He did point out, however, that "the newsreel offers everyone the opportunity to rise from passer-by to movie extra," while the use of nonprofessionals as actors in both documentary and fictional motion pictures offered the tempting possibility that "any man might find himself part of a work of art." This statement is remarkable for its prescience, considering that Benjamin wrote before cinema verité, for example, or the expansion of television news, with its endless need for stories and faces, greatly enhancing the possibility that the "passerby" will enjoy his democratic right to a moment of stardom.

From the moment movies were established as a national habit, we would forever stand, all of us, in tenuous balance, stretched between admiration and envy of the favored. A paradigm occurs. In 1910 an English comedian named Charles Chaplin embarked for America as part of a touring comedy company. He did well, well enough to be signed in 1914 for work in the Keystone Comedies, at a salary of $150 a week. After two years in Los Angeles (and Chicago) he returned to New York to sign a contract that would pay him $820,000 to make a dozen two-reel comedies in a little over a year's time. As he journeyed east the railroad telegraphers along his route wired their colleagues down the line of his presence on the train, and so at each stop, crowds of admiring gawkers awaited him. In New York it was necessary to take him off the train at 125th Street to avoid the crowds gathered to greet him at Grand Central Station. Even so, police protection was required for him as he transferred from train to limousine.

HE'S HERE, one newspaper headlined, and everyone knew who *he* was. Later that day (Chaplin recalled in his autobiography) he strolled aimlessly about the city—"all dressed up and no place to go." "How does one get to know people, interesting people," he mused as he wandered anonymously among the anonymous, knowing then that if he introduced himself to anyone a discomfiting scene would follow (as it did when a waitress in Child's Restaurant recognized him). "It seemed that everyone knew me, but I knew no one."

His experience would be echoed by others of the famous for the rest of the century. And his feelings, too. Not too long ago Johnny Carson used almost exactly the same words to describe his passages through the common streets. One can but wonder, did Chaplin sense an undercurrent of malevolence in the greetings he had received? Did he feel the instability of his admiration? In time, as we all know, he would come to understand both all too well. One wonders, too, did he sense the price he would pay when, out of self-defense he, like so many others, would be forced to retreat deeper and deeper into that isolation that struck him first on this night? Did the shadow of the artist he would become in his last years, that purveyor of gaseous humanitarian platitudes, that rich man cut off from the roots of his genius and walled off from his past by the Alps of Switzerland, fall across him as he watched his name and his new salary pricked out in lights, circle the Times Tower? One utters a sad "perhaps."

The great personal change Chaplin was confronting was, clearly, a function of vast social change, the dimensions of which he could not possibly have perceived. No one could, though surely some saw that World War I would accelerate the rate of change in many realms.

For example. Very shortly people would be wondering why Chaplin did not return to England to defend his native hearth against the hated Hun. Curious, this, for at least part of the passionate feeling against Germany was the creation of Chaplin's own profession and the press with which he was symbiotically related. From the start of the war in Europe there had been a steady flow of inflammatory American films about the way the Germans were conducting themselves. Most of them seem to have featured young girls falling into the rapacious and sadistic clutches of the Kaiser's soldiery. These fit with suspicious neatness into the line then being promoted elsewhere, everywhere, by the notorious British propaganda machine, which kept saying the Germans were beastly chaps. Indeed, there is evidence that D. W. Griffith's somewhat belated effort in this vein, *Hearts of the World,* was directly subsidized by the British Government. Doubtless other American films were as well. As a result, Chaplin and others—particularly males of fighting age—had a need to demonstrate their devotion to the cause of freedom.

Fortunately, the same machine that created this need provided the means of answering it. Especially after the United States entered the war, and George Creel's Office of Public Information had been set up, no screen personality had the slightest difficulty finding ways to prove his devotion to the ideals for which we allegedly fought. The archives are full of short subjects featuring the leading players of the day urging enlistment and support of the Red Cross. That sort of thing. And then there were the Liberty Loan drives, familiar to modern students of picture histories. They provided classic images of the great stars— Chaplin, Pickford, Fairbanks—touring, selling investments in the cause. As well, these photos afford the first tangible evidence of star power. The crowds have the dimensions of a sea, threatening to engulf the principals. As a busy participant in all this, Chaplin had no trouble convincing people that he was far more valuable to his country by lending his gifts and his popularity to the propaganda effort than he ever could have been entrenched in Flanders fields.

Chaplin was victim and beneficiary of a force as unprecedented in history as war on the scale that it was being practiced in France was. In its calculation and expansiveness, nothing like the internal propaganda campaign practiced in the United States had been attempted before anywhere, if only because no mass communication system like the one suddenly in being had existed before. But then, the situation was unprecedented too. As far as the United States was concerned, Germany posed no perceptible, immediate threat to its citizens, its property or, for that matter, its honor. Only its ideals were in danger.

Practically speaking, this was a tenuous excuse for a fight. It was particularly true in a country that had absorbed much immigration and was not, therefore, as ethnically cohesive as it had once been. The fact that there had been much internal immigration—from country to city, from sea to shining sea—also presented a problem. How identify the least common denominator among these restless folk? How make certain they would accept the inconveniences and impositions of wartime life when the war itself was such an abstraction? The need for individuals easily recognized and generally liked was answered by movie players. This search for the simplifying symbol thus proceeded with the full faith and credit of the government behind it—though it was still quite simpleminded, this effort, compared to what would come later. Still, it was a beginning.

For the stars caught up in it, the experience was heady. In the past glamorous actresses had, of course, been privy to the affairs of state because of affairs of the heart, but this was something new. One small example: the Chaplin, Pickford, Fairbanks Liberty Loan tour concluded in Washington. There was an invitation to the White House and pictures were taken of the Hollywood swells hobnobbing with the Washington power elite. Fairbanks was particularly impressed by the youthful assistant secretary of the Navy. He told Franklin Delano Roosevelt that he had the personality to succeed as an actor if he wanted, which later, in a certain sense, he would do.

In effect, this was the beginning of celebrity desegregation. The isolation of the envied West Coast community was then seen to be breachable if the cause was correct. And that community, so recently removed from contemptible servitude, at humiliating prices, in one-reel movies, gained a sense of its power as its members were courted by statesmen, world leaders.

D. W. Griffith may have been the first to sense this, when in 1915 *The Birth of a Nation,* the first American film of truly epic proportions, was screened at the White House (as well as elsewhere in Washington for congressmen and Supreme Court justices). Woodrow Wilson even gave the picture an endorsement, later denied when a public outcry over the film's racism arose. In that instance Griffith had been seeking favor and may have been surprised by the ease with which it was won. But just three years later it was he whose favor was being sought. When he went to England not only was he received in the great houses, but titled ladies agreed to appear before his cameras. He was then a valued ally, his cameras and his skills needed in the fight for England's survival. He was even granted an audience at 10 Downing Street by Lloyd George, and the fact that the British Prime Minister would take time out from running a war to meet him so impressed Griffith that, years later, it was this scene with which he began the autobiography he never completed. It was his best measure of how far he had climbed from the Kentucky farm on which he had been born. Perhaps, too, he reflected in that moment that just a decade before he had been an out-of-work stage actor receiving five dollars a day for working in a Western shot in New Jersey.

In effect, a beginning was being made here, under the impress of wartime exigencies. An establishment, a power elite, call it what you will, which had previously been confined geographically to the eastern seaboard, and which had comprised the banking, industrial, and political managers of the nation, was being expanded and democratized. After all, the movie people then earned salaries comparable to theirs, and the business in which they worked was then beginning to refer to itself as an "industry." As well it might, since feature films, which in the years between 1914 and 1918 had mostly supplanted the short pictures of earlier years, required large financial services and the companies that produced them were entering upon a period of consolidation and turning themselves into an oligopoly of a sort familiar to the leaders of more traditional enterprises.

In short, the war years demonstrated to everyone that a new force had arrived in the society, one that might well have its larger uses if properly handled. Even nicer, this new power was fun power. The people who possessed it were pretty and exotic and quite jolly in their innocence and their new-rich expansiveness.

Some, of course, were too jolly. "Swimming pools, wild parties, you expect every girl to fall in a dead faint at your feet." The indictment of the movie star breed is Debbie Reynolds in that lovely period piece, *Singin' in the Rain*. But it is an accurate enough statement of the impression they had made on the plain people by the end of the 1920s.

The famous scandals of the 1920s—sex (Fatty Arbuckle), drugs (Wallace Reid), murder (the William Desmond Taylor case, with Mabel Normand and Mary Miles Minter tainted by their involvement with him)—did much to fix this impression. Eden had been breached. That brief sense of being sequestered, free in one's isolation, that picture people had enjoyed before World War I was over. Yes, Tom Mix, the cowboy star who had passed enough of his time in the real West to understand something about boomtowns, might choose to spell out his name in lights taller than a man atop his house, or to install in his house an uncowboyish fountain on which colored lights played, or to appear at a wedding driving a coach-and-four. Gloria Swanson might lead her peers to Europe in search of titled mates. Everyone might compete in the creation of fantastical housing, and the world might watch with amused wonder. But over time that wonder had to become tinged with malice. And the scandals focused that malice; they were the smoke that seemed to indicate fires down below, their extent unknown, perhaps unknowable.

Maybe there were no fires. Or maybe there were a few fires here and there, but nothing to worry about, no threat to the youthful morals pious people were always fussing over. But reality was of as small concern to Hollywood's critics as it was to the dizziest of its denizens. And even the soberest of its citizens, those performers who were now putting themselves forward as industry leaders, often did so in ways more colorful than those of the leaders of other one-industry towns, Detroit or Pittsburgh, Akron or Washington, D.C.

Consider the careers of the four people who had emerged from the century's teens as the movies' top people in the public mind. They are, of course, the four pioneers of film celebrity we have already mentioned—Griffith, Chaplin, Pickford, Fairbanks. In 1919 they combined to form United Artists to distribute their own films. Fronting for them was no less a Washington personage than William Gibbs McAdoo, former Secretary of the Treasury and Woodrow Wilson's son-in-law. They would be entrepreneurs as well as "personalities." They would thus be taken more seriously in the world than mere movie stars ever would be. They would pass the classic American test of responsibility and grown-upness; they would meet a payroll. And they would be spokesmen for their industry, the way, perhaps, Morgan was for Wall Street, or Ford for Detroit.

It worked out least well for Griffith. He had enjoyed performerlike fame when *The Birth of a Nation* burst on the world and sustained that fame for several years thereafter, even when films like *Intolerance* and *Hearts of the World* did less well at the box office. But his name on a film was not a guarantee of success, not the way those of the artists with whom he had united were. Try as he might—and his publicists helped him to try mightily—he could not compete, from behind the camera, with those who were constantly in front of it, placing their well-defined images before the public. His partners all had studios devoted to turning out their films, and they made money with them. His studio, located unglamorously back East, quickly became a burden to him as his pictures, lacking among other qualities major stars other than himself, failed commercially.

Chaplin, on the other hand, did all right financially, maybe better than anyone, but his heart was not in leading the industry. He wanted, maybe, to lead the world, anyway to be taken seriously as a moral and intellectual force, the way writers and artists of a more traditional kind sometimes are (the example of Paderewski must always have been before him). Anyway, he became a rather tiresome lecturer in moral and political philosophy. Also, of course, he undercut his position as the years wore on with his many peculiar romantic arrangements—better said, entanglements.

That left Doug and Mary, whose liaison, when both were married to others, was greatly facilitated by their Liberty Loan tour. Of more significance, in the history of celebrity, however, was a date two years earlier, June 24, 1916, to be precise, when "Little Mary" signed a contract with Adolph Zukor of the Famous Players corporation—the movies' first million-dollar contract. She had been goaded to seek it by the steady rise in Chaplin's compensation in the years prior to it, and though the $1,040,000 the document called for was, in fact, payable to her own production company and was for a two-year commitment on her part. Details. Details. What the public apprehended was a new and heady essence—that someone was being paid a million dollars merely to appear in the movies, never mind for how long, never mind to what entity the checks were made out. It was at the moment this deal made headlines that reward began to detach itself from effort and from intrinsic merit, when the old, reasonable correlation between what (and how) one did and what one received for doing it became tenuous (and, in the upper reaches of show biz, invisible). In this circumstance one of the bases for public morality began to disappear. Salary, reward, became an end in itself, the largest basis for judging success. It followed from this that merit of all kinds—including the aesthetic—could be ascertained by consulting the net worth of the worker in question. At last American democracy had achieved what no other system had achieved—a means of quantifying the sublime. It is amazing that it took as long as it did to bring over from the movies to literature, to painting, to all the arts, a means test for merit.

Be that as it may, in the years ahead—as if caught up in a cautionary fairy tale—Pickford would pay a stern emotional price for her economic pioneering. For she was, at heart, rather a shy type, and it would appear that her reclusive tendencies were reinforced by several frightening experiences with out-of-control mobs when she and Fairbanks took a wedding trip to Europe in 1920. Poor, innocent Europe.

It did not understand what had happened while it was preoccupied with war and its aftermath, did not understand that a film star now required the sort of security arrangements previously reserved for royalty and heads of state. Pickford was very nearly trampled on her way to a London garden party, menaced by the crush of the crowd in Paris, and in Oslo. Yes, Oslo.

In the years to come her naturally reclusive nature would win out. More and more she would retreat to the safety of Pickfair, though until the 1950s she could occasionally be lured out for social and charitable gatherings of suitably impeccable nature. And, until age and illness rendered it impossible, she was pleased enough to receive members of the movie peerage and visiting celebrities.

Of them all, only Fairbanks seemed to have had the social imagination—or perhaps it was simply a curious nature—to see how his fame could be traded on for more than mere monetary advantage. In the 1920s and early '30s it was said that his annual trip to Europe was made mainly to line up the following year's Pickfair guest list. But that was not a joke. The English peerage was particularly well represented at his table. But so were sportsmen, writers, intellectuals, performing artists from every field. One of the few movies of Pavlova dancing was made when she visited his studio. And Henry Ford was once encouraged by Fairbanks to join his host on a climb, via vines and drainpipe, to the eaves of Pickfair to enjoy the view.

Whether he consciously envisioned it or not, Fairbanks was clearly experimenting with the creation of an international fellowship of the accomplished, a multinational celebrity community that was, to borrow a phrase, a sort of moveable feast for the famous. He was ahead of his time. Transportation and communication were not quite yet in a state where these ties could be maintained as they now can be. Yet it does seem that the great circle Doug drew about him prefigures the envied circles drawn from quite disparate public professionals who seem always to be kissing one another in the pages of *People* and, as outsiders imagine it, have one another's unlisted telephone numbers and hitch rides in each other's Lear jets.

Of course, they were the lucky ones—these top-of-the-line stars. They managed to represent something of our best selves to our best selves—or seemed to. Within reason, therefore, they were granted the same sort of indulgences we would grant ourselves. Flagrant immorality, for instance, would not have been countenanced; but a certain liberality was in order. Pickford and Fairbanks, for example, were not punished for arranging the divorces that permitted them to marry. Doug went right on publishing the little books of peppy advice for young people that his ghostwriters ran up for him.

Others were not so fortunate. Forced to live within images that had been concocted for them, or had fallen to them as the result of some early role, stars became restive, even self-destructive, as a result of living up to the lie off-screen. This was more acting than they had bargained for. Gilbert, Garbo, Valentino—how could they possibly be in reality what they so exotically represented on screen? And yet they had no choice.

The goldfish bowl image Adela Rogers St. Johns used to characterize early Hollywood life has more than a cliché's resonance. Goldfish are pretty and harmless, anonymous and useless. They are entirely segregated from the life around them and powerless to affect it. Nothing depends on them. Such attention as they attract is idle, without psychic freight. But this image, once applied with fine accuracy to Hollywood people, suddenly a few years later applied not at all.

They were now the basis of a big-business's prosperity. Large sums of money had to be risked on their ability to carry full-length feature films. It was increasingly borne in on people that that popularity was based, in large measure, on what they stood for—or seemed to stand for—in people's minds. Since, manifestly they could set standards of personal style—bobbed hair for women was a big item of controversy in the twenties, as long hair was for men in the sixties (odd this American obsession with the moral qualities of a coiffure)—then they might —horrors!—be capable of setting standards of conduct as well.

Now, many of the sometime goldfish wished to continue to swim round and round, not bothering anyone, lest they in turn be bothered. Others decided, as did Chaplin and Fairbanks in their different ways, that they were victims of mistaken identity. They were not goldfish at all. Maybe they weren't quite sharks, but they were big strong fish nevertheless, and they would leap the aquarium walls and find a large pond, or the mainstream. Or maybe, as they were relatively smart fish, they saw that the safe, nice days inside the glass bowl were numbered anyway—too many people crowding about, armed with nets and strange, popping lights. They were roiling the water, muddying it. And some of these intruders were clearly killers. Best to break the metaphor, cease being pets, and evolve not merely defense mechanisms but aggressive presences that would command a higher respect.

🦇 🦇

It was time. The press, like the movies, and coincidentally at the same historical moment, had come of age as an enterprise. In 1919, the same year United Artists was formed, a new publication appeared on the newsstands of New York. It was called *The Illustrated Daily News.* The descriptive word was dropped from the logotype within a year. It was superfluous. Everyone could see that the tabloid was illustrated. Halftone engraving, a quick process that permitted photos to be used despite the exigencies of the daily deadline, had come into fairly common usage by the turn of the century. But pictures had never been used as the *News* used them. Any picture would have loomed large on its pages, half the size of those of a standard newspaper. But the editors employed them with a boldness their full-page competitors never attempted. The news stories nearby were, in contrast, very short. But they were written in snappy, punchy style and topped by brash headlines. The manner was idiomatic (to say the least) and subjective. The ideal of objectivity was not much treasured here. Heads, prose, photo imagery—they seemed to leap out of some mass stream of consciousness. The boldstroke style aimed at a kind of low-life impressionism: its vision of big city life was of a series of shocks, in which the untoward became commonplace; each fragment was perhaps, comprehensible, but the whole scene was one of anarchy. Reading the *News* was like tuning in on a New York cabby's monologue, shrewd, vulgar, ultimately half-witted.

Crime, sex, movies, sports, and helpful tips for the distaff side—that was the basic tabloid formula. The events, by and large, were recurring. They differed in detail, of course, but not in their emotional tone to the reader. One could actually count on the tabloid product being essentially the same, day in, day out—like television, its successor. In the end repetition assures meaninglessness. In the world of the tabloid, there is little in the way of cause-effect relationships, no flow or continuity, no attempt to impose even a spurious sense of logic on life. One gets one's bearings there very largely through imagery. How comforting to come across the familiar face of a movie star or other celebrity in this collection of tales from messed up lives.

One might argue that the tabloid is a truer portrait of life in our times than one finds in the New York *Times* or any other publication that attempts to impose order and meaning on the day's events, or any publication that clings to the belief that debate over public policy or the flow of diplomatic cables has anything to do with reality as most of us experience it. Maybe love nests and axe murders are a truer projection of our times, our inner lives.

Yes. But there is an old, self-justifying city room definition of journalism. It is "history in a hurry." In other words, the thoughtful journalist likes to think that besides informing his contemporaries about what's going on around them he is also providing the historian of the future with an important source of raw material. In other words, he operates "within the hierarchy of what is powerful in history."

The quotations here are from *The New Yorker,* wherein an anonymous but brilliant contributor to "The Talk of the Town" section took up, at last, the problem of defining the operating principles and functions of high journalism and low at a moment—now—when they have become far more blurred than they were sixty-odd years ago. The point this writer makes is that the tabloids (and two more, the *Graphic* and the *Mirror,* soon followed the *News* into the New York market) have always dealt in what he calls the "emblematic." By which he means that certain people, certain events, when mentioned in a headline or glimpsed in a photo are emblematic not just of themselves, but of similar people and events throughout history. They evoke in the reader raw excitements, basic emotions remembered from other times and places—including sometimes his or her own childhood.

It is true, this anonymous media philosopher allows, that occasionally the tabloid press takes cognizance of "the quality of the presence of a man in history . . . as he has moved through history. He is angry. He is sad. He speaks from the soul." In other words, he appears in a context that renders his behavior explicable. But more often than not journalism in the emblematic mode provides neither context nor a sense of the continuity of the lives and happenings it chronicles. Everything it reports exists outside history entirely, is made to live on the page only for the reader's instant emotional gratification. Murder, corruption, cruelty, love blighted or perverted—in a sense, this material is not news at all, precisely because it happens all the time and has since the beginnings of time. It is naturally the stuff of novels, and it might be that the tabloid journalist could revise the old saw and say he is writing "fiction in a hurry." But, of course, the newspaper dealing in this material does not treat it as the novelist does, probing for cause and effect, for example, or seeking the subtle nuance in the intersection of personality and action. No, it is using it only emblematically, or symbolically, aiming simply at a frisson of emotional identification on the part of the reader.

The New Yorker writer goes on to say this: "An image, which may, in ways we do not completely understand, evoke all of human experience, is complete in itself. The implications of the power of the image are large, but one of them may be noted especially; an image does not seek context. It carries some some small context within it, sufficient for its own nourishment, and may disdain to be placed in history."

Obviously, what he has just described here is the screen star, par excellence, an image requiring no context for recognition, an image we apprehend instantly (or think we do) as a result of the amalgam of old roles, old gossip, old publicity photos. Such a figure is, in fact, a walking context, perhaps not sufficiently self-nourishing to satisfy his own requirements (particularly if he likes to think of himself as an artist), but providing plenty of psychic vitamins for the fans.

Equally obviously, in the 1920s the media, newly abustle, had discovered techniques whereby almost anyone could be wrested out of whatever context had originally nurtured him and turned into images of this kind. We think of Charles Lindbergh, of course. He is forever and always at the center of the twenties montage. Around him—your choice. You might want Al Smith and his derby, Calvin Coolidge in his Indian headdress, or Louise Brooks under her bangs. From the animal kingdom there might be Man-O-War or Balto the Hero Dog. Al Capone or Legs Diamond can represent organized crime, Ruth Snyder, snapped by an enterprising tabloid photographer at the moment of her death in the electric chair, unorganized crime. And there's Red Grange and Babe Ruth and Big Bill Tilden. Valentino in some exotic get-up and Clara Bow as the flapper's flapper. F. Scott Fitzgerald should be there, and, of course, Shipwreck Kelly atop his flagpole, a parody of heroism but a paradigm of "celebrity" in the decade of its birth. Even as the images fade and curl, they somehow retain their evocative power. They "read"—strong and simple, supplying their own contexts even at this late date.

Two things must strike us as we contemplate this montage. The first is that for no previous era is it possible to make a history out of images, that for no subsequent era is it possible to avoid doing so. For most of us now, this *is* history—this jumble, this incoherent impressionism. We are forever the prisoners of the montage, and to a degree, the overtones of celebrity go resonating down the corridors of time, fixed and immutable, stumbling blocks to reinterpretation, just as in life their famous images also resisted interpretation beyond the first powerful impression. The second point to be made, and it is perhaps the more important one, is what a crowded and disparate canvas we confront here. It is like looking at a photograph taken at the reunion of some very large family. It is impossible to sort out the hierarchy, to assign significance to these figures. They clamor equally for our attention, jostle one another for place. And there are no clues to help us in their environment, for as we earlier observed, there rarely is any environment in the modern portraiture of the famous. They are always glimpsed against some neutral background, which can always be airbrushed out. We can pick them up like paper dolls, place them where we will, in juxtapositions that suit the pure fancy of the moment.

There is another kind of paradigmatic figure we should deal with here. That is the press photographer, that rude fellow elbowing his way to the front of the crowd, setting off flash powder (later flashbulbs), ordering strangers around by either getting them out of his way or bending them to his crude will, so that his snap will sell. The paradigm of the paradigm was the lensman assigned by the tabloid to a ship's newsbeat. His task was simply to join the harbor pilot on his tug, meet incoming liners, and take pictures of the famous people on board. "A little more leg, Queenie," one is alleged to have yelled at Marie of Rumania. This was the historical beginning of the paparazzi, that disgusting herd of photographers to be found elbowing and trampling one another (and anyone in their way) now that the ships don't run and all travel lacks even a spurious sense of occasion, at any event the well-known are likely to attend, in order to get pictures of the celebrated. Note that from the beginning their subjects were not doing anything newsworthy. They were simply beginning a journey or arriving at the end of one, something everyone does all the time. It is the same now—celebrities are seen entering or leaving a building where a premiere or a charity function or some other quite ordinary event is taking place. It is merely that for the length of time it takes the star to get from limo to entrance he is unguarded, a "photo opportunity." Sometimes during the event, the pack, shepherded by press agents, is unchained and given five or ten minutes to shoot inside and work the room. One of the strange things is that an occasion does not seem quite as glamorous, quite as memorable if camera persons are not present, their flashguns winking.

But the future (or our present, if you will) is a digression. The point is only this: these pictures of the famous coming and going are perfect examples of the contextless image, or of the image that provides its own small context, whichever one prefers. Do note, however, that if the tabloids created the demand for this sort of thing, that demand has outlived the tabloids, only a few of which continue to totter on into our own time. In short, there are fewer such publications, but the paparazzi are more numerous than ever. Better equipped, too. Which means the tabloid spirit now infects all of journalism.

It may be argued that the tabloids were nothing new, just a further extension of the old Pulitzer-Hearst style, technologically updated. It may also be argued that outside of London (where the format originated with Lord Northcliffe's *Daily Mirror)* and New York, the form did not spread widely or prosper greatly. But the fact is that emblematic journalism remains a growth industry.

In the newspaper field, in the twenties, two factors encouraged that growth. One was the rise of the feature syndicates, with their need to provide least-common denominator imagery to their far-flung clients. Movie news, gossip, and photos, retailing information and pseudo-information about the doings of a class of people already "well-known for their well-knownness" (to borrow Daniel Boorstin's phrase, which has, in itself, become well-known for its well-knownness), was a necessity for them. The rise of the chain newspapers, with headquarters providing material that all member papers could use, also found film people of inestimable value.

Nor were newspapers the only form of mass journalism to take a quantum leap in reach and prosperity during these years. The popular magazines—*The Saturday Evening Post, Collier's,* the women's books —all selling for a nickel, had grown enormously. The circulation of the *Post* alone had risen from 314,671 per week in 1902 to 2,187,024 in 1922, during which period its advertising revenues had grown seventy-eight times as great. They, too, had a need for emblems, figures who had an instant recognition factor, profiles to be profiled as it were.

And then there were the innovators, most notably *Reader's Digest* and *Time,* both of which began in this period. Like the tabloids, though at a slightly more elevated level, they catered to the public perception that the world had speeded up, that there was both an increased flow of information and diminished time in which to absorb it. Obviously, there was a need to provide vehicles that could boil everything down to basics, make people feel "well-informed," (that civics class desideratum) on the cheap. Equally obviously the way to do so was with some form of emblematic journalism. "It's a basic premise at *Time* magazine that people are interesting *per se,*" says a recent ad for the magazine, "and *Time*'s founding fathers prized the nuggets of information, the unexpected facet, that make newsmakers come alive on the page."

Yes. The cover portrait and the story inside about the individual portrayed thereon constituted a masterstroke. The original rule—since rescinded—was that the cover figure had to be a living man or woman —no historical figures and no abstract representations of trends or ideas. The notion was that by investigating the intersection of personality and achievement in the life of a single individual, the magazine could offer its readers an approachable emblem of any matter that might otherwise prove to be disagreeably abstract.

The technique was employed in miniature (but in increasing degree as the years wore on and success mounted) in each section of the magazine. Since it undertook to organize the week's events under section headings—a very useful function, considering how jumbled an impression the world made on one as the flow of information increased—the necessity was to find as many people as possible on which to peg stories.

The whole was given a tone, almost but not quite, a point of view, by much-parodied *Time*style, as zippy and cheeky as anything in any tabloid, but more literate. This was said, by co-founder Britton Haddon, to have been derived in part from Homer's epic manner, very suitable for a publication that took the view that the week's events constituted a kind of epic in themselves. There was in this style a kind of omniscience of tone, a knowingness, that was reassuring to the reader.

Yet there was a kind of youthful playfulness in it too, a sense that puns and gags, neologisms and fanciful references were requisites if the multiplicity and simultaneity of events were to be adequately— that is, catchily—portrayed to the somewhat backward reader. It is perhaps worth reflecting that around this time, in another, far higher cultural realm, a great writer had also gone to Homer for his model and was also playing dazzlingly with words while celebrating, and organizing into artistic form, the quotidian. That, of course, was James Joyce. One wishes to do no more than point the parallel. And, by so doing suggest that journalism, at its humble level, was modernist too. Had to be. The search for the overpowering image, the one that might at least resolve for a moment the individual's sense of being awash in incomprehensible events and inundated by inchoate emotions, can be seen as a humane enterprise, an act of charity for the increasingly befuddled.

It is perhaps worthwhile observing that in the age of television the newsmagazines are, by and large, much less emblematic in their journalistic practice than they were in the beginning. Their original function having been preempted by the newer medium, they have prospered by counterpunching. More than half the time now their cover image will not be of an individual, but will be an abstraction calling attention to some social or political trend. Or it will be a news photo lifted out of the rushing stream of current events and implying that inside the magazine the reader will find the kind of reportage that will interpret last week's major happening with the thoughtfulness (and perhaps the grace) that hard-charging TV news cannot provide. Such stories may now take up to ten or twelve pages and they will be based on extensive, original investigation by the magazine's staff of reporters and correspondents. Moreover, the giddy prose of the journals' youth has disappeared, replaced by a tone more suitable to responsible maturity.

All of which is fine. They are now, most usefully, a force slowing down the pell-mell stream of events, permitting and encouraging at least a moment's reflection on them. But that does not invalidate our basic historical observation: the newsmagazines principally, but all magazines to some degree, in this their greatest era of innovation and of domination in the media mix, were the carriers of emblematic journalism from its place of origin, reporting about show people, into new realms—the political, the social, even the literary. They focused and fixed simple, simplifying images of all kinds of people, undertaking all manner of complicated endeavors, in terms any dull wit could comprehend. Shaggy Einstein was the symbol of intellectuality; fierce-featured Toscanini was the artistic temperament personified; Hemingway was the artist as adventurer; Gertrude Stein the artist as incomprehensible. And so on, through every form of human endeavor.

Can an argument be made that the obsessive interest of the press in the private lives of the well-known represents an effort to redeem them from their photographic images, from the limbo of public role playing? Do the words that accompany the pictures have the effect of reinserting them in a context that we all share?

It would be nice to think so. The balance restored and all that. But it does not seem to work out that way. The press could never really penetrate the mysteries of Einstein's imaginative universe. Or, for that matter, Hemingway's. Acts of high imagination remain inexplicable to the rest of us. And it really tells us nothing useful to report that Einstein had trouble with his income tax forms, just like everyone else. Even if the person under journalistic investigation is beautiful or glamorous, it may be consoling to the less favored to hear that much of their lives are as humdrum as ours, or that we share certain problems —ungrateful children, say, or an unappreciative spouse. But it does not enhance understanding—only our sense of identification.

And, anyway, the press and its subjects have long since entered into a kind of unconscious conspiracy. The well-known person wishes to preserve some measure of privacy—and some sense of mystery, since there is power in that. Therefore he agrees to limited intrusions on his time and space and gives out to the journalist just enough to satisfy curiosity and serve his own ends—the book or film or idea he is currently promoting. Or so he hopes. On its part, the press is by and large satisfied with this arrangement. Too much material needlessly complicates the story and renders first editor, then reader, restive with the accumulation of nuance, the loss of a clear story line. And besides, if his subject is prominent enough the reporter wants to stay on friendly terms with him. Never can tell when you might want to come back. And so a conventionalized portrait is agreed upon in unspoken terms. And what emerges? The equivalent of a photo in words, an image or emblem by other means. This basic method of conducting business was arrived at, of necessity, in the twenties and continues to pertain.

It was not arrived at without confusion and pain. They were, in fact, basic to the bargain, which was defined during and after the great Hollywood scandals that began with the Fatty Arbuckle case of 1921–23. Arbuckle was the popular over-sized comedian who had begun in pictures in 1913. It has become clear since—indeed, it was clear to the jury at his third trial, which took just five minutes to acquit him of a murder charge and compose a statement asking fair play for him after his ordeal by publicity—that the worst he could be accused of was a careless display of libidinal energy.

There had undoubtedly been a large, long party over the Labor Day weekend in the suite Arbuckle and some Hollywood pals had taken in San Francisco's St. Francis Hotel. Women had been present and one of them, a prostitute named Virginia Rappe, had taken sick at the party and subsequently died. There was no evidence that her illness had anything to do with her sexual activities at the party or that these necessarily included making love with Arbuckle. There is every evidence to suggest that it was alcohol, exacerbating a chronic bladder condition, that led to her hospitalization and subsequent death. It also appears that she suffered from venereal disease and that she was pregnant at the time of the party. It is also likely that the woman who recruited her for the party had it in mind, from the start, to work a badger game on Arbuckle and friends, to entrap them in sexual misconduct for purposes of blackmail. It appears possible that even after Rappe's death this woman's continued incriminating statements to the police had as their purpose an attempt to make Arbuckle buy her silence.

So much for the facts. They soon ceased to have much influence on anyone. For as Betty Harper Fussell has observed in her recent book on Mabel Normand, Fatty's costar and friend and a victim herself of subsequent trials by publicity, the public, "conditioned by and responding to a decade of faked images, was now taking revenge by inventing mythic images of its own." The controlling image, in the rumors that circulated at the time, and ever since, was of Arbuckle, huge and baby-faced, doing fatal damage to Rappe (even the victim's name, by terrible ill-chance, conjured up sexual violation) either with his great weight or by use of a Coke bottle as a dildo. As Mrs. Fussell writes, "By 1921, a generation of moviemakers had betrayed the innocent imagination of America, and like other professional virgins, America cried 'Rape!' Since a baby could not rape without aid, what could be more monstrous as his tool than a bottle of soda pop, symbol of youth and refreshment?"

People may or may not have been revenging their betrayed innocence at Arbuckle's expense, but Arbuckle, who was, in his person and in his comedic style, very much a symbol of their cheeriest and least sophisticated days, surely dismayed people. He, of all people, did not belong at a wild party; he, of all people, should not have been placed in a position where he personified everyone's worst imaginings about

Hollywood life (and the rumors, especially about drug use, had begun to circulate earlier). For someone like him to be associated with the orgiastic was simply too much to bear. If he was involved in such goings-on then who could or would not be? Yes, Mrs. Fussell is right, Hollywood's biggest baby, someone the nation had loved and indulged had turned into a Golem and, by extension, the whole innocent-seeming world that had produced him and promoted him turned monstrous with him.

Rich psychic stuff, this. And if the press did not fully apprehend all its dimensions, it could recognize that it was onto something very powerful, something that stirred people in some new and astonishing way.

There had been nothing like it before, so there was no machinery in place that might tame the tide. And, anyway, the story had happened in San Francisco outside the movie capital, where even such primitive accommodations as had already been reached with its kept press could not be invoked. Arbuckle had to be sacrificed for the greater good, just as later people accused of communism (also in arenas where the moguls had no power to silence their accusers or control how the story was reported) had to be sacrificed.

Nor did Arbuckle's destruction end the matter. The death by drug addiction of Wallace Reid, the popular romantic star, which occurred in the midst of the comedian's three trials, seemed to confirm everyone's worst imaginings, as did the mysterious murder a little later, of director William Desmond Taylor, who had been romantically linked with Mabel Normand, the charmingly hoydenish comedienne, and Mary Miles Minter, a promising ingenue. No one ever connected either woman to any wrongdoing, but it is worth observing that, like Arbuckle and like later stars whose careers were damaged rather than enhanced by their off-screen misadventures, both women had projected essentially innocent images on-screen. They rudely shocked people's expectations, and where contemporaries like Gloria Swanson or Clara Bow might have survived connections with scandals of this sort, they could not.

Hollywood, of course, hurried to repair the damage not to its people, but to itself as a burgeoning institution. Will Hays, a starchy middle western politician then serving as Postmaster General (and as Waspish as the industry's leaders were Jewish), was appointed head of a new Motion Picture Producer's Association, given power to censor on-screen material and to act as moral guardian of the performers' off-screen behavior. He could—or so it was made to seem—ban any and all players from the screen if they offended, and compel studios to bury any unreleased works by these pariahs. All contracts were provided with a morals clause, permitting the studio to abrogate them should the parties of the second part bring shame on their masters with their conduct. As far as one can tell, such Draconian measures were never employed after the Arbuckle case. The threat was enough.

It was enough because as the studios consolidated, power was concentrated in a few hands. By the end of the decade the half dozen heads of the half dozen major studios could literally blackball anyone who got out of line. And, controlling the then severely limited number of news sources, they could manage the press quite easily—at least up to the point where some unpleasantry actually got to court, which aside from matrimonial matters and the odd nightclub brawl, was not very often. The deal was simple: access to the stars when stories were needed; in return, silence, or anyway, vast discretion, when the studios required it. From time to time, in addition, the Hollywood columnists were used to punish and reward stars who showed too much individuality (or too little gratitude) in their dealings with their bosses.

Amusing things would continue to be reported from Hollywood, and movie stars would continue to symbolize changing masculine, feminine, and romantic ideals, but aside from Errol Flynn's statutory rape case, and Chaplin's paternity suit in the forties, after the Arbuckle case, the movie industry rarely produced a major symbolic crime, something for the social historians and moralists to sink their teeth into. From the Lindbergh kidnapping to the Jean Harris trial, they would have to look elsewhere for the stories that would purport to tell us about social change, revisions in mass psychology.

In the manipulation of publicity, as in everything else, practice makes perfect, and as the years wore on, Hollywood had plenty of practice in this dark art. But there were other factors at work here. The change in movie technology, from silent to sound production, affected the relationship between the public and the movie stars. So did the huge change in attitudes when prosperity gave way to economic depression. But the largest factor in stabilizing Hollywood's relationship with its journalistic auditors was the result of changing organization and technology in journalism itself. Hollywood became big, oligopolistic business and, increasingly, so did the press. Big was now speaking to big; symbiosis was setting in. Crude symbolization, by no means confined to movie figures, but with the process of using these symbols modeled on the star system, was beginning to become a standard operating procedure in all the media.

Sometime in the 1920s a journalist of traditional stripe traveled by train from New York to the Middle West over a weekend. At each stop —Buffalo, Cleveland, Toledo, Indianapolis, Chicago, St. Louis—he purchased the Sunday paper. And, once they were jumbled in his compartment, he found it near impossible to tell from which journal he was reading. The wire service stories and pictures were the same in each; so were the columns, whether political or gossip. Most carried the same syndicated comics and magazine supplements. Most carried very little local news that might have helped the reader differentiate one publication from another. At around the same time other travelers began a complaint, scarcely diminished today, about the decline of regionalism in everything from cooking to spoken language. Everywhere a homogenization process had set in.

This devastation (and that is how it was perceived by those who cared about such matters) was the result of an explosion in image technology. It was as powerful in its way as the television explosion was three decades later. It loosened this decade's connections with its past as surely as TV loosened us from our moorings to the period preceding its appearance. Indeed, as the emblematic journalism of the twenties preempted the more sober and traditional journalistic forms that went before it, so television preempted the preemptors. Almost everything discussed in this chapter has either disappeared or changed form. The tabloids are almost all gone, and the daily press, especially the afternoon daily press that faces the most direct television competition, constantly dwindles. The big general weeklies have folded, and the newsmagazines have reversed their former function. *Time*style is no longer its jazzy, almost self-parodying self. The writing there is sober and straightforward, and the articles are longer as befits a magazine that sees itself providing the contexts, the historical and social perspectives, television news cannot provide. It still has its occasional emblematic cover, to be sure, but as often as not, the cover story will explore some general issue rather than a personality. In short, the newsmagazines, alone of the general interest magazines, prosper mainly by being less of what they were at the start, not more.

Except to the degree that reiterated banality lowers the general tone of life, it must be understood that, as fiction, television poses no active threat to anyone, the strictures of the PTA and the various fundamentalist crusades against it to the contrary notwithstanding. No, it is in the realm of reality, or what passes for reality, on television that our interest must lie. For it is here that the pacified and the inert, gather their weird, incoherent impressions of their world—from the talk and interview shows, from the news and pseudonews shows (which now proliferate in the hours before the network evening news programs). Television news is, by traditional standards, inadequate. The people who produce television news are themselves always telling us that. They offer, they say, "a headline service" and urge us, with becoming modesty, to look elsewhere for background and perspective.

But they are not modest enough. Headlines are what we get on news radio. What we get on television is not a headline service but a tabloid service. It takes that old format to its logical extreme, since manifestly television is *all* pictures, for which anchormen and reporters merely provide captions. Some stories, alas, cannot be illustrated. Usually they are the complicated and boring ones—about the economy or foreign policy, let us say. The inherent demand of the medium is to get through this stuff as quickly and painlessly as possible, cut from the talking heads to the crying heads (disaster victims, let us say, or political loonies), or better still, running feet or rapidly moving vehicles—explosions, riots. Like the tabloid journalists before them, the television crew is always on the alert for an emblematic figure and will thrust a moment of fame on anyone who is eyewitness to a disaster. To the degree that such stories can be universalized, made to seem a threat to everyone's well-being or complacency, they improve. A mine disaster is not what it once was—few of us are miners. A commercial airline crash is excellent—we all fly and somewhat fear it. And so on.

When the issue is more abstract, or anyway less naturally pictorial, different emblematic figures are required. Heads of state and other powerful politicos perform this function ex officio. Others acquire it. These celebrity authorities may be known for their well-knownness, but they are also known for their knowingness. Their presence when they appear, talking, carries an aura of expertise, which may have begun years ago in public office or with a book or even a moral act they committed, but after a time that aura is a compound of all their previous television appearances, supported by their magazine articles, quotations in the newspapers, busy work on lecture platforms, at symposia. Pictures of them chatting with a movie star at some bash *People* has covered even make their contribution: Steinem=feminism, Nader=consumerism, Mailer=literature, Walesa=dissidence. And so on. For every ideology there is a spokesperson, an emblem. We do not have to ask, no one needs to waste valuable seconds explaining, what gives them the right to speak or whether we should believe what they're saying. They are the movie stars of the world of (simplified) ideas; they are capable of reducing any complexity to the time span of a commercial. Indeed, if they were made to put on white coats before they fixed us with an earnest eye and started lecturing, we might at least be aware, as we are when someone so garbed points to an impressive-seeming chart, that we are in the midst of a pitch.

All this comes at us out of a void. These people do not seem to live anywhere specific, even walk the same streets we do. Impossible to imagine them at the supermarket. Edward Epstein called television news the "news from nowhere." George W. S. Trow says we exist in "the context of no context." What I am saying is that nowhere came into existence longer ago than they say it did, that our public context began to lose touch with our private context some sixty years ago. We did not happen to notice it back then, because the means by which images were hawked—that is to say, networked—still bore some relationship to traditional forms. Newspapers still mostly looked like newspapers, magazines like magazines. Even the big new form, the movies, invention of which provided model and impetus for changing our perceptual mode, was for a long time misunderstood. It is only very recently that people have stopped chastising the movies for not being more like theater, for not being more literate and linear and logical the way plays are—or were. It is only recently that people stopped hoping movies would "grow up" and be elevated and elevating the way the theater could sometimes be.

By the time the 1920s ended, our world had not so much changed as it had bifurcated. Or had begun to bifurcate. Our immediate, physical surroundings had not changed, and our immediate personal concerns had not changed—not very radically at any rate. We were even still permitted public life of a sort in our communities. But there was this trouble with it: it seemed to be very small potatoes. Its rewards and recognitions seemed paltry compared to what was going on elsewhere, where the images were made, where the truly glamorous made work seem like play and fame was the spur.

It was not too bad for a while. The images from that "nowhere that was everywhere" (everywhere that we were not, that is) were still murky, still arrived in consciousness travel-stained and a little tired in those preelectronic days. They did not soak up so much of our time and the means by which they were disseminated were neither so sweetly seductive nor so brutally domineering as television can be. A certain distance was maintained, therefore a certain skepticism.

Nowhere, the context of no context, could yet be tuned out as easily —or almost as easily—as it could be tuned in. Only a few people had confused image and reality. Only a few manifestly crazy people labored under the delusion, now common, that nowhere was somewhere and that somewhere was bound to be a nowhere—that is to say, a place where nothing good, interesting, or important ever happened. There was still, in the 1930s and the 1940s, a tenuous balance between the two, maybe even a certain energizing tension between them.

THREE

Where I Came In

Objectivity is all right, as far as it goes. But celebrity is singularly a subject that reaches into everyone's brain in strange and irrational ways. If you write about it you are obliged to come to terms with the ways in which you think it may have affected your own sense of reality —declare your interest, as it were, to the degree that you can determine what it is.

For example. I was born in a large middle western city in the early 1930s. I grew up in a middle-class suburb of that city, among people who were, it seemed, quite contented with their lot. Restlessness was not something I saw much of in those days. Where mine came from, I cannot say for certain. But I think it came from outside, from the things I heard and read and saw.

That is to say, it came in from the movies, from radio, from the press. Of these I don't know which was the most significant to me, but I do know that when I was nine or ten I began going to the movies at least once a week—more often if possible. Even before that, the radio had been a large factor in my life—almost as important as television has been to later generations, though of course it was possible to do one's homework while listening to it, which is at best an improbability when the TV is running. One tuned in to the serial adventures for kids in the late afternoon, took a dinner break, and returned to the mysteries, comedies, and quiz shows that were supposed to interest the whole family.

My favorite program was "The Lux Radio Theatre," in the days when its host was Cecil B. DeMille. It was on CBS on Monday nights at eight o'clock. It offered hour-long radio plays based on some current film and generally featured the stars of the picture in their original roles. I especially liked the chats DeMille held with them at the end of the show, when they told him what their next pictures were going to be and he acted surprised and delighted at the brilliance of these projects. When he announced what his next "Lux" offering was to be, the audience, carefully cued, would draw in its breath sharply and break into "spontaneous" applause. And when DeMille said good-night "from Hollywood," he had a peculiar way of rolling the word off his tongue, with a rising, glamorizing inflection on the second syllable—very impressive in the hinterlands.

We had, in our town—or as it would now be known, "metro area" —one rather distinguished daily newspaper (it was always making the ten-best lists) called *The Journal,* and another that was rather less so —a Hearst paper, in fact—called *The Sentinel.* The former, for a long time, reviewed movies in only the most perfunctory way (there was no regular critic) and did not carry news or gossip about them or about show business in general, except in its Sunday "Screen and Radio" section. Special indulgences were, however, granted local men and women who had achieved stardom or even starletdom. One thus learned a disproportionate amount about Spencer Tracy, Pat O'Brien, Jack Carson, Dennis Morgan, and the man who played "Mr. District Attorney" on radio, all of whom had been born locally. *The Journal,* incidentally, took considerable pride in the fact that it carried no syndicated columns of any kind. All opinions were homegrown and confined to the editorial page; there was no gossip anywhere about anything, though hard news involving the well known (i.e., Tommy Manville's divorces when a court officially granted them) was dutifully but very discreetly, noted.

The Hearst paper, in contrast, often seemed to consist of nothing but columns, the vast majority of which emanated from elsewhere. Winchell and Louella were, naturally, staples, and so were the editorial page cranks—Pegler, George Sokolsky, et al. There were also loads of King Features Syndicate stories about glamorous folk of every ilk. This newspaper was regularly deplored in our house, but it was read, especially by me.

I do not wish to imply that these were the only publications that entered our house. Many magazines came as well—*The Saturday Evening Post, Time, Life, The Saturday Review, The New Yorker,* my mother's women's magazines, even the Sunday edition of the New York *Times,* which arrived by rail Monday and could be purchased at one, and only one, downtown newsstand. All in all, I was subject to a singularly rich "media mix" as we would now call it. For that time and place, indeed, it was richer than that of anyone, young or old, whom I knew.

No doubt my subsequent career was greatly influenced by it. One could not help but gain a sense that there was out there a place—lots of places, really—where interesting and exciting things were going on. I didn't know quite how or even where I might fit into that larger scene, but I began wanting to, and when I was quite young, I somehow gained a sense that writing was a respectable occupation for which I might have some gift (surely I had none for math or the sciences). It also became clear to me that writers were employed in all the fields that purveyed entertainment and information to me, and soaked up so much of my time. Then, too, it seemed better to be in on things as they were happening, to be at what seemed the center, rather than to be trapped out there where you always felt you were the last to know what was really going on.

To a degree, I glamorized the process of gathering and disseminating information, and of putting on the shows that so bemused me on the air and on the screen. I checked out library books that purported to explain how movies, radio, newspapers worked. Did I think I might myself become famous by writing my way into this world? I think I must have hoped so, without having any sure sense of how that might happen. From the distance at which I observed the great world I could not, certainly, see that there was a distinct pecking order in it, that though many of the journalists I read implied intimacy with the powerful and the favored, they were deluded. Or were trying to delude us. As I would come to know firsthand, journalists are courted, flattered, used by their subjects, occasionally even feared by them, but they live permanently under suspicion—which is as it should be if you are a sort of double agent in the celebrity system—because they are trying to get ahead by writing about those who have already gotten ahead.

A romantic image that. But, of course, the notion of being a spy in the house of self-love did not occur to me when I was a youth. What I could dimly sense at that time was a different element in journalism's appeal. I liked the possibility of being a gadfly, a cynical idealist, knowing yet independent. And there were, of course, examples before us all the time of very successful newsmen—famous columnists, foreign correspondents who wrote best-selling books about their experiences, great crusaders, Waspishly quotable critics—who seemed to have transcended the limits of the profession. You could hear them on the radio; they came through town and gave lectures; they were somebodies. It seemed if you were lucky and talented you might have your integrity and be a success in worldly terms, as well. Matter of fact, it looked easy. And rather fun, too.

This illusion was the product of two fictions, one of which was more or less consciously formulated and presented within a formal fictional framework. The second was the product of a felt commercial necessity —one of the largest efforts at reeducating an instinctive perception of reality one was ever witness to, somewhat the victim of. It was pervasive and it was quite subtle in its workings—so subtle that I, at least, was unaware of its existence until some years later.

Let me set it aside for the moment. Let's talk first about the more formal fiction and its workings. If you are born and raised in the boondocks and have the slightest sense of ambition, one fact becomes clear as soon as you become aware that the world is wide: that out there, away from your little bend on Moon River, people are doing interesting things, having more fun, and, in the end, accomplishing things that one cannot undertake locally. In the United States achievement obviously has several venues—New York, Los Angeles, Washington, for certain, and out beyond them the other world capitals of art, entertainment, thought, politics. In due course all these places tend to merge into a single country of the mind, The Great Other Place, as I came eventually to think of it.

It was a place where people tended to be beautiful (or at least well-dressed), witty, thoughtful, sexy, and able to handle wine lists, menus printed in French, and registering together at a hotel even if they weren't married. The men were often to be found in dinner jackets or even tails. At play, yachting costumes and jodhpurs were favored by both sexes. In the evening the women wore dresses that were, to our untutored eyes, barely distinguishable from their negligees, in that they were cut of shimmery white satin that clung sensuously to their bodies. These people lived in penthouses also very white and high-key, glittery with mirrors and appointments we can only in retrospect identify as art deco. They often had white pianos.

For the weekends, there was always Connecticut. In his study of what he terms "the comedy of remarriage," Stanley Cavell notes the prevalence, perhaps the necessity, of "a green world," a place where the perspective of posh people can be regained, psychic renewal obtained. This was always identified as Connecticut in the movies. It existed in films of a less comic nature. And it persisted in movie iconography well beyond the 1930s, this rural Eden of lovely stone houses and converted barns. It seemed to be peopled with comically practical rustics who existed mainly to form a contrast with the brittle sophisticates who had the leading roles—escaping ad men, magazine editors, theatrical producers, heirs and heiresses. An oddity of these movies was that when the city folk threw open the doors to their retreats the fire was always crackling, the lights were always softly glowing, the tray of drinks was always set out. By whom? one wondered. And how did they know master and mistress were on the way? One never heard the warning call being placed. Did these unseen servants keep the fires going always, just on the off chance . . . ? Or were the woods outside populated by benign elves? It made no difference. This, obviously, was *the* life.

What was being purveyed in these films, though we were unaware of it at the time, was a version of café society life, that unintended by-product of prohibition. As C. Wright Mills pointed out some years ago in his pioneering study, *The Power Elite,* it was bootlegging and the speakeasy that created the first alliance between organized crime and the respectable world, and brought the criminal elite into contact with the other elites—financial, literary, show biz, and hereditary. All of them began to meet and mingle rather glamorously in the Manhattan clubs where illegal booze could be obtained. It was to this world that, when sound pictures were invented, Hollywood turned for people who could write dialogue. Journalists, one-shot novelists and playwrights, fringe *littérateurs* who were either down on their luck or had never had much luck, headed west at glorious salaries to write about what they knew—or claimed to know. And while it was at it, Hollywood scooped up the Broadway comedies that also purported to show how the swells lived. And, above all, talked, since the need was for something attractive and stylish to place on the sound track. Pauline Kael has wisely observed, in her "Raising Kane" essay, that there was a cultural lag there—that what the writers brought to Hollywood in the thirties was really the Broadway spirit of the twenties, a fast and fizzy farcicality that was at once cynical and sentimental.

Watching from our provincial shadows we did not know that. We

did not know that what we were seeing was, probably, inappropriate—
even a bit weird—in an era of vast economic dislocation. We did not
even know that what we were watching was not a realistic vision of a
social milieu that had in any case largely disappeared before we were
born, but rather a highly conventionalized commercial formulation.
What we did see was that no matter how brittle their talk, how grand
their surroundings, or how fatuous some of their friends and relatives
were, the heroes and heroines of these comedies and romances were
good guys and gals—essentially democratic in their attitudes, sweet,
affectionate, and decent in their manners. One could identify with
them, project oneself into their shoes. In other words, and in subtle
ways, The Other Place, The Better Place, seemed to be attainable. The
passport, one guessed, was talent. And niceness, of course.

The movies were not the only place we obtained this information.
The radio was not all Fibber McGee and Molly. It had, for example, a
large population of society detectives ranging from Nick and Nora
Charles to Ellery Queen and Nero Wolfe, and their investigations always uncovered hints of the good life. The public library in my town
had everything from P. G. Wodehouse to John O'Hara (I told you the
geography of The Other Place was quite delightfully vague). Every
once in a while a touring play came through town, and it carried the
perfume of distant glamour. And then, of course, there were those
columns in *The Sentinel* every morning, in which the names we saw in
the credits every week at the movies jostled on apparently equal foot-
ing with other names, the occupations and preoccupations of which
were extremely vague: Hope Hampton, Cy Howard, Greg Bautzer,
Jock Whitney, Steve Crane, Lady Mendl, Herbert Bayard Swope, Jed
Harris. One had no sense of their comparative social status or, in some
cases, what they actually did for a living. All one knew was that they
could all, apparently, get in where we could not, trade quips (and
escorts) quite indiscriminately, flit about the world at will. Their
names became tags mingling with other tags—Butterfield 8, the Al-
gonquin Round Table, "21," "Good Evening, Mr. First Nighter,"
"The Manhattan Merry-Go-Round."

It was not quite a delirium. But it was a confusing, seductive buzz in
the back of the brain—this erratically delivered blend of information
and misinformation. It fed one's own innocent and highly speculative
gossip mills ("Boy, I betcha . . . ," the sentence always started). And
for a few of us, discontented in some vague way, though not actively
unhappy in that benign backwater (where even World War II, when it

came along, seemed quite safely distant, even rather entertaining), this stuff fed dreams of escape and achievement (yes, I think the word order there is correct), quite unfocused, quite grandiose, quite impractical. This imagery did not make us what we are today. But it did make us want to be something like what we are today.

🍂 🍂

There was a power in all this. There is power of some kind in the creation of any imagery that is pervasive and memorable. But in the midst of a depression, comedies in which rich people, no matter how cute, do silly things, are unlikely to be regarded by masses of people as anything but a cheerful form of escapism. Even among my youthful, innocent peers, I was so far as I can see (looking back through the mists of time) the only one who found some kind of loopy inspiration in these films. But then, I was the only one nurturing fantasies of fame on a scale that was more than local. And I was pretty circumspect about it. For public consumption, I'm sure that I couched any discussion of ambitions in terms that the good paper, *The Journal,* would have approved.

Community service was a basic good. No man in our town was regarded as successful if he did not "head up" some charitable enterprise, work in the PTA, serve his church as a Sunday school teacher, Cub Scout leader, or vestryman. A little later, when the war came along, the range of possibilities was greatly increased. Scrap drives, bond drives, work with the draft board or the rationing board, even being an air raid warden—these were worthy occupations for a responsible male and accepted, as political nominations were, reluctantly, as a call to duty. Always, one was expected to carry oneself with dignity, with due modesty and circumspection, while keeping any outlandish opinions one might entertain to oneself. One did not lightly set these standards aside, even if one's eye was roving toward more distant horizons.

In those days, indeed, except for the very occasional work of an exemplary nature, some movie, for instance, that it was thought particularly instructive for the young people to see *(Going My Way* was such a one), popular entertainment was rarely summoned to the cause of moral edification. If you were a male child, sports were, and stars in that field were, made to loom large in your emulative fantasies. Those who were known to gladly grant autographs to importunate youngsters—perhaps even pause to chat with them about how to hit a curve to get some distance on their punts—were always well thought of. Visits to hospitals, bearing gifts of balls autographed by the entire team, were looked on with particular favor. An annual newspaper feature was the snap of the college all-stars, members of the East and West teams in the New Year's Day game played for the benefit of crippled children, while visiting the tykes whose limbs would be magically healed by their athletic toil on the gridiron.

In those days, of course, amateurism was much admired, professionalism was not. To play a game for money—especially football or basketball, which were associated with bright college years—seemed somehow to detract rather than to add to a man's stature. Proof of this was supplied when we heard reports of Ted Williams's arrogance and general snappishness with press and public; he was heartily disapproved of. And snorts of disgust arose from behind *The Saturday Evening Post* or *Collier's* when my father or grandfather ran across an ad in which some athlete was seen to be endorsing Camels or Lucky Strikes. This was definitely not setting a good example. In fact, all endorsements of commercial products, whether by jock, actress, or bandleader were looked upon dimly in our town; one was not supposed to trade *virtù* for hard cash.

Still, it appears to me, looking back, that the properly conducted sporting life—complimentary toward opponents, modest about one's own achievements, exemplary in one's conduct off the field—was as close to paradigmatic as any public life could be. For it must be remembered that, in those days, athletes were, if anything, underpaid rather than overpaid and were not expected to have opinions on social and political issues, for which, in any event, there were no forums available to them.

Males achieving success in other lines, business or politics, for example, more or less followed the athletic model, for as with the sports stars, their occupations in and of themselves guaranteed their manliness, thus their credentials as right-thinking citizens. They had no need to prove anything to anybody. And when the war came along the heroes it created were expected to follow this basic line as well. Their manner, when they were sent forth on their morale-building, war bond-selling tours of the home front, was very much that of the Western movie stars. They were shit kickers, thus good examples to youth, to everyone.

Good examples! One could almost grow nostalgic for the term, once so prevalent, now so disused. In the thirties and the forties it was the simple basis for reaching a judgment on whether or not a prominent person was to be permitted permanent residence in our fancies or would be asked to leave town before sunset.

It was a matter of great moment in the motion picture industry, though I did not know it at the time. In those days I had only the dimmest awareness of what had gone on in the scandalous twenties, but in the very year I was born, the production code was strengthened —to the point where industry censors could force editing or reshooting of a scene if the inside of a female thigh was exposed or if both a male lover's feet were seen to leave the floor while he was wooing a lady reclining on bed or couch. And so on. These antique sillinesses require little rehearsal now. If they reflect anything more than a craven response to pressure from the Catholic church, especially from its more morally enthusiastic laymen, it may be that they can be seen as a response to more sober and sobering times.

Politically the mood swing was to the left, of course, and it was incumbent on everyone in the public eye to be serious, even when they were advocating optimism. The old Hollywood flightiness, its former youthful exuberance, did not suit. Well-known people were supposed to celebrate, or appear to celebrate, the values of the common man in what was supposed to be his era, maybe even his century. This included, for movie stars, a certain modesty of dress and lifestyle. And deportment. Marrying foreign royalty was distinctly not done now. Ranch houses went down better with the public than did castles as places to hang your hat. Emphasis in studio press releases shifted from how hard the stars played to how hard they worked.

Coincidentally, the shift from silent to sound productions reinforced this stress on commonality. Simply stated, the addition of the voice to film (music had always been present via orchestras, organist, or humble pianist in the theaters when silents were shown) added new notes of reality and intimacy to the film-going experience. We were no longer dealing with an essentially iconographic and (at least potentially) poetic cinema, in which the performers, in order to convey emotion and idea, had to resort to unrealistic pantomime while directors developed the symbolic language of montage to get their points across. The development of a purely cinematic language of artistic expression by and large declined in the first decade or so of the sound era, but dialogue, as supplied by those newly recruited playwrights and novelists, exploring what amounted to a new medium, and exploiting—almost as a game—its potential for innuendo that could be sneaked by the censors, made an impact on the sensibilities of the moralists that was extraordinarily powerful.

Beyond that, the psychological distance between stars and their audience was radically shortened with the coming of sound. What seemed to be their last significant secret, their tones of voice, was now revealed—or so it seemed. And, of course, talk permitted them to appear more comfortably in realistic (or realistic *seeming)* contemporary settings. It was no longer easy to refer to them as gods and goddesses, or even to think of them as democracy's surrogates for royalty—though social commentators continued rather mindlessly to do so. More and more they seemed—or were made to seem—like prettified versions of the folks who lived just down the block or, at the farthest, up the hill, in the better part of town.

So, once again, technological development had its effect in changing the nature of our relationship with the celebrated and refashioning the unspoken, near unconscious links between performer and public. And it was no more than common sense to stress the commonality of the uncommon and the common in a new political climate by emphasizing not the differences between them, but their oneness.

Oneness! What a curious moment in the history of press agentry this was! During the period stretching from the early thirties to at least the middle of the fifties, a massive effort—of just how much consciousness on the part of those engaged in it is impossible to say—was made to reeducate the public. The old exotic fancies were, in large measure, canceled out, a new fiction of ordinariness created. It was a fiction in which extraordinary people—if not always in talent, then assuredly in looks and income level—were supposed to be seen as entirely like their audience in basic values and desires. To put it in my familiar terms, the characters of *The Sentinel*'s columns were then to be seen behaving on the national stage as the responsible Rotarians of *The Journal*'s superb local coverage did.

Here was a fiction that went beyond the formal fictions of the screen that were so engaging to me at the time, a fiction of great surface modesty and simplicity and all the more remarkable therefore. Because it stands to reason—stood to reason at the time—that setting aside all questions of comeliness and money, these were a chosen few—albeit haphazardly so. At the height of Hollywood's power over us there were, after all, no more than a couple hundred people who could be called stars—and that is stretching a point—including character players who commanded top billing on occasion, short-lived phenomena that the studios failed to put over, starlets who lost their hold on their producer-mentors after one or two films, a dog here, a horse there, and so on. In truth there were perhaps not more than a hundred real stars in those days, actors and actresses who could adequately fulfill the basic demand of their trade, which was to pull us into the theater no matter what the monstrosity in which they were playing.

Yet these amazing creatures were constantly portrayed, when I was growing up, as absolutely regular guys and gals. The men seemed always to be out hunting or fishing or rounding up cattle on their ranches. (Interesting how this old ranching fantasy is continued by Ronald Reagan, whose taste in public relations imagery was obviously shaped permanently in those simple days when his largest ambition was to be what he never became—a star of the first rank.) The women, it seemed, labored under the impress of what we might now perhaps be permitted to think of as the "Mommie Dearest" syndrome. That is to say, no matter how glamorous they were, or how possessed by careerism, they had to be seen as devoted mothers, endlessly helpful wives—even if they had no gift for either role and even if, like Joan Crawford, they had in effect to hire children to play the supporting roles in a domestic drama.

Neither sex any longer dwelled in the crenellated fantasies of the silent movie kings and queens. When we were permitted a glimpse of them at home, in *Life* or *Look* or the fan magazines, these houses had about them a distinctly suburban air. They were larger, of course, than our houses and came equipped with swimming pools and tennis courts, but they were recognizably like the places where the most successful people in our town lived. They were, in fact, very like the houses these same actors inhabited in movies where they were required to play middle-class couples—aggrandized projections of the ordinary. In the movies these visions excited a certain amount of criticism at the time; people of the income level these characters were supposed to represent simply did not have the grandeur about their settings that the production designers imputed to them. But we are talking about fantasies, and these were fantasies well within our range, unlike, say, Falcon's Lair or Pickfair, or Harold Lloyd's grand, cold pile.

In short, the news from the rumpus rooms and the barbeque pits of the famous, conveyed through the picture layouts in the Sunday supplements, the profiles in the thick, slick magazines, was not only that their pleasures, but their most basic values were virtually indistinguishable from our own—despite the fact that they were better supplied with terrific recreational equipment.

I know it seems improbable, this sense that people so beautiful and so favored could be so precisely like us in the matters that really counted. But it must be remembered that, at least in the middle classes, we were terribly content with our world, and it seemed completely logical that the achieving others would want to go on living pretty much as we did. The goads toward dissatisfaction among us watchers would come later, paradoxically as our prosperity rose, bringing with it that familiar malaise of modern bourgeois life, the revolution of rising expectations. But forty years ago the carburetor setting on the communications machine had not been changed, enriching the fuel that fed our fantasies, encouraging our dreams of easy and instantaneous emulation. Aspiring to little more than more of the same, it was simple enough—and pleasant enough—to believe that movie stars and suchlike wanted pretty much what we wanted—to move the family into that nice big house out in the new section of town, to buy a new car, to bring home the new console model Magnavox as a surprise for the household. I mean, what more was there to life?

If that makes it seem as if, for many of us, the conventional relationship between media figures and their auditors was here reversed, that the movie stars were imitating us, so be it. Something like that, to some degree, was going on, for it was child's play to feed those childish fantasies of ours, easy enough in those slow and simple times to smother—much of the time—such dubiety as might seep into our contemplations of the rich and famous.

And what a pleasant fiction this was! So seemly. And so innocent. And how uncomplicated it must have been—compared to the way things are now—for those performers who chose to live within it. Insofar as they were not seen to rip up the nice white picket fences that had been metaphorically placed around their lives by the publicists, insofar as they were able to pull themselves together when *The Saturday Evening Post*'s Pete Martin decided to call on them, then they were granted a certain paradoxical freedom, that freedom, so often remarked by philosophers, that is to be found when free will is constrained, when a limitless array of choices is not available to bedevil the self-bedazzled.

In time it became possible to maneuver right up to, and even beyond, the edge of scandal. For example, the divorce rate among the famous did not decline, it was just that divorce, among other domestic anomalies, ceased to be seen as it had been by the public, as the wages of sin, and became what it was in our hometowns—a surprise and a minor tragedy, which remained so even with the fourth trip to Reno. The same applied to all the other sadnesses and disappointments of life, such was the detached sympathy we felt for the favored in those days.

Underlying this myth of ordinariness was another one, a myth of hard and often anxious work, insisting that whatever the stars had, they earned. However luxuriously they might disport themselves in the Sunday rotogravure, however carefree they might look in the snaps from Ciro's and the Mocambo (for it was not necessary that they be complete homebodies, anymore than our parents were prohibited from dining out or even going dancing from time to time), it was constantly put about that, for all the ostensible glamour of their occupations, the stars worked farmers' hours in factorylike conditions. Why, it was often said, they could not even enjoy their on-screen lovemaking, what with all those grips standing around, and the cameraman fussing about the shadows their noses cast, and the director telling them what they could and could not do in the shot.

In time, actually, the emphasis on the early hour at which they were required to report to the studio for makeup and hairdressing, the exigencies (and the occasional danger) of the working conditions under which they toiled, came to seem self-satirizing, even to us in the faraway provinces. So did the reiterated portrait of the atmosphere in which these exertions took place, an atmosphere in which a few flop films, a public relations error, a falling out with someone like Louis B. Mayer ("You'll never work in this town again"), an inability to cope with some understandable human weakness, like alcoholism, could, under pressure, destroy a career in a matter of months. But, for a time, we believed.

A Star Is Born (1937), itself a variation on the earlier *What Price Hollywood?* (1932), made this lesson clear, and the fact that it has been remade twice, with the end not yet in sight, suggests the power of this, the central self-referential show biz myth. So does the fact that it is but the most famous of what amounts to an entire subgenre about the

making and unmaking of movieland greats (cf. *Hollywood Boulevard,
Hollywood Cavalcade, Sunset Boulevard,* etc.). Indeed, in the first version of *A Star Is Born* my basic theme could not be more clearly
stated, for the star about to be born is, in effect, discovered in a man-
ger, that is, in her hayseed living room, while listening to the radio
broadcast of a Hollywood premiere. All her relatives disapprove of
these faraway carryings-on, but not Vicky Lester. She is—there's no
other word for it—starry-eyed, already transported in spirit to Tinsel
Town, where soon enough she will be transported bodily.

But as the movie makes clear—and it is interesting that in the subsequent remakes this prelude is dispensed with as being too obvious—
you can take the girl out of the country, but you can't take the country
out of the girl. Despite her meteoric rise, she continues to live by the
good, solid values of her youth. Which makes the contrast between
her and her discoverer, lover, and, finally, husband, the more poignant. For poor Norman Maine, it is clear, has lost touch with the
basics if, indeed, this addled matinee idol ever understood them at all.
The implication is that the public has turned against him because he is
so lacking in homely virtue. And, throughout, the industry types—an
avuncular producer, a cynical press agent—keep proposing that he
will regain his magic (and his following) as soon as he stops indulging
his quite un-American egomania. His boozing, the visible cause of his
downfall, is seen as a symptom of this deeper malaise, for even when
he gives up the bottle, his fundamental weakness, his refusal to behave
within the conventional rules, leads him to his final assault on those
rules, which is, after all, what his suicide is, however much the film
tries to make us see it as an act of altruism and contrition, rather than
of contempt.

In a sense, cautionary tales like *A Star Is Born* rendered it all the
more remarkable that stars could be pictured in the press as they
enjoyed the quiet pleasures of hearth and home, very often with children glimpsed in cheerful frolic about them. That, as well, they could
find time for the vast round of civic and charitable duties that they
were carefully portrayed undertaking in the best of spirits made them
seem all the more wondrous. One could not help but speculate, should
a good fortune comparable to theirs be visited on us, whether we could
manage to maintain, as so many of our favorites apparently did, our
bourgeois balance.

The nonsensical apotheosis of all this occurred during World War II. It is an ill wind that blows no good, and the winds of war particularly favored Hollywood by allowing its good citizens to undertake, on a global scale, what the rest of us could manage only on a more humble one, with our little victory gardens. The stars literally traversed the globe to bring a touch of homegrown fantasy to our troops and exhausted themselves on cross-country treks by selling war bonds, launching ships, autographing bombs and other armament as they bucked up the factory workers' productivity. Not a week went by in which one of them was not seen in a trailer at the movie house, in an effort to urge us on to this or that patriotic endeavor. Stills and newsreel sequences gave us glimpses of people like James Stewart being sworn into the service, or Tyrone Power good-naturedly peeling spuds in boot camp, or Clark Gable (a particularly poignant figure since his wife, Carole Lombard, had lost her life in a plane crash on the way home from a bond-selling tour) going about his air force duties—doubtless with good effect on the enlistment rate, certainly on our feeling that we were all, the favored and the unfavored, in this thing together, democratically serving and sacrificing.

In effect, the war as seen from the home front might sometimes have been mistaken for an epic production that had opened its run—as the really good pictures always seemed to do—in some faraway place and that what we were witnessing was some huge prerelease publicity campaign, a buildup for one of DeMille's mammoth spectaculars. Of course, an informal bargain had been sealed between the entertainment industry and the government. The government got, virtually free, highly professional assistance in publicizing almost anything it decreed as useful in prosecuting the war—including such dubious works as *Mission to Moscow*, with its remarkable apologies for Stalinism (and its endorsement, controversial when the film was released, of a second front), and *Victory Through Air Power*, which powerfully argued the case for strategic bombing, otherwise known as blasting civilians to smithereens. For its part, the movie industry received favors that ranged from stock footage to delays in the induction of stars who had pictures to finish. And, best of all, a heady sense of participation in the higher councils of state along with the right to toot its own horn about its contributions to the common weal in a time of danger. The show biz-government alliance of World War I was renewed with unprecedented intensity.

But perhaps the largest benefit the entertainment industry derived from the war was the opportunity to complete the decade-long process of demystifying and democratizing stardom. It gave the favored an opportunity, thanks to their USO tours and so on, to mingle with commoners suddenly rendered heroic by government issue, and to acquire, by these exertions in army camps at home and at sites excitingly near the front lines abroad, an opportunity to definitively reacquire the *virtù* that had been dimmed by the excesses of the early, or mining camp, days of filmdom. This was a blessing no one had foreseen when the bombs fell on Pearl Harbor, but it was one that was easily turned to account.

Indeed, there was a short-lived, but quite intensively developed genre of uplifting and self-congratulatory film and stage productions in which the business side of show business reaped direct commercial rewards for these allegedly altruistic efforts—*This Is the Army, Winged Victory, Tars and Spars, Thank Your Lucky Stars, Star-Spangled Rhythm, Hollywood Canteen, Stage Door Canteen*—near plotless revues for the most part, in which, generally, movie stars appeared as themselves, or more properly, as comfortingly ordinary versions of themselves, doing specialty numbers and then permitting themselves to be observed performing humdrum services for our boys in uniform —washing dishes at one of the canteens or waiting a table—in the course of which they often offered advice to lovelorn youths in uniform even to the point of arranging dates for them with the starlet-hostesses.

Hollywood Canteen offered the most risable and exemplary such tale. In it, a young soldier played by Robert Hutton falls for Joan Leslie, playing herself, a demi-star. When she shyly encourages him, he is permitted two boons—a tour of the Warner Bros. lot and a home-cooked meal at her house, which turns out to be, wonder of wonders, a little bit of the Middle West plunked down in the middle of Hollywood. There is warmhearted Mom. There is wise and patient Pop. There is Kid Brother, only a little bratty. There is a white picket fence. There is a porch, with an old-fashioned swing where a fella and his gal can sweetly spoon. What was not there were white pianos, mirrored walls, shimmery gowns, servants or, for that matter, even a hint of a liquor cabinet. One seems to recall someone saying grace before dinner.

Skinny, gawky, with an ever-bobbing Adam's apple, Hutton was an almost paradigmatic GI in the movies of the war years, exactly what we thought—or someone thought—a democratic hero should be, that is, modest to an inarticulate fault. And when the real-life models for the kind of figures he and a dozen other 4-F juveniles played shot down an astonishing number of enemy planes, or led some reckless charge up some godforsaken beach, or saved their patrol by risking their lives in some amazing way, they were fed into the wartime publicity machine, treated to motorcades and White House receptions and hometown welcomes, and generally processed as if they were movie stars on personal appearance tours. If a man were cynical, he might have thought for a moment or two it was worth risking his life in some faraway place in return not just for the adulatory publicity, but for the business and political opportunities that would follow in its wake. Of course, just as there were no atheists in the foxholes, there were no cynics, either.

In fact, many wartime heroes were quite bent by the experience. Not a few of them became drunks and emotional cripples in slightly later life, with their struggles to reclaim themselves in the aftermath of their glory becoming the stuff of TV dramas in the fifties and sixties. At the time, however, most of them came on becomingly boyish, very much in the manner of Western movie heroes. The interesting exception was the most decorated hero of the conflict, Audie Murphy. Later on, when one encountered it, one would see that he somehow exemplified D. H. Lawrence's bleak description of the American character: "hard, stoic, isolate—and a killer." At the time, those coolly appraising eyes, set in his baby face, uncomfortably reminded one of his origins as a small-town juvenile delinquent, the kind of kid who hangs around the garage, being sullen when he wasn't being insolent. One saw that he might well have drifted into a life of adult crime had not the war offered him an acceptable outlet for his sociopathic impulses. His subsequent career as a curious but interesting B movie star (his thin, flat, ungenerous voice was particularly chilling) also discomfited. This was endorsing Camels on a grand scale, and not at all what Sergeant York or Eddie Rickenbacker had done. In fact, Murphy put one somewhat in mind of Jacky Smurch, "The Greatest Man in the World," who was the Anti-Lindbergh of James Thurber's short story. This character was a heroic aviator of the early thirties who upon returning from his welcoming ticker tape parade in New York greeted the President of the United States with a wave of the hand and a distracted "How ya cumin'?," his mind being occupied by the thought of booze and broads, which he understood to be a hero's just, if unpublicized, reward. At the end of the story it became necessary to push Jacky out of the window, and claim it was an accident, before he could set a bad example for American youth.

🍂 🍂

And what of American youth, or for that matter, American adulthood, at this time? Were we as dumb as I have portrayed us, as the manipulators of the growing celebrity system clearly took us to be? No, not quite.

It is true that the process of creating an image had grown, in this period, somewhat more subtle and sophisticated. But the gossip columnists had not disappeared. Hedda, Louella, Sheilah Graham, Jimmie Fidler, to name just the Hollywood contingent, were still in full, yelping cry. And Walter Winchell, who appeared to be bi-coastally informed, led a New York pack that was always busily asniff. Even Washington was not immune, what with Drew Pearson circling in from the left, the vicious Westbrook Pegler cutting traces from the right. And there was always plenty of grist for their mills. To speak only of the movie people, it is perfectly clear that roughly the same percentage of them as ever continued to mess up their marriages, their careers, their lives. Reports of dismaying behavior in the "movie colony" continued to circulate. As before, as now, there was no shortage of alcoholism, weird sexuality, scandalous affairs, and general tastelessness out there. And all that was alluded to—in nonlibelous terms, of course—in *The Sentinel*. But only a handful of these tales were ever fully laid out for us (when, all compromises and flummery having failed, they got to court). Yet that steady, spattering shower of tersely phrased, gnomically worded column items had a cumulative effect on us. They provided a dim, double vision of celebrity life, a shadowy sense that it was not always as bright, well-favored, and quotidian as the picture stories in *Life, Look,* and the fan magazines (to which I was sometimes treated when I had to stay home from school with a cold) constantly insisted. Always, that sense that we didn't know everything that went on in the glamour capitals nudged and nagged at us, and with it a sense that what we didn't know was the really good stuff. Indeed, that sense of underlying wickedness was an essential element in attracting and holding everyone's continuing interest. And the purveyors knew it, too. Their trick was not to let tales from the dark side of the woods get out of hand and shame the whole movie community.

In this effort, as we did not discover until some years later, the columnists, the whole shabby show biz press, were used as enforcers, whipping wayward players into line by the threat of printing damaging stories if they refused to abandon bad habits, or even if they became rebellious over roles or salaries. Usually the threat was sufficient. Or maybe publication of one or two carefully worded blind items, warning shots as it were. After all, a career destroyed was an investment destroyed—all the time and money a studio had invested in building up a star had to be weighed against the need for discipline. As a result, the columnists in those days spent more time covering up dubious behavior than they did exposing it. And when something went really wrong, it was not unusual for the police, arriving on the scene of some potential scandal, to be greeted by a studio press agent with a smooth explanation of the untoward prepared—and any embarrassing evidence safely in his pocket. Possession of that, of course, gave the studio enormous power over the miscreant.

From the viewpoint of those who made their livings by being well known, from the viewpoint of the studios protecting their investments, this system of information control, crude as it may look in retrospect, worked quite surprisingly well. If one lived within one's image, did nothing to disappoint those behavioral expectations that image induced in the public, it was possible for a star to live as peacefully as he or she lived prosperously. Indeed, it was possible to live the life of a roué or an "I-don't-care" girl (to revert to a quaint descriptive phrase) —if that mode matched the public perceptions of the star. For example, when Errol Flynn was hauled into court on what turned out to be a bogus (or anyway, unprovable) statutory rape charge, it did him no harm. Everyone knew he was a raffish fellow. "In like Flynn," we said cheerfully when good fortune, sexual or otherwise, struck us. One was titillated, but hardly appalled, by his trial. A little later, Rita Hayworth, who had played a number of women, notably *Gilda,* who were not better than they should have been, disported herself all over Europe with Aly Khan, to whom she was not married, most everyone hoped she had a swell time. She was doing nothing that was not expected of her.

Trouble came only when someone rebelled against expectations. Charles Chaplin, for instance, was placed on trial in a paternity suit around the time everyone had grown heartily tired of his widely disseminated leftist political views. As it happened, he was adjudged guilty of being an unwed father and required to pay support for his alleged offspring. But the results, as far as the public was concerned, would have been the same had the blood tests come out differently. He was pilloried and driven into exile. The Dear Little Fellow, the beloved tramp who had once symbolized an innocence and sweetness now seemingly lost (this was, incidentally, a very simple reading of a complex screen characterization), was not expected to be found in compromising situations—especially since he was, by then, a man of some years and the offended plaintiff was very young. Then there was the matter of Ingrid Bergman. She had played nuns and saints, and even when not so engaged, had (mostly) played women of solid virtue. She was denounced from the floor of the House of Representatives and rendered unemployable in American films for almost a decade, when it was discovered that she was conducting an affair with her director while on location—a situation not exactly unknown in movie annals—and was going to bear his child. She was just not supposed to do things like that—especially when he was a snaky foreigner (and a director of art films as well), and both had left apparently trusting spouses at home. She, too, had flouted her image.

It should also be noted that neither Chaplin nor Bergman were then under long-term studio contracts, as Flynn and Hayworth were at the time of their derelictions. They thus had no access to the protective machinery the studio press departments provided their people, no way of walling themselves off from the ravening press.

One cannot stress too strongly the value of the press agent's services in this regard. It was as protectors, not promoters, of images that they best earned their keep. Consider what they had done for the star class in two realms entirely unrelated to sexual activities. They were extremely successful in quieting the doubts that arose from the frequent lack of correlation between a star's skill and his or her success. Too many people seemed to rise to the top almost immediately upon being spotted at some drugstore soda fountain. And while stories like that fed a certain hopeful feeling of identification with the lucky ones, they also fed our least-elevated, or spoiled-child, fantasies, in which rewards came to us just because we sat around looking adorable. The stress on how hard the stars worked once they had received their lucky break, and the exemplary nature of their private lives thereafter, were reassuring. A component of effort and modesty was, after all, present in these lives. It was not all done with mirrors.

The second dirty little secret was money. There was no hiding that inconvenient fact. But in this period the stars were still salaried, and few, if any, received percentages of a film's profits or grosses. None held even partial ownership of their films. Both had been factors in creating the first generation of show biz superwealth in the twenties. Both would be factors in the creation of a new generation of multimillionaires starting in the mid-fifties, when the studios ceased to bind players to long-term contracts. The stars of the thirties and forties lived well—better than anyone except the possessors of old, eastern money—but they did not live as their once and future peers did. If the Lear jet had been invented, most of them could not have afforded one. The possibilities of unseemly materialism, not to mention wildly decadent behavior, were thus decently circumscribed. A mistress kept quietly in a West Hollywood apartment was a possibility; the opportunity to load her and the entire entourage on a private plane for a weekend in Paris, where the trail could be picked up and made public by the paparazzi, was not. To put the matter simply, great prosperity was present, but it was easily played down. We really did not think those nice folks out West had moved that far upscale from where we were.

One must be careful. One must not forget *The Day of the Locust.* Very simple people were sometimes driven crazy by stardom in those days. They did journey West and were lured by the belief that, since the institution appeared to be so democratic, they too could claim its benefits. And, since they lived in close proximity to the ease and glamour of the movie capital, the possibility of riotous assertions of those claims, if only as an expression of perverse and unrequited love for the system's godheads, was a possibility.

One must recall, too, the cautionary myth about how Hollywood exploited, and then destroyed, literary and theatrical talent. In real life F. Scott Fitzgerald was the paradigmatic case. And he crossed over into fiction as the victim-protagonist of Budd Schulberg's *The Disenchanted.* But, of course, there were dozens of other books, plays, and even movies on this theme—at every level of aspiration and taste. (And they continue apace, witness the recent movie and television program about the sad adventures of Frances Farmer in Movieland.) This fictive tradition is late-blooming, the first Hollywood novels having tended toward a sort of innocent bedazzlement (for example, *Merton of the Movies).* The business of the later fictions was chastise the upstart film industry—after all, a powerful competitor to novels and the stage—by imbuing it with an evil, destructive power out of all proportion to the facts. Ignored in all these tales, whether romans à clef or not, was the *self*-destructive capacity of their protagonists. One is inclined to believe that Fitzgerald and Farmer would have ended up drunk and disorderly no matter where they worked. Similarly one is inclined to believe that the second-rank writers who insisted that crass Hollywood was destroying their delicately flowering talents, or found themselves being drawn toward guilt-ridden Stalinoid politics, were copping a convenient plea. It is perfectly true that writers, being the least expensive to replace cogs in the machinery, tended to absorb more abuse than anyone else in the studio system. It is also true that their values—literary values only erratically useful in the process of making a movie—naturally placed them in an adversarial position vis à vis producers. Given these facts, and given the fact that their stock-in-trade was articulateness, it is easy to see how the self-romanticizing myth of Hollywood as an anti-Eden, a veritable fiery furnace where the artistic soul was terribly tested, and often consumed, was propagated and grew. Never mind that many talented, well-adjusted writers, ranging from Dudley Nichols to Nunnally Johnson, found happiness and even a degree of fulfillment there, never mind that one of the greatest writers of the period, William Faulkner, uncomplainingly moved in and out of town for over a decade, using his craftsmanlike labors on various screenplays to finance his novels, which remained utterly uncorrupted by their author's Hollywood experiences. The myth was too precious to the literary community, to the middlebrow world in general, to let reality even partially contradict it.

None of that was clear to the rest of us. Or even known to us. What had been created for us, or perhaps one should say we had somehow arrived at, was a workable contradiction. We had been led to believe, by all the publicity, that there was a psychological continuum between ourselves and the inhabitants of The Other Place, that we, the humble, were at one with them, the mighty, in values, in spirit. We began to think that the grace, wit, and style they had attained in The Other Place we might attain in ours—and without too much distortion of our best natures. At the same time, distances being what they were, and the media being what it was—not yet in a position to place us in what appeared to be close psychological connection with the famous still controllable by those with a vested interest in control—we were held, hesitant, at arm's length.

And there were yet separations between the various areas of attainment. However much the political world, for example, might wish to use the entertainment world, and however much entertainers might be flattered by that use, there was no sense that power was transferable between those worlds. And in the world of, let us say, serious writing, or art, there was no sense that one might conduct his career as a movie star might. Or be entitled to the same sort of mass interest in his life, work, and thought. On the contrary, by the time I reached the later years of high school, and college, there was considerable contempt for that sort of thing, much talk about people who "sold out" to show biz. For by this time we were beginning to be aware of the pictures I've just described, appalled and titillated by them. But unless we could imagine ourselves going into the movies—and no one I knew could make that leap—this was strictly the stuff of fairy tales, no more than metaphorically relevant to us. In short, it was only within a very narrow professional realm that one might dream of (or worry about) getting famous, becoming a "celebrity" as we now define the term.

"This celebrity business is quite chronic," Virginia Woolf once remarked as her work began to be noticed. But it was not—not by modern standards, anyway. Whatever excesses might be satirized (as Hollywood itself often did in those days, in good-natured films like *Blonde Bombshell)* or deplored, whatever sillinesses we might indulge in our fantasies, the fact is that the "celebrity business" worked quite well, quite proportionately. Nostalgia is a dangerous, and false, emotion, but we are not wrong to exercise it in this regard, about this period. Our bedazzlement was part-time. We might have been bemused by celebrity, but we were not yet obsessed with it, for there was, besides distance, decorum in our relationship with the famous.

FOUR

Super Hero, Super Victim

Some of that decorum was the product of a commonsensical definition of stardom by some of the stars themselves. For example, Cary Grant. In her long, provocative essay on the screen self he created, Pauline Kael writes: "He became a performer in an era in which learning to entertain the public was a trade; he worked at his trade, progressed and rose to the top. He probably never had the sort of doubts about acting which have plagued so many later performers, and he didn't agonize over choices, as actors of his stature do now . . ."

Yes, very sensible. In Grant's case, his course was set not merely by temperament but, one suspects, by early conditioning. He had come into show business as an adolescent working in an acrobatic act in the music halls. At that level, at that early an age, one learns to be, as we now say, "job-oriented." One is not concerned with "making a statement." One is concerned with getting bookings, and with saving enough money to tide oneself over when there is a gap in them. There is not time for excesses of temperament or, for that matter, brooding about the state of one's art or the state of the world. Mooning about in that way can interfere with the basic task of pleasing managers and the public, and that can, in turn, interfere with eating on a regular basis. Whatever inclination one might have to act the role of artist-rebel-hero is likely to be trained out of one in the scuffle of two-a-day life. Later, when one has money and a certain power to make choices in one's professional life, the memory of being at liberty is likely to temper one's actions. One wishes never to be poor, or insecure, again. It is more important than making elaborate, or self-conscious, artistic statements.

Englishness comes into it, too, of course. One thinks of Grant's friend Laurence Olivier and his repeated assertion that he is not Hamlet at heart, but Archie Rice, "the Entertainer" of John Osborne's play, arguably Olivier's most perfectly realized stage role. That is to say, even at its highest level, at the level where actors win knighthoods, there is a sense of acting as an honorable and respectable profession which consists not so much of serving oneself as of serving the work at hand, the play or the film, and only after that sparing a thought for the public's hopes and expectations from the star or the star's hopes for further glory. Ralph Richardson often spoke of himself as a "printing press"—that is, as the humble and impersonal machine by which a writer's words are spread. He was too modest, of course, and one does not wish to imply that the typical English actor is a shrinking violet (no one who happily displays himself in public is). But the length and stability of so many English acting careers, the relative lack of lunacy there, must commend itself to the American.

Even at the less grand levels of achievement, there are examples that suggest alternatives that our actors have not been able to explore. One thinks of the great repertory companies that nurtured not only talent, but a sense of theatrical tradition and a feeling for camaraderie as well. Besides rep, and stretching still further back into theatrical history, there was the tradition of the actor-manager, putting together companies each season to tour either in the classics or some vehicle that set him (or her) off to good effect. Frequently these vehicles, generally melodramatic in nature, were either commissioned or bought up and thus entirely controlled by the star, who would often grow old in the part, without thought of any obligation to novelty or of asserting a personal or political vision through his craft. Ultimately, operating out of both these traditions, Olivier used his star's prestige in aid of establishing the National Theatre which performs in repertory style, but in which Olivier acted as a sort of actor-manager to the entire nation, and at once guarded and refreshed a great tradition.

The peer and his peers were served not merely by tradition, but by happenstance and geography. It happened that film production did not take hold in Britain as quickly and as strongly as it did in the United States, perhaps precisely because the theatrical tradition was so much more deeply rooted there. Its show people had something strong and worth defending to cleave to, and were thus much less easily swept away by movie stardom than their American counterparts. Our first great playwright, Eugene O'Neill, did not arrive until roughly the same time the movies did, and setting Shakespeare aside, the plays with which our actors had been occupied were no better than the movies. Indeed, they served as structural and thematic models for the early films, when they were not simply adapted whole for the cinema. As for geography, the schism between theater and film (and later, television), which occurred in the United States when the movie business moved to Los Angeles, simply did not happen in England. All three major branches of show business continued to center on London. A performer can, therefore, spend his days in a supporting role at one of the studios outside town or at the BBC, and his nights in a leading role in the West End. And no one thinks the less of a Richardson or a Gielgud for so doing. It is how one makes one's decent but not mind-twisting livelihood. It is how one keeps all one's skills in trim. And it is how one keeps in touch with the workaday realities of one's profession, keeps up those fraternal ties that were often the first great attraction of show business for the children of broken or unhappy homes, which is what a disproportionate number of actors and actresses are. A "dazzling land of smiling, jostling people," is how Grant once described show business as it first appeared to his young outsider's eyes, "classless, cheerful and carefree." As long as one is in touch with that sense of things one is likely to be all right. It is isolation, geographic and economic, that causes most of the trouble in the "dazzling land." They give one space and time in which to brood about the strange inequities of life at the top, to brood about one's inability to assert one's singular self and remarkable visions, make a difference in the world, *be* a hero instead of merely acting one.

Put so baldly, the ambition seems feckless, if not downright comical. What *are* these favored people fussing about? Yet the dissatisfaction has been there almost from the beginning of show business's modern era. It crystallized sometime in the 1920s, around the time movies had left the Age of the Nickelodeon behind and got themselves listed on the Big Board. The capital requirements of this new enterprise were too intensive, the system of producing and distributing the product too complex and too mysteriously risky, to be left in the hands of flighty artists. It required men who had heads for figures and eyes for the main chance to make such sense as could be made out of this unprecedented "industry." And an "industry" it had to be—Americans do not know how to organize anything except on an industrial basis. The same thing, of course, would be true of all the other means of communication as they came along. Whereupon a funny thing happened.

Previously, success in America had been a unitary thing. If, let us say, you succeeded in inventing something and developing an "industry" around it, your reward consisted of three parts—wealth, fame, and power. They came together in a package. That was not true in show business as it was redefined. Everybody who succeeded in it got money—pots of it. About that, there was no dispute; the wealth was shared. But here and here alone the other two items were divided up—fame to the performers, power to the producers. It was galling to both sides. The producers, who fancied that they did all the hard, smart work, got almost no recognition, while these wayward children they employed, these actors and actresses whom they were always having to guide in the paths of righteousness (and bail out of trouble), got all the adulation. It is conventional not to waste too much sympathy on the producers, and it is a convention that it is always easy to honor, though it ought to be recorded that among these vulgar buccaneers there were men of shrewdness, energy and, in their way, vision. But their problem was not as galling as that of their celebrated employees, who had the trappings of success, the money and the fame, but not its essence, which is power.

There are three elements in this, too, as it has been traditionally defined in America. First of all, power must include the power to do what you want with your life—with no one ordering you around anymore. Second, it implies ordering other people around—the people in your factories, for instance. Finally, it means being listened to in high places: presidents consulting you, newspapers listening respectfully when you talk and dutifully reporting your views on tariffs, immigration, world peace, public morals—all those stupefying grown-up topics. Conversely, no one ever asked Thomas Alva Edison if he slept in the nude.

None of the above was possessed by the stars. If they wanted to give orders to anyone above the level of hairdresser they had to create entourages. Meantime, they were themselves constantly ordered about by the studio bosses. They did the pictures they were assigned, and they were assigned to things that others deemed to be within their range—and within the range of the audience's expectations. These expectations had the paradoxical effect of further limiting a performer's choices even as his skills improved with use and maturity. For his fans were like children, demanding to hear the same bedtime story over and over again, with their attention wandering if they were not given it. The most a star was permitted to risk were minor variations on his basic characterological themes. That would have been all right if he defined his function modestly, as simply giving delight to people, as some of the theatrical stars of the nineteenth century must have done as they set forth for their silver anniversary tours in *The Two Orphans* or *Way Down East*. But the discrepancy between near heroic monetary rewards and less than heroic professional activity rankled numbers of movie stars.

Why couldn't they work creatively, daringly, express their most profound feelings, their deepest wishes, their most thrilling insights to the world? To put the matter as simply as possible, why weren't they taken seriously? It seemed the ultimate celebrity—immortality—was being willfully denied them. (They did not see that a preserving technology would grow up and tend that need.) At the same time, at the more immediately ironic level, despite their fame and wealth, they were not being permitted to assert themselves fully. And, if you cannot assert yourself, then, in America, you are not an adult. At one level pampered, cosseted, their tiniest needs attended to; the male stars felt on another level, emasculated, felt actually as if they were sort of kept women, overpaid to look beautiful and to be charming and sexy upon whimsical demand. It was just as bad for the women. Hollywood had—and still has—a contemptuous way of making its female stars feel whorish. Even if they were among the strong ladies and avoided that degrading sense of themselves, they felt their powerlessness in the same way that so many of the male stars did. Whatever the gender, they all were, after all, Americans, and therefore shared the basic, national definitions of success and failure. Maybe Rudolph Valentino spoke for the whole starry breed when he said, not long before he died, "A man should control his life. Mine is controlling me. I don't like it."

There was an essential absurdity in all this. Probably we are dealing with a form of what we would now call the revolution of rising expectations. That is to say, the more favored a group is, the more favor it expects. For, to put it simply, actors are, rather obviously (and at best), interpretive artists; it is a misunderstanding of their function for them to take on or fantasize a primary creative role. Certainly it is damaging to them, conceivably to everyone involved in the creative endeavor, to undertake such a role. It is just here that the division of power within the new show business did incalculable damage.

In 1922, D. W. Griffith, then at the height of his fame as a director and master (briefly) of his own studio and production company, gave two interviews. In one of them, he reflected on the nature of heroism in America. "Your hero is yourself," he declared, so "the national hero becomes the one who expresses in the highest degree the achievement the people of the nation would like to achieve individually." At the moment, he thought Henry Ford was the most admired leader in the country, but he noted with interest that despite having just fought the greatest war in our history, no military heroes seemed to have even temporary residence in our pantheon. This betokened to him a large shift in spirit; from being a "fighting people" we had become a nation preoccupied with material progress. If we could, in a short period of time, replace the soldier with the industrialist as a heroic model, then was it not likely that in fifty or a hundred years "America will awaken to an appreciation of art," with the artist then replacing the industrialist as a popular heroic figure? The possibility seemed to him distinct and, he added innocently, "Perhaps motion pictures will do more to stimulate this interest than any other force."

Of course, Griffith, who suffered from the visionary gradiosity that is common to the narcissistic temperament, imagined that it would be people like himself, the people who conceived movies and fought them through to fruition, who would be the heroes, should be the heroes, in all justice. The thought of actors playing this role seemed to him nonsensical. And later in 1922 he complained about the public's lack of perception in this regard. He observed to another reporter that there were two classes of picture fans, "those who worship the star, and the thinking class interested only in pictures that reach an artistic standard and not known for the actors." These last were obviously his kind of people and it was on their increase, of course, that he placed his hopes for his future, and that of his medium.

Poor Griffith! His observations and to a degree his predictions would prove correct. By the time a half century had passed, the "thinking class" had reached numbers sufficient so that director *auteurs* could play the role of beleaguered cultural heroes, struggling to impose their singular visions upon a crass and unfeeling world. The name of Francis Ford Coppola springs to mind, with his carefully orchestrated (and commercially successful) attempt to enlist the world in the drama of bringing his financially out of control films—*Apoca-*

lypse Now, One from the Heart, The Cotton Club—to market, his long-running serial melodrama about whether the wicked bankers would foreclose the mortgage on his studio and whether he would ever get untied from the tracks of his loony ambition. By now, Griffith himself (who pioneered this drama) would have been delighted by his posthumous reputation as an artist thwarted by unfeeling commerce. And, of course, there beside him in this new pantheon we can find his old assistant Erich von Stroheim and his old admirer Orson Welles, both premature rebels with expensive causes—the assertion of their egos. Indeed, in the movies about moviemaking, a lively and extensive genre of the 1930s and 1940s, the visionary director, pretentious, temperamental, troubled, and gifted became something of a stock (and usually comic) figure, achieving his apotheosis in Preston Sturges's great satire of 1941, *Sullivan's Travels,* in which the director of *Hey-Hey in the Hayloft* and *Ants in Your Pants of 1938* aspires disastrously to the seriousness of adapting a proletarian novel called (a perfect Sturgesian skewering here) *Brother, Where Art Thou?* In these fictions he usually ended up either dismissed or chastened, and that was, at least, true to life at that time. In the real life of our time, they merely go over budget with the screams of the cost accountants drowned out by the awed murmurings of the multitudes.

But we are getting ahead of our story. For before the director's status was advanced from that of near anonymous technician to cultural hero (in the film magazines recently they have been advertising a T-shirt that bears the legend, ". . . but what I really want to do is direct"), we had first to pass through a terrible time of testing in which the actor struggled noisily to assert his right to be *auteur* of something larger than his own screen persona.

What he was looking for was nothing less than a kind of transcendence. For consider, a star actor in a film is, de facto, as much the "author" of any movie he appears in as anyone else involved in creating it. His personality, his strengths and limits, are at least as large determinants of the film's content as any other factor. The writers write with him (or her) firmly in mind, and the director generally doesn't get the job unless the persona and the person behind it detect a certain empathy with what the star is—or thinks he is. The trouble is that this truism is something of a dirty little secret in the movie business. Worse, this power is an unearned increment, and effortlessly earned power is not as efficacious, or as satisfying to use in America, as power that is effortfully gathered. It is suspect, and it makes its bearer feel vaguely guilty. We finally want our games to involve a test of wills. That is especially true of show people, with their inherent sense of drama. The thing just doesn't work as well, doesn't engage the emotions as thrillingly, if everyone feels all along that he can eventually walk away unscathed.

This game, or drama, could not have been played widely or seriously without the intervention of a historical coincidence; a radical change in the system under which movies were produced and the creation of what amounted to a philosophical rationale justifying the performers' desires to take the authorial role in production. The very "star worship" that Griffith had complained about so early in film history was something more than an aberration in mass psychology. Within a matter of years it would be the basis for the industry's organization as a rational economic organization—rationalism based on irrationalism. Wonderful!

At the moment Griffith was voicing his complaint about the system's growth, his industry was consolidating, turning into a classic oligopoly; the era of clamorous independence in which many small producers colorfully competed was ending, an era in which the means of producing, distributing, and exhibiting was controlled by a handful of large concerns was beginning. Their need was to turn out as many films as possible, on as routinized a basis as possible. Their ideal was a variation of Henry Ford's ideal of mass production. The trouble was that movies were not motor cars to be identically stamped out on an assembly line. But you could aspire to coming as close as possible to Fordian nirvana. Genres helped; the audience for a Western or comedy or a romance was fairly predictable. But putting a star in a genre picture that suited him or her helped to refine this calculation, and if he or she was particularly well-liked, to maximize it. The studios quickly learned that writers might go off on tangents, that directors might nod, but that the best and brightest stars had surprisingly long periods of ascendancy and could be literally counted on as no other element in a movie package could. With many major chains owned by the same concerns that controlled the studios, this made for a very tidy business method. And the theaters that were not so controlled would buy a major star's pictures sight unseen. Indeed, under the block-booking system these vehicles became the basis for selling a package including many lesser items. It therefore followed that a studio wanted to have as many of these blessed creatures under long-term contract as possible, and since this linkage of corporate and individual fates was so close, it also followed that one wanted the performers to see themselves not as romantic rebels in the cause of art, but as tradespeople—sober, steady, reliable. The standards of nineteenth-century theatrical professionalism would be most suitable, most suitable indeed.

And the system worked surprisingly well for about three decades. To be sure, there was sometimes restiveness in paradise. A Bette Davis or a James Cagney would occasionally come to so deeply resent either the quality of their typecast roles or the contrast between their salaries and what the studio was making on their work, that they went off and sulked (it was called going on suspension) until some adjustment was made. Usually that was arrived at quite quickly. The star's contracts naturally forbade them to work for other studios and they could not long survive without their contractural stipends, so they were in the weaker bargaining position. But the studios, committed to implacable production schedules that called for delivering virtually a picture a week to the theaters, needed their most important assets at work, not improving their tans poolside. Of course, there were players who were seriously troublesome—the drinkers, the sexually scandalous, and (later) the politically outspoken. They sometimes had to be dealt with harshly. Finally, there was a handful that just simply rubbed one of their bosses the wrong way (when John Gilbert punched out Louis B. Mayer in public it did not exactly help his career) and they, too, were sometimes crudely and cruelly banished.

On the whole, however, the stars permitted themselves to be treated as favored citizens of a more or less benign dictatorship. And, on the whole, they derived great benefits from the system. These lay in the constant exposure, in three and four films a year as they were being built up, in constant publicity when they arrived and were required to make fewer films, that imposed them on the national consciousness—which paradoxically gave them the power to oppose the studios in argument and negotiation, often at least with partial success. In effect, they were the managers of wholly owned, but prosperous subsidiaries of the studios, the stock-in-trade of which consisted entirely of themselves. The smart ones, and some who were merely docile or agreeably unadventurous in the realms of art, did very well under the system.

Around 1950, however, it all began to break apart. As everyone knows, television networking began in 1948, and very quickly it undermined the movies' prosperity. Within a matter of a few years the weekly audience for films had shrunk by two thirds. At the same time, a consent decree in a long-fought antitrust suit forced the studios to divest themselves of their theater chains, and the practice of block booking was also ended. The need for a large number of productions and of large numbers of stars to appear in them declined and the institution of the long-term contract binding players to studios virtually disappeared. But for the greatest of the stars, the ones for whom there remained a demonstrable, consistent demand, the rewards were now larger than ever. They could get more for a single picture than they might have made over several years on a contract and, as freelancers, they now had many highly agreeable options. They could function as their own producers if they wished; bringing stories, directors, and costars and whoever, to the studios for financing, which gave them a far larger measure of creative control than they ever enjoyed before. At the very least they could insist on approval of all these elements when they signed on for a project and receive percentages of gross or profits for their efforts besides. Beyond that, they were now free of the personal constraints the old contracts imposed on them. They could live as they pleased, go where they wanted, do what they would, and in an era that grew ever more tolerant in the realm of personal behavior—morals if you insist—suffer no consequences. Indeed, people quickly became eager to hear any confession any prominent person cared to make about any aspect of his life—and pay good money for it, too.

There were a few who handled this situation very easily. The aforementioned Cary Grant, for example. He had, for most of his career, managed to escape exclusive contractual commitment to any studio. And he slid smoothly into the era of independent production. He had no message to impart to the world—except the splendid one of charm, wit, style, and vitality that he had always offered—no social or political statements to make. He just went on doing what he had been doing —at better pay, with, perhaps, greater comfort. For others, however, life was not so pleasingly simple. For in the immediate postwar era, there had grown up a new method of theatrical self-presentation (called simply, "the Method") and there agglomerated around it a mystique and a politique that implicitly promised not just personal reward for the devotee but reformation for the entire theatrical enterprise as well.

In and of itself the Method was, for some performers, a useful technique, which through various exercises (pioneered, of course, by the Russian director Stanislavsky) enabled the actor to get in touch with such emotions as were buried within himself that were analogous to the emotions of the character he was portraying. Slickness, superficiality, the merely elocutionary or the merely mnemonic were not good enough now. One must use the character as a metaphor through which the deepest and most universal behavioral truths could be illuminated by the serious and striving actor. It seems obvious that the best actors, throughout human history, must have devised ways of making this connection between self and fiction. But never before had these techniques been codified so that they were generally teachable, not just as the Method's temple, the Actors Studio in New York, but wherever an adept could find loft space and some aspiring disciples.

Nor was the cultural ground ever previously so fertile. By the 1950s the metaphors of psychology had ceased to be the exclusive property of the advanced intellectual class. The movies, popular fiction, and theater were full of them and an acting technique that, broadly speaking, did for performer what psychoanalysis did for the ordinarily bedeviled citizen—permitted him to plunge creatively, redemptively into the abyss of himself, his buried past, his hidden thoughts, was bound to be alluring. Superficially at least, the performer could present himself not merely as an entertainer, but as an artist engaged in an artistic and intellectual endeavor every bit as serious as that of the great writers and thinkers, an activity that had its obvious links to the main currents of artistic modernism.

Nor was that an end to the new actor's ambitions. Many of the people who founded the Actors Studio (including its great guru, Lee Strasberg) had strong links to the left-wing theatrical movements of the 1930s, notably the Group Theatre, which numbered among its most important objectives the reformation of the American theater, by turning it from the superficialities of bourgeois comedy and parlor melodrama to what its members were convinced was a more profound engagement with the realities of everyday life and the political and social issues of the day. They first came to know of Stanislavsky's theories as a result of their interest in his Moscow Art Theater. Be that as it may, Waiting for Lefty was not enough for the theatrical left —they would work actively to bring him to the center of the stage, the center of consciousness. For the rest of the nation the Fervent Years were well past by the 1950s, but serious-minded show people saw that the theater still required reformation. The ferment of the 1930s, so full of promising experiment, had dwindled; what had once looked like the beginning of an artistic revolution now looked to have been little more than a cultural fad. As for the movies, they remained, as ever, profoundly unredeemed.

But all was not lost. Not quite. For it seemed, in the fifties, that the corrupt old institutions of the business, vulgar commercial Broadway, vulgar commercial Hollywood, could not long endure in their present state. Hollywood's faltering state was well-known; wishing television would go away was not making it go away. As for Broadway, each year it seemed to shrink a little more—fewer theaters, fewer new shows opening, fewer profitable runs, the road near defunct. Meantime, off-Broadway, with its economies of (small) scale, offered new hope for the venturesome, and yet another challenge to the decrepitly ruling oligarchs of the Main Stem.

Now, suppose actors and the craft of acting could be reformed. Suppose that a sufficient number of them could be sent forth, cleansed and purified, into a profession now confused and weakened as it attempted to grapple with its own changed economic conditions. Might they not, by their presences (and their refusals), cleanse and purify the ancient corruptions of show biz? The idea did not seem so farfetched, especially since this new breed of performers was being trained to a new subjectivity of style that seemed to suit the new subjectivity of an apolitical audience rather morose in its materialism, slightly guilty about its self-absorption. All the other revolutions promised by the 1930s had turned rancid with delay. But perhaps this one, also too long denied, might at long last, and almost by chance, have its moment.

All revolutions, we know, begin in the yearning hearts of a few courageous individuals. Those there were aplenty in the 1950s—actors and actresses by the score whose youthful idealism had been fired, as their skills had been tempered, not merely by "Lee," but by "Herbert" and "Uta" and "Sandy" and "Bill" and all the other legendary teachers whose first names rolled so trippingly off so many tongues on so many unemployment lines in New York in the 1950s. They wanted what young actors had always wanted—work!—but there was a special agony for many of them when they got a TV job or their first small part in a Broadway show because they thought they were selling out before they had even got going (a roommate of mine contrived to lose the lead in a bit of Lindsay and Crouse commercialism less than a week after rehearsals started). In fact, they seemed to worry more about selling out than getting jobs; so much so that when I hear people talking about the bland and unprincipled materialism of the fifties I think of my contemporaries in the theater and how little they suited that image. I think, too, of how the blacklists and graylists imposed on show business by McCarthyism helped to staff the New York acting schools' faculties with gifted unemployables who added their bit to the antiestablishment fervor that one soaked up there.

If this was a conspiracy, it was, I hasten to say, an entirely unorganized one. No plot was afoot—just a shared set of attitudes based on a set of shared experiences among the older generation, a set of values eagerly embraced by the younger crowd. Both groups had come to agreement, through no conscious consensual process I could discern, on a hero and exemplar, a man on whose fate as an artist they had staked their largest hopes for change. If he could succeed in imposing his style and values on the world of mass entertainment, if he could transcend himself, become something more than a mere star, become a moral and intellectual force (and be recognized for those qualities, not just within the profession, but by the public at large), then there was hope that others might follow. If he failed they would doubtless continue their assault on the citadels of show biz power (and the public consciousness, of course), but in grimmer mood, a martyr in mind. We are, of course, talking about the greatest of the fraternally dropped first names, Marlon.

Already in the middle and late fifties people were worrying about him. The great run of films that had established him—great at least in the sense that they permitted him to indelibly impress himself on a generation's consciousness—was complete. From *The Men* in 1950 through the film version of his stage masterpiece, *A Streetcar Named Desire*, to *Viva Zapata, The Wild One*, and the Oscar-winning culmination of his first phase, *On the Waterfront*, he had laid out his credentials and by 1954 they had finally been accepted by nearly everyone (witness the Academy Award) as genuine. Moreover, he had done it his way. He had worn his blue jeans in Bel Air (long before it became fashionable; indeed, he probably established the fashion), he had insulted Louella O. Parsons, he had picked his nose in public and said terrible things about mighty people. He was the star as antistar. But now, as the Chianti went 'round in the lofts and railroad flats of lower Manhattan the discussions of Marlon and his future course grew hot with anxiety, cool with gloom. Why was he staying so long on the Far Coast? When would he return home to his roots, enter again upon that temple of truth, the theater? Was it possible—darkest of all possibilities—that he, of all people, was now in danger of "selling out"? Was it possible, perhaps, that the deal had already been struck. *Désirée* did not encourage.

"The national hero becomes the one who expresses in the highest degree the achievement the people of the nation would like to achieve individually." Well, perhaps not the *whole* nation. But it is unarguable that Brando was something new in our experience. He was the first actor to be burdened not just with the weight of a significant and interesting career, but with the weight of history as well, an obligation to transcendence. His selections of roles, his actions off-stage—these had symbolic implications, even cultural consequences, that no performing career had previously had in the minds of a substantial portion of his audience. He had thrust himself—more likely, had been thrust—into precisely the heroic position that Griffith had predicted would one day come to the American artist.

Indeed, from today's perspective, his career can be made to fit the classic pattern Joseph Campbell discerned in his classic study of *The Hero with a Thousand Faces*. In it the great scholar tells us that all godlike heroes, Western and Eastern, ancient and modern, are embodiments of what he calls a "monomyth." That is to say, each in his way, acts out a version of the same archetypal three-part story. In the first act there is the drama of separation and departure; in the next there comes a series of initiatory trials, leading to a victory of some sort; finally there is the triumphant return and reintegration with society. Let's set Brando's life to that music.

Act One. The departure was psychologic and aesthetic. You can still find tradition-minded people in New York retrospectively offended by his Marchbanks opposite Katherine Cornell in *Candida*. You can still find aesthetic radicals who can feel in their tissues the electrification he administered in Maxwell Anderson's short-lived *Truckline Café*. And people who saw him as Stanley Kowalski in *A Streetcar Named Desire* in 1948 cannot forget the sense that they were seeing the beginning of something for which there was no precedent. The performance, of course, is preserved on film—perhaps even enhanced by film, with its opportunities for intimate observation. It is breathtaking still. The more so in that Brando disliked the character. "Kowalski was always right, and never afraid. He never wondered, he never doubted . . . And he had the kind of brutal aggressiveness I hate. I'm afraid of it. I detest the character."

The performance's greatness is born of that detestation. Brando in those days was an utterly beautiful young man: his chunky body was sculpted almost like a weight lifter's, there was a dark and enigmatic depth in his eyes, something noble about his brow and nose. The contrast between this (by stage and movie standards, unconventional) handsomeness and the literally cocksure qualities of the character he was playing (not to mention the brilliant vocal manner he concocted, the very voice of modern mass man) made us understand how the genteel Stella fell under his sexual thrall: he may have been a brute, but he was a beautiful one. More than that, one sensed in his characterization unspoken dimensions, dimensions that were no more than shadows in the writing. For Tennessee Williams, one senses, it would have been sufficient had Stanley been no more than a brute force, crushing the fragile and poetic flowers of dreaming Southern womanhood. But Brando gave him something more—an instinctive intelligence, a satiric (not to say, satanic) humor and, most important, a yearning quality that informed his thrashing bafflement with Blanche and the airs that she put on. Somewhere under his cheap knowingness, his confident sexuality, his sadistic humor (which perhaps no other actor could have made us laugh at so genuinely) Brando suggested a sensitivity so buried that Kowalski himself could not recognize it, even a vulnerability that, long ago perhaps, Stanley saw as weakness and hid under every kind of male denial. This untutored, unspoken sensitivity informed all of Brando's early roles, and the suspense in all of them revolved around whether or not he would acknowledge his best self, articulate his aspirations and his pain.

"Oh, Charlie, Oh, Charlie . . . You don't understand. I could have had class. I could have been somebody, instead of a bum—which is what I am." One could almost hear the national sigh of relief rising when, at last, he uttered, in *On the Waterfront,* what would turn out to be the most famous lines he ever spoke. Here at last was the articulation not only of his own needs, but perhaps of all our needs in a decade where, by common consent, no ambition was to be vaulting. The film itself insisted that Terry Malloy, the ex-pug now living on the small change the waterfront mobs scattered in his direction, find his best self in narrow and peculiar political action. The director, Elia Kazan, and the writer, Budd Schulberg, had both suffered calumny as a result of their cooperation with the House Un-American Activities Committee's investigations into show biz Communism, and Malloy's heroism consisted of being what they were accused of being—a stool pigeon—and then of suffering a terrible beating for it (the poses of a pietà are employed to emphasize his martyrdom).

But no matter. Or small matter. Official recognition of Brando's gift could no longer be denied. And the calumny he had suffered—the cruel parodies, the intellectual clucking over his lack of the classic actor's graces (which included the canard that he mumbled), the fuming and fussing over his antisocial behavior—these were now stilled. One could not resist, especially if one were his contemporary and partisan, drawing analogies between his life and his role. There was heroism in his individuality, his resistance to the publicity mechanism (giving interviews he would later say was "Navel picking—AND SMOKING IT"), his challenge to the tradition of the well-made actor.

His achievement seemed, then, to consist of two parts. He had redefined and expanded our notions of what constituted the heroic on stage and screen, so that it could include visible self-consciousness and visible self-doubting, which is the simple way of saying that he had brought the spirit of modernism over from literature and painting (where, increasingly, the subject of the work was the work itself) and applied it to performance. And, as a public figure, he had brought the same qualities to celebrity existence. We were involved, as we never had been before, in the actor's struggle to find and realize himself as an artist, and this experience was different, shall we say, from our sympathetic enlistment in the causes of performers who made their personal troubles public, different from our worries over Judy Garland's struggles with booze, pills, and victimization by her producers and managers.

We actually knew very little of Brando's personal life. All his struggles were aesthetic. And by insisting on that metaphor, he changed the terms of the discussions his peers would have with their public, with their ostensible employers. There was a certain strange and wild humor in Brando, and there was an element of put-on in all this. But as always with movie stars there was a seepage between his public persona and his screen roles and, in time, one began to detect on the screen glimpses of the star profession's essence—its insecurities, its endless, quiet-bubbling contempt for the people they work for (which includes the audience), and, above all, the nagging, peculiarly American fear that acting may not be suitable work for a grown-up, heterosexual male. ("Why does anybody care about what any movie star has to say? A movie star is nothing important. Freud, Gandhi, Marx. These people are important. But movie acting is just dull, boring, childish work.") Only by the assertion that acting has a moral dimension, may have at its best social and political effects, can one still these nagging doubts and fears, salvage one's soul and the audience's too, perhaps. Not to make this unprecedented exertion was demeaning, perhaps unmanning. Earlier I interrupted Pauline Kael. Let her finish her thought: "A young actor now generally feels that he is an artist only when he uses his technique for personal expression and something he believes in. And so he has a problem that [Cary Grant] never faced: they also became sellouts. They began to feel emasculated when they played formula roles that depended on technique only, and they had to fight themselves to retain their belief in the audience, which often preferred what they did when they sold out. They were up against all the temptations, corruptions, and conflicts that writers and composers and painters had long been wrestling with. Commerce is a bind for actors now . . ." Yes, and that bind was the creation of Brando and the aesthetic revolutionaries standing behind him and cheering him on. Ironically, he was to become something besides its creator; he was to become its first victim.

Act Two. We perhaps misunderstood him. Perhaps he misunderstood himself at times. He is a shy—and in later years, even reclusive —man. If, at first, we thought he was of that breed of actors who go on stage because it offers unparalleled opportunities to show off, it is obvious that we were wrong. He appears actually to be of the second type, which is composed of people who are mimics and impersonators, people who like to assert themselves without actually revealing much of their insecure and often unformed selves. "Actors have to observe, and I enjoy that part of it," Brando once said. "They have to know how much spit you have in your mouth, and where the weight of your elbows is. I could sit all day in the Optimo Cigar Store telephone booth on 42nd Street and just watch the people pass by." Besides, he said, an actor, if he is working well and truly, has to "upset" himself, to dive down deep and examine the junk and offal buried at the bottom of the psyche in search of the pearls that are also buried there; and the supreme effort of will that those explorations required grew increasingly difficult for him. "There comes a time in one's life when you don't want to do it anymore. You know a scene is coming where you'll have to cry or scream and all those things, and it's always bothering you, always eating away at you . . ."

Here was irony! The man whom everyone expected to lead the heroic modern thespians' expedition to the heart of our twentieth-century darkness, the route to which perforce lay through his own soul, had finally no spirit for the job. If he could have stayed on the surface, achieve his effects technically, could have been, actually, a movie star of the old-fashioned stripe, he would have been happier. That was, he said, "a perfectly reasonable way to make a living. You're not stealing money, and you're entertaining people." But on this point he was speaking more out of envy than out of experience. For the ironic fact is that there is more self-exposure in being Cary Grant or Gary Cooper or any other long-lived star you care to name than there was in most of Brando's roles after *On the Waterfront.* For a star's screen persona must be based on some true aspect of his personality—not all of it, surely, but some part that is authentic and can thus stand the test of repeated examination. And that Brando did not wish to present to the world. For almost two decades he hid out in what amounted to a succession of character leads, roles that required a succession of odd makeups and accents. To name a few of the best remembered of them is to suggest the lengths to which he would go in his attempt to hide in plain sight, a purloined letter somehow mixed in with all the special delivery parcels of stardom: a Damon Runyon gambler in *Guys and Dolls,* a Japanese interpreter in *Teahouse of the August Moon,* a Southern officer fighting his own racial prejudice in *Sayonara,* a German soldier de-Nazifying himself (a character development he had insisted upon) in *The Young Lions,* the vengeful antihero of the Western he took over direction of, *One-Eyed Jacks,* Fletcher Christian played, daringly, as an aristocratic poof in the remake of *Mutiny on the Bounty,* a homosexual shuffling off his repression in *Reflections in a Golden Eye.* And so on. In retrospect the gallery's range is remarkable, and one ventures the thought that it will seem the more so as time goes on. For in each of the roles there was a teasing moment (or two or three) in which he took your breath away with some bit of acutely observed behavior by which he revealed some simple truth about his character—perhaps about himself—that no conventionally disciplined movie actor would ever have dared. And in almost all of them there was, indeed, a technical competence for which no apology need be made.

Except that people kept wanting him to apologize. His old support-ers felt betrayed. Where were the classic roles they had yearned to see him test himself in? If not those, then where were the deeply serious new works that would permit his voyage inward—to his soul's depths. And ours. His old enemies felt justified. They could claim now that they were the first to see that his promise had been a false one, that he was just another broody hunk of actorish sound and fury, signifying nothing very much. In the sixties he became more sulky and uncoop-erative on the scts than ever. He was costing people money now—and no longer bringing it in at the box office. His pictures became more marginal, more absurd. He was finally playing a murderous chauffeur one year, an Irish gamekeeper who liked to tie up the governess when his lordship left them alone in the great house the next. There was much contempt in all this—for himself and for the world. Considering him in 1966, Kael quoted Emerson to the effect that the American artist "must pass for a fool and a churl for a long season." She added: "We used to think that the season meant only youth, before the artist could prove his talent, make his place, achieve something. Now it is clear that for screen artists, youth is, relatively speaking, the short season; the long one is the degradation *after* success."

Act Three. The year of his redemption and reintegration was 1972. There was *The Godfather,* of course, the culmination of his career as a character actor. His Don Corleone was old and sweet and deadly—cunning in both senses of the word. He deserved the second Oscar he was awarded for the performance, and show biz deserved the fake Indian princess he sent to pick it up for him. In that same year, however, there was also *Last Tango in Paris.* Kael may now regret announcing that the date it premiered at the New York Film Festival, October 14, 1972, "should become a landmark in movie history—comparable to May 29, 1913—the night *Le Sacre du Printemps* was first performed—in music history." Only a decade later *Tango* seems more a curiosity than a precursor to anything very much. But as a date in the history of modern celebrity, why yes, it has a certain resonance. Bernardo Bertolucci, who both wrote and directed the film, said at the time that he liked to create characters based "on what the actors are in themselves," instead of asking them "to interpret some-thing preexistent." This, after his years in the wilderness, was some-thing Brando needed, and something his reputation needed, too. Time —long past time—to go pearl diving again.

Seeing the movie again, a decade later, one sees, as one did not amid the hoopla attendant on its initial release, that its sole significant business, the place where its vitality now resides almost exclusively, lies in this opportunity it provided Brando. *Le Sacre du Printemps,* indeed! The thing is the star vehicle to end all star vehicles. Yes, it aspires to something more, to some pure and daring statement about the relationship between man and woman. But no, on that level, its intellectuality is strictly soft-core.

The story has a nameless man and a nameless woman (she is played by Maria Schneider) meet in an apartment both are thinking of renting. Having checked it out, he falls upon her and she, in the modern manner, accepts him for a quick, brutal fuck. Thereafter, they meet for increasingly vivid fornications (the classic porn structure is followed with the domineering male and the submissive female isolated and thus freed from all restraint, which permits escalation in the intensity and daring of their sexual feats). Outside the apartment we see that she is involved with a young filmmaker, who is recording their affair (he will eventually propose marriage) and her biography for a documentary. He wishes to impose the spurious order of art on life. The Brando character's wife, it is revealed, has just committed suicide, and that has summoned both reminiscence and remorse on his part—along with the need for the affectless sanctuary the apartment and the girl afford. Eventually, and banally, there is a role reversal. He proposes a conventional living arrangement to her, just as she decides that she has got all the good she can out of the degradation (in slavery there is freedom, as the cliché goes) he has imposed on her. He follows her to the home she shares with her parents (Father is an Army officer, no less), and when he violates that bourgeois sanctuary with his importunings and his presence, she kills him with her father's revolver.

But all of this—whatever it started out to be in Bertolucci's original conception—serves Brando, and only Brando. Maybe originally, it was supposed to be a duet, but it plays as an aria, with Schneider (a newcomer, who brought no resonances with her) serving as an accompanist (in modern film we can tell who the star is not by who has the most lines, but who has to take off the most clothes, and she is the most exposed here). Be that as it may, the apartment is an existentialist symbol as well as a pornographic device—a central void in the universe, to be filled in the absence of God (or whatever) as we do these days with sex and autobiography. It is value-free, history-free, future-free, and Paul and Jeanne (as they are finally labeled) furnish it only with a bed, a plain table and chairs, lust and memory.

The sex, as Norman Mailer pointed out in his remarkable essay on the film, is faked—well faked, to be sure, but nevertheless visibly faked —and it is, as a result, in this context, strangely disappointing. As Mailer wrote, "Brando's cock up Schneider's real vagina would have brought the history of the cinema one huge march closer to the ulti- mate experience it has promised since its inception (which is to re- embody life)." The reason for our disappointment with this material lies precisely in the contrast between the filmed sex and the filmed talk. There, we feel, no niceties have been allowed to intervene; Brando, in particular, gives the impression that he is being allowed to say anything that comes into his head, or anything that came into it during rehearsals and was saved for the takes.

This material is of two distinct characters. The first is pure autobi- ography, a rehearsal of the character's history from childhood to the present. It is full of snips and snaps that remind us of things we seem to remember hearing about the actor as well as oblique references to his film roles—an exquisite blending of private and public history. Here, then, we witness Kowalski-Malloy-Brando arrived at the mid- life crisis, the concluding unscientific postscript, as we were led to think, to the life in which we had taken such an avid interest these two decades, this life we thought we had shared. The authentic air of this dialogue is further reinforced by Brando's behavior throughout. As an actor he has been—notoriously—a motherfucker to handle, a man rendered quickly bored and restless by repetitive rehearsal, by the stock conventions of his trade, yet also hating to appear bald-faced in roles where the public might mistake what it is seeing for his true self and where other actors hide out behind technique and their self-pro- tecting mannerisms. That is why there is so much makeup, so many accents, in his history. Here Bertolucci makes capital of Brando's frantic burrowings to escape his own skin. If the actor wants to drop into an English accent or adopt the mannerisms of a bouncy adoles- cent, he lets him. Brando can mumble his lines or stumble on them, he can strike poses or he can sulk. Best of all, he can indulge his free- associational humor, which leads him inevitably toward the sexual and scatological. And the more he tries not to be Brando, the more he is Brando. For the essence of his art has always derived from the tension between his impulse to truth and his instinct to hide.

And so, autobiography and behavior combine to guarantee—or

seem to guarantee—the truth of the second major portion of his dialogue, the sexual fantasies, which up to a point his partner must act
out for him. And if, whether fantasized or acted out, these disgust or
appall, so be it. All right, he seems to say, you wanted the truth about
me. Well, here it is, go gag on it. When Brando buggers Schneider's
chic, saucy, *cultured* little bourgeois ass, he is buggering all and everything that has bugged him. And when he forces her to explore his own
fundament, the while describing his fancy of her copulation with a
dying pig, he is saying something about the fate he has reserved for all
who have tried to probe him for his secrets these many years. In these
moments, we are all Blanches to his time-warped Stanley, allowing
ourselves to be reamed breathless by his contempt.

Mailer: "The crowd's joy is that a national celebrity is being ob-
scene on screen. To measure the media magnetism of such an act, ask
yourself how many hundreds of miles you might drive to hear Richard
Nixon speak a line like: 'We're just taking a flying fuck at a rolling
doughnut' or 'I went to the University of the Congo; studied whale
fucking.' Only liberal unregenerates would be so progressive as to say
they would not drive a mile. No, one could start mass migrations
. . .''

It is surreal, says Mailer, but he adds, surrealism has become the
objective correlative of our time. "A private glimpse of the great becomes the alchemy of the media, the fool's gold of the century of
communication. In the age of television we know everything about the
great but how they fart—the ass wind is, ergo, our trade wind. It is
part of Brando's genius to recognize that the real interest of audiences
is not in having him portray the tender passages and murderous
storms of an unruly passion between a man and a woman, it is rather
to be given a glimpse of his kinks. His kinks offer sympathetic vibra-
tion to their kinks."

But—and this is a crucial point Mailer did not explore—we do not
certainly know that these kinks are really his kinks. For all we actually
know Brando may prefer the missionary position—in the dark with
his pajamas on. In 1972 when the lights in the theater went up, the
possibility of a splendid duplicity lingered. Let us posit, for the moment, that the scatological is not his bag. Let us propose instead that
he was speaking in the tongues of metaphor, that Bertolucci had presented him, in this film, with the long-dreamed-of opportunity for
apotheosis, and finally, that he intended to use it not for the minor and
dubious "bravery" of confirming the gossipists' speculations about pri-

vate life, that he was not some Shelley Winters naming the names of good and bad lays in her autobiography. We can see, as well, that he was not making, herewith, some simpleminded statement of political belief or social protest. If he wasn't Shelley Winters, he wasn't Jane Fonda either. No, he was finally doing what he was supposed to have been doing, speaking from his depths.

But these were now polluted depths. What was once a pure and authentic spirit—that of an idealistic artist, as he perhaps saw it, certainly an uncorrupted individualist—now carried the poisons of fame in his system. It was this bile that he would spew here, under the not entirely erroneous assumption that we, the audience, were as much responsible for its creation as he was and deserved a sample of its bitter taste. And so what we had was the first (and so far only) performance in which the fact of the star's stardom—not just the idea of stardom, which we sometimes get in movies about movies and the theater—was the subject of the starring role. Brando had taken all of it —his conceptions and misconceptions of himself, our conceptions and misconceptions about the same subject, and made a role out of the mess. And we are not talking here about just a few scribbled rewrites on the set, designed to match image and skills more closely to the demands of the writers' blueprint. No, we are talking about an organic symbiosis—something that does not, I think, exist in nature but can perhaps be used as a term of description in the unnatural world of celebrity. Brando, especially toward the end of the film, when he puts on his fallen angel mask, begs for a tragic interpretation of all this, and one feels like conceding it to him in gratitude for the high-grade farce that went before. And our gratitude, as well, for the Bronx cheer (or was it authentically a fart?) he sent in the direction of his critics and the volunteer keepers of his conscience.

Somehow, his old, good instincts had been made to function once again, and he had shown us where the demand for subjectivity, for "truth," unguarded, unshaped by psychological distancing and stylization, is bound to take us in the age of celebrity. That is, toward a confusion between personality and product that can never be art, must inevitably end up in publicity. He had better reason to know this than anyone, for self and statement are inextricably bound together for the performer, with his power to command his own fate being utterly dependent on his fame. In the age of celebrity the only truly heroic act an artist can perform is to protect his vision and his virtue by cloaking them in a modesty that is near to the secretive. And that, as a practical matter, amounts to taking a vow of poverty—especially for actors. Brando's *Last Tango* whirled us to the center of this knowledge. His final act of heroism lay in his despairing acknowledgment not of his "kinks"—that was just sleight of hand—but of the terrible confusions that had brought him low, and by which he would then, at least briefly, restore himself.

Briefly indeed. There is no need for an epilogue to the story of the hero with a thousand faces. But the actor with a hundred faces lives on in our messed-up world, with a leftover life to kill in a culture that offers no rest, no home. It was as if *The Godfather* and *Last Tango* exhausted Brando. Now there was only silliness and money to occupy him—*The Missouri Breaks, Superman, Apocalypse Now, The Formula*. The disgust with the public, with oneself for paying attention to it, endemic in all performers, especially as they age, is now in full heat. His final disguise is as a fat man too lazy to learn his lines, pasting them on the camera, on his fellow performers' foreheads for the close-ups. In this, too, he becomes a paradigm. Even his self-loathing has a scale about it that might, perhaps, be termed heroic.

🌿 🌿

Celebrity can sometimes be understood as a kind of algebra, a system of equations: where there is a hero there is often a victim to balance him. If Brando can be seen as a new sort of cultural hero, striving in his ambivalent and self-destructive way for a kind of transcendence, then his contemporary Marilyn Monroe can be seen as a very familiar sort of show biz victim—the dumb blonde done wrong. If, except for self-destructiveness, she was as unlike him as it is possible to be in most respects, she was like him in the one that counted most. For she too craved transcendence, and she too discovered that the time was right, the machinery in place, to magnify, amplify, sentimentalize qualities that were in themselves not uncommon. Just as Brando was scarcely the first or the last actor to want to be taken seriously, Marilyn Monroe was not the first pneumatic starlet to wish to symbolize something other than sex. The difference was that now a melodrama, larger, richer, yet more apparently intimate than anything she ever appeared in on the screen, could be constructed in real life around this yearning. In the end, it would carry subthemes of social and cultural criticism more potent (and infinitely more approachable at the most vulgar level) than anything in the Brando story. And, of course, a firmly tragic denouement that has assured it a resonance that, if anything, seems to increase with the passing years. It was, and is, great stuff: from the level of *The National Enquirer* to that of Norman Mailer everyone is presented with something to gnaw on.

Hers was a story—a "legend" as any competent tabloid deskman would automatically style it for his headline—that depended on our awareness of a larger legend. As early as 1921, five years before Marilyn was born, the Hollywood Chamber of Commerce was taking out ads in papers around the country warning the impressionable against trying to break into the movies without prior invitation. Already there were too many waifs on its doorstep—sleeping on it, in fact—and that message was reinforced, in the years Monroe was growing up as Norma Jeane Baker in Los Angeles, by a thousand movies, radio shows, magazine articles, and fictions. Well before she attained her majority, these cautionary tales had become part of American folk knowledge. Impossible to say how many thousands were thus saved from misery. Equally impossible, however, to estimate how many thousands ignored the warnings, for along with them, in the same journals, ran tales of the favored few who accepted the risk and beat the odds. There is, after all, a level of psychic impoverishment more grinding than any amount of economic impoverishment, a level where hope—a realistic emotion that can motivate and sustain the development of talent—is crushed, and pure fantasy, loosened from its anchorage in reality, takes its place.

Hollywood drew thousands from this huddled mass to it, and for its members, just reaching a casting couch represented a triumph of sorts, a welcome respite from eight hours afoot as a carhop, a welcome alternative to prostitution of a more formal kind, or the stag reels. Of them it might be said that even their degradations were at least livelier than the mundanities they had escaped. They were the locusts who swarmed in Nathaniel West's novel, and it is not too much to say that Norma Jeane Baker was a first-generation child of this underclass. Her mad mother worked as a negative cutter (a skilled but not a creative motion picture craft) before she was institutionalized. When she was not in an orphanage Norma Jeane numbered among her foster parents, extras and stand-ins. She married for the first time when she was sixteen, and while her husband was serving in the merchant marine during the war, she found work in a plant where a photographer, assigned to do a picture story for *Yank,* the serviceman's magazine, on a pretty war worker, discovered her. Soon she was modeling full-time for the *Clic-Pic-See* magazines. Awaiting the barber's ministrations in those days one must have skimmed her. It is said that she rejected a photographer's plea for nude poses on the grounds that someday she intended to be a movie star and wanted nothing rising up out of her past to haunt her, though even in the Middle West we had heard of *Ecstasy* and Hedy Lamarr's husband who tried to buy up all the prints that evidenced his bride's youthful shame, had pondered the legend of the skin flick Joan Crawford once allegedly made and we knew that such youthful indiscretions did not necessarily harm a career. There follows for Monroe the small-time agent, the helpful males with whom use is traded for use, the studio contract, the small parts, the bigger parts, the ever more important men . . .

But wait. This is not a life we are reading. It is a novel or a screenplay, or maybe a novelized screenplay. And not a very good one. Its author must be named Irving and this must be his "searing indictment" not just of Hollywood, but of the American Way of Life, its corruptions and tawdriness. In short, we are dealing here in archetypes if not stereotypes. There is something almost moronic in the story's simplicity, the way it seems—not halfway through—to be pointing the most obvious moral. There is also something shrewd in it. Irving, after all, has many bestsellers to his credit, and the reason is that he gives the people what he knows they want. And he knows what they want because he knows his own mind, its needs and limits, and he knows, without cynicism or condescension, that it is perfectly in tune with the sensibilities that compose his audience. But, of course, Irving did not write this particular tale—just the urtexts on which it was based. The author here is also its subject and is working not on traditional foolscap but on the many and wide screens the media have placed before the modern artiste, on which she projected the only materials he had, her thin and unsingular autobiography, around which she placed in the only intellectual framework she knew the fantasy into which she was born. Which is, of course, precisely the point Norman Mailer argued in his longest, looniest, and most compelling meditation on celebrity, the introduction that grew into the book *Marilyn,* the deepest caption in the history of picture books.

For him, the turning point, the moment at which she ceased to be merely the passive player in the publicity game, agreeably falling into whatever poses the cheesecake chefs demanded, arrived when a blackmailer came forward asking ten thousand dollars not to disclose the fact that she had once abandoned principle and, for fifty dollars, posed in the nude in a photograph that was suddenly turning up on calendars all over America. The criminal had gone to the producers of a picture she was making at RKO on loan-out from her home lot, Twentieth Century-Fox. They, as it happened, thought the publicity would, in the short term, do them good, and had small concern for Monroe's or the rival studio's long-term interests. Fox, naturally, disagreed with this assessment. But Monroe, who by this time had access to advice far shrewder than one finds in a corporate executive suite, advice that came from men who had lived by their wits in the jungle just outside the studio compounds, opted for disclosure. She had, indeed, stripped and lain down before the lens on the crumpled red velvet of the offending still. Luckily the pose was not lubricious; it was definitely of the "art" variety. And the paltriness of her fee made one feel sorry for her. In those so recently innocent days, before large numbers of people took to exhibiting themselves naked, one imagined it would require much more than fifty dollars to get any decent woman to undress and disport herself with a camera present. Poor kid! To have to embarrass herself like that for a lousy fifty bucks! She really must have been up against it. And there she was, being so sweet and honest about it.

But what a masterstroke! What a subtle sense of the shifting of the national consciousness was here displayed! And what an acute prescience as to where we were about to go. Before anyone, even before Hugh Hefner, she had judged that nakedness need no longer be automatically equated with promiscuity, that there were ways of restoring a childlike innocence to the display of flesh, of disarming all but the most avid moralists by talking naturally and unthreateningly about it. Like all the girls next door who would soon start folding out of *Playboy*'s center pages, there would be a sort of good sport naughtiness in her quotes ("Did you have anything on?" "Yes, the radio") that made one think, perhaps, of a cheerfully frank cousin who had become a stewardess, or Aunt Peggy, Mom's youngest sister, who had a lusty wink and a few snappy jokes for the teenagers when she came home from the big city at Christmas. Maybe a little fast, but basically good as gold. Swell kids!

But besides initiating an era in which the nude model no longer had to keep the seventh veil of anonymity draped around her (and conversely, the well-known might, if they chose, discreetly strip in public), she also initiated a new age of bold confession. No longer did public figures have to hide their guilty secrets. Quite the opposite. Properly handled, they could enlist public sympathy, help explain and justify one's weaknesses and more recent errors. It did not happen all at once—*Confidential* was still around, terrifying and titillating—but the trend was announced, and with it, incidentally, another large chunk of studio power began to erode. If very little about one's past was truly shameful then the threat of exposing a star's youthful (or subsequent) indiscretions in order to discipline him was a hollow one. *The Big Knife,* Clifford Odets's play on this subject, was a dull blade by the time it reached the screen in 1955, though still full of superb Hollywood caricatures, however pompously they were presented.

For Monroe in particular, confession was a vital part of her success. As Mailer has demonstrated, she tended to make her early life sound even grimmer and more melodramatic than it actually had been, for by novelizing her autobiography and giving it still greater pathos, she linked her myth to the preexisting myth of the victimized starlet, struggling to retain respectability in a cruel world. Had she possessed a subtle and ironic mind, had she been Charles Dickens instead of an Irving, she might have lived the great novel of our time instead of its most enduring potboiler.

Still, she did all right. When she first walked through the gates at Fox everyone saw her as the latest bimbo. She looked like a bimbo, acted like a bimbo (that daily appointment with Joe Schenck, founder of the studio—"I'm always done with Mr. Schenck by 3:20"—seemed to suggest the traditional service starlets perform for moguls), and was generally cast as a bimbo. All right, she was a bimbo. And if it was that less than exalted state she had to transcend, then she would have to do so. She would make people understand that bimbos had feelings too, and, as they say in the trade, back stories. The measure of her achievement lies precisely here. Think of all the girls who have played bits and posed with their breasts bulging out of their bathing suits, and given blow jobs to the boss, and then think how few have gone on not just to stardom, but beyond it into "legend." It was as Mailer put it: "She . . . has burst out of all the standard frames of reference for publicity . . . Our heroine has been converted from some half-clear piece of cheesecake on the hazy screen of American newspapers (where focus always shifts) to another kind of embodiment altogether, an intimate, as real as one's parents, one's family, one's enemies, sweethearts and friends. She is now part of that core of psychological substance out of which one concocts one's life judgments . . . Marilyn had become a protagonist in the great American soap opera. Life is happy for her one hour, tragic the next; she can now appear innocent or selfish, wronged or wrongdoer—it no longer matters. She has broken through the great barrier of publicity—overblown attention—and is now *interesting;* she is a character out there in the national life, alive, expected, even encouraged, to change each week. The spirit of soap opera, like the spirit of American optimism, is renewal! God give us a new role each week to watch, but a role that fits the old one. Because that, Gawd, is how we learn!"

In this passage we understand why Mailer's caption grew and grew. For he himself had long ago announced his entrance in the race for transcendence by way of his imagined competition with Ernest Hemingway, or should one say the ghost of Ernest Hemingway as, in the fifties, he appeared to us, courtesy of everything from beer ads to *New Yorker* profiles, talking in that weird clipped way of his, a parody of his written prose, achieving in life what his sometime friend F. Scott Fitzgerald was achieving in death—trademark status. They were the images that sprang to impressionable or illiterate minds when the word "writer" came up in conversation. Neither could threaten anymore with complicated or dangerous thoughts, both had lead, and one was still leading, romantic and glamorous lives, both offered, should one actually choose to go past image into works, E-Z "classics." One had come to a comprehensibly tragic end, and one appeared heading there—good suspense in the journey—though he had time to knock off a "hymn to the human spirit" which bowled everyone over when it ran in *Life.* Of course, Fitzgerald's heroic status had been thrust upon him a decade or so after his death, and he perhaps did not consciously seek it. But Hemingway demonstrated for Mailer, for all of us, that you could work for it if you were bold and clever enough in your manipulations.

One has to think that D. W. Griffith was by no means the only American artist of the 1920s to sense the potential for heroics in the artistic vocation, that Hemingway began turning himself into a "legend" almost as soon as his work began to be noticed. By 1935 Edmund Wilson was writing of *The Green Hills of Africa,* "the self-dramatized Hemingway we get has the look of having been inspired by some idea of what his public must expect after reading his rubbishy articles in the men's-wear magazine, *Esquire"* and "the Old Master of Key West . . . has a way of making himself ridiculous." And so on, for years, by critics less prescient than Wilson.

There was, perhaps, a trifle more to this matter than Wilson realized at the time. In *Fame Became of Him,* his excellent study of

"Hemingway as Public Writer," John Raeburn persuasively argues that the novelist's pose as he-man adventurer at least began as a strategy for disarming his critics, to whose doubts and strictures he was preternaturally sensitive. The implication of his image—a construct of brawls, hunting expeditions, war correspondence, and mighty fishery —was that no man clinging tightly to his effete urban comforts could possibly comprehend him, thus was in no position to effectively criticize his work. He was, in effect, appealing over the critics' heads to a larger public, the sale of his books and his viability as a popular magazine sage, giving the lie to their increasingly negative natterings, his enviable lifestyle—he was always giving his fans very precise instructions on what wine to drink in this or that circumstance, how the fish or game he killed should be prepared for table—demonstrating how to live well and truly as an artist who yet drank deeply of the most basic human experiences. What he sensed was what people in the movies had known from the beginning, what all kinds of writers and artists would soon sense, namely, that despite all the talk about the increasing power of criticism, "The Age of Criticism" as some in the years after World War II would dub it, criticism was actually an irrelevance, or could be made into an irrelevance by a shrewd publicist. The point was to become a brand name if you could—the equivalent of a movie star, splendidly free of the finespun meshes of the theorists, free to play the game by what seemed to be your own rules.

The tactic, of course, infuriated his critics, assuring Hemingway of still more vicious attacks in the literary journals, and perhaps driving him toward the prodigies of self-parody that marked his later years, perhaps deepening his inability to write confidently, perhaps deepening that despair that led him to suicide. What if they were right? About this, of course, we can never be certain. What we can say is that neither his pose nor his prose improved with the passage of time. By the time Mailer announced that he wished to arm wrestle him for the top rung on the ladder of American literature, it should have been apparent to the younger man that this was a mug's game, for which, actually, Mailer was ill-suited. Hemingway was not an intellectual, which Mailer was. The range of Papa's interests, like the range of his prose, was really quite narrow. He could define one form of masculinity imagistically in his prose and in himself, but he could not go much beyond a vignette of surfaces in other matters. Mailer, on the other hand, could write quite seriously, when he was only thirty-six, that "like many another vain, empty, and bullying body of our time, I have been running for President these last ten years . . ." and we understood the irony to be seriously meant, especially after he ran for mayor of New York in reality, went in for filmmaking, took up journalism with an eye to recasting the form itself, all the while leading a private life that kept getting as spectacularly into the papers as Hemingway's had. All this, of course, distracted from the imminent leap at the throat of the "big" novel the self-conscious attempt at the immortalizing masterpiece that he announced and announced, turning that oft frustrated effort into a kind of serial drama that was not so very different from Monroe's quest for the great role that preoccupied her later years. When, people kept asking, when was he finally going to do it? Or would he never find this fulfillment?

Whether he did or didn't in *Ancient Evenings* is not relevant here. The point is that his obsession with Hemingway and, latterly, with Monroe, his implicit envy of the ease with which they inserted themselves into "the national life," "the great American soap opera" was, in some sense, misplaced. That a movie star starts with an edge in this respect, an edge based simply on the wider interest that naturally accrues to someone in her line of work as opposed to someone following the writer's trade in a functionally illiterate society, seems not to have occurred to him. Nor did he seem to notice that Hemingway's narrow, indeed obsessive, self-absorption was of an intensity he could not hope to match given his infinitely distractible nature.

Hemingway, wrote Wilson in 1935, was "his own worst-drawn character," by which we must assume that this hunter–bullfighter–war-loving he-man failed to meet the classic specifications of a literary construct; he had no depth, not enough curious contradictions, represented not a concatenation of qualities but a single one played to the hilt. In short, he was what popular novelists (and movies, of course) give us, a type not an individual. It was the same way with Monroe. She had taken her basic bimbo's understanding of the world, and her instinct for leveraging it, and played her bimbohood for all it was worth, just as any popular novelist would have, and for the same reason: it represented her full understanding of the character, the best that she could do with it, and we sensed that she was not cheating or talking down to us through it, even though it read easily and did not tax us as it touched us. And, yes, it did touch us. For all women have something of the bimbo in them, subdued though it is by moral instruction and by life's demands for other subtleties. Similarly, the analogous male quality, the fucker's impulse—use 'em and lose 'em.

She was, finally, the embodiment of the dream that never dies, the dream of the transfiguring one-night stand.

Poor Norman! He could analyze creatures like Monroe *en passant,* scandalize and stimulate in the process, but he could not become as they were. Complexity blurs. Complexity confuses. Complexity does not come across in the picture mags or on TV. He has done better with it than most, thanks to his dramatic poses and adventurings. But he cannot quite break through. His works are nattered over on the front page of the New York *Times Book Review,* but the great mass of people do not know or care. The Irvings all outsell him, Hemingway and Fitzgerald are still the Great American Novelists. And Marilyn, despite his clever understanding of her, is the tragedienne of our times.

But we are perilously close to digression. There is yet the rest of the Monroe character's arc to contemplate. Or should one say the limits of that arc? Yes. For there is only one place that victims can logically go, and that is to destruction. Her triumph may be that she delayed it for a full decade. For all that time she remained under contract to Fox, and it continued to serve her as an antagonist. The moguls didn't understand her, they typed her, they didn't value her aspirations, but they would not let go of her either, not in these hard times when she was virtually the only star worth holding on to. Stupidly, they kept underpaying her; they might at least have given her what she was worth and so subdued that complaint. Not so stupidly, they kept casting her as a bimbo—a star bimbo now, instead of a featured player bimbo. And they let her, at least, kid the part, satirize hot sex while still embodying it. She complained. She said she wanted to play Grushenka in *The Brothers Karamazov* (Who put her on to that? one wonders). She went off to the Actors Studio and tried to improve herself (night school is full of Marilyns). She acquired Lee Strasberg and his wife, Paula, as gurus, and they took her seriously, since they were incapable of an unserious response to anything, and besides her enlistment in their cause was a coup. It almost compensated for the way Marlon had drifted away. What a heady triumph if their "Method" could turn the bimbo into an actress even as the actor was turning into a fucker. "Lee" worked with her on *Anna Christie.* And she wet herself when she had to do one of Blanche Du Bois's scenes from *Streetcar* at the Actors Studio.

For she was not yet, and never would be, an actress, not in any reliable and effective sense that she or her employers or her co-workers could count on. Which is, perhaps, the main reason why she was so frequently tardy or entirely absent from her sets, why she drove the professionals she worked with, the directors and the actors, crazy. (It was after a simple scene that she required more than forty takes to complete that Tony Curtis made his famous remark that kissing her was like kissing Hitler.) In a remarkable analysis of her work and personality in *Film Comment,* David Thomson writes: "No other famous movie actress is so scattered or blank on the screen. She has the handicap of nervousness that could never settle into shyness. If that seems too dismissive, look instead at the authority she had and the pleasure she took in stills. In her movies, time and again, there is a strain, in the editing and among the actors, as well as in her woefully distracted face, that tells us about the communal worry as to whether she would remember her lines and know when and where to move. The white lie must be told smoothly; falter and it begins to stink." Thomson adds: "There is not one film in which she is the pulse of its *mise en scene."* And "Far from deriving from her, films had to wend their way around her shortcomings." And "She is not with the other actors but imposed upon the scene like a special effect."

The contrast between Marilyn on motion picture film and Marilyn as she was captured on the still photographer's film is extraordinarily vivid. For in the stills she was like Archibald MacLeish's classic definition of a poem, she did not have to mean, she had only to be. Or, to refine the thought a bit, she had only to be a very simple thing, one that was within her range: she had only to be the stuff of a wet dream. The stillsmen, as Thomson says, were "her escorts to immortality and the great public, the visionaries who saw she was in the realm of perfection whenever she stopped. In the middle of a movement or a thought, being arrested gave a promise of continuity," the very quality her herky-jerky screen work so rarely had. The still photographers' response to her, as a person, was directly the opposite of that of her movie directors. Where the latter saw only meanness, madness, and panic, the former were aroused to passionate awe, and perhaps something more than that. "This is love," writes Thomson, "when the sight of the beloved seems to enhance and celebrate the lover's watching." And, of course, the same grace is extended, even unto the pimpliest little whack-off artist contemplating the glossies.

In the stills, one feels, she is in command, as she could never be on the sound stage. She is at the very least the co-*auteur* of these images, and working well within her natural range. In her own way she knew as much about passive fantasy as any adolescent mooning over her

half-naked images, for had she not spent many a dreaming hour similarly agog over the pages of the fan magazines when she was that age?
And still, these two decades and more later, she commands us from
the page as she cannot from the screen. It is as Thomson says: "Forever humiliated by seeming dumb in movies, in stills Marilyn tran-
scends intelligence. As Mailer guessed, the man looking at stills of
Monroe hears her private voice, and even if it is the pit of superstition,
that bestows a great knowingness on her, a thorough command of the
medium such as a witch enjoys with spells. No one asks if a soothsayer
is intelligent when she is right . . .'"

All right. She had transcended. But she was a hollow star. She was
still a joke among her peers and so long as she lacked even the rudimentary professionalism that very often can be inculcated in reformed
carhops who are willing to learn their new trade, she was doomed to
go on repeating herself—the bimbo on screen, the victim in the rest of
her public life and in her private life. It was quite enough to sustain
the mouth breathers' concern for her. But the thing the orphan girl
most needed, that sense of a creative community sustaining and supporting her, was denied her. It is built up on sets and on locations, out
of sharing with colleagues the difficulties, complexities, and (often)
sheer lunacy of the motion picture or theatrical enterprise. He or she
who adds to those difficulties and complexities is shut out, isolated,
turned into a scapegoat, the object of derisive gossip.

As if in compensation for that isolation she offered no resistance
whatever to the celebrity high life, which looks like a community but,
since there is no sharing of craft or trade, no true community of
interests, is not. She married a legendary athlete. Then she married a
legendary artist-intellectual. And if there is anything that gives credence to the gossip that, at the end of her life, she was having an affair
with Bobby Kennedy, it lies in the fact that he would have represented
the third leg in her triple crown, a legendary politician. (What she
might have represented to the Attorney-General, namely justice,
makes the possibility of a liaison between them still more intriguing.
For the famously faithful family man, younger brother to the most
famous fucker of them all, to err with her was not only to err, but to
err spectacularly. To have saved it all up and then to have spent it on
the ultimate movie star—that would have been a competitive statement to reckon with. To have been "just good friends"—which they
seem probably to have been—was not nothing. It offered both an irresistible frisson.

For her, however, all openings became traps. In her last interview (with *Life*'s Richard Meryman, published just after her death), the sad litany concluded unchanged in tone: "People took a lot for granted, like not only could they be friendly, but they could get suddenly overly friendly and expect an awful lot for very little." And "Everybody is always tugging at you. They'd all like sort of a chunk of you. They kind of like to take a piece of you. It stirs up envy, fame does." And "A sex symbol becomes a thing. I just hate being a thing." And "When you are famous every weakness is exaggerated." And, finally, "It might be kind of a relief to be finished."

She was, one feels, entitled to her self-pity, as she was perhaps entitled to her self-destructiveness. By this time, with her comeback picture shut down, and openly besieged by the studio and its lawyers —they weren't just tugging at her, they were tearing at her—she surely sensed that the transcendence she had been reaching for in her dim and inconstant way, the transcendence to "acting," was now beyond her. At thirty-six, with her health and her mind perhaps permanently destabilized, with experience now reinforcing her instinctive understanding of F. Scott's dictum that there are no last acts in American life (by which surely he meant there were no good, inspiring, upbeat last acts), it occurred to her that the only transcendence reality could still offer was the slow one of decay. She also understood that what becomes a legend most is tragedy and so, finally, reached for her pill bottle, and reached for a resonantly cautionary conclusion.

In a sense she was right. Think, two decades later, how it would feel to come upon her puffy and lined in the Blackglama ads. It would have been a comedown not merely for her, but for us, for the fantasies we poured into the empty vessel that was her. In death she became, as Thomson says, "all conspiracy theory." And, as he also said: "Perhaps that's the way she wanted it . . . for, 'Like Marilyn Monroe' is a directional arrow implanted on modernity. It quickly transcended any duty we might have felt to the facts of life, to whether it was decent to wonder if she was good as an actress (or in bed), or whether we liked her. Legend doesn't deal in analysis or approval; it does require an actual nonentity, a vagueness of life or reality, a subjunctive pervasiveness . . ." Or, as David T. Bazelon put it, "The real Marilyn Monroe is a proper appreciation of her fictions, even if they are facts; or her facts, as long as you're not sure they cannot serve as fictions."

But still. She—or rather that construct-projection that we assumed to be her—was assuredly a tremor. And whether it was a consequence or a coincidence, when it had passed we could tell that the ground had shifted at least slightly under our feet. We have to think now, briefly, about sex as she affected its symbolization. And about death as her death affected its symbolization.

We have to go back, again, to the nude on the crumpled velvet, taken in anonymity but claimed (and proclaimed) in fame. Monroe could not have calculated the picture's ultimate effect, counted on what it would eventually do for her. She can claim wit only in the improvisation she came up with when it brought her career to its first crisis. But if she could achieve what she achieved through accident, then it occurred to others that they might achieve something similar through design. It was not long before other actresses began discreetly to shed their clothes in public. Art was, of course, the first great justification for this activity. Wicked Europe, much less addled on the subject of nudity than America, permitted not just its Bardots but its rather more serious actresses this freedom when the plot demanded it —or could be made to seem to demand it—so a precedent was already present. And an imperative, too. For the movies now required (heh-heh) "mature themes" if they were to differentiate themselves from television. What could be more mature than naked lovers atwitch on bed or beach? (The answer is, almost anything, but let it pass.)

Known women who had a taste for this sort of thing—or anyway, no revulsion to it—were thus encouraged to reveal themselves. Much more interesting, unknown women who wished to become known were similarly stimulated to "progress" from the rather demurely exposed breasts of Hefner's pioneer bunnies of the fifties to the beaver-splitters of today's *Hustler* and its ilk. The impulse for self display being an essential part of the performing personality, the slight escalation of that impulse required for an actress to do a modest movie skin scene requires little comment. Nor is it an impulse confined entirely to performers, and so one can readily appreciate the exhibitionistic and/or narcissistic frissons available to the pretty young secretary, receptionist, student, unmarked by the years (or by thought) as she corkscrews this way and that for Bob Guccione's camera. Her inevitable rationale that there may be some long-term advantage for her in this display, and that at any rate this offers an immediate buck easier and more glamorous than her usual employment offers—yet another opportunity proffered by the Land of Opportunity—seems reasonable enough, though the fact that no one has yet made the ascension from centerfold to significant stardom over these many years ought really to be borne in mind.

Perhaps, indeed, the strange adventures of Vanessa Williams, quondam Miss America and overnight sensation in the summer of 1984, will prove exemplary in this regard. It will be recalled that prior to winning the great beauty contest Williams posed for some nude photographs—two sets of them, for two different photographers it was finally revealed—a fact that somehow slipped her mind when interviewed by the rectitudinous managers of the pageant, but not, of course, the busy minds of the lensmen for whom she had toiled. They now found their routinely raunchy "smudges" (to borrow the lovely term the English paparazzi employ for their work) had been transformed by her title into that greatest of boons in the skin trade—celebrity skin.

When publication of the first set of photos was announced, Williams attempted a variation on the old Monroe ploy—frank innocence. Yes, she had done the deed, but it had been just a larky, girlish indiscretion. And anyway, the photographer had promised that she would be seen only in silhouette. She was outraged by his betrayal. It washed well for a time. People were tired of the pieties of the Miss America moguls, and many—including the New York *Times* editorial page—observed that there was not a lot of difference between posing nude and parading about in "swim suits" and high heels on national television, which contestants have been doing for decades in September in Atlantic City. It was a good point. It could be argued, in fact, that straightforward nudity was less kinky than the weird get-up insisted upon by the pageant. The appearance on the stands of the *Penthouse* carrying the now infamous pictures alas spoiled this scam. For Vanessa was observed to be miming the postures of lesbian sex with another model, and to have permitted close-ups of anatomy that approached the clinical and could not have been taken while maintaining the fiction of silhouette work. We were very far away from Marilyn on her red velvet. Light years away from it, shall we say.

Sympathy turned quickly away from her. The lie was too blatant, and it betrayed a lamentable understanding of the fitness of things. One can cross over from the discreet and artful nude to respectability —and back in the opposite direction, as well. Any intelligent (or intelligently managed) actress whom the bourgeois moviegoer or television watcher is led to believe is hot stuff—a Joan Collins, a Bo Derek, a Pia

Zadora—may go before the still camera and coyly reveal breast or bum, but the conventions of pose and drapery that have pertained in this line since the Renaissance are sternly observed. And the young woman who wishes to emulate their prosperous careers is well advised to observe similar discretion as she clambers up their heights in their direction. Excesses of nakedness, in the public's mind, betoken excesses of ambition (and, of course, possible brain damage). And all the propaganda of the Hefners, Gucciones, and Larry Flynts to the contrary notwithstanding, have not moved it from this position. It is a bitter irony that the most famous former centerfold is—Dorothy Stratton. She of the senseless murder and *Star 80,* subject now not of sexual fantasy but of moral example.

But yet one would take no bets against more Vanessa Williamses briefly claiming our startled attention. For there are depths of dumbness (and degradation) yet to be explored while we are on this subject. One thinks now of *Hustler*'s most curious and imitated innovation, the "Beaver Hunt," a section of the magazine that encourages husband or lover to haul out Polaroid and have his naked mate drape herself over bed or couch, then send the resulting snaps in for publication. Here one's curiosity turns completely from the sexual. Indeed, pity and sadness attends one's shamed and hasty perusal of these pages. At least, one assumes, a few dollars pass hands in the world of professional porn. And one understands how the lies of the photographers and promoters working that world may delude the silly and the stupid and the merely overeager. But these poor creatures, smiling foolishly into the moronically manipulated amateur camera, all nature's ineptitudes, all the years' misuses of their bodies pitilessly revealed in the hot, flat lights—what profit, psychic or otherwise, can they hope to realize?

This is not the nude as art—not even in parody. This is the nude as confession, as desperate assertion, as, perhaps, a special plea. We seem to be looking not at flesh, but at souls consenting to their own degradation. We here touch the country of Diane Arbus, for these fallen breasts and flaccid bellies direct our thoughts not to the erotic (unless we are sadists) but to the quotidian. One finds oneself fantasizing not about these sad asses, but about the florid floral couch on which they seem inevitably to be parked—how many time payments are still due on it, and what the beaver magazine's honorarium will contribute to the early retirement of the finance company's lien. One thinks, too, of the camera's careless employment. The professional stillsman is, at the very least, a skilled artisan. He brings to the sitting, perhaps, a certain professional respect for his co-worker, some training and discipline, some sense of his genre's conventions, even possibly some desire to aestheticize the experience. In contrast, embarrassed giggles seem to rise from these Polaroids. On the page the women are lined up in a row, vulnerable and defenseless. Poor butterflies! There they are, pinned down for cool and casual study—not of their beauty, but of styles in humiliation.

They are stripped even of the primitive defense that is customary in porn film or the more elaborate skin book picture acts, some simple story line or biographical sketch, which serves as a diversionary tactic, permitting both subject and viewer to maintain the fiction that the business at hand is not really the business in hand, as it were. These verbal fancies surrounding the pictorial ones help to keep our minds from straying to the occasion of the photo session—the technicians gawping at actress or model; the director shouting (or whispering) instructions at her, urging her to abandon more and more inhibition (and amour propre); the exertions of her partner(s); what she is thinking about as she works; all the mysterious goings-on of this line of endeavor.

When we contemplate the beaver page in the skin book our attention shifts decisively from fantasy to occasion. There is nothing to distract us here. The professional model, or even the amateur working for *Playboy,* works on a neutral set or location, conventionally understood not to be her home, not to reveal anything further about her. Beavers are stalked and shot in their lairs. This is her shower, her bed, her patio—whatever. And these environmental glimpses lead us on to even greater intimacy of speculation. We begin to wonder about the relationship between her and the photographer. Did she propose this adventure or was she talked into it? Is the picture emblematic of their free and easy sexual relationship or does it bespeak a desperate effort to rescue it from boredom or worse? Were joints or booze employed to ease the sitting? What happened after the roll of film was exposed? Did second thoughts occur? Were there arguments about mailing them off to the magazine? Are they still together now? Or is this publication an act of vengeance? And so on.

Here, at the meanest level of porn, we are arrived at its contemporary essence. If it is not confessional, it is pseudoconfessional. Once the nude model ceased to be anonymous, once her name was attached to her pictures (and these were surrounded by the "factoids"—Mailer's neologism—contained in the accompanying text blocks), once she ceased to be an abstraction, that arrangement of light and shade the classic nude was thought to be, then we lose the protective mantle of convention, that invisible shield that separates nudity from nakedness. Instead of participating in a process that more or less by common presumption is accorded the legal and social defenses of art, or at least the striving toward it, the new model instead finds herself acting as a symbolic representation of one of the age's great animating impulses, which holds implicitly that straightforward self-display—honesty—is entitled to a reward, too. That reward, of course, is notoriety, which (as in the case of Monroe and her calendar pose) can turn into celebrity. And it is so easily claimed. One can will oneself to truth telling; one cannot will oneself to giftedness (as Monroe's career after the calendar proved).

In the spring of 1982, a reporter from *Los Angeles* magazine was permitted to attend a meeting where Hugh Hefner and some of his associates were going over pictures of the candidates for an upcoming "Playmate of the Month" pictorial. One of the aides, plumping for the candidate that most appealed to him, summed up her virtues with breath-taking succinctness, "Great nipples, sincere bush and she looks uncomfortable." Here, obviously, was a man for Hef to treasure; here in his employ was the perfect *Playboy* gawker. He had the adolescent's absurdly clinical eye for fine distinctions of physiology (the body as Talmud, to be debated into meaninglessness). More important, he understood that the great pussy picture must have about it an element of awkwardness, embarrassment, to impart to it girl-next-door authenticity. If a woman in this situation looks too comfortable she is assumed to be a professional something—hooker or stripper, a crass veteran of wanton display—and her ease drains eroticism from the photos. No, what the model must hint at is what, blatantly, the beaver shots loudly proclaim—shame brazened out, and the avid-eyed strangers knowing, or thinking they can perceive (for, after all, it could be just an act), her secret.

This element was added, ex post facto as it were, to Monroe's first nude—sleek, distant, anonymous, and traditionally "arty" in pose. But there was a final set of nudes, made just weeks before her death, a few of which are contained in Mailer's *Marilyn,* a larger number of which are to be found in *Final Sitting,* which appeared at the twentieth anniversary of her death. These are by Bert Stern, they are technically proficient to the point of artfulness, and Monroe, as always, conspired erotically with the lens and the photographer. She curves her body flirtatiously; she manipulates her props coquettishly, her smile is a glistening invitation, her laugh looks as if it would sound full and throaty and satisfied. But there is something cruel in many of the pictures. The silver eye makeup in some of the shots appears to have been applied too heavily, almost as matrons err toward paintpot excess in their desperate struggle with age. In other shots the lines around the eyes are deep and unmediated by the tricks of lighting a photographer of Stern's skill knows how to use almost without thinking. You could, if you wished, count the many small imperfections on the flesh of her arms and back. An abdominal scar is entirely unhidden. And her most famous feature, her breasts, are photographed naturalistically, with no effort made to compensate for the droop the years have imposed. You can, kindly, read the entire take as a sort of liberation from the fantasy of perfection. Or you can see it as a confession that is also an accusation. Look what you, your demands, have done to me! Look what I've done to myself living my life for you! Here, at last, is the intimacy the strangers always wanted. Here, at last the goddess does not tease, is not merely nude, is frankly naked, and displaying the first, and for her devastating, hints of mortality. She could do no more than this. She could do no less than this. And with these images she completed the arc of her public life; it seems no accident that she ended it entirely just weeks later. For her final statement she had chosen the perfect medium—her one true medium—and in her way said what she had to say, by way of conclusion—in a time and place of her choosing, without fuss or squabble, misery or fear. There is a poignancy in this final statement of her vulnerability that she did not achieve on the screen or in her publicity, a resonance that echoes down the years.

Monroe's death or rather the way it has been dealt with, predicted other deaths. In the apocryphal story, the first Hollywood type proclaims the news, "Elvis Presley is dead," and the second responds, "Good career move." Yes, but as Monroe proved, only if it is premature and only if it is surrounded by ambiguity that supports continuing tragic or at least cautionary speculation. "Marilyn Monroe is all conspiracy theory now." So is Presley, of course. And Judy Garland. And the trashed rock singers, Joplin, Morrison, and Hendrix. And all the other prematurely dead pop artists—Bill Haley, Buddy Holly, Sam Cooke, Otis Redding, Jim Croce, Cass Elliot. And the murdered

John Lennon. They are our permanent icons of confused values—their own and society's. They are kept alive in memory by the messy untimeliness of their departures. This is not unprecedented. Maybe Byron was the first great figure of permanent posthumous romancing. In our time Fitzgerald and Dylan Thomas join Hemingway as analogous literary figures. And maybe, in the show biz end of things, Valentino's early and sudden death offers precedent, though the riotous hysteria surrounding his funeral seems to have offered instant discharge to simple emotions, and to have shifted subsequent speculation from the man himself to the nature of fandom in a mass society. Certainly Bogart's gallant passing in 1957 and his instant elevation to cult status in the sixties deserves note. At any rate, new candidates for secular canonization as martyrs to the fast track appear each year. Freddie Prinz appears not to have made it; the committee is still out on John Belushi; silence surrounds Natalie Wood. "And so it goes."

The crucial issue appears to be this: Can the fictions that their public lives were support new fictions after they are gone? That is to say, after the first simple and largely journalistic reprocessing of their lives—the lengthy obituaries, the retrospective picture displays in the magazines and on television, the critical appreciations, and the hasty moral and philosophical ruminations—is there another, mythic and transcendent plane that can be ascended? Here we arrive at televised docudramas, thinly disguised novels and films (both theatrical and television), the Mailerian "novel-biography," all the weird trappings of our modern funerary art.

They are the instruments by which, after death, we are finally allowed to take full possession of these lives. At the commercial level these images may now be manipulated in any manner the masters of the media choose, without regard to inconvenient facts, inconvenient temperament or, for that matter, inconvenient agents. The libel laws no longer apply, nor those designed to protect privacy. All stars, in death, turn into Mickey Mouse, that most agreeable of the great ones, who passively allowed himself to be drawn and redrawn until his creators had him just where they wanted him to be. But, of course, a larger possession occurs for the deceased star. It is a public possession, in which his or her image is completely internalized by the fans. In death, *we* have them exactly where *we* want them. Those elements in the biography that discomfited fantasy in life now wither and eventually disappear, while the fantasies that we wished to impose upon them can now be freely grafted on their unresisting ghosts with no inconvenient facts to interrupt our reveries. Nor can fresh events trouble our contemplation of the beloved objects. Drug busts, sexual anomalies, unpleasant rumors about their off-screen personalities— none of these can interrupt our dreamy relationship with the objects of our affections. Death is a kind of airbrush, whisking away the imperfections of reality, glossing over and imparting a satisfying glow to its subject. The analogy between its work and that of the retouchers bending over the Playboy bunnies need not be stressed.

And, as death becomes yet another media event, it loses its sting. Artists in particular have always been motivated to greater or lesser degree by the desire to leave something behind, something that will outlive them. What no one realized about movie stardom when the institution was created was that the stars were in a unique position; they could, they inevitably would, leave their selves, their living selves, behind them. When you interview people who worked in the early movies, you always hear some variation on this thought: "If I'd known they were going to last this long, I'd have tried to make them better." It was, depending on your point of view, either an unanticipated blessing or a curse. But the joke is not quite a joke; death *can* be a career move, for the careers now have a theoretically infinite life, thanks to television and video cassettes, thanks to revival houses and film festivals and the academicizing of film.

This is true of the most modest movie star. The possibility of a second chance at greatness is always there. Who would have guessed, for instance, that a quite obscure silent picture actress, no more than a cult figure during her ascendancy, and a player who made her last movie, a B Western, in 1938, would emerge in the late seventies and eighties as a cultural heroine, playing her variation on the victim theme, while a finer actress, and a much greater star in their day, Mary Pickford, would become a kind of joke, perhaps because she had been a lifelong winner? Yet that is what happened to Louise Brooks. For that matter, who would have thought, at the time, that John Wayne, the costar of her last little Republic picture, *Overland Stage Riders,* would turn into a legend, while the great Westerner of that day, the far more graceful, and perhaps more naturally accomplished, Gary Cooper, managing his life and death more quietly, would have faded as he now has? It seems you can go on seeking transcendence not only to the end of your days, but beyond. You must merely pay attention to the way you play your final card, the trump of death. One cannot help but think that, there being no end to media lives, death itself loses some of its power for some of the watchers in the shadows. Drawing a bead on a famous person they may conceive themselves not as the agents of death, but as the agents who arrange the star's biggest deal yet, the multi-pic pact with immortality.

I have used two symbolic figures of the 1950s symbolically in this chapter. I do not wish to imply that they were alone. They had their peers. I have mentioned, in passing, the figures of pop music and the posthumous power of Bogart. Surely Sinatra should be mentioned, rescuing his faded career as a teen favorite by winning an acting Oscar for *From Here to Eternity* in 1953, moving on, then, to multimedia stardom, many famous affairs (including, it appears, a brief encounter with Monroe), many controversial contretemps, alleged shady connections (the mob) and demonstrable sunny ones (the Kennedys and, latterly, the Reagans)—all the stuff of transcendence. One might, as well, mention Grace Kelly and the masterstroke of her royal marriage, her soap opera children, *her* premature death. And, of course, there is Elizabeth Taylor, up from innocent child stardom, now embarked on her multiplicity of marriages, touched equally by tragedy (the death of Mike Todd) and farce (Eddie Fisher, cuckolded by Richard Burton in the course of making the ill-starred *Cleopatra*). She, herself, had a heart-stopping, heart-winning brush with death, and her recovery was rewarded with her 1960 Academy Award. She was, in those days, our lovably wayward daughter, and her endlessly stormy, jewel-strewn marriages to Burton kept the drama alive, literally for decades. People didn't go to see her pictures, but they paid attention to her. It was, by and large, the same way with Sophia Loren. Her films were not wildly popular, but there was the enigma of her beauty-and-the-beast marriage, and her long struggle to bless it with a child to occupy our speculations. For a long time she was, by common consent, the great icon of the women's magazines, a surefire circulation builder when she appeared on the cover. Thinking of enigma, one thinks of deeper mysteries, the perverse celebrity accorded those who shun all display—Garbo, for instance, and J. D. Salinger. It became clear in this period that this, too, could be a strategy for holding the world in thrall. Some remarks of Roland Barthes on Garbo seem particularly apposite, for alone of the great beauties she made a drama out of refusing to participate in the archetypal drama of the female star, the fight against fading. He writes: "How many actresses have consented to let the crowd see the ominous maturing of their beauty. Not she, however; the essence was not to be degraded, her face was not to have any reality except that of its perfection . . . The Essence became gradually obscured, progressively veiled with dark glasses, broad hats and exiles; but it never deteriorated." In the celebrity family, she became the eccentric aunt in the attic, but by her absences she became, paradoxically, a compelling presence, a force in fantasy that she never could have been had she attempted to exert herself in the real world. Many and curious are the means by which power is gathered and held by those who transcend, who escape the confines of the Bijou's casually consulted screen, who find a way of casting themselves in the only movie that counts, the one that runs in everyone's head all the time.

They are obviously not numerous, these creatures of self-created legend, but they are not few either. And, like a special television broadcast that preempts the regular schedule, they now, in a sense, preempt ordinary life, make it seem less interesting, less valuable than it is or ought to be for the groundlings. It is that particular sense of things, the result of a new technology's interaction with new levels of education and prosperity, that began to be hinted at in the fifties.

But that is also a pattern I have retrospectively imposed on that decade and on the first few years of the sixties, which were, socially and politically, an extension of the previous ten years. I want to make it clear that neither I nor anyone I knew or read in those days, perceived any of this at the time. Afflicted by what Michael Arlen once called the "bookish, culture-conscious, giggly-Brahmin" state of mind, we came to mass culture eager to deplore it, unwilling to admit its formative fascination for us, and distinctly unwilling to make the effort to reinterpret it or to understand it, except in the inappropriate terms of traditional critical and psychological practice.

In the one comparatively simple realm that is our subject here, the workings of the celebrity system, we were witnessing in the fifties the birth of what we now think of as "superstardom," but the term did not even come into common circulation until the late sixties (and then, as we shall see, in suspicious circumstances) and we did not see that a quantum change in the institution as it was most narrowly and obviously defined, that is, as the most visible aspect of show business, was taking place before our very eyes, that it was now possible for stars to escape the categories of their origins, to take on both a wider public life and to make a more profound emotional impact on the individual's inner life than had ever been possible. Certainly we could not have predicted that, within a decade, the machinery and trappings of this new thing, superstardom, would be available in many new and surprising realms, altering our consciousness of almost every aspect of human endeavor. The next territory it would conquer would be politics, and it would begin its incursions there as the decade turned, in 1960.

FIVE

The Politics of Illusion

"The 1952 political conventions were the last to which a man could come with any real cause to doubt the outcome or to hope for excitement. The delegates to a modern convention have become mere members of a studio audience. The campaigns are like that, too, great leaps by plane for brief stops to serve a studio audience. By all accounts, the 1960 election was decided in the empty television studios . . ."

The words are Murray Kempton's. Their occasion was the brief introduction to a section of his superbly observed convention and campaign pieces in a collection of columns *America Comes of Middle Age,* which was published in 1963. Several of those pieces have to do with the stage-managing of what the television audience was supposed to perceive as spontaneous political events. But Kempton saw, far more clearly than most at that time, that this new instrumentality had a potential for the mischievous manipulation of public opinion greater than any previously devised and clearly, often wittily, pointed that out. Still, wise as Kempton was (and is), even he could not see how the collusion (collisions occur only when someone breaks an unspoken agreement) between the political process and the quickly developing processes of the new medium would alter not only the landscape of politics, but the landscape of our minds.

For example, he wrote in the same short piece that he had favored Stevenson over Eisenhower in 1952, not because he thought the latter would damage the nation, "but because he had no sense of style or tone" (and also "no sense of sin," about which there can be little dispute). But as late as 1963 even Kempton could not quite see that politics was becoming almost entirely a matter of style and tone (as transmitted by television). And now we have all lived to see that among the factors contributing to the upwardly revised estimates of Eisenhower's presidency is a nostalgia among latter day, up-market political writers precisely for the apparent artlessness of the general's self-presentation, that bluff refusal not to seem other than he was, and let the media experts fall where they may.

In the early sixties, Kempton, like all of us who are of a liberal turn of mind, set aside his lingering affection for Adlai Stevenson and permitted himself to be beguiled by John F. Kennedy. On the face of it, this was a simple matter. After the bumbly good nature of Eisenhower and the personal nullity of the people around him, we were all hungry for a touch of wit and glamour, a bit of dash and style. And, yes, romance. On the campaign trail in 1960 Kempton saw how Kennedy's skills as a womanizer (a subject of entrancing rumor then, of documented fact now) could seduce female voters en masse. One of his leads was: "John F. Kennedy treated Southern Ohio yesterday as Don Giovanni used to treat Seville."

But there was more to this matter than simple sexiness, personal qualities. What we are dealing with here is a recognition on the part of the candidate and his managers that traditional debts and alliances within the party and among various outside interest groups were, in the age of television, of less significance in winning elections, and in governance itself, than the creation of an image that gave the illusion of masculine dynamism without sacrifice of ungoing affection. Which is, one hardly need add, exactly what a successful male movie star recognizes his job to be.

This recognition, in turn, was based on a sense, a divination really, that certain subcurrents had been eroding, for longer than anyone realized, the traditional underpinnings of our politics. This was more than a recognition that the old pressure group arrangements were breaking down. It contained an acknowledgment as well that party allegiances based on principle and ideology were also coming unglued —a lesson very broadly hinted at by Eisenhower's two electoral victories of the fifties.

Kennedy is, then, a pivotal figure in the history of our practical politics. In manifesting what had been largely hidden before his appearance, he also summarized a group of unspoken trends. By taking advantage of them, he determined the course of politics to come, by turning them definitively into a branch of that greatest of postindustrial America's industries, public relations. From his time onward, the game has been played his way, with all of our major political figures (and everyone who hopes to become one) working their personal variants—often grotesquely—on his basic methodology. But we must not get ahead of ourselves. Let us see what predicted the predictor.

🌿 🌿

An odd time to bring up politics. The fifties! Everyone knows about the fifties. Eisenhower asleep in the White House, the students adoze on the campuses, the reformist thrust of the New Deal, the one-world idealism of the war, waning memories as a kind of middle-aged spread afflicted American politics, its soft center flowing out in all directions, so that perhaps 90 percent of the population embraced its principles—modest welfarism at home and less modest anticommunism both at home and abroad. The center of debate was whether as the lunatic right, led by the careerist-adventurist, McCarthy, charged, there was a domestic threat from the "Comsymps" or whether that was all a wicked fantasy. About the threat from external communism there was no doubt at all; everyone supported the defense budget, and there had been a war in Korea to prove its necessity.

Actually, of course, there was a large indifference to all these matters much of the time. This, after all, was the age of the Lonely Crowd, the Organization Man, the Man in the Gray Flannel Suit, an age when our private concerns—the little house containing the little woman and the little kids which men left each day to pursue their little careers—were far more involving in their paltry ways than public affairs were in theirs. Even the arts, both high and popular, were for the most part in an as unadventurous and unenergetic phase as they had ever been in this country in this century.

My generation, graduating first from high school then from college in this period, was widely regarded as a symbol of the sad malaise afflicting the body politic. "The silent generation," was the epithet that stuck, but there were others: "a generation of jellyfish," "the vacuum-tube generation," for example. All implied that in comparison to the culturally rebellious youth of the twenties, the politically rebellious youth of the thirties, the heroic adventurers of the forties, we were an apathetic, inarticulate, and self-absorbed lot. At the time I felt that, like most journalistic summations, this one lacked a certain subtlety. In 1955, the year I was graduated from college, I wrote an essay for a small liberal monthly that I called, "The Island of the Present." In it I argued that the immediate, or New Deal, past no longer seemed particularly usable to us, while the future was so murky that it was impossible, not to say foolish, to make any bold plans for dealing with it, lest they turn out to be disastrous miscalculations.

I was speaking, in the main, politically. What I was trying to say was that all the liberals were offering at the time was a Rooseveltian program with a coat of paint splashed on it and some flower boxes in the windows, while the conservatives had nothing but a disused mansion for sale in a run-down neighborhood—"a handyman's special" as an eighties' real estate ad might describe it, a "fixer-upper." Neither, it seemed to me, was relevant to a new time, or worth working up a passionate desire to invest further energy in. Rather than running off toward either, it seemed to me, and to most of my contemporaries, only common sense to set one's own place in order and await developments. Hence, I argued, we had taken refuge on the island of the present, confining our concerns to the short-term and the concrete, to ourselves and our immediate circle. When, a little later, Daniel Bell proclaimed "the end of ideology," I did not disagree, and subsequent political events did not contradict him. Surely Kempton's complaint about the tame predictability of our political conventions (in which centrists, and even moderate ideologues who could be made to look like centrists for the national audience, were typically coronated rather than chosen by the delegates) can be traced in part to the demise of ideology; there would be no more Tafts fighting to the bitter end for principles. Even when the politics of protest disrupted this even tenor in the 1960s, ideology was only an afterthought, a set of nonsense incantations designed to rationalize a mass adolescent hysteria that was implicitly encouraged by television, which knows a good set of images when it sees one.

But I am being less than forthcoming. The fact is that a corner of my heart cheered when the death of ideology was proclaimed. For I now believe that the reason my generation was so withdrawn, so seemingly apathetic, was that we sensed what has now become apparent but did not yet have the tools to discuss or to come to terms with, namely, that all modern politics is an illusion, a show. We knew, without knowing we knew, that torture the language and gestures of traditional politics however anyone might, they could not be made to address the issues that most profoundly moved not only us, but everyone. That is why they have become the stuff of show biz—and show

biz at its least elevated, and least emotionally involving level, a qua-
drennial Golden Globe show.

Writing in 1969, when a new generation of students had proved
themselves to be as strident as we were quiet, one of my most brilliant
contemporaries Renata Adler made the first, and still the most intelligent, attempt to summarize our generational sensibility. In the fifties,
she wrote, "a center of action seemed to have broken down for us." By
that she meant that the kind of political ideologies (and the social and
cultural ones, too) that had motivated previous generations simply did
not exist for us in sufficient strength or appeal so that we might find "a
generational voice." As a result, "we knew what there was of our
alienation privately and not yet as a claim or a group experience." Our
ties, she wrote, were, and remain, vertical—to people of different ages,
to the ideas and idioms of different ages, too. This lack of a common
rhetoric to which we might lay proprietary claim turned out to be an
advantage. It liberates us to be quizzical and skeptical, to be eclectic
and unbeholden. Above all, as Adler says, in culture and politics "we
are the last custodians of language—because of the books we read and
because history, in our time, has wrung so many changes on the meaning of terms . . . we, having never generationally perpetrated anything, have no commitment to any distortion of them. Lacking slogans, we still have the private ear for distinctions, for words."

It is, needless to say, precisely from this platform that is not a
platform at all, that I am writing (and wish I could say that I have
always written). But that is not the reason that I have invoked Adler.
Young people never actually know much of anything that they, or
anyone, can coherently set forth. But their instincts function rather
well. They are, perhaps, the antennae—the perpetually renewing antennae—of a society as it crawls along, beneath the indifferent stars, to
its inevitable doom. What we sensed, and transmitted to the society
three decades ago, was unease—an unease with received opinion, received political and social practices. This activity was, I think, every
bit as profound as the next generation's—more profound, because we
did not take to the streets to make a fake revolution and achieve with
it a fraudulent generational celebrity.

But, of course, we were very lucky. Not just in our leisurely prosperity, though that was certainly good. No, the source of our luck lay
in just this: we were the last generation to make it all the way to
adolescence unaccompanied by the day-long drone and whine of the
television set. If our politics, in the fifties, was a politics of quizzical

quietism, I do not think most of us expected to stay that way. As I said, we on the left were holding the line for common decency (supporting Stevenson, opposing McCarthy, and tolerating Eisenhower) while we waited signs of something better, more positive, more relevant to our understanding of what was really wrong with the world, to take shape and then command our rational hearts.

What we did not see until it was too late was that television, this amusing novelty in the living room, was going to begin to literally dictate events. In effect, it was going to flow into the vacuum that had developed in our political life at the end of World War II, a vacuum that had been created not only by the decline of ideological debate, but by the steadily increasing impotence and stasis of lumbering government to act decisively and imaginatively on the issues that most affected us. The play of personality was substituted for the play of ideas and for the play of authentic as opposed to staged events. Imagery would subsume everything in the political realm, and what had seemed but a pause in the march of events, a regrouping of a kind that was hardly unknown in political history, turned out instead to be the beginning of a revolution—a revolution in sensibilities that was the more profound for having been based on unacknowledged forces and for continuing in an unacknowledged way. Sometime in the 1950s a neutron bomb of the mind was set off, leaving the structures of our politics intact but killing most of the life that had gone on within them. The survivors are mutants, mutants who are still not aware that they have been struck by a new and terrible force.

To understand how we arrived at this condition, it is necessary to pause for a bracing draft of theory. One of the most important and— in this country, if not everywhere—one of the most neglected volumes of contemporary social commentary is Jacques Ellul's *The Political Illusion.* Had it existed in the 1950s, the puzzled and puzzling behavior of the young electorate would not have been so enigmatic; if it had been heeded in the years since, much that is troubling about our political life would at least be explicable.

In *The Political Illusion,* Ellul, who is a professor of law and social history in France, argues that in our time all problems, even including those of individual morality and taste, family arrangements and personal psychology, have become, in the largest sense, politicized. "It is not just a question of accepted political procedures being applied to questions that at first glance do not seem political. The point is that these questions *are* by now in the political realm, and political procedures are applied to them"—willy-nilly, as it were, whether or not such procedures are appropriate or useful.

As a result, we have evolved a political system the surface of which consists very largely of impotent rhetorical posturing by political personalities mostly concerned with fostering agreeable images of themselves while, beneath the surface, the real work of government—often quite at odds with what its public figures are saying—proceeds under the guidance of a faceless and generally unaccountable bureaucracy.

All of this, Ellul observes, is a relatively recent historical development, the unintended creation of a political system—liberal democracy—that was spawned by rationalism, the Enlightenment. Prior to the eighteenth century, the prevalence of autocracy in one form or another as the principal mode of government had the obvious effect of keeping the masses at a distance, uninterested in politics. Neither a nostalgist nor, in the full sense of the word, an elitist, Ellul refuses to paint the predemocratic era as a golden age. But he does point out that the rise of mass communications followed very closely on the rise of popular democracy, with the result that the means for fulfilling one of the chief ideals of the latter, the "well-informed" citizen, was provided by the former.

With a vengeance. For as Ellul says, a simple classical view of modern man would see him as a "self-contained individual who merely has been placed before an array of news and information and, in some fashion, absorbs his dosage of information, swallows it, digesting and utilizing this mixed food for his greater benefit," becoming thereafter "somehow more intelligent, better informed, and more able to be a good citizen." But that, as common sense and common observation tell us, is distinctly not the case. In the first place, news comes at us daily, hourly, from everywhere, the relevant and the irrelevant vulgarly, unselectively mixed in a communications "environment" over which the individual, himself a "changing, susceptible being," has at best only partial control. The result of all this "input" on the individual is "not to make him more capable of being a citizen but to disperse his attention . . . and present to him an excessive amount of information too diverse to serve him in any way whatever . . ."

The day's news has another characteristic. It tends to evaporate with the rising of a new day's sun. That is to say, yesterday's current events will always be replaced in consciousness—blotted out really—

by today's—and so on. "In order not to drown in this incessant flow man is forced to forget." And so attention is, almost self-defensively, dispersed and rendered discontinuous. And no one can entirely avoid the consequences of this immersion in the ephemeral. As Ellul observes, we derive much of the vital sense that we are participants in a community by taking this daily bath. The media, more and more, *are* our community. No other in which we take part imparts the same feeling that we are connected with large, significant, exciting events, that we are on intimate terms with people who do big things, are in themselves amusing, entertaining, glamorous. Surely the recent legitimization of gossip by respectable journalism is a function of this new sense of where our true community lies. For, as Ellul says, prestige accrues to the knowing, even if one's knowingness derives, somewhat pathetically, from being the first lady on the block to get hold of the latest issue of *People*. Given our present day scheme of values it is inescapably exciting "to be privy to a secret that one can transmit to others, to wait for their reaction, their surprise, and by one's superior knowledge undermine the standing of those who are not 'in the know.' "

But that is, for the moment, a digression. What is essential to bear in mind is that the rush of news, and the rush of our lives, effectively prevents us from behaving as reflective political creatures. This accounts for the weird anomalies that are always turning up in political polls, which, for example, may report a majority of respondents disapproving most of the specific policies of a national leader yet generally approving his conduct of office. Nowadays we hurry past (or are hurried past) our contradictions. Unable to fully grasp the news as it flashes past, how can we possibly pause to reflect upon it? And if someone does make the effort to connect the fast flowing surface of events with the slower moving historical currents beneath them, the chances are he will not be heeded except in the most elite and unworldly circles. He will seem not "with it." What the sage is trying to say cannot be summarized in headline or lead or in forty seconds on the evening news. Him, too, we are compelled to hurry past, as "Current news pre-empts the sense of continuity, prevents the use of memory, and leads to a constant falsification of past events when they are evoked again in the stream of the news."

But it is not merely the conversion of history into instant nostalgia, memory rendered useless by trivialization, that threatens us. The business of being "steeped in the news" (one of Ellul's favorite phrases) also devastates foresight. At best current events offer us only false continuities and foster the politician's incessant reliance on the public opinion poll, which although it has become the chief policy-shaping tool of our times, is useless as a predictive device. This weekly testing of an opinion that is formed and reformed by the most transitory of occurrences has the effect of tying the politician's fortunes, therefore his choices of action, ever more tightly to the news. His energies must always be directed toward statements and policies that are essentially reactive in nature. They are mostly responses to immediate events and have as their aim some immediate effect—influencing tonight's news broadcast, tomorrow's front page, next week's straw poll: New York's mayor, Ed Koch, speaks for all of them when he cries to his fans, "How'm I doin'?"

In these circumstances it becomes equally impossible to (a) pursue a policy that will not bear fruit for months or years, or (b) adopt a policy of watchful waiting, in which events are permitted to run their course until a rationally planned and timed intervention might prove effective.

The attempt to tune—and keep in tune—the economy is perhaps the paradigmatic example of the political illusion at work. When it is ticking over in a generally pleasing fashion, that is, in a mildly inflationary mode, no consensus can be developed to address those long-term issues that pose a possibly mortal threat to its health—the astronomical federal deficit and the equally astonishing foreign debt being currently the most obvious of these. Neither is an issue that can be dealt with adequately in the usual American manner—by adjusting the demands of competing interest groups through political compromise. Neither can be adequately managed by the bureaucracy doing business as usual. And neither can be adequately discussed in a sixty-second television spot—or even in an hour's special—so no consensus for policy can be popularly developed. As a result, although short-term responses to temporary problems are made (i.e., adjustments in credit rates and money supply) nothing is done about the underlying issues, for these can be addressed only through patiently worked out policy decisions, requiring months, perhaps years, before they yield results. The electorate is unused to such approaches—and is, indeed, bored by them. Action—or the illusion of action—is what it wants from a leader. A stir. A flurry. Ideally an air of pressure and crisis around the White House, the limousines coming and going in the night. That is what we have come to expect. Indeed, our current President came to office largely because his predecessor responded to a different sort of crisis—that of the Iranian hostages—with a measured care, a sense of the practical limits of his—the nation's—power, that looked like—and may have been—weak-minded dithering.

The result? Russell Baker put it well: "It got people's goat. Sitting tight wasn't what Presidents got paid for. Presidents got paid for doing something." Or, as the great theorist puts it, the citizen "only knows what happened yesterday, excites himself only over the latest events, and demands that the politician should take a position on it. All the rest matters little to him. And the politician knows well, in turn, that he will have to respond accordingly. He is therefore led to keep himself tuned continuously to this level of current events."

Democratic electoral politics is, by all of this, reduced to a kind of sport. Its interest resides almost entirely in the question of who wins, who loses. To be sure, a few small consequences may derive from an election. Depending on who won, the defense budget may go up or down a miniscule five or ten billion dollars, there may be some small variance in the income tax or the social security impost. And there may be some small change in how the money is spent—a little more or a little less for the poor or for the highways or whatever. And colorful quarrels will arise in legislative halls among passionate supporters and detractors of measures that affect matters of personal morality—between pro-abortionists and right-to-lifers, for example, between anti-pornography groups and those who favor free speech at any cost, between those for the ERA and those against it, to name three of the more prominent recent battles over issues that are largely symbolic—and probably would never have reached our legislative halls were they not so gaudily telegenic.

But, one notices, the American government has galumphed along a predictable policy path for at least thirty-five years, probably for a half century since the first wave of New Deal legislation took effect. For all the alarums and excursions one has lived through, nothing has much changed as the result of official political activity. The domestic policy consensus that has obtained for the length of my entire life has not varied in its essence at all. The foreign policy consensus that has obtained all my adult life has also changed only in its details. The really great changes that have taken place, especially in the latter time span, changes in the ways we think about the races and the sexes, for example, changes in the ways we live our domestic lives, our working lives and our leisure lives, have all resulted from changing technologies and from new, spontaneously arising moral agreements. Television we have talked about, and will continue to talk about. By capturing its attention, blacks, women, homosexuals have forced the beginnings of a redefinition of their place in society. But other technologies—the jet plane, the computer, the photocopier, to take just the readiest examples—have also done more to change the quality of our lives as individuals than anything the government has accomplished in the last three decades. Indeed, its role now is to run rather clumsily and inefficiently after both the moral and technological changes, attempting not so much to control them—though that is what organizations like the Moral Majority would like it to do—as to attempt to rationally codify their effects in law.

Ironically, as political creatures we do not seem to notice the laggardly nature of institutional politics. We keep insisting that "they"— our elected representatives—do something about this or that issue that interests us without observing that something has already been done— outside of political channels but, as it were, inside the TV channels. Herein lies the first significant practical effect of the political illusion, namely, that what we do or do not do at the polling place has but small effect on the workings of our government. This oversight is obviously further encouraged by the immediacy with which television now places us in touch with our leaders, even with some of the more public processes of government. But, as Ellul says, "All of this is just a spectacle, appearance without root, a game . . . all the more so as the flickering little screen fixes the individual's attention on the spectacle, and prevents him from searching deeper, and asking himself questions on the true nature of power."

The true nature of power? What is the man talking about? We understand unquestioningly that the President of the United States is the most powerful man on earth, that senators and congressmen who have been blessed with seniority (and news-magazine cover stories), governors and mayors who have been anointed at the polls, have a sizeable ability to command our destinies. Yes, so we have been told. Mostly because it is convenient for journalists to tell us so, and convenient for the men and women who posture before them as persons of significance to foster the illusion. The ego rewards for the latter are obvious; the professional rewards for the former only a little less so. For, to put the matter simply, it greatly facilitates the task of the journalist in search of a "handle" or "peg" for a complex story if he can find a single politician whose grapplings with an issue symbolize its difficulties and humanize the problems it presents.

But, of course, true governmental power does not rest with these figures. It resides elsewhere, with the much despised bureaucracy, that portion of the government that is now so famously "on the back" of the people and about which, in the 1980 election, there were so many promises to dislodge from that inconvenient location. These promises are as Ellul described them, mere "litanies," "on the order of magic incantations, and absolutely no genuine modification of bureaucratic autonomy can ensue from them." Why? Because "the bureaucracy really *is* omnipotent. Omnipotence lies in behemothic size and functional complexity . . ." The fault for this more than likely lies with ourselves, or anyway with the citizenry of past generations, since it persistently indicated a desire for state intervention in almost every aspect of life and "A state that wants to do everything and change everything can do so only with help of an enormous bureaucracy." And "it is precisely here that the political illusion resides—to believe that the citizen, through political channels, can master or change this state."

Yet, that is what the citizen expects his elected representatives to do, although in practice they cannot. They are both overworked and underinformed, and lacking the time and the knowledge (both of which bureaucracies always have plenty of) they avoid basic confrontations with the seat of true governmental power and content themselves with obtaining from it a few favors for themselves and their constituents.

All of us—elected politicians, journalists, academics, ordinary citizens, the bureaucrats themselves, lurking behind their breastwork of paper and trying to maintain the faces of earnest and innocent servants—have a vested interest in maintaining the political illusion. To abandon it, and to embrace the chaos implicit in our political reality, is to ask too much. We cannot dismantle the system; we would not know where to begin or where we might end. Worse, we would be abandoning the comfort of something that can be diagrammed so neatly that an eighth grader, studying his civics text, can easily grasp. We need the memory of that chart to invoke against the Kafkaesque reality we reluctantly confront and leave as quickly as we can whenever we are forced to do business with government. We need it, as well, in order to maintain belief in what we read in the papers or see on TV, the belief that the news is, in fact, news, a record of events that have genuine consequences and a real relationship to our lives. Without that belief we would be cast adrift on a chartless existential sea, without means of taking our bearings.

But what has all this to do with celebrity? Everything, it seems to me. The rise at this historical moment of an instrumentality, television, which has as its inherent imperative a need for individuals who can be used to personify current affairs, may be an accident. But it is no accident that everyone has so happily and thoughtlessly fallen in with that demand, no accident that the rest of journalism, competing with this new power, makes itself over, coming more and more to resemble its dominant competitor. It is, as we have seen, something it wanted to do anyway, and started to do before the beginning of this century. An impetus was all that was required to complete the process. And TV was precisely that.

Ellul has little to say about the function of celebrity in sustaining the political illusion, doubtless because he lives and works in France, where, even today, well over a decade after he wrote, television is still not the dominant force it has become in the United States. But it is obvious that celebrities are an essential part of the "spectacle" of which he writes—that, in fact, they *are* the spectacle. Their lives and careers give such form to the news drama's formlessness as it may be said to have.

We are scarcely working Aristotelian territory here. But a drama it surely is. To begin with, it proceeds within highly conventionalized bounds. It is never admitted that an election campaign, or what poses as an ideological debate, is, in fact, a contest between personalities, but that is what it has become. The issues merely provide the occasions for testing the personal appeal of the contenders. It is immaterial what a candidate says in response to press interrogation or in a televised debate. Everything hinges on the tremble of the hand or voice, the glimmer of sweat on brow or upper lip, one's general air of ease or unease under performance pressure. Beyond these rituals we also hang suspensefully on the other turning points, crisis, of the politician's life. And one of the clear and present dangers of modern political life is the temptation a politician must feel either to invent a crisis if matters have proceeded eventless for too long, or to turn some modest contretemps into one. Of the six crises, for instance, that gave Richard Nixon the title for his first bestseller, not one involved mortal danger for himself or the country. And surely the ludicrousness of Jimmy Carter trying to convert a simple request to put out the lights, turn down the thermostat, and ease up on the gas pedal during the oil shortage into the moral equivalent of war cost him the regard of such sensible people as are left to muse on such matters. One suspects that some of the more dangerous-seeming crises of our time may have derived from a similar need to create drama on a more heroic and gripping scale than the ordinary run of events typically provide our leaders.

This is a matter to which we shall return. For the moment it is enough to note that though the ups and downs of a political career do not generally provide us with either genuine comic release or a purging sense of pity and terror, they do have the capacity to humanize abstract ideas and distant events, to involve us emotionally in them. Occasionally they even offer the mild catharsis we feel when some ambiguous ending to some murky political drama is finally sensed. In short, if there is any continuity left at all in our political life, any coherence, it does not derive from long-standing party principles to which, as was formerly the case, many citizens gave life-long allegiance and from which they derived (as they did from the city and state in which they lived, the church they attended) a significant portion of their individual identities. No, such coherence and continuity as we can find in politics derives from the lives of the people who gain their fame by following this branch of the performing arts. Far away from us, they are yet made to seem very near by the media. At the same time, political opponents unconsciously conspire to make themselves appear to be far apart on the issues when, in fact, they are very close together.

If there were hints that the political spectacle was being reshaped in these terms before him, and if during his two terms in office the new dimensions of the spectacle eluded even the most astute observers, still we must date the beginnings of our new politics from the presidency of Dwight David Eisenhower.

George W. S. Trow: "In the phrase 'I Like Ike,' the power shifted. It shifted from General Eisenhower to someone called Ike, who embodied certain aspects of General Eisenhower and certain aspects of affection for General Eisenhower. Then it shifted again. From 'Ike' you could see certain aspects of General Eisenhower. From 'like,' all you could see was other Americans engaged in a process resembling the processes of intimacy. This was a comfort."

Eisenhower, in Trow's terms, had gained his powerful repute by acting within history. That is, he had played a leading role in one of the unarguably significant events of that "record of growth, conflict and destruction" which is how Trow defines our formal history. He was thus acceptable, this transitional figure, to traditionalists, who liked their political leaders to have been blooded, but not bloodied, by great events. Conversely, despite the fact that he had a good deal of iron (and conventional ambition) in his character, he was an outwardly amiable and, it would seem, entirely decent man, who also had about him that air of worldly innocence that often marks men who have passed their entire careers in the military. It required some months, it may be remembered, to determine what he was, a Republican or a Democrat, and his grounds for deciding finally that he must be one of the former were so softly put that they are lost to memory. The point was that he saw himself, as many American soldiers had, not so much as a leader, but as a servitor—not of any ideology, but of his country, which was defined, so far as one can tell, mythically and perhaps even mystically. In short, he was easy prey to a high-minded pitch for a new and higher service by the hucksters of Eastern liberalish Republicanism, who spent four years and more working to gain a commitment from him. One imagines the calculating and manipulative nature of their enterprise passed beyond his ken, if not beneath his contempt, as would most of the machinations that surrounded him—surround anyone—during his White House years. One always imagined that the Vice President with whom he was so oddly yoked was something of a mystery to him, a representative of the otherness of electoral politics, not better but perhaps not worse than the other strange birds now perching on his epaulets.

These men who had persuaded Eisenhower to run, and who were to share the spoils of his triumph, were, for the most part, not professional political workers. They were, rather, establishment figures who gave time, money, and advice to the party. After twenty years of defeat they mostly wanted to see a return on a political investment that had not paid a dime in dividends since 1932, and did not much care how they finally found prosperity. Unpreoccupied by the awful dailiness of life down in trenches, they were free to perceive what the Republican troops—who wanted Taft as their candidate in 1952—could not see. Which was that he could not win.

This was not just a matter of his being too starchy, too glum, and unattractive compared to easy-grinning Ike, though that is what everybody said at the time. What they sensed, probably without being able to fully articulate it, was that the very process of history was being redefined. By 1952, as Trow said, traditional history's "booming" voice had become something of an embarrassment. People had begun to redefine it, so that it no longer had to do with "the powerful actions of certain men, but with the processes of choice and preference." History, that "record of growth, conflict and destruction," was now starting to become another kind of record, that of the "expression of demographically significant preferences: the lunge of demography *here* as opposed to *there.*"

What a perfect presidential candidate Eisenhower was for the moment of this great shift! Far from being a defect, his lack of powerful identification with one party or the other was a great asset, just as his Republican opponent's identification as "Mr. Republican" was (except among the poor, dumb party faithful) distinctly disadvantageous. For almost everyone's sense of party loyalty was beginning to weaken. Then, too, Eisenhower had no deep roots anywhere. He had, to be sure, grown up in the Far Midwest and the Near Far West, and the mild accents and not too stern style of those most difficult-to-define regions clung to him. But his adult life had been spent moving from army post to army post, which were at home touched by the exotic and, in more exotic climes, touched by the homely, but which were basically neither one nor the other. In a sense, he was quite literally, in 1952, the "News from Nowhere," a man who had lived all his life "within the context of no context."

That, of course, was the very place many Americans were now taking up residence. Levittown with its streets and houses indistinguishable from one another, with its constantly shifting population, is as close to army base living—and not just in looks either—as a civilian can come. It is no mystery that Eisenhower was "a comfort," to this newly rootless crowd. He might previously have served the "booming" voice of "history" as it was traditionally defined. But his personal qualities were those of the people now living outside that history, in demography. They liked Ike because, well, he was likable. And likability—shallow, thornless likability, which definitely includes the ability to avoid pointless arguments about matters that make a lot of people hot under the collar, matters like religion or politics—is a primary requisite for quickly and pleasantly establishing yourself wherever the Army or the company decides to transfer you. He came across, as the novelist Thomas Rogers once put it, as "a cheerful bustling, helpful soul who would have made a good male nurse."

These qualities, lacking hard edges, were very reassuring, and are, of course, extremely telegenic. The ongoing joke of his presidency, especially in liberal circles, was the way Eisenhower would bumble and fumble through his press conferences, entangling himself in his constantly unraveling syntax. But that was no defect in the eyes of most people, who rather imagined that they might not do any better (and possibly a good deal worse) in such circumstances. Besides, the point, which was always nonthreatening, and mostly nonurgent—generally soothing—somehow got across. The intervention of actor-director Robert Montgomery as television advisor to the President (scandalous to the opposition, since it smacked of Hollywood trumpery invading the sacred preserve of politics, which never never deals in fakery) seemed to make no discernible difference in the performance. And the reason for that was simple: it was not a performance at all, but a true reflection of the man.

Yes, people said, he's a dope. But they were wrong. What he was was a bureaucrat who had mastered the bureaucracy. Or anyway, *a* bureaucracy—the U.S. Army. And his much satirized public style was really that of the bureaucrat *in camera*. That is, he had learned to raise obfuscation to the level of artless art, to give an illusion if not of action, then of, perhaps, meaning to act, or at least agreeing that some action is definitely necessary. The point is to give the clientele the impression that whatever it is that they think they want to have happen may very well be going to happen, but not to commit yourself to anything that could be held against you later when things go wrong.

This makes Eisenhower sound cynical, but that is a disservice to him. I have come to believe that he was operating out of a higher vision. I think he actually had an instinctive understanding of almost everything Ellul would later codify. To begin with, he created his own mini-bureaucracy, organized along military staff lines (which is to say that it looked efficient on paper, but wasn't in reality) as a kind of countervailing force against the established bureaucracies of Washington. Its ostensible function, of course, was to free its leader for the really important decisions. Its real function, naturally, was the opposite—it was supposed to take the blame for inaction and misadventure. As for freeing the President from the nagging details of command, it did so, but only as a fringe benefit of its other main job which was to keep Eisenhower the symbol unsullied by failures of policy and failures in the execution of same. And in this sense it worked superbly. Indeed, all subsequent presidents have cause to envy Eisenhower, for he alone of the postwar chief executives was free of alarming downward swoops in the public opinion polls. He reigned without ruling, attempting little and accomplishing less. But in his person he pretty much suited everyone's idea of what a president should be—benign, agreeable, requiring very little of the individual citizen, yet somehow in charge of things, seeing to it that the government ticked along, providing undiminished that level of services that the New Deal's revised social compact had established as roughly what the government could offer without strain either to its skills or the citizen's checkbook.

Did Eisenhower sense that some sort of domestic equilibrium had been arrived at? Or was he simply too lazy, too old-fashioned, and too unimaginative to push on to new, and perhaps more creative, levels of government exertion? Hard to say, though surely there were domestic issues on which he might well have expended some of the treasure of esteem that had been heaped up around him; he might have employed that unprecedented symbolic power of his on just and moral causes. One, which was before us even as he ran for President, was McCarthyism; the other was desegregation. On both issues he was notably silent, and even though everyone was pretty sure that he was against McCarthy and for racial equality (how could so decent a chap be otherwise?), he refused to commit himself publicly and unequivocally. It is, of course, impossible to say what might have happened to bring us more quickly closer to a better society had he done so, though an argument can be made that nothing was lost and perhaps something was gained by his silence, which permitted broad consensuses against McCarthyism (a matter to which we shall return) and for desegregation to develop to what finally amounted to irresistible levels. In the case of the latter issue the passage of time also permitted a truly effective symbolic leader, Martin Luther King, to arise spontaneously, as it seemed, out of the ferment.

But on other domestic matters, Eisenhower's instinctive grasp of what Ellul would later describe served him well. Given the complexity of the issues confronting the large modern state, and given the intractability of the legislative and bureaucratic processes with which it confronts those issues, all a leader can do within official channels is a bit of tinkering here, a bit of cosmetic surgery there—creating an illusion of action. One instance indicates the point. Eisenhower did almost nothing directly about poverty, though in the course of paying his Republican debts all sorts of favors and advantages were accorded business. Somehow, over the span of his presidency (and continuing on over the Kennedy years, when nothing much was done in this realm either), the percentage of the U.S. population living below the poverty line declined from 32.7 percent to 19.5 percent, a trend that was reversed only in those years in which the gross national product declined. By contrast, after Lyndon Johnson declared his famous War on Poverty, annual federal expenditures on programs aimed directly at improving the lot of the poor reached as high as $21.8 billion—with a reduction in their numbers to about 12.8 percent of the population. And it is at that level that their numbers have stayed through the seventies and eighties although there has been no significant diminution in the programs designed to aid them. Given the cost-effectiveness of such activities, and given the amount of time and energy necessary to bring them into existence, there is something to be said, obviously, for going out and playing another round of golf.

Still, we know from Ellul that the illusion of activity and concern is essential to political success and here Eisenhower was particularly blessed. His predecessor had actually been forced to make a stern and real response to Communist aggression, and mobilized the nation for an undeclared and hard-to-explain war in Korea before the Cold War consensus had fully developed among the populace. This exertion had been difficult, painful, and costly to him and his party—as genuine political activity, requiring hard choices (in this case the choice to expend lives, not merely treasure and rhetoric) always are. But from Truman's commitment Eisenhower reaped many benefits. He was elected on the promise to end the stalemated truce talks, which he did. Thereafter, he had only to maintain a posture of militancy against the allegedly encircling menace of global communism. And this was comparatively easy. Public consensus had hardened on this point during the Korean War, and better still, Eisenhower saw that there was in the branches of government directly concerned with foreign affairs no bar to the appearance of decisive action. A president has in this realm broad powers to act which, as a rule, Congress can do little to halt. His instrumentality is, of course, the executive order, which most dramatically has provided the legal basis for the undeclared wars we have fought since World War II, not to mention the many less lengthy military adventures we have undertaken in those years. Executive orders are used with great abandon in foreign policy, but much more cautiously in domestic affairs, where outcries from interest groups can be expected when anyone attempts to do anything, and the executive fears to move without fully mobilized public and congressional support.

Until the Vietnam War reached nightmare status there was no questioning of the executive orders under which it or any military or foreign policy matter was prosecuted, and the congressional outcry over Vietnam arose only after the cries from the streets could no longer be denied. Until then, the consensus against the Communist "menace" was broad enough to legitimize almost any action a president felt moved to take against it, and it was further supported by something known as a "bipartisan" foreign policy, based on the wartime model when opposition to presidential conduct of hostilities is deemed unpatriotic, if not downright traitorous. As for the bureaucracies, they were easy. The thing the Defense Department does best is procurement and the Cold War offered it prodigies of activity in that line, which activities, obviously, had much to do with the country's continuing prosperity. In the realm of foreign policy itself, the bureaucracy is relatively small and remains an extension of the foreign policy "establishment," that congeries of well-to-do gentlemen, scholars, international businessmen, and Eastern lawyers bored with torts who like to theorize about these matters, drift in and out of the official government on the tides of the election returns at the sub-Cabinet level, and, above all, have the ear of the national media. One of their numbers had, in fact, devised the national policy regarding communism—"containment"—and it was evoked from Korea's 38th parallel to Lebanon to the Berlin Wall to Cuba for something like a decade and a half. Indeed, although the word is scarcely used anymore ("detente," through the process of Orwellian Newspeak, has replaced it), it is difficult to see where or how the policy that word summarizes has greatly changed even now.

Be that as it may, this general situation suited Eisenhower's nature very well. Containment is a passive and reactive mode, requiring but small imagination and little initiative to sustain. It suited the "cheerful, bustling, helpful" side of his soul. It made him male nurse to the free world. The policy also suited his work methods. You could staff out a finite problem, get some choices of action down on a page or two, and then order the one you liked into being. There was no opposition, little ambiguity, and the results were concrete. If you put the troops on alert somewhere you could damn well see them snap to. It wasn't like fooling around with the welfare system, where the benefits might not be visible for a generation or two. (It may be that the

Eisenhower domestic program concentrated so heavily on highway construction and urban redevelopment programs because—aside from satisfying construction industry pressures—there was the immediate gratification of quickly seeing literally concrete results.)

It is true, of course, that Eisenhower had at his side for much of his term of office that militant and dedicated cold warrior John Foster Dulles, who was always talking about "rolling back" communism or "unleashing" Chiang. He used to scare people. But that, apparently, is what Eisenhower liked about him. Recent evidence indicates that he had in his own mind, concocted a sort of good cop-bad cop routine with his Secretary of State, although he never let grim old Foster in on his little secret. The idea was that he would offer atoms for peace while Dulles offered atoms to go blooie. Thus with threats and promises did they soften up the suspect world. Beyond the creation of little frissons of hope and fear, few practical results flowed from this routine. But it gave everyone a distinct impression that someone was on duty at the precinct house.

So it went with our first media President. One despairs of ever ascertaining how much he calculated his effects, how much we were simply witnesses to a natural fit of personality and historical moment. What we can see now is that Eisenhower's failures lay not in the policy realm (he was, sensibly, not trying there) but in his inability to see just how great the power of his personality, his celebrity, was in the new media context of his presidential years. He simply could not appreciate or perhaps believe, how his symbolic charisma, magnified by television and by the rest of the media as they redefined themselves in its rapidly lengthening shadow, might have been employed in aid of selected, urgent matters before the country.

In other words, he saw the growing discontinuity between the traditional poses of political leadership and the practical ability of the leader to move the lumbering legislative and bureaucratic machinery more than infinitesimally in the directions he wants. What he did not grasp was the power he had to move outside of the customary party legislative and bureaucratic channels, to use himself, the self in whom the vast majority of his countrymen saw so much of their best selves, as an instrument of moral suasion. So, instinctively attuned to the historical flow in one area, he still did not see where that flow was heading, did not see that a significant measure of political power in our society was in the process of relocation, moving out of the halls of duly constituted authority and into the living room on its way to the mean streets of the sixties. Or, to put the matter still more simply, he did not know his own strength, did not see that a gently likable man such as himself, placed in the one position in America where the television networks were literally at his beck and call, could focus our attention on all our unfinished moral business, summon us to a spring-cleaning of the soul at the start of a new historical season.

Eisenhower's moment of truth came at the time of the school desegregation crisis at Central High School in Little Rock, Arkansas, in 1955. At that time it was publicly suggested that the way to solve it was for the President of the United States to fly there and walk the black students through the jeering mobs and into the school they were then legally as well as morally entitled to attend. If he heard the idea, Eisenhower did not acknowledge it; melodrama was not his style. He sent troops instead of himself.

Nothing immediate was lost. The symbolic entrance was eventually made. But we would, in the decade to come, pay for the large failure of imagination that this specific failure to act implies. We would pay for it mainly in the arrogation of moral authority in our society by people who lacked other forms of authority, notably those of maturity and wisdom.

Still, one cannot leave this general without noting that whenever he comes to mind, another general also appears there: Tolstoy's Kutuzov, as that historical figure is fictionally refracted in *War and Peace*. They were both simple men of fundamental good natures. Both were attuned, as more complex personalities often are not, to the murmur of deep historical currents proceeding beneath the clamorous surface of events. In war, both accomplished the same thing—the defense of their countries and the unquestioned values each represented—through the defeat of enemies seemingly more brilliantly commanded. Both did so by finding ways of harnessing themselves to the secret tides of history—"going with the flow" as we would say—and thus gaining their ends with an effortlessness that puzzled and infuriated their activist critics. The historical Kutuzov made no attempt to employ the power of his instinct in the trickier waters of peacetime politics as Eisenhower did. And he was perhaps wise. It seems likely that one requires the isolation of a far-flung army, not to mention the comfort of military secrecy, if one is to make the patient search for historical necessity into a policy. At any rate, it is evident that such a policy is more easily employed in the vastness and fastness of nineteenth-century Russia than it can be in twentieth-century Washington, with its huge press corps constantly looking for and demanding news-worthy action. Above all, one must bear in mind that the passive turn of spirit that permits a Kutuzov or an Eisenhower to identify the salient historical current of the moment is essentially an amoral skill. If it were otherwise they would be confused by fashion and personal preference like the rest of us. Another way of putting it is that they were looking for opportunity, not for trouble. And the taking of moral stances is always trouble.

But that is perhaps beside the point. Eisenhower, as the record of his successors, not to mention Ellul's theory, shows, was at least half right in his reading of the times. Every major attempt by government, outside of enforcing court orders, to redress the grievances of our age, both foreign and domestic, have been abysmal failures, costly beyond measure in every way that one can count. As for the rest—the moral failures that nag at one—who can argue with the self-imposed limits he placed on himself in his relationship to television and its era? Mea-sured by the simplest of tests—his ability to retain the confidence and affection of the electorate—he was far more successful than all the willful men who came after him. His very lack of moral and policy ambitions, his refusal to be tiresome, a scold, or a conscious manipula-tor, prevented him from wearing out his welcome. He was the Law-rence Welk—or, to name his own favorite, the Fred Waring—of presi-dents, the one true genius of the political illusion we have yet witnessed. If that statement seems excessive, we have only to look at the record, as they say in politics, of his contemporaries and his suc-cessors.

In the politics of the fifties, Eisenhower had his dark double, his great opponent and, in his very camp, his almost parodistic opposite. The first, the double, had risen to terrifying prominence, though never to official power (only tolerance), before Eisenhower declared for the presidency and, in fact, the general would receive a certain amount of support he might not otherwise have obtained because it was thought that his moral weight and his correct connections might counterbal-ance the reckless adventurings of Joseph R. McCarthy (Rep., Wis.).

This did not happen, because in confronting McCarthy, Eisenhower was at his most Kutuzovian. History would take care of the problem better than he could and, as a general, he was used to the tragic necessity of sacrificing a few lives while waiting for historical necessity to do its work. Indeed, very few lives were lost to McCarthy and his ilk—only careers and reputations, which were small enough sacrifices to make as, perhaps, the old soldier saw it. Anyway, we know he tolerated vicious criticism of his friend and mentor George C. Marshall, even going so far as to excise from a prepared speech an attack on McCarthy for the latter's assaults on Marshall.

As for the senator himself, he had, in his ever-questing ambition, stumbled on the very essence of the political illusion. When he went off to Wheeling, West Virginia, to make his charges that there were a certain number of Communists (the number kept varying in subsequent discussions of the speech) "working and shaping policy" in the State Department, he was employing only the crudest sort of attention-getting device. He intended to create a sensation, not to totally reshape his obscure career.

But McCarthy was a sort of perverse populist from a genuinely populist state, the state of the La Follettes, one of whom ("Young Bob") he had defeated for his Senate seat. It had always been good politics in Wisconsin to place as much blame for whatever was wrong with the world on "Eastern interests" (the banks, the railroads, etc.), and it was well understood there that the Washington bureaucracy, especially the foreign policy bureaucracy, was an extension of that establishment. Now those fellas had gone and "lost China" as well as got us mixed up in this Korean mess. What better way for a rather lackluster junior senator to show his constituents that he was up and about, on the job. And, as illusionary politics, it was safe enough; recall Ellul's observation that such assaults on bureaucracies are in the nature of "magic incantations." They normally do neither harm nor good, since that bureaucracy simply shrugs them off and proceeds under its own power on its self-determined path.

But the linking of a standard attack on the lack of institutional accountability with the issue of communism and the growing fear of its secret ways, produced an explosion of interest far in excess of McCarthy's provincial dreams. His hoped for one-day sensation was not over in a day, or a week. He was suddenly under pressure to produce proof of his allegations in some quarters, while in others he was instantly accorded heroic status. In any event, he was a celebrity. And the rest of his career was an acting out of Ellul's doctrines.

To begin with, the prestige of knowledgeability instantly accrued to McCarthy. He gave the impression of having information no one—not the President, not the press, not even the sacred FBI—had. And even when this or that spokesman rose quietly and rationally to defend the official record, insisting they were attending to the matter and had turned up nothing to support McCarthy's charges, it made no difference. For the senator would be on to the next case, and the next. He had stumbled on the most important fact of life in the modern media world, the central point in Ellul's argument, which is, it will be recalled, that "steeped in the news," the typical citizen loses all sense of continuity, finds his memories of even very recent events either blotted out or distorted. The way at least a few people said it at the time was that the denial, the counterevidence, never seemed to catch up with the sensationally phrased, front-paged, initial charge. And as these last piled up, stupid people kept saying things like, "Where there's smoke, there's fire." Or they simply found the rebuttals too subtle and therefore too dull to think about in comparison to the simplicity and sensationalism of whatever original charge the senator (or one of his several imitators) had made.

Had the effect of what he did not been so evil there would have been something comic about him. His principal personal prop, for instance, was a bulging and battered lawyer's briefcase, which accompanied him even to the podium when he spoke. In the beginning he had simply waved a sheet of paper and cried that he had there in his hand a list of the State Department's secret Communists. Then, the well-stuffed briefcase implied that his information had multiplied and required this commodious file just to serve his immediate needs. Occasionally, when pressed, he would dig into the thing and haul out some dubious document and press it on an inquiring reporter, who would generally not see its relevance. McCarthy would often agree with him (he was personally a rather agreeable fellow) but say that this tattered shred fit into a larger pattern of evidence that he was, in his patient district attorney's way, fitting together for some latter-day devastation that somehow never arrived.

Another thing people said at the time—earnest, serious people, that is—was that McCarthy and his brethren seemed to be abusing Congress's investigatory power. It was supposed to be linked to the proposal and passing of laws, but no legislation ever seemed to come out of all this harrying about. This was very sweet and innocent of them. But, of course, legislation was never the point. The point was "spectacle, appearance without root, a game" diverting the audience and fixing its attention on matters of no consequence.

Yet another thing that surprised earnest people was how much of the press, though not the best of the press, seemed to go along with McCarthy, though obviously his methods, should they have become institutionalized, posed a threat to the freedom of the press. What they did not see was that, on the whole, it was involved in the same enterprise as McCarthy, which was entertainment masquerading as a serious involvement with the issues of the day. The papers liked him, even when they loathed him, for he was an endless source of copy, and he was very obliging about it, even with the individual representatives of journals that opposed him. The only thing he was ever punctilious about was seeing that his press releases got out in time for the reporters to make their deadlines. And he was fair about it; if the AMs got a break one day, the PMs would have one the next. And he always gave a Willy Loman–like impression of wanting to be liked, even by the people he tried to ruin. Better than his opponents he seemed to understand that he was just running a game, a show. Why did people keep taking him so seriously?

The answer, of course, was that there were real consequences to his symbolic activities. Unlike Eisenhower, who committed no active harm out of the same instinctive understanding of the requirements of the political illusion, McCarthy and his imitators did. They got personal, and there were cries of individual human pain, and individual human sympathy for the pained, that arose in their wake.

One likes to think that, in time, this chorus of protest would have swelled to irresistible volume, that simply by consulting their individual senses of decency and fair play a majority of Americans would have swung over from approval, or anyway acquiescence, to outright opposition to the man and his ism. But that was not the case. So far as one can tell, there was no significant diminution of his support until there was a decisive intervention in the matter by television, which brought the whole sorry business to a screeching, and, at the time, startling, halt.

McCarthy had not had much access to television in the early days of his career which, of course, coincided with the early days of television. But as his power crested, television's too was burgeoning and, to put it mildly, he was not a natural for it, any more than Richard Nixon was. There was the matter of his beard and his unpleasantly thinning hair. There was his manner, which featured a nervous, breathy, near giggle that arose at inappropriate times. There was his prosecutorial style, much too sharp-edged for the medium. But, for the most part, he was not often exposed on TV, and when he was, his appearances were brief—a news clip here and there. He was essentially a creature of print where his voice could not be heard and his style, with its dependence on "documentation" (however phoney), was dignified by the implication of authenticity, rationality, that print imparts.

What he could not withstand, but what neither he nor his opponents knew in advance he could not withstand, was relentless daily exposure in an unrehearsed, free-form forum, which is what the Army-McCarthy hearings turned out to be. The issues debated therein have faded from memory (he had accused the Army, Eisenhower's beloved home, of knowingly harboring traitors), but the images, thirty years later, remain indelible. They continue to constitute a portrait of a bully, a tiresome and not very bright man who presented a feeble case very badly. Except for the pioneering television broadcast of Estes Kefauver's hearings on organized crime, this was television's first sustained employment as megatheater, cast with accidental brilliance, dramatically hypnotizing and, in the end, morally satisfying.

For though he had begun to totter after just a few days' exposure, what brought McCarthy down was a comparatively minor miscalculation, an attempt to smear Fred Fisher, a young associate of his chief tormentor, Joseph Welch, the leading attorney for the Army. McCarthy accused the young man of having once been a member of a legal organization that was supposed to have been a Communist front. It was not different in kind from literally hundreds of similar charges he and his kind had made in the past, but this time millions saw the desperate reach for a diversionary weapon, saw the sniveling manner in which he did so, and witnessed Joseph Welch, a man they had come to like and trust, the very picture of the foxy, witty, humane, and eminently sensible lawyer we all hope we'll find if we ever get into trouble—a regular Mr. Tutt from *The Saturday Evening Post* stories—react not with more legalistic palaver, but with the decent outrage of a father defending his son.

It was wonderfully appropriate. McCarthy died as he had lived not on the issues, but in between them, on a question of imagery. Ironically, indeed, he died correct. No one ever claimed his facts were wrong in this particular instance—Fred Fisher had indeed once belonged to the front McCarthy said he belonged to. But he had never hidden the fact, and everyone understood that it had always been all right for bright young men in America to sow their wild ideological oats as long as they outgrew that activity. Since basically that was the worst McCarthy had actually ever proved any of his victims had done, it became vividly clear that he was wasting everyone's time in addition to being, visibly, a much more awful fellow than the newspapers had let on.

So television emerges, briefly, in a heroic light. But only briefly. The next McCarthy, when he comes, will be slicker. He will not have a ghastly giggle and the makeup guys will do something about his beard. He may look something like Johnny Carson. Or like Eisenhower. Or maybe even Joseph Welch. For the fact is, television is quite amoral and apolitical in what its cameras like and don't like. It can undo good men as well as bad.

Take, for example, Adlai E. Stevenson, who was everything McCarthy was not, but was also everything Eisenhower was not. In his vaguely academic, vaguely patrician way, he sensed that the rules of political warfare had changed, but he entirely misjudged the nature of the change. The traditional flummeries of the campaign trail were, indeed, outworn, the old bold oratorical flourishes, for example, gave off a comic air. It was time for something cooler, more natural. Stevenson perhaps thought that meant we were as a society getting more grown-up. In fact, it was just the opposite; we were becoming more childish. As Trow says, when we fall out of conventional history into the world of demographics, where we count everything and value little, then a child's opinion carries as much (and in many realms of our culture, more) weight as that of an adult. It follows, therefore, that it is pointless to act like a grown-up. It was a cliché of the time that Eisenhower was a father figure to his followers, and there was an approximate sort of truth in the observation. Anyway, it is characteristic of fathers and father figures that they reduce the complexities of their thought and rhetoric to that of the youngsters they seek to influence. If you are attempting to do that to large numbers of people via television, the likelihood is that you will still further simplify things, for it is in the nature of television to reduce to its scale everything it observes, thereby trivializing all who speak through it.

And here came Stevenson, at least in 1952 fulfilling his promise to talk sense to the American people and trying to impress them with his gracefully turned ironies. It was a disaster. Irony is a quality much valued in the high culture; it is virtually unknown in the low, and what is lower on anyone's cultural scale than a national political campaign? It went over well enough with the journalists, the intellectuals, the rest of us junior and aspiring members of the new class, who wanted to prove that something in our college educations had rubbed off, that the virtues of civility were not lost on us even as we scrambled for beginners' niches as "manipulators of symbols" (to resurrect one of sociology's then fashionable descriptive phrases for the fashionable media occupations). But to the majority a taste for complexity came across as a sign of weakness. Eisenhower's simple insistence on simple virtues, or anyway on the implication of a return to them by the assertion of his manifestly virtuous personality, was, in a sense, a benign version of McCarthyism. That is to say, he offered a simplification of the issues of the day that was no less radical than that of the junior senator, no less of a falsification of what the world had become. And, anyway, it *was* time for a change, especially since he was offering as his running mate a man who not merely appeared to be in touch with the grimy realities, but was one of them, that member of the *lumpen bourgeoisie,* that classic American careerist, Richard Milhous Nixon. He would see to it that Eisenhower did not drift too far off into the cloudland of goodwill.

In some respects, Richard Nixon presents the most interesting case of all the politicians who came to prominence in the 1950s in that he was the one who most consciously recognized that political success had come to depend almost entirely on the presentation of a pleasing personality. This was not news that he reveled in, for he had enough self-awareness to recognize that a pleasing personality was precisely what he did not possess. And so his entire career, culminating in the ghastly Watergate farce, must be read as a desperate attempt to compensate for what he saw, in his endlessly self-pitying way, as a tragic flaw.

Now many politicians are not to the media manner born. But it is not a fatal defect. They learn to compensate by presenting to the camera a reasonably honest, decently modest, recognizably human version of themselves, neither spilling their guts nor totally hiding their hearts. This, however, requires a certain contentment with oneself, and a certain confidence that what one has to offer will not too greatly displease strangers. Poor Nixon! He appears from the beginning of self-consciousness to have been aware, as Gertrude Stein's *mot* about another California phenomenon has it, that there was no there

there. He seems also to have resented the fact that he was born at the wrong—or receiving—end of the media chain. It was his only known populist attitude, but it was a powerful one—this feeling that the press and the networks were controlled by faraway and malevolent forces that might either misunderstand him or understand him all too well—find him out, by which one means, expose his emptiness.

There was in all this an element of disappointed envy. He had once entertained a wistful boyhood fantasy of being a sportscaster; it is said he accompanied his youthful sporting adventures by giving play-by-play accounts of them. But, of course, lost deep in his provincial glooms, he could not imagine how one went about getting such a job, though it is a shame he could not have made that imaginative leap. He had a lifelong passion for sporting statistics that was almost as profound as his gift for political calculation (his worst enemies always conceded that Nixon had no peer at the technical side of politics—interpreting polls, for instance, or predicting the way a fellow professional's mind might change under pressure). He also had a voice well suited to the work, mellow and resonant. And, of course, the lack of a strong, well-defined personality is an asset to a sports announcer, who is supposed to describe the action, not intrude upon it. It would have been an ideal job for someone like Nixon, a man of generalized ambition and no qualities.

But the path was too exotic, and so he set forth on a more conventional route. Cruel people would say later that he was the candidate not just of those who had trouble with adolescent acne, but of all of night school America, of all those of unpromising background who thought they might amount to something by working overtime or learning some job better than those their fathers held. And, indeed, Whittier College was that kind of an institution—a night school that happened to meet by day. Duke Law School was not a night school; it is merely second-class, the safety school for marginal applicants to Harvard, Yale, Columbia. It didn't, in Nixon's day, get you an interview with Cravath, Swaine & Moore when you graduated; it helped you to catch on with OPA during the war. And that probably didn't hurt when he was trying to wangle a nice, quiet desk job in the Navy, which carried with it that striving young pol's essential, a military record of some kind.

Still, if he could not quite imagine himself Graham MacNamee, one can't conceive Richard Nixon imagining himself a vice presidential or presidential candidate, either. A small-town law practice, party committee chairmanships, later a run for the assembly or the state senate, that was more his speed. He was a hard worker, and that quality brings its modest rewards in politics. But the party was shorthanded in California after the war and needed someone to run for Congress against the seemingly unbeatable Jerry Voorhis. Nixon won, of course, and in the process discovered one or two interesting things. The first was that one no longer needed a personality of one's own in order to stand for public office. There were now people who could make one up for you. It might not be much, but it would do. It would do especially if these same craftsmen could distract the voters' attention. We're not talking veterans' bonuses here, or a new post office. We're talking real sensations—the implication that the other fellow or lady was a Communist. Well, not exactly a Communist, but in all fairness—looks of earnestness and piety here—a dupe, an unwitting ally. Just look at this voting record here, voted the straight party line X percent of the time. A dirty trick, the first of many, the beginning of a lifetime habit; a habit that would first raise Richard M. Nixon up, then cast him down, over and over again.

Well, what else could you do? It was pointless to try to create a permanently pleasing public personality for this unctuous, sweaty man, who could not tell the simplest joke, whose attempts to evoke any sort of personal emotion always seemed to involve stealing them from some lowest common denominator in the popular culture, who could not even coordinate gesture and facial expression with what he was saying, so it often seemed that his dialogue had been dubbed in later. No wonder, as the years wore on, we were treated to one new Nixon after another, with the press falling over itself to pick up this or that hint of new maturity or growing statesmanship whenever his handlers dropped one. In a lifetime of diversionary tricks, this was the big one.

It is a tribute to the American citizen's innate sense of fair play—or is it simply gullibility?—that Nixon could win as often as he did before turning into our ultimate loser. Poor guy, people would think, he can't help it if he's a klutz. And then they would shut out the sorry spectacle he made of himself and attend his words, which often contained a certain plausibility, even if one happened to disagree with him. His success may even be attributed to the persistence of the political illusion, that is a great will to continue to believe that personality (or lack of same) doesn't count, that we are all gathered here by the television set to discuss the issues. How else explain his survival of such truly terrible performances as the Checkers speech, the humiliation at slick-ster Kennedy's hands in the presidential debates (when Marshall McLuhan said he looked like a railroad lawyer signing leases that were not in the best interests of a small town), the awful self-revelation of the "You won't have Nixon to kick around anymore" press confer-ence when he lost the California gubernatorial race? Right to the end he was tacky; one recalls one of his several feeble explanations of Watergate, with bound volumes of the transcripts of the famous tapes next to him and, over there, at the edge of the screen, unmentioned, but not unseen, a bust of Lincoln, "Honest Abe," to link him to the great tradition of his party and his country—about as subtle as a blow to the head with a two-by-four.

There is, of course, one other explanation of his persistence in our lives. That is, as politics turned into megatheater we needed him as our dark star, the visible manifestation of the dingy side of the Ameri-can character, that side which has always relished frauds, cons, scams, and especially envies, even admires, people who keep pulling them off. He was, perhaps, the W. C. Fields or the Willie Sutton of politics—though without the former's comic genius or the bank robber's insou-ciant charm. "How he fascinated me," the novelist Julia Whedon has one of her characters reflect. "I listened to him lie and bully and swagger and whine and wheedle and admire himself and wondered how he got away with it. He stunned people with the sheer force of his bullshit, that's what he did. He would do *anything.* And we knew it." In other words, no character (in the moral and psychological sense) finally became character in the theatrical sense, maybe the greatest, finally our age had yet produced, the one who will forever draw us back to search our seamy side. It may be, indeed, as David T. Bazelon has speculated, that no nation achieves maturity without first endur-ing the reign of some figure who encapsulates and forces it to contem-plate the most evil aspects of its nature—Ivan the Terrible, Napoleon, Mussolini, Hitler. If that be so then we were lucky; Nixon was a far more paltry figure than any of those monsters of the grand scale. But, in the end, Otis Cribblecobble, Willie Sutton was transformed, becom-ing—appropriate coincidence of names here—a sort of Richard III.

🌿 🌿

The politics of the decade, then, varied from the benevolently dis-mal to the dismally banal—with the occasional side excursion into evil of the peculiarly small-minded sort that McCarthy and the rest of the investigators practiced. No wonder that one more and more withdrew from involvement, even from the distant emotional involvement of rooting for somebody or other in this or that election. Even a degree in political science taken with the thought that it would aid a career in political journalism was not proof against an indifference that was often indistinguishable from disgust. By the end of the fifties, one's path, not entirely unthinkingly, had gone in unexpected directions. One then read the political news as one read the sports pages, with a sort of distant bemusement, but the heart was surely elsewhere. And there was no sense that one was isolated; many a contemporary had taken analogous steps during that time.

Yet one had not yet entirely abandoned hope for a change. If a heroic political age seemed beyond reach, a slight brightening in the political weather seemed likely, if only because a natural cycle of dark and light had always operated in these matters in the past.

One's initial response to John F. Kennedy's candidacy in the primaries and his nomination by the Democrats in 1960 was not enthusiastic. He seemed an agreeable fellow, and certainly a pleasant contrast to Tricky Dick. But one imagined that if one ended up voting for him at all it would be because one willed a disregard for his inadequacies, not because one thrilled to his adequacies. People kept arguing in print, for example, that his awful father should not concern the voter because Kennedy was not close to him (far from true, actually). Out of print people said his Catholicism shouldn't be a concern because he appeared to be a bad, or anyway indifferent, Catholic, a point that was reinforced by his growing underground reputation as a cocksman. Then, however, as Kennedy and Nixon started to slug it out, one's perception began to change.

It was not just a case of Kennedy being more attractive than Nixon. Who wasn't? Nor was there any compelling position on some issue or other that caused one to lean in his direction. Did anyone really care about Quemoy and Matsu? Did we really believe that feckless Republicans had permitted a dangerous missile gap to develop between us and the Russians? No, one began to sense, as the campaign wore on, that something new was in the air and that Kennedy had caught that fresh breeze.

Hard, now, to sort out what we only unconsciously understood then and have come to understand more rationally since. But from the start we saw that the tailoring and the figure were better than Nixon's. And the cool, occasionally self-deprecating humor worked well both outdoors on the platform and indoors in the television studio. The unruly shock of hair, the stabbing forefinger, the refusal to wear an overcoat even in the coldest weather, bespoke youth and energy in such a way that Kennedy would never have had to speak directly of these qualities (though "vigah" became, in due course, a national catchword). In a sense, Kennedy was the candidate of joggers as yet unborn. Buttressing this near-subliminal appeal was another, that of a thinker—not some Wilsonian doubledome or some Stevensonian introspective—but of a man who, with the same ease and grace, tossed off quips as he tossed off books (though even at the time there were nasty rumors that both were largely the products of other craftsmen). Finally, there was the sense that, like a talk show host, he was at ease in many worlds. The rat pack, connected through Peter Lawford, who was a junior member and also a junior Kennedy by virtue of his brother-in-law status, gathered at his side. Then there was the Harvard contingent—eager to prove that academics could be men of affairs, given half a chance. And there were carefully cultivated connections with the world of arts and letters. And not a few athletes, run in as ringers in the Kennedy clan's much photographed touch football games. Even the humble world of journalism sent its representatives to the forming court. At the time this all seemed quite spontaneous, though in retrospect it comes to seem more and more the result of careful calculation.

What has also come clear now is that Kennedy was different from the politicians who preceded him to prominence in the fifties in that he required little adaptation to fit into the new, television-dictated way of presenting oneself, whereas they had all had to shape their preexistent personalities, formed in earlier days or in the deep provinces, to this new reality. He was to this manner trained by his privileged life, his father's connections. Indeed, in his shrewd, rude, new-rich way, Joe Kennedy had often said, based on his forays into motion picture production, that "after the New Deal had completed the destruction of the old social hierarchies begun by the Depression, Hollywood, with its ability to manufacture status overnight, would provide the aristocracy of the coming era" (as Peter Collier and David Horowitz put in *The Kennedys).* And the elder Kennedy had taught his family another basic lesson, which was that among the most entertaining thing power could buy was entertaining connections—useful too, of course. Wonderful to be in a position where no one could refuse your phone call or your invitation. But movie stars, writers, the nonpolitically prominent in general, did more than decorate your table, they bedazzled the groundlings, "the beggars of glamour" as Norman Mailer would style them, by imparting a sheen to one's achievements that could not so easily or so cheaply be obtained in other ways. Good to have splendid houses, cars, yachts, but if you really wanted to impress people, proof of access to the celebrity world offered larger, more generally visible benefits.

These lessons were not lost on John F. Kennedy. We have seen that, since Woodrow Wilson's day, movie stars and the like have been welcomed at the White House on state occasions, sometimes *as* state occasions. FDR, for example, had recruited them for activities like the annual March of Dimes ball and radio broadcast even before they were pressed into wartime public relations services. After the war actors had been increasingly employed in political campaigns, and there is reason to speculate that a more cynical connection of this sort was manifested by the House Un-American Activities Committee investigations into the "infiltration" of Communists into show biz. The Committee too, in its bizarre way, wanted to associate itself with big names. Remember that before they got down to the small-fry Stalinists they actually had something on (basically the possession of party cards and a set of inappropriate beliefs—the politics of Hollywood self-hatred), they held a parade of "friendly" big name witnesses—Gary Cooper, Robert Taylor, Adolphe Menjou, Walt Disney—who made various sorts of fools of themselves attempting to explain how the great conspiracy was sapping the vital bodily fluids of the movie business. But, really, the worst they—or anyone—could say about the handful of performers who had innocently worked for the party fronts was that they understood (misunderstood, actually) the petitions they signed and the benefit appearances they made to be not different from their officially blessed work for other equally good-seeming causes. The worst they could say about the nonperforming leftists, the few writers, directors, and producers caught in the Committee's net, was that like everyone who has ever worked at any art, they occasionally slipped in a few hints of their personal views on current public issues. Given Hollywood's endless propagandizing, both conscious and unconscious, in aid of the most bourgeois forms of "Americanism," these almost imperceptible (indeed, never concretely identified) moments must be seen as inadequate to the task of restoring even a modestly balanced view of the world. But, of course, the Committee, and the eager blacklisters who followed in its wake, was actually working off the dark side of our celebrity infatuation, working off our envy and resentment of people who wrested personal privilege from the thrall-dom in which their commercialized fantasies held us. It was excellent for many people to see them reduced to penury because it could be made to seem that they had attacked the very order that had raised them up—poetic justice and all that. This was the basic *Star Is Born* story line projected into a more pitiless arena, one where the morons could cloak their meanspiritedness in what they saw as the higher political morality, while giving no thought to their own envious psychodramas.

Be that as it may, Kennedy, whose brother Robert had worked for McCarthy and who had himself spoken well of the senator, changed the nature of the connection between political celebrity and show biz celebrity. What had formerly been a matter of trying to achieve momentary glamour by brief and rather carefully controlled social and (in the broader sense) charitable association, now became an attempt to create real intimacy. Or, at least, a powerful illusion of it. For a long time we had been given the impression that a president could get a movie star on the phone when he needed him. Now, it seemed, certain movie stars could get a president on the phone when they had needs. Or just a juicy bit of gossip to impart. In the past, it was understood that it was the performer who had everything to gain from these connections with the politically mighty. In this brave new world it was clear that the politicos had much to gain as well.

The new order of things was stated very clearly in an incident that occurred after Kennedy's election, when Sam Rayburn, Speaker of the House, and, for generations, a man identified—often reverently—throughout the press as one of the two or three most powerful men in Washington, a true maker, shaker, and breaker in its corridors of power, importuned Frank Sinatra for some favor at some function. Sinatra affected not to know who the old gentleman with the bourbon and branch water accent was. Sam apparently could not believe such a show of ignorance and persisted, even unto taking hold of the singer's lapels. Whereupon he was told, "Take your hands off the suit, creep."

Here, indeed, was the new order proclaimed. Maybe, just maybe, a president had status of a magnitude sufficient to treat a show biz superstar as an equal. But a working pol? No. Never. One imagines chortles over at the White House. The old politics humiliated by the new. And this boring old dodo they had to pretend to take seriously all the time, and actually had to take seriously some of the time, when a piece of legislation was in trouble, put in his place by the Wop from

New Jersey and Las Vegas. How sweet power of this new kind could be.

In other ways, too. Henceforth, presidents, ex-presidents, and presidential aspirants would be weekend guests at the movie stars' splendid houses in Palm Springs and similar venues. The implication that they gossiped together, quipped together, and, indeed, slept together gained general credence. We know, now, that one of John F. Kennedy's many mistresses, a sometime gangster's moll he had inherited from Sinatra, was particularly appealing to him because of her background. And since she was still in touch with the singer, the Leader of the Free World enjoyed getting the latest word on Sinatra's current liaisons from her. Of course, the tales of Kennedy's affairs with actresses are legend and legion, and no longer denied by anyone. If we have the names of some of his star-fucks wrong, we assuredly have the quality of his sexuality right. It was, not to put too fine a point on it, show biz sexuality—casually macho, risky from time to time (to keep it interesting), and exploitative of the women involved with him.

The sexual connections were kept as quiet—officially—as the social connections were not, but rumors of the latter were every bit as titillating. As is so often the case in these matters, Norman Mailer caught the drift of things first. In his famous *Esquire* article "Superman Comes to the Supermarket," which appeared just before the election in the fall of 1960, he wrote, "America's politics would now be also America's favorite movie." More so, perhaps, than the novelist realized.

He wrote the piece, though he did not publish it, before the television debates that tipped the election from Nixon to Kennedy. They hinged almost entirely on appearances, and in them familiarity with and acceptance of show biz illusionism stood Kennedy in good stead. Poor Nixon understood that a real man did not wear makeup in any circumstances, certainly not during one of the most important public appearances of his career. He may also have feared that Tricky Dick could not afford a leak indicating he had applied to the cosmeticians for help. Kennedy had no such compunctions. What actor refuses any bit of help he can get as he essays a difficult role? And so a blue-jowled Nixon, sweating lightly (about the amount a bit of powder would have invisibly absorbed), took his menacing, prosecutor's manner out into the ring and got jabbed to death by the Irish dandy. It was John L. Sullivan vs. Gentleman Jim all over again. And so John F. Kennedy—

with a little help from the stuffed ballot boxes of Cook County—
became the thirty-fifth President of the United States.

And founded Camelot. At the time, of course, no one referred to his
regime that way. It was posthumously identified as such when Jacqueline Kennedy called in Theodore White, the journalist, for an interview just after her husband's death and revealed to him that the President liked to repair to their private quarters and play the Broadway
show album. Once he had commented that he hoped his term would
be remembered as Arthur's court had been. Only recently, in the last
of his series of books on our presidential elections, has White gone
back beyond Lerner and Loewe to an earlier reteller of the Arthurian
myth, Alfred Lord Tennyson, to quote this passage: "The city is built/
To music, therefore never built at all,/And therefore built forever."
White quotes the line approvingly—he believes Kennedy to have been
a "great" president—but we are not talking mythology when we are
discussing modern American political leadership. Imagery maybe,
mythology no. Anyway, in this context Tennyson's lines ring ambigu-
ously. The city built to music is never built at all, he says, meaning
that it is a construct of spirit and ideals, therefore of small metaphorical relevance in considering the work of a modern leader in a realm
where all historical judgments must finally be based on practical political achievements—on the construction of real palaces in the real
world.

Besides which, there was something fishy about Kennedy's spirit
and ideals anyway. What did his Camelot really consist of? Robert
Frost proclaiming a new age of "poetry and power" on Inauguration
Day? Invidious comparisons of the musicians Kennedy and Eisenhower invited to the White House (Casals vs. Fred Waring), with
Arthur Schlesinger, the court historian, moved to write, "I would
hope that we will not leave it to the Soviet Union to uncover the Van
Cliburns of the future?" (As Gary Wills says, "Poor dumb Eisenhower
—he not only lost Cuba, he lost Cliburn. He created the pianist gap.")
Mrs. Kennedy redecorating the White House with antiques more appropriate to the period in which it was built?

And? . . . Well, no harm was done by having Isaac Stern drop by
and play the fiddle now and then. But to argue that these gestures had
any substantial effect on the national cultural climate is nonsense. To
argue, indeed, that they had an interest for the general public comparable to its concern for the relationship between rat pack and White
House is ludicrous. They helped keep the intellectual and artistic com-

munity in line on the cheap, and they may have offered a certain amusement to the culturally aspiring middle class. But the White House musicales were the equivalent, on a grandish scale, of a Book-of-the-Month Club subscription for the occupants.

There was, however, a more dangerous component to the Kennedy administration's flirtation with the things of the mind. That was the conception of the presidency as an arena for existential heroism. This was a notion set forth first by Norman Mailer in his "Superman" article. The context was this: a distinct lack of excitement about Kennedy among the better class of Democrats—Stevensonians sulking in their tents, the rest of us affecting a certain cynicism. Throughout the late summer and early fall of 1960 people were going around saying there really wasn't much to choose between Kennedy and Nixon. It was just a matter of style (yawn).

Whereupon Mailer published his article in *Esquire,* which he would later say "had more effect than any other single work of mine." In it, he pointed out that "since the first World War Americans have been leading a double life, and our history has moved on two rivers, one visible, the other underground; there has been the history of politics which is concrete, factual, practical and unbelievably dull . . . and there is a subterranean river of untapped, ferocious, lonely and romantic desires, that concentration of ecstasy and violence which is the dream life of the nation." It was Mailer's thesis that these streams "had diverged too far. There was nothing to return them to one another, no common danger, no cause, no desire, and, most essentially, no hero," that is to say, no man "whose personality might suggest contradictions and mysteries which could reach into the alienated circuits of the underground . . . capture the secret imagination of a people and so be good for the vitality of his nation . . ."

But, as Mailer acutely realized, the hero of our time would not resemble the grand wistful projections of the untutored folk imagination. He would not be Homeric or even Arthurian in dimension (how right, in the end, that the "Camelot" reference was to an indifferent musical comedy reduction of the great myth). No, the new heroic figure would be of more cinematic proportions.

This, surely, was a prospect to engage the novelist's imagination. A movie star is, after all, only an approximate lust fulfillment, one refracted through a mechanized, corporatized, and commercialized system that is bound to distort our dreams. And now that model was to be projected into the political arena, an arena where far less control could be exerted over its presentation, and none could be exercised over external events affecting its presentation.

Mailer put his argument's historical rationale excitingly and attractively: "The film studios threw up their searchlights as the frontier was finally sealed and the romantic possibilities of the old conquest of land turned into a vertical myth, trapped within the skull, of a new kind of heroic life, each choosing his own archetype or a neo-renaissance man, be it Barrymore, Cagney, Flynn, Bogart, Brando or Sinatra." And, yes, though the "regulators"—politicians, professors, psychiatrists, policemen (just to name the *P*'s)—had bricked in modern life "with hygiene upon sanity, and middle-brow homily over platitude" the myth had refused to die, needed, at last, to will out someplace. One must pause, just a moment, to applaud the power of illumination inherent in the workings of a good novelist's mind. The writer had intuited what was not documented until two decades later, when one of Kennedy's more observant chums, Charles Spalding, recalled a period when Kennedy came down to Hollywood from San Francisco (where he had been desultorily covering the founding of the United Nations for the Hearst papers). He was on what he called a "hunting expedition" (the prey, of course, were starlets). Rubbing shoulders with the likes of Gary Cooper and Clark Gable, Kennedy found himself obsessed with trying to discover the secrets of their success. As Spalding was to put it for Collier and Horowitz: "Charisma wasn't a catchword yet, but Jack was very interested in that binding magnetism these screen personalities had. What exactly was *it?* How did you go about acquiring it? Did it have an impact on your private life? How did you make it work for you? He couldn't let the subject go."

Obviously, he never did. But salutary as it might be to have a president who projected movie-hero values—well, anyway, entertaining— an involuntary shudder, half-risible, half-horrific, runs through one almost a quarter century later as one rereads Mailer's characterization of the archetypal existentialist of the silver screen, "it was almost as if there were no peace unless one could fight well, kill well, (if always with honor), love well and love many, be cool, be daring, be dashing, be wild, be wily, be resourceful, be a brave gun."

One understands the appeal of such a figure to the literary man, one admires and still agrees with the daring (not to say dashing) imaginative connection Mailer made between image and political man. Yet it must be recorded that finally one is dismayed that having caught on to Kennedy's game, Mailer so wholeheartedly approved of it. To be sure, a change from Eisenhower and his appeal "to the needs of the timid, the petrified, the sanctimonious and the sluggish" was in order, and perhaps, in purely political science terms, it was time, again, to try to get outside ossified bureaucratic channels and stir things up a bit in Washington. Assuredly, there needed to be an implicit recognition, by a national leader, that nineteenth-century America, small-town America, was no longer the only, or the most significant, America, that power in the society had passed to a (somewhat) more youthful, more worldly, and more urbane crowd. Most assuredly, given a choice between Kennedy and Nixon, one had to choose the former, however dubiously.

But in the light of the history that has intervened since 1960, one must ask oneself, who was in the long run healthier for a society, Eisenhower or Kennedy? Which of the two had the more realistic sense of the limits of formal politics? Which of the two offered fewer false hopes, thus fewer embittering disappointments? Which of the two, sensing the illusionary quality of modern politics, acted more responsibly on that knowledge? Which one, in short, dampened the political illusion, which attempted to ignite it anew?

Brave guns, indeed! What were the "New Frontiersmen" supposed to do? Challenge the entrenched committee chairmen of the Hill to walk-downs on Pennsylvania Avenue? Get up a posse to chase down the rustlers of our dreams? Circle the wagons against the marauding rednecks? The images may have worked as a Mailerian literary conceit, but if you try to translate the metaphor into the language of practical (as opposed to imagistic) politics, the results are ludicrous.

But there is a problem with writing well, anyway vividly, about politics, a field that generally attracts the conventional and the sententious. The sheer force of an original thought, arrestingly phrased, gives it unwarranted power. Mailer himself would later claim that in a narrow election, one which finally turned on something like one hundred thirty thousand votes, his piece, appearing just as people were making up their minds, may have been as helpful as Mayor Daley's machine in turning the tide for Kennedy. Impossible to tell, of course. But one can attest that it perked up a lot of people, made us think that four or eight years of Kennedy would be somewhat more tolerable than an equal number of Nixon years—precisely because the style around the White House would be more agreeable.

More important, the piece was read where it counted—in the White House. It lent legitimacy to the instincts of the Kennedy team. It turned out that a highly regarded social-psychological diagnostician agreed with the course of treatment they, the political sawbones, had been prescribing.

And now, a word from academia. From Harvard, no less, where Richard Neustadt, the political scientist, had just finished *Presidential Power*, which as Gary Wills says, "became the 'hot' item of the transition." Wills quotes a salient passage: "When Roosevelt let his channels and advisers become orderly he acted out of character. With Eisenhower, seemingly, the case is quite the opposite . . . For Eisenhower the promotion of disorder was distinctly out of character. When he could not work through a set procedure, or when channels failed him, or when his associates quarreled openly, he grew either disheartened or enraged. . . . Eisenhower had been a sort of Roosevelt in reverse."

The obvious model for a Democrat, and a dynamic one at that, was the Rooseveltian one. We would have, in Arthur Schlesinger's admiring phrase, "a fluid presidency." The cabinet would meet only as a formality and favorites in it, like Robert Kennedy and Robert McNamara, would be encouraged to flow out of their tanks into other people's ponds, while rocks like Stevenson and Dean Rusk would be ignored and, behind their backs, derided. Eisenhower's cumbersome committees would be dismantled in favor of smaller more "supple" instruments, which the "brave gun" disdained ever to call into formal conclave. As the other court historian, Theodore Sorensen, put it, "He paid little attention to organization charts and chains of command, which diluted and distributed his authority. He was not interested in unanimous committee recommendations which stifled alternatives to find the lower common denominator of compromise."

The admiring metaphor here was of a basketball team calling out plays to one another on the run—nothing set, improvising like crazy. Except, of course, that description fits a school yard kind of game, not the NBA level of play to which the New Frontiersmen must have aspired. What they were really doing was running patterns, trying to set picks so their big man could get loose and score. If he did some colorful juking and jiving when he went one-on-one with some recalcitrant statesman, if he could bring the crowd to its feet when he put his moves on a tough problem, that was all to the good. It diverted attention from the fact that the Frontiersmen were, in fact, a low-scoring club. "Dee-fense" was what got them through their short season. That, and a schedule loaded with setups. They weren't the Celtics, they were the Globetrotters, traveling with a group of opponents who were supposed to lose.

But that metaphor should be no more than spot player. Theater, not sport, was their true passion. A couple of years into their run, Mailer returned once again to his theme: Kennedy was himself Kennedy's only great and lasting creation. *He* was his own idea . . . "His impulse, that profound insight into the real sources of political power in America came from a conscious or unconscious cognition that the nation could no longer use a father; it was Kennedy's genius to appreciate that we now required a leading man."

And this: "This impulse—to create and forever re-create his nature—has been the President's dominant passion. There is no other way to comprehend him. From the Hairbreadth Harry of his P.T. boat exploits through the political campaigns with their exceptional chances (who could beat Cabot Lodge in Massachusetts in 1952?) through the lively bachelordom, through the marriage to the impossibly beautiful and somewhat madcap wife, the decision to run for President, a decision worthy of Julian Sorel, the adventure in Cuba, the atomic poker game with Khrushchev . . . when the biggest bluff in the history of the world was called—yes, each is a panel of scenes in the greatest movie ever made."

And, as Mailer could not have known when he wrote, almost all of them were near frauds. The PT tale was greatly exaggerated with a little help from John Hersey, another of the friendly journalists constantly cultivated by the Kennedys, who retailed it in the impeccable pages of *The New Yorker* during the war. The marriage, given what we have since learned about the husband's sexuality, was, at best, a convenience, at worst, a sham. The Cuban adventure? The Kennedy forces hoped to pick up a cheap and flattering victory, executed by some surrogates, were told by competent military authority that the odds were against the plan working, but went ahead anyway, good little existentialists that they were. Then, when it indeed failed, they left their surrogates to die on the beaches of the Bay of Pigs. After which they put it about that they had merely been the inheritors of one of the previous Administration's bad plans, too far advanced to be stopped. Besides, there was by this time this new scheme to put defoliants in Castro's beard to amuse themselves. And that atomic poker game? Gary Wills, among others, proposes that the famous missiles could as well have been described as defensive rather than offensive weapons, and that if they had been, there were means short of precipitating a world crisis for dealing with them. But, of course, it was time for another melodrama. The Kennedy group needed it—the feel of the adrenaline coursing through their nervous systems—needed it as much as their public, whose attention was beginning to wander, needed it.

There was in all this a huge element of macho posturing. The missile crisis was used to recoup the tough image damaged by the Bay of Pigs fiasco. But there was something more besides. Kennedy and his circle had by now passed beyond the business of creating and re-creating a self for the President. They were now in the business, it seems, of creating dramas in which, it was hoped, that self would be exhibited in the best, most dramatic light. If the first of these Latin melodramas flopped ignominiously, the second was a huge success. It is, in fact, the one "achievement" of the Kennedy administration that everyone acknowledges and agrees upon. Of course, there might have been another alternative to the Kennedys' Castro obsession (which may have stemmed, Wills suggests, from a horrid suspicion that he was a real leader, commanding his people through the strength of his character, not a fake one "creating and re-creating" himself in search of the winning—or should one say winsome?—image). That alternative was simply to recognize Communist Cuba as an inconvenient but scarcely deadly fact of life, to patiently work for a normalization of relations with it. How successful such a course might have been, and how soon it might have brought advantage to the United States, is problematical. But if one were serious about governance, if one were seeking to expend the goodwill that automatically accrues to a new president in a useful, rather than a theatrical way, if indeed one wanted to show the difference between a new administration's philosophy and that of the one it had replaced not by heroic strokes but by patiently reeducative means, if one were interested in writing history rather than megatheatrical screenplays, then this would have been the proper course.

And what of the other achievements of the Kennedy regnancy? As fans of flexibility Kennedy's people encouraged the growth of counter-insurgency military organizations like the Green Berets and, by employing them, began our involvement in Vietnam. Once again masculinity was looking for an inexpensive way to assert itself. There was the Peace Corps, and it turned out to be a good thing, but it began as a rather casual bit of public relations and it was only when it achieved genuine success in that realm that it was wholeheartedly embraced at the top. Legislatively, though, the Administration's accomplishments were small. It turned out that existential adventuring was useless in breaking the connections between Congress and the entrenched bureaucracies and lobbies of Washington. Might as well have spared the effort and maintained the sleepy equilibrium of the Eisenhower years. For good or ill (mostly the latter, it would seem) Lyndon Johnson, that master of congressional manipulation, was the one who actually —if briefly—"got things moving again" on the Hill.

What really marked these years, what will give them their historical resonance, was the Civil Rights Movement, ending segregation in the South and in the schools, and making a powerful beginning at laying the legal groundwork on which, at last, the assertion of moral principle could possibly stand in years to come. And this was an issue Kennedy funked. The appeal of Martin Luther King, not only to his fellow blacks, but to everyone of decent impulse, was enormous. He could not be disowned. But he could be urged toward caution. And, with Robert Kennedy's knowledge, if not at his orders, the FBI compiled a dossier on King's sexual activities, just in case the ultimate weapon of blackmail was required to keep him in line. Tough guys they were, or wanted to think they were, or wanted us to think they were. One recalls Donald Barthelme's brilliant parody of the kind of reportage that came out of Washington in those days in "Robert Kennedy Saved from Drowning":

"He is neither abrupt with nor excessively kind to associates. Or he is both abrupt and kind.

"The telephone is, for him, a whip, a lash, but also a conduit for soothing words, a sink into which he can hurl gallons of syrup if it comes to that.

"He reads quickly, scratching brief comments ('Yes,' 'No') in corners of the paper. He slouches in the leather chair, looking about him with a slightly irritated air for new visitors, new difficulties. He spends his time sending and receiving messengers."

And so on. Decisiveness. Hardness. Efficiency. Manipulativeness. This was the imagery of the New Frontier distilled. In this context Martin Luther King was a distinct inconvenience, often an active embarrassment as well as—of course—a competitor. His rolling preacher's rhetoric, his ability to meld a thousand cries from the formerly silent hearts of a people into a chorus—and then draw from that chorus a courage that went far beyond toughness, a courage that sent Southern children into the streets filled with sheriffs' deputies with their clubs and cattle prods and dogs, to claim their rights, sent them through the menacing night to register votes. All that rang with a truth, and an honorableness beyond the reach of the best and the brightest publicists.

To be sure, Dr. King used the media to amplify his voice and the Gandhian techniques he used to call attention to his cause were used, a little later, by others whose causes were more dubious and whose motives, in calling attention to them, were suspect precisely because there was an element of personal aggrandizement in them that seemed to be missing in Dr. King, just as the elements of private willfulness and the need for power for its own sake were missing in him. As a result, as Wills says, the power he came to command was real "because it was not mere assertion—it was a persuasive *yielding* of private will through nonviolent advocacy." But there was more to him even than that. For, by forging "ties of friendship and social affection," by eschewing the use of "violence or stealth . . . manipulation or technological tricks," he alone of the great public figures of recent times "came across"—came across as both authentically great and authentically human. Even television could not trivialize him and it never crossed anyone's mind to think of him as a "celebrity." He was, quite literally, selfless not only in his service to his cause, but in his refusal to offer up himself to the media's demands for intimate exposure. We do not know what he liked for lunch, what his office routines were, whether or not he slept in the nude. We cannot imagine a *People* photo of him and Coretta sharing a bubble bath. If on his long and lonely road he slept with women who were not his wife, none has published her memoirs of the encounter. Indeed, as a personality he has virtually slipped out of history. It is his work that has not, for it has changed our lives as individuals, as a nation.

Wills puts the matter elegantly when he notes that all the tricks and trumpery that attended Kennedy's public relations had as their aim to hide when necessary, to assert when he needed to, the most primitive definition of power, the power to combine "resources and will" to destroy—to assassinate Castro as he fantasized, or sabotage his economy, or wipe out his missiles. But this power must generate a backlash, especially when it is cloaked in the kind of dramatic glamour Mailer noted. It has its refutation in the ability of almost anyone to destroy the destroyer. Or as Wills puts it, "as children can wreck TV sets, so Oswalds can shoot Kennedys. The need to believe in some conspiracy behind the assassination is understandable in an age of charismatic pretensions. The 'graced' man validates his power by success, by luck. Oswald, by canceling the luck, struck at the very principle of government . . ." One wishes to pause here for emphasis. "The very principle of government." Yes. The principle of government through bedazzlement, through show, through the staging of celebrity events. But Wills goes on: ". . . it was hard to admit that he was not asserting (or being used by) some *alternative* principle of rule," for "Oswald was a brutal restatement of the idea of power as the combination of resource with will. Put at its simplest, this became the combination of a Mannlicher-Carcano with one man's mad assertiveness. Power as the power to *conquer* was totally separated, at last, from ability to control."

A dreadful thought occurs: perhaps the mad search for a formal conspiracy that killed Kennedy is a way of denying the simplest and best conspiracy theory, which is that we were all enlisted in an informal one, enlisted in it unconsciously of course, out of our bedazzled need for intimacy with our movie star President. Murder is, of course, the ultimate intimacy. Maybe we sensed, from the moment we came in, about halfway through the picture, where this scenario had to end. We had, after all, been raised on Westerns, and knew that, of late, many of the best ones, the ones that partook of the truest spirit of our times *(The Gunfighter, Ride the High Country, Lonely Are the Brave)*, had ended with the "brave gun" not triumphant, but dead, killed by some punk envious of heroic celebrity (the first named) or by the workings of modernism itself, which has a tendency to ride roughshod over the puny posturings of traditional heroic imagery (the last two). We must know, we must surely know, that at any given moment there are in our society a few hundred, a few thousand men (not many women) who truly believe that the king must die, die for reasons that are entirely private and mad. We must also know that the more we worship a heroic image of the leader, and raise it up, and him up, the more we conspire to create the circumstances that encourage tragic apotheosis. "We kill our heroes nowadays," Edward Hoagland, the essayist, wrote in 1974. "As too much admiration fixes upon them, a killer emerges, representing more than just himself." The result: "Afraid of what will happen if we admire somebody too much, we look a little to one side, take care to hedge our praise, until, like other feelings that go unsaid too long, it loses immediacy." One wishes one could be certain he was right, that the guardedness a man of Hoagland's civility is bound to feel in times like these is universal. But one is not certain. Other feelings—damnable feelings—surfaced at the time of the Kennedy assassination. They were present, I think, in the best of us, as well as the simplest and the strongest.

"Where were you when you heard Kennedy was shot?" It is, or was, a question often asked and always answered. And by our ready answers we assert that we were at least, at last, admitted to the sound stage, permitted to don extras' costumes in the epic of our lifetimes. And did we not, over the endless grieving weekend that followed, finally achieve some kind of devoutly wished for communion—not, of course, with the fallen leader, but certainly with his intimates? At last we shared perfectly in their thoughts and feelings, knew inescapably that we were so doing. And one among us, Jack Ruby, stepped forth on Sunday afternoon and, in his derangement, ended his anonymity, arrogated to himself both momentary fame and a place in history. And, of course, expressed the worst that we were feeling.

After that, the tawdriness. The jostling of the memoirists and memorialists, the scuttlings of the conspiracy nuts, the cries of the vendors hawking a few last souvenirs outside the suddenly darkened coliseum, in the shadows of which the pathetic young men lurked, fingering their revolvers while awaiting their opportunity for the bath of fame that would cleanse them of their failures. A face in the crowd, caught hauntingly by Jean Stafford, was Marguerite Oswald, mother of the killer, Lee Harvey Oswald, and now self-styled "a mother in history," the phrase that became the title of Stafford's brilliant exercise in bitter irony.

Mrs. Oswald had, of course, a desperate, pathetic, and understandable need to justify herself. What parent would not be haunted by memories of things done and undone in the childhood that had led finally to calamity on this scale? But when Stafford came to interview her she found something more than puzzled grief. She found, indeed, a celebrity manqué, a woman whose son's infamy carried with it—as Mrs. Oswald saw it—the potential of fame for herself. Indeed, as she sometimes seemed to see it, she, having already been projected by events from grinding anonymity and bad luck into the immortality of "history," already *was* a celebrity, with all those obligations to her public that weigh so heavily on the well-known. A motif of Stafford's reportage is Mrs. Oswald's silent implication that she is speaking not to a single interlocutor, but to a crowd—sometimes, perhaps, the audience at a lecture, at other moments to a group of reporters. There are, of course, things that the famous cannot discuss with their importunate public, for chilling example, how she might have voted in the 1964 presidential election: "Why, honey, you know I can't discuss my personal politics. After all, I *am* responsible for two Presidents." Later, she apes the manner of official spokesmen, press secretaries, and the like, as she has learned it from television: "No comment . . . I do not comment on my statement." Needless to say like any prominent controversialist, she numbered among her highest wishes the one of reaching young people with her story, that they might "know the truth of history." Weirdly, or not so weirdly, come to think of it, Mrs. Oswald, in the mid-sixties, did have a small public life, for as the conspiracy theories multiplied, she was invited to speak her piece at various public forums, on TV talk shows, and the like. She was, of course, often interviewed by reporters from the newspapers and magazines whenever some new theory of what had happened that bad day in Dallas surfaced. Some seemed to exonerate her son, all mitigated his guilt, by diluting it among a larger group or seeing him as an innocent dupe of dark forces any of us might have succumbed to. All, of course, tended to reinsert him into what most people think of as the rational world, by supplying him with explicable ideological reasons rather than inexplicable personal reasons for his crime.

Still, her life as a celebrity did not entirely satisfy Mrs. Oswald. She was, for example, miffed about the lack of financial rewards that had so far come her way. Her son's diary and childhood photos had not fetched the price from journalism that she thought they should have, and there had been no offers from the publishers for the story of her life and anguish. Her speaking fees (her subject, she claimed, was "the American way of life") were minuscule and she complained to Stafford about a television show that had paid her only a hundred dollars for an appearance while the very next night Richard Burton had received five thousand dollars from the same source. He could afford to give the fee to charity, she noted, whereas she didn't know "where the rent money was coming from." And he was not even an American citizen! She could not help but note in this context that each of the other females in the case—the President's widow, the widow of police officer Tippit, her daughter-in-law, Marina—had become "a very wealthy woman" as a result of her son's actions, while she, with "two Presidents in my life," was still scrabbling. Poor Mrs. Oswald. She lived too soon. Can anyone doubt that had it all happened twenty years later, the publishers would have beaten a path to her door?

But, she insisted, she was not bitter, and having delivered herself of her amazing thoughts, she would always pull herself together and put on a plucky face for her invisible audience. "I have my health. I eat well. I'm not brooding." As she had obviously learned from a lifetime of exposure to dramas of the show-must-go-on sort, no one likes a whimperer or a whiner. One must soldier on until, at last, the respect one deserves is finally won. By the time Stafford woke up for the last of the three days she spent with Mrs. Oswald (this one included a Mother's Day trip to Lee Harvey Oswald's grave), her impulse was "to eliminate the day by taking a sleeping pill," and one sympathizes. Even today, rereading her short book so many years after the fact, a chill settles down over one.

It is, in the final analysis, a reflective chill. George W. S. Trow has theorized—and we will have reason to return to this thought in other contexts—that in the years after television entered our lives "the middle distance fell away, so the (psychological) grids (from small to large) that had supported the middle distance fell into disuse and ceased to be understandable. Two grids remained. The grid of two hundred million and the grid of intimacy. Everything else fell into disuse. There was a national life—a *shimmer* of national life—and intimate life. The distance between these two grids was very great. The distance was very frightening. People did not want to measure it. People began to lose a sense of what distance was and of what the usefulness of distance might be."

But we know, don't we, precisely what that distance is? It is the distance it requires for a bullet to travel from a man who lives enviously in the intimate grid to a man who lives enviably in the national grid. There is this one method, this one brutal and shocking method, of connecting the two. And now no person who lives prominently in the national grid, as it is daily projected into the intimate grid by television, can afford to forget the possibilities of this connection via short circuit.

A movie star president? It was a nice conceit, and its appeal to a man of John F. Kennedy's background, temperament, and age is obvious. But it was a conceit that was outdated as it was annunciated. The screens of his youth, Mailer's youth, my youth, were large screens and the figures that appeared upon them were awesome in their size and distanced from us by the exoticism of the contexts that were created to set them off properly. And they did not come into our homes, except as disembodied voices or as silent images on the printed page. To commune with them we had to leave the context of normalcy, enter into darkened picture palaces, often themselves overwhelmingly exotic in their decor. In short, a rich middle distance was created for us to traverse, with each step of the way reminding us that what we wished to embrace was not real but mythic and chimerical, a fantasy . . . which we were invited to enter on tourist visas, not as permanent residents.

To project images of that power, without the old distancing protections, to project them directly to the audience "where they live" is to court a terrible danger. Of course, in 1960 it was not entirely clear that the Age of the Movie was finished, that there were unseen sophistications beyond the sophistication of Kennedian politics and Mailerian analysis that had not yet manifested themselves. But Trow's grids, besides being psychological, are, in effect, basically electric circuits and, again in effect, the equipment of a mighty broadcasting station had been wired into lines that had been designed to carry, at most, a string of forty-watt lights. The system had to blow in 1963. And it has blown in the years since. And it will continue to blow.

For all their sophistication, Kennedy and his people were, finally, as innocent as the rest of us, could not see the danger they were courting. To put the matter as simply as possible, what happened was that by becoming the existential author of himself, and in the process introducing a new and highly volatile kind of imagery into the political context, while that context itself was being altered by vast technological change, John F. Kennedy became at least the co-author of his own doom. And the madness of "the mother in history" begins to seem less mad. After the terrible fact she made—dimly to be sure—certain connections that the rest of us, in our sanity, resisted, and are bound still to resist if we are to keep our grip on reason, on the coherence of the connections between our traditions and our new reality.

There was, of course, an alternative ending to the Kennedy script. The possibility of greatness, as well as martyrdom, was inherent in it, too. It was that possibility that Mailer had quickened to, and that the rest of it had less consciously sensed. And our hopes for it persisted, perhaps unreasonably, during his term of office, despite the lack of programmatic progress, despite a growing sense that his critics were right, that there was more style than substance to the Kennedy Presidency. It was as if we were finally beginning to implicitly admit the existence of the political illusion and, having made that acknowledgment, were willing to extend a certain patience to a man making an increasingly conscious attempt to master one illusion with another kind of illusion, gain an effective purchase on political problems through the application of, to put it politely, the performing arts.

Maybe these were not, of necessity, black arts. If, increasingly, traditional politics, the attempt to blend and balance competing interests through compromise, had led to stasis, if it was, in fact, impossible for the elected politician to gain mastery in his relatively short term over the entrenched bureaucracy through traditional means, then perhaps untraditional means were the answer. That, at any rate, was the best hope we had at the time, and the process of watching Kennedy simultaneously attempt to invent and master the techniques of this new politics had its fascination.

It was fascinating precisely because it was a conscious effort. The other great presidential performer, Eisenhower, had been a mesmerist ("You are growing very sleepy") and his routine, though it was as irresistible as hypnotism well-practiced always is, had obvious limits. It is always said of hypnotists that they cannot make anyone do anything he or she does not want to do. They cannot move us anywhere against our will. But Kennedy was, at his best, a magician, so part of our minds attended to his technique, and fascinatedly looked for the card up the sleeve. But a part of us also sensed that he just might have the skill to move us where, out of laziness and caution, we did not want to go. Like a magician he seemed sometimes to possess a capacity to force a suspension of disbelief. For a moment or two he could even conjure up positive belief—in our best national self, our proudest possibilities. During his Thousand Days, when, disappointingly, politics as usual were more often than not played, a saving thought recurred: a second term. It is taking longer than he thought, or so we thought, to make the transition from the old politics to the new—and maybe, after all, the effort will fail. But a second term! When he will have settled on his final self (he was, after all, still short of that final sense of himself that often comes to men in their late forties and early fifties). When he will be free to attend to his immortality instead of tending to the next election . . . a second term! Of the possibilities before us in 1963, it was surely the best.

And after his death, and after the slow poisoning of the war in Vietnam had taken palpable hold, one began to see that the transformation one had hoped for in John Kennedy might actually be taking place in his younger brother Robert. Once the toughest of the tough, the true-believer-as-hardballer, tragedies both personal and national, seemed to be working a genuine change on him. Or maybe he had always had more passion than his cautiously calculating and essentially light-minded brother had and was now free to let it flow beyond his family, beyond his brother's career, beyond even his own ambitions. It began to seem that, perhaps, he had the soul to complete the psychic connections his brother had divined, might be able to complete them more effectively than the older man could have, since he seemed more truly the natural-born existentialist, more visibly the product of human forces rather than of imagistic longings. He was shaped, in his last years, less by the fading images of the movies' great age, more by the fresh memories of the anguish we all shared. There was less of the fictive brave gun about him, more a presentiment perhaps of a figure like *M*A*S*H*'s Hawkeye in him now. Or so one dared hope, until the lightning struck again.

Hope was, by this time, a desperate imperative, for that chain of ineptitude and disaster that would mark our politics up to the present time was now being formed. At every level of public life, the Kennedy legacy was turning out to be one of technique, and nothing but technique. This was nowhere more apparent than at the lower levels of politics, where, in everything from advertising to haircuts and wardrobe, the Kennedy manner was aped. This had nothing to do with "style," defined as the outward manifestation of at least an aspect or two of inner substance. No, it was pure mannerism. Down to the humblest candidate for city council or state assembly, we were suddenly confronted, on the hoardings, with the interchangeable images of tieless young men, coats slung over their shoulders, hair tousled by the wind, a cityscape out of focus in the background, dynamism their implicit message. At least the elder Kennedy had imagined himself. They had merely fashioned themselves in his image. And so there was nothing for our imaginations to fasten upon. Like the models in the after-shave and beer commercials, they all looked alike, agreeable and empty. At a certain level politics began to take on the air of a singles bar.

At the upper level, confusion reigned. The presidential candidates would attempt to gather to their side the show folk celebrities (poor Nixon, in 1968, was stuck with such has-beens as Anita Bryant—then selling orange juice before briefly reviving herself with her audacious attack on homosexuals—and Connie Francis); they would all attempt to master, and in one way or another, fail to master, the new art of television self-presentation (none tried more devotedly or, at first, successfully, than the new, new, new Nixon of 1968); they would all experiment with the merchandising of what pass, today, for political ideas via television commercials and reach what it is doubtless too soon to call a nadir in 1982 when the Republicans actually hired look-alike actors to impersonate such easy-prey opponents as Jimmy Carter and House Speaker Tip O'Neill in little playlets of contempt. Yet none of the major political figures of the last two decades achieved, with that audience that it is no longer quite accurate to call an electorate, those psychic resonances that Kennedy seemed so easily to achieve. Maybe there was some truth, after all, in the old Hollywood dictum that stars are born, not made, and that mass affection, at its most profound level, cannot be bought by even the most expensive publicity campaigns.

What a collection they are, the Presidents of these last two decades! Lyndon Johnson, for example. He did not, in the end, yield even to Richard Nixon in his distrust and hatred of the press, which appeared to be based on the same underlying emotion—a bitter envy of Jack Kennedy's easy mastery of the boys in the bus. Indeed, as his term wore on, he established a pattern that was to hold until the present time—honeymoon, disenchantment, and then a fatal paranoia in the leader's relationship to the men and women who covered him. One cannot help thinking he was the first President undone rather than made by modern communications. First of all, having done the thing he thought deserved the most praise (pushing Kennedy's stalled civil rights program through Congress, then launching his own Great Society schemes), he was dismayed to find the press largely indifferent to these slightly sexless but nonetheless genuine achievements. Then, having turned his hand to that area where the modern President has been most untrammeled, namely, fighting the Cold War, he found that besides the doubtless insuperable difficulties presented by his chosen battlefield, the increasingly sophisticated capabilities of television balked even a will as powerful as his in three ways.

The first, and most basic, was that it had the capability of relaying, almost instantaneously, the horror of war (and this would have been true, and will remain true, of any war not fought in some remote arena like the Falklands) directly to the civilian population. Much was made of this fact at the time, and television was seen by at least some commentators as a moral force. But, and this point cannot be too forcefully made, television is morally neutral. It will take and use to the fullest the grabbiest, most emotional-laden pictures of any subject toward which its lenses are directed. Had it existed in World War II, it might have been impossible to prosecute that war, "just" as it is still deemed to be by common consent. Surely, Korea, not much different, morally, from Vietnam, and equally "unwinnable," might not have elicited the response it did domestically (a sort of puzzled and weary acceptance) had TV been on hand to record the retreat from the Chosen Reservoir.

And then, having stirred our emotions, television kindly provided a place for us to vent them—in marches, rallies, riots, sit-ins—all, in effect, staged for the cameras. "Part vaudeville, part insurrection, part communal recreation," Abbie Hoffman called his often witty and well-staged acts of guerrilla theater, which began as a series of jujitsu holds on the American press, attempting to turn the force of its mindless lungings after the colorful feature or the neat snap back on itself, so that its power was used to subvert the very order for which it stood. The way in was through the back of the book sections of the newsmagazines, the "happy news" feature sections toward the end of the local news shows, and the trick was always the same—to do something outrageous and sufficiently lacking in subtlety that its essence could be captured in a few words and images (a hippie duck loosed in a talk show studio, money dropped from the visitors' gallery onto the floor of the stock exchange, free sample joints mailed to a random list of New Yorkers on Valentine's Day). Later, of course, the tricks stopped being funny, and they moved from the back of the book and the back of the news to the front. But Hoffman's description of the basic technique holds true. And surely had an effect he did not calculate, reinforcing the suspicion of Johnson and people like him that if the press was not covering these activities out of hostility then it was guilty of near-criminal incompetence.

Finally, for Johnson, there was the matter of his own image on TV. Intimates were always saying that there was something larger than life about the man—his passions, his rages, his glooms—something that was, perhaps, too powerful to be adequately communicated through a twenty-one-inch screen. One suspects that may be true, and that a Johnson presidency conducted prior to the invention of television might have been more successful. At a distance, not as a living presence in the living room, he might have been converted into something of a legendary figure. Personal force of his arm-twisting, jaw-to-jaw kind becomes much more attractive retailed in print, where it can be reshaped as a kind of tall tale. As it was, he had to go on television, where he did his best to cool off and scale down to the temperature and size the medium required. The voice would soften to an unctuous whisper, the regional accent would sound at once wheedling and pious. The words, of course, were remarkably platitudinous. But the total effect was of a man not only telling lies, but of living one. For the tales of advisors abused and humiliated (and being forced to wait on him in his water closet), the beagle picked up by its ears, the fresh operation scar flashed for the cameramen, the hints of venality as regards the television station he still owned in Texas, all passed into the folklore of the moment. Here, indeed, was a father figure for his times—a father figure who fulfilled rebellious youth's worst fantasies about the older generation. In a society that, excepting Kennedy, had always leaned toward the patriarchal (the influence of the Judeo-Christian tradition, as some tiresome academic was sure to point out when the subject arose), this represented an extraordinary reversal—the focus of our loathings instead of our longings for such a figure.

Nowhere in our politics had such a creature ever arisen. One had to look to the theater to find the appropriate archetype—Big Daddy in Tennessee Williams's *Cat on a Hot Tin Roof,* that self-made man, brutally willful and manipulative, sententious and hypocritical, financially and psychologically grasping, destructive not merely of dissent, but of any manifestation of inwardness or sensitivity.

Williams's Big Daddy carried within him that virus of self-destruction, cancer. Politically too, the virus arises from within. Or so it seems nowadays. Men carry within them weaknesses that, even when they are quite successful in the ordinary theaters of achievement, do not show up in destructive strength. Lyndon Johnson's need to personally manipulate people ("press the flesh"), and see them bend to his implacable will, served him well as his party's leader in the Senate. But place such a man in the White House, surround him with the panoply of power, isolate him so that he is dependent upon third parties for information about the world and for the means of communicating his own thoughts and wishes to that world, and a magnifying distortion is bound to grow, cells that were once benign, or at least not threatening to life, begin to grow uncontrolled.

In his hubris, Johnson thought he could bend an entire nation, if not the great world itself, to his will, as once he had the Senate. But the gossip leaked, the snoopers and the critics were omnipresent, the secrecy his wiles required was lost to him. The techniques that had served him in his private preserves, the techniques with which Big Daddy had ruled "ten thousand acres of the richest land this side of the Valley Nile," were cruelly self-defeating when processed by the image-mongers and projected out into the air across a vast nation which had different—albeit equally childish—notions of how a democratic leader was supposed to behave. And no matter how deeply he retreated into the Situation Room, there to personally select the targets for "his" bombers in Southeast Asia, he could not recoup. That paranoia which is the occupational disease of the modern president soon followed. He became convinced, according to one biographer, that he was in personal touch with the deity, just like Joan of Arc. And then the bitter retreat homeward, the inevitable book, the equally inevitable plans for a grandiose presidential library. We give our deposed leaders plenty of Elbe room. And then settle back to watch the drama unfold again. "The fall of great personages from high places," writes George Steiner, "gave to medieval politics their festive and brutal character. [They] made explicit the universal drama of the fall of man."

It is curious to reread now, after Watergate, Joe McGinniss's brilliant report on the Nixon campaign, *The Selling of the President 1968*. To its obvious qualities of bitter humor and carefully controlled irony, one must now add prescience. The situation was this: a candidate who was almost pathologically afraid of print journalists—only psychiatrists with, to Nixon, an apparently magical ability to ferret out a man's weaknesses, frightened him more—wished to appeal to the voters above the heads of the press and speak directly to them via television. Yet, as past experience had shown him, he was hopeless on television, a stiff. Or as Roger Ailes, who produced the carefully managed "talk shows," in which Nixon appeared to be responding spontaneously to the unrehearsed questions of ordinary citizens, put it in what remains the most memorable passage in McGinniss's book:

"Let's face it, a lot of people think Nixon is dull. Think he's a bore, a pain in the ass. They look at him as the kind of kid who always carried a bookbag. Who was forty-two years old the day he was born. They figure other kids got footballs for Christmas, Nixon got a briefcase and he loved it. He'd always have his homework done and he'd never let you copy.

"Now you put him on television, you've got a problem right away. He's a funny-looking guy. He looks like somebody hung him in a closet overnight and he jumps out in the morning with his suit all bunched up and starts running around saying, 'I want to be President.'"

Yes. But Nixon had finally found engineers to match his dreams, and with his book bag earnestness, he studied their lessons hard, and for the first time he came across as, well, presidential. He was rather an old-fashioned model, almost McKinleyesque in manner, but, as McGinniss makes achingly clear, his team was adroit. They kept steering him away from the jugular where Nixon's older political advisors, when they turned up belatedly on the scene, kept telling him to go. Dignity, statesmanship, maturity—remember, you're the new Nixon. They kept the pesky print press away as much as possible, even out of the studio when one of his carefully rigged "Meet the Citizens" shows was going on. Those citizens, of course, were carefully chosen, so that no one would throw any high, hard ones at the candidate, and the panels were neatly balanced ethnically, occupationally, and in terms of age and sex (a little crisis occurred when a psychiatrist almost got booked on one show).

The advisors knew their man. They knew that if anything upset his rather delicately balanced equilibrium, if, indeed, anything forced him to deviate from his well-rehearsed, standard answers to the campaign's basic questions he might revert to meanspirited, or cornered-rat, type. Throughout, McGinniss kept picking up hints of the shape of things to come from the candidate's aides: discussions of how this or that network was subtly shading its coverage of Nixon in unfavorable ways, threats to bring this or that network chairman (NBC was particularly in disfavor) to Washington after the election and ask him some embarrassing questions, with just the hint of license revocation for his owned and operated stations if things did not improve. Even before the election we were but two or three steps from the threats of IRS audits for opponents, the infamous enemies list, of a few years later.

Of course, Nixon won a squeaker, having almost snatched defeat from the jaws of victory with a campaign that, finally, seemed too well-managed, too antiseptic while Hubert Humphrey, who was to say that the biggest mistake of his political life was his failure to learn to use television, plugged along, inept, windy, but at least authentic. And four years later Nixon had it made—even Nixon couldn't figure out a way to lose to George McGovern. What he could manage, as a substitute, was a way to dishonor himself permanently—as it seemed at the time. And people kept wondering why. Why, with the only question of the campaign being how large his landslide might be, why would he countenance Watergate?

But the answer is obvious. Trusting nothing, he could not even trust good fortune. Even at this late date he was not convinced that the heart of his emptiness would not be penetrated by the press. But where once he might have feared to use illegal means to secure his last advantage, now he was President. He could order up his plumbers, and, as he thought, cover up their doings ("Well, when a President does it, that means it is not illegal," he would later say). As it had with Johnson, the office granted him the opportunity to exercise, without restraint, his darker impulses, for like a movie star's entourage, a president's retinue contains no one who will deny him his whims. On the contrary, all are there assembled to cater to those whims, and more, to anticipate them. But darker impulses be damned; he should have recalled his first instinct, which was to fear the press, guess that among its numbers there might be a couple of reporters with nothing to lose, everything to gain, by investigating the odd occurrences at Democratic National Committee headquarters. Hubris. Star tripping. The follies. That is what undid him.

His immediate successor, Gerald Ford, never having dreamed the great dream, having thus the true soul of the hack, need not long detain us. Dagwood Bumstead in the White House. Shuffling down to the kitchen to make his own snacks, joining good-naturedly in the laughter at his own clumsiness, he was like one of those characters in a thirties movie who wakes up one day to find that a rich uncle has left him a few million and then has the good grace not to change his simple ways just because he happens to find himself living in a mansion. We attached ourselves to him in the simplest possible way, as a man acting out our simplest fantasies. And when, after a couple of years, we determined he had had all the fun and good luck we could stand, we unmaliciously turned him out and wished him well. Time to get back to reality.

More or less. "We've got the biggest star in television. Jimmy Carter may be the biggest television star of all time." The speaker was one

Barry Jagoda, media advisor to the President. This was the time of euphoria, a few months after Carter had taken office. His interviewer Richard Reeves wondered, as the comparisons with Johnny Carson and Walter Cronkite rolled on, if the Man might not burn out, become overexposed. The Milton Berle phenomenon was not exactly unknown.

No, no, no. "He is the first television President. He looks normal on television, natural; most of all he's *comfortable.*" The secret? "Television has become a regular part of his life, as natural as anything else in his life. It's not a big deal. That's what we set out to do; to make television neutral." Jagoda passed on the remarkable thought that there is no such thing as overexposure on television. "You are only overexposed when you run out of good ideas on how to use television."

But, of course, the Man was not a natural. He seemed hushed and pinched with reverence for his own success, or perhaps his born-again status. And, besides, there are limits to what a president can do on TV. The news keeps an anchorperson fresh; his writers and his guests keep Carson fresh. But you can't freshen up a president by putting him on "Battle of the Network Stars" or off-casting him as a rapist on the "Movie of the Week." You can tell him to put on a sweater when he's making his thermostat speech. You can send him to the mountaintop to reexamine his soul and then have him come back down and inform everybody that the trouble with his soul lies with them. But somehow the sourness and the whininess keep coming through. And the provinciality. His Southernness, therefore his "otherness" for most Americans, kept coming through. Piety, careerism and a darkling soul—what an exotic puzzlement that crowd was—the hard-mouthed mother, the Bible-thumping sister, the ne'er-do-well brother. What kept springing to mind was the Snopeses: *The Hamlet, The Mansion, The Town,* and now, at last, the concluding volume that even Faulkner had not dared to imagine, *The Capital,* last stop on their seemingly irresistible rise. But though they were like the great writer's inventions in their lack of lovability, they were unlike them in their lack of fascinating qualities. Their moral blather seemed too large for their souls and lacked the note of hypocritical falsity which might have given it a certain comic resonance. And so it went at every turn. Restraint in the Iranian crisis looked more like ineptitude and cowardice. The sulky withdrawal from the Moscow Olympics seemed an impotent response if the invasion of Afghanistan was indeed a threat to the status quo that Carter claimed it was—and mostly worked a hardship not on our enemies, but on a handful of American citizens for whom this competition represented a once-in-a-lifetime goal. Or, to put the matter simply, he had trouble matching means and ends, just as he had trouble matching the statesmanlike image he wished to project with the small-town arriviste's manner that he could not shake. He, too, came to believe that the press had done him in.

And then, at last, came the Actor. It was as if, in despair at seeing so many amateurs fail in the part, the public finally decided to turn it over to a professional, a professional of a peculiar sort. Ronald Reagan was not the sort of person who dreamed all his young life of being an actor. Far from it, he had been the kind of good-looking young hunk Hollywood swept up by the trainload in the thirties, hoping that one or two among the called would be chosen. It was a clean and decent job, better than most, and in his modest and agreeable way Reagan worked hard at it, owing his rise as much to his pleasantness around the studio as to gift—or to huge public demand. He was not a bad actor, though most of his movies are indifferent, but he was not a good one either. Just competent. One was always pleased to see him turn up in something like *King's Row* or *The Hasty Heart*—better than William Lundigan, let's say. On the other hand, he was not a Brando type either, someone discomfiting or dangerous. There was no obsessive search for behavioral truth in him, nothing unbalanced or unbalancing. His politics might have veered, over his lifetime, from left to right, but his personality was always middle-of-the road, the kind that wears well over the years. It is interesting, for example, that at seventy-two he still projected something boyish. Even age did not unduly affect him, and people marveled indulgently at his splendid hairline. The right had finally found a representative who was not scary. One imagined he would be to the great presidents what, let us say, Ronald Reagan had been to the great stars of his generation, the Grants and Tracys and Cagneys—a not unpleasant alternative when one of their pictures was not playing.

And so, up to now, it has been. He has accomplished little, but he has also offended little. And he has brought back just a touch of show biz swank to Washington. Nothing awful will have to be undone when he departs, and the temptation to showy initiative in foreign affairs, so attractive to presidents who wish to place their mark on history, has been entirely lacking. His anticommunism, for example, is far more ritualistic than Kennedy's: he will make no quagmires. And no Watergates, either, for he long since possessed the public affection Nixon ached for and has no worry that the press will alienate it. Nor has he so far made any ringing calls on the citizenry for heroic exertions or sacrifices. His basic, conservative constituency complains that his foreign policy lacks strenuousness where the Red Menace is concerned while domestically he has moved disappointedly closer to the center than they thought he would. Actually, he reflects no ideology beyond the basic prejudices of his new rich friends and backers from the Sunbelt, and the largest imperative before him appears to be the easing of their economic path while continuing to be, like Willy Loman, "well-liked" by the public in general. In short, we now have, at last, a president who truly operates outside of history, who seems to understand that immortality is nowadays best obtained not through dreary political achievement but through the attainment of a celebrity so large that it dissipates only very slowly, in the process turning into beloved legend.

The model, again, is show biz, where we witnessed certain contemporaries of Reagan's—the Cagneys and Fondas and Grants—making that transition. Reagan, as a star, could not have made it—no AFI tributes for him, not even a special Oscar. Logically, what he had to look forward to was more corporate spokesmanship, cameos in not very distinguished movies, maybe, God help him, episodic television and the dinner theaters. Instead, as if by a miracle, he was granted the role of a lifetime, a role he can produce and direct himself, with no interference from Jack Warner, a role that consists very largely of those favorite actor's moments, entrances and exits, most ceremoniously stated. His business with us is really no more than to convey his enormous pleasure in the part, and his gratitude for being allowed to play it. He must understand that he need do nothing from here on out to assure himself of posterity's continuing interest, for the big thing has already been accomplished, namely that a man of his peculiar profession has finally succeeded to the Oval Office.

This represents an epochal change in our perception of the nature and duties of the presidency, a semiconscious coming to grips with its true nature. A few years ago the common wisdom about permitting a rich man to hold office was that his wealth offered a form of assurance against corruption; having no need to steal, he would not be tempted. It seems possible now that a similar thought operates in the case of

Reagan; that it makes sense to elect to high office a man who has had the experience of stardom, and thus is inured to its ups and downs. And so far, it must be said, it has worked out. It is true that Reagan is heard occasionally to grump about the treatment of his national programs by the press and television, with their tendency to accentuate the negative. But the angry outbursts—and the paranoic withdrawals of a Johnson, a Nixon, a Carter—are missing from his performance. Like every actor he has reason to understand the show biz adage "When you're hot you're hot, when you're not you're not," and to understand that both conditions are subject to change almost without notice and for no very logical reason. Over a long career at his level one learns to ride out these ups and downs with a certain equanimity. All politics and principles aside, one could not, these days, ask for a more suitable President. If personality tests were a requisite for the job, his would be the ideal profile on which to base the exam. As his smashing victory in 1984 proved.

Consider the handicaps he overcame. One had imagined, for example, a continuing longing for a figure a trifle more classical in his fatherliness than Reagan or any recent president has been. Patriarchy (of a socially acceptable kind, that is) has not come easy to any of them and Reagan lacks that full measure of reassuring qualities that people still like to find in their presidents. A little too much he and his clan seem like the family up the hill who did rather better than the rest of us expected them to do, but who have not yet achieved that sureness of taste and solidity of manner that we still like to believe should follow in the wake of success and comfortable wealth. He is, after all, a divorced man, and though we have progressed sufficiently since 1952 that this does not actually cost a candidate votes, as it did Adlai Stevenson, it is slightly discomfiting, particularly since the children have grown up to seem a trifle unstable. Then there was the Nancy problem. Up to a point, she is useful to Reagan politically in that she is both grimly spendthrift and prissily pretentious, with a taste for expensive wardrobe and decor that bedazzles the impressionable and irritates the envious, which is also valuable because she directs ire away from her husband and onto herself. The fact that she continues to practice the traditional show biz art of trading the promotional value of wearing some designer frock for a break on its price hardly smacks of corruption, however much the press once made of it. It is difficult, indeed, to see how the course of clean government is diverted because one homosexual or another gains her favor. What should have been unambiguously a detriment to the President's re-election campaign, her propensity for backseat driving, made highly visible when she was caught by the cameras prompting his reply to a question at one point in the campaign, was, if anything, passed over more lightly than her adventures among the couturiers.

And that should not have been. For the incident should have reinforced in everyone's mind the largest question about the personality of a man whose entire career had been based on the assertion of an agreeable personality. That, of course, was whether or not age was beginning to dim that personality, diminishing his capacity to effectively deploy his only known asset as a statesman. Thereafter, of course, his somewhat befuddled performance in his first debate with Walter Mondale, his only slightly more creditable one in their second engagement, taken together with his long record of faulty memory for facts and figures, should have sent a tremor of fear through any reasonably senescent electorate, should have stirred memories, perhaps, of the stricken Woodrow Wilson, virtually helpless to intervene while his wife and his White House staff ruled in his stead. Or if that history was too ancient, surely the tragic image of FDR in his last term, visibly failing, clearly incapacitated to some immeasurable degree, should have come to mind. One does not suggest—certainly does not hope—that such a fate awaits Ronald Wilson Reagan. But equally one must think that however pleasant the majority finds him to be in his projected person, some recognition that he was, at his age, in his position, more than usually susceptible to the ills that aging flesh is heir to, should have become manifest to large numbers of people.

But, as the returns demonstrated, that was not to be. Even though poll after poll showed large numbers of the citizenry disagreeing with him on many of the most significant issues of the campaign, they could not bear to face the future without The Great Communicator (as he had long since been styled) beaming into their living rooms on the nightly news—even as a senile shadow of his former self. In the divorcement of the election's results—a landslide victory—from any discernible connection with ideological realities—there was no vivid evidence of a profound shift in the nation's mood on the issues—it seemed we had reached a turning point so clearly marked that even a professional politician could not miss it. A few days after the election Walter Mondale was heard to sadly muse: "I think you know I've never really warmed up to television, and in fairness to television, it's never really warmed up to me. I don't believe it's possible anymore to run for President without the capacity to build confidence and communications every night. It's got to be done that way."

Not bad. It has taken only a quarter century for this simple, basic truth to dawn on him, on his generation of politicians. But one should not be too hard on Mondale. It is hard for everyone in politics to abandon his or her traditional habits of mind. As the Reagan rout proceeded on election night, television turned to ideologically balanced panels of pundits to assess the damages, and it was amusing to watch the right wing attempt to reclaim the balloting from personality, attempt to cast it as a national embrace of such ideas as their man could lay claim to. If the leftists, who saw it correctly as a purely personal victory for the incumbent, struck the observer as closer to the mark, one still had to concede their hidden agenda, which was to assert the viability of the old liberal consensus. All it needed, they implied, was a front man as adorable as their opponents had stumbled upon. What no one wanted to admit was that both ideologies were in essence irrelevant to almost everyone, that henceforth personality would be everything in electoral politics.

What was wanted now by both parties was a leader whose image people could live with through many a long season, someone who would never abrade, never whine or bully, never wear out his welcome. Reagan had proved to be just the genial host the great American talk show—which is what the evening news is in essence—had been looking for without knowing that it was. And the general facing up to that fact in the wake of the 1984 election may well come to seem in retrospect a good thing. We may, at last, begin to honestly face up to the way we are.

But we are not yet arrived at perfection with Reagan. There is something a little unsettling about the obvious second-rateness, the unseriousness of his show biz past. One wonders if he could pull us through a genuine crisis if one should arrive. One wonders if, in such an event, we might not yearn for someone with the same soothing capacities but with a little more solidity, sobriety in his background. And one wonders, too, if such a figure would not be even more appealing than Reagan in a national election. There is, one cannot help but think, still one more short step to take down the road toward a perfect politics of personality. And the minute that thought occurs, one begins to wonder if Walter Cronkite, if his soul has dark nights, regrets having been born just a shade too soon, before he, or we, could quite imagine him in a part yet grander than the one he so admirably played.

Remember that he emerged just when we needed him, not long after Eisenhower's retirement from office, as a man we could turn to for reassurance as successive presidents failed us. If he was not quite the father figure of our yearnings, then he was an excellent substitute, an admirable stepfather. He was, indeed, not just a network's anchorman, but the nation's, granting to his job title metaphorical overtones, since for many he was, indeed, an anchor, preventing them (or so it seemed) from being wrecked by the gale force winds of change, or by the ugly riptides of reality as they tore at us in the past two decades: "the most trusted man in America," according to a survey, and with good reason. We knew that he worked hard at his job—arriving at his desk early in the morning and staying straight through to airtime, shaping what seemed a calmly accurate, carefully objective portrayal of the day's events. Yet we knew, as well, that he was not without his human sympathies—you could hear the anxiety in his voice when an astronaut was in trouble, the sorrow when a great figure passed from the scene, the struggle to suppress his anger and do his job correctly when the Iranian hostages were taken. He did not abuse his welcome in our homes anymore than he abused his power when he was invited into the presence of the mighty. His private life—what little we know of it —was exemplary, his interests—tennis and sailing—were suitable to a responsible figure, tony, but not exotic. Above all, he was not an ironist. He exemplifed the solid value of small-city America, where he began learning his trade as a wire service reporter.

But Cronkite's biography is significant only to the degree that it presents no facts at odds with his image. The main thing is that if Daddy were to disappear, this is the sort of man we would like Mommy to find as a replacement—which is, of course, more or less what happened when Cronkite came into our lives, not long after the last great presidential good father left the scene. Like all wise stepfathers, Cronkite seemed to sense that he could not shape us, lead us, inspire us as a natural father could. He could do only what he so responsibly and carefully did—act as a discreet example, a steadying influence, a benign and supportive presence in our lives during a rough passage. It is no wonder that, as the 1980 election loomed before us, another poll showed a large, wistful percentage of the population would be glad to see Cronkite declare for the presidency. It is difficult to imagine such an endorsement coming to any other television figure that we yet know about. Certainly his visibly ambitious, rather abrasive replacement, Dan Rather, is not going to gather that kind of affection to him—no matter how many sleeveless sweaters he dons to warm and soften his image—and, not incidentally, improve his ratings. Of course, Cronkite as candidate rather than objective commentator would soon have dissipated the affection that had gathered around him by the necessity of taking positions bound to offend this or that element of his constituency. Or would he have? Perhaps he might have managed a sort of Eisenhowerish remoteness from the dailiness of politics, found a way of beaming benignly down on the hurly-burly of the political trading floor, as he did when he so soberly contemplated our political conventions—"old iron ass" as he was sometimes called by colleagues. About this we will never know, since—further proof of his wisdom—he politely quashed this yearning discussion of a possible candidacy, the value of which was mainly symbolic, a reflection, among others, of the quiet but persistent unease that has grown up over electoral politics in the last two decades.

"Unease?" The word is too mild. "Indifference" comes closer to the mark. We have reached a point where even in a presidential year only slightly more than half of those registered in the nation vote—and, of course, in all other elections far less than half so trouble themselves. We have a two-party system all right, but as Gore Vidal says, one is the party that votes, the other is the party that doesn't. As a result, "presidential elections are a bit like the Grammy Awards, where an industry of real interest to very few people honors itself fulsomely . . . on prime-time television. Since the party that does not vote will never switch on, as it were, the awards ceremony, the party that does vote has to work twice as hard to attract attention to get a rating."

But the situation is actually worse than that. Assuming a relatively close race, the winner gets just a little more than half the votes cast, which means that he is the choice of approximately one quarter of the electorate. Another way of putting it is that *all* our presidents are, theoretically, minority presidents. Talk about symbolic leadership! Practically speaking, it is the only kind of leader a modern American president can be, for given the inertness and disaffection of the electorate there is no ultimate force he can mobilize, no effective power of public opinion he can summon in order to persuade Congress that it will suffer dire consequences if it fails to follow him on some issue or other.

Of course, in former times that would not have made so much difference, since party discipline could always be invoked to sway significant votes: the promise of a favor here, the threat of withholding one there worked wonders when proffered by a master like Roosevelt or Johnson. But television—and electoral reform—have diminished that unwritten presidential power greatly. National candidates cannot yet abandon their party labels, but candidates for all the offices below the presidential level can and do play down their affiliations. There are recorded instances of congressional candidates failing to print that once-vital identification, "Republican" or "Democrat," in their campaign literature, while television spots are now almost entirely identified as being sponsored by this or that bland-sounding citizens committee. Politicians are nowadays able to change party affiliations without fear of effective reprisal and in places where it is legally permissible they run on more than one party's ticket with equanimity. Meanwhile, the effect of well-meant, antibossist reforms—our proliferating primaries, the funding of campaigns not by wealthy individuals whom a party's leaders can control, but by ad hoc political action groups—further diminishes the number of persuasive weapons a leader has at its command.

This is particularly disastrous now, since the problems of a modern technological society are so complex and so delicate. Literally dozens of ideas—some of them quite good—are afloat, have been afloat for years, and are worth trial applications to such persistently intractable issues as energy conservation, inflation, taxation, environmental management, unemployment. But the political parties are unable to perform their traditional functions, which are to organize possibilities and to exert discipline in aid of their choices, presenting clear-cut alternatives which, finally, their candidates can symbolize for the public. A young congressman is quoted in *Time,* "We get to Washington and we're not prone to look for leadership the way they used to; we don't owe anybody anything." The Washington *Post*'s political analyst, David Broder, writes: "The individualistic instincts in this society have now become much more powerful in our politics than the majoritarian impulse. It is easier and more appealing for all of us— leaders as well as followers—to separate ourselves from the mass than it is to seek out the alliances that can make us part of a majority."

One must be careful, of course, not to romanticize the years when the parties were all-powerful. They were obviously prone to corruption, crudity, and compromise. But the situation now is worse. From his exile Richard M. Nixon comments with sour acuity that "television is to news what bumper stickers are to philosophy." But there is no doubt that television has further vulgarized the already vulgarized process by which ideas are translated into political action. By going always for the shrillest advocate of a program or policy and then juxtaposing with him its most outraged and outrageous opponent, it parodies, in a thirty- or forty-second spot, the best traditions of democratic debate. "It excludes the third or fourth choice," Adlai E. Stevenson III said, having given up his Senate seat at least in part because he no longer wished to participate in a process of this kind. The media in general—not just television—he added, "establishes the issues and then reduces them to simple and sometimes meaningless formulations."

He does not mention another factor, recently isolated by political scientists. It might be termed the Idiot's Delight Phenomenon. It is based on the fact that 20 to 30 percent of the audience for the nightly news broadcasts use these shows as their sole source of information about current affairs. They read no newspapers or magazines, and they represent the low end of the scale educationally and economically— emotionally, too, one may speculate, since we know that the incidence of mental illness is highest in this class too. We may also be pretty certain that they do not vote, since voting on a more or less regular basis is essentially a middle-class phenomenon, based on the fact that members of this class continue to take their civics lessons seriously and thus cling most closely to the political illusion. Be that as it may, Professor Michael J. Robinson, a political scientist at Catholic University, identifies the denizens of the socioeconomic lower depths as the "inadvertent audience" for news, people who, before the advent of television, were stable in their opinions and passive in their political behavior. Now, even though they don't vote, even though they are precisely the Grammy Awards audience that Vidal is talking about, they actually exert what might be called an "inadvertent influence" on political life. They are, to begin with, the least common denominator at which news programs must be aimed, for Nielsen naturally includes them in its ratings. Since like all the rest of television, the news shows are dependent on the numbers for success, it is understood that this lower third must not be allowed to become bored and start switching channels. Lively pictures and pleasing personalities—that's the ticket to their contentment. So, through the years, television news drifts ever downward in its aspirations and its appeals, particularly at the local level with its "action news teams" miming the busy toughness of the city room in an old Cagney movie—and, between stories, the kidding camaraderie of those movies as well. But if Nielsen picks up these absurdities, so do the other pollsters when they are testing the waters on other matters, and Daniel Yankelovich, the public opinion sampler, attributes the sudden, violent gusts and eddies that blow through his polls to this volatile, perspectiveless mass. And, of course, the politicians, no less than the TV people, must play to that mass since they cannot be certain that they don't vote (almost no one, queried by a pollster, will admit to that immorality). Thus the imperative to keep the dullards pacified. Thus the tendency for the political personality to detach itself from close identification with any specific issue, to instead be rather vaguely connected with vaguely defined positions, stressing rubbery image over concrete positions. One keeps one's options open, eschewing only that dislikability which is bound to come when one takes a stand on an issue firm enough to cost one a few points in the polls. In this context a president like Reagan, who maintains his personal popularity in the polls while the respondents reject such policies as they identify with him, becomes not an anomaly, but, it appears, a historic inevitability. And the little Cronkite flirtation of 1980 begins to seem a notion only historical minutes ahead of its time. All that is required for the next Cronkite to be taken seriously is for the parties to decline a bit more, so that in their disarray they will reach out for a figure whose detachment from their traditions (and from whatever transitory issues are agitating people at the time) is perceived not as a false disadvantage but as a distinct advantage. Thus, it seems, everything Ellul theorized in far-off France becomes a reality in too-near America.

But, it will be argued, things continue to get done politically. In the two decades from Kennedy to Reagan the protection of law has been extended into areas previously undreamed of. Begin with the mighty effort to secure in law, if not in every prejudiced soul, the civil rights of blacks and then note how those rights, by virtually automatic extension, have been guaranteed to other minorities. Women, the handicapped, the consumer, the homosexual, even that impersonal entity, the environment, have all benefited by increased concern not just for their rights, but for their well-being. The facts are undeniable, even if, in the event, we have come to see that this or that specific protection has had this or that unintended social effect that may now require some new remedy.

To which one enters this mild demurrer, "Yes but . . ." Yes but, much of what has been accomplished has not been done in legislative assemblies but in the law courts, to which in despair those who are aggrieved, or who merely think they are, turn when the stasis of formal politics frustrates them. The consequences of this endless litigiousness is, of course, social policy made without benefit of true social compact. A highly specific law, or a specific judicial precedent is tortuously—not to say, torturedly—applied in areas where no one intended it to be applied by the courts' interpretations. Whereupon those whose way of life or way of business is afflicted by this, as they see it, sneak attack on them, apply, in their turn, for relief. The controversies over school busing, affirmative action in employment, all the outrages of reverse discrimination, are the most visible signs of this process in action, and we must, finally, ask ourselves if, in terms of cost effectiveness, not to mention moral effectiveness, the price has proved too high. And, beyond that, there is the whole question of whether the defects of laissez-faire in the regulation of commerce has not been converted into another sort of defect, that of excessive regulation, which greatly burdens an already struggling economy.

But set aside the whole matter of legislation by judicial fiat. Turn to the matter of legislation by legislation. In rough terms, the system now works like this: a need is felt. Agitation in the form of a series of media events occurs, and these may take forms ranging from the publication of a well-publicized book to confrontational debates on televised forums to marches, rallies, sit-ins, picketings that may or may not become riotous (though the threat must always be implied or the television cameras will ignore the event). Out of these excursions and incursions symbolic leaders will arise, possibly spontaneously, more likely through design. They then become the spokespeople for the cause, organizing principles now being replaced by organizing principals. It is their duty to be, in their persons, the ongoing symbols of what purports to be a cause that is widely embraced, since the cry for justice seems to be arising on all sides. The basic methodology here was pioneered by the civil rights movement but now it is employed in far more dubious enterprises, which manage things rather in the manner of clever movie directors, who by selectively employing their cameras make a crowd of two hundred lackadaisical extras look like a determined army of ten thousand. Ultimately, a legislative response is made in the form of some placatory and piecemeal set of laws. This does not cause the agitators to disband, but it does, for a while, dampen their outcries. And begin the process of civilizing them as Washington understands the term. By which one means they open an office there and convert themselves into lobbyists, jostling at the public trough just like the more traditional members of the tribe, the representatives of big steel, big labor, and all the other seekers of the more customary political favors.

In essence what this process does is convert what may or may not be moral fervor (but always *looks* like it) into what amounts to a commercial transaction, known around Congress as "throwing money at problems." No single such action can break a rich nation, and nearly all that we have witnessed in the last two decades were, as Theodore White says, "passed through Congress in the name of virtue. No single program could be denounced, vetoed or buried in committee without the objectors being shamed for their indifference to the call of conscience." But, as White makes clear in the last, sad volume of his *Making of the President* series—a set of books which began in tones of authoritative not to say sententious hope with an account of Kennedy's election, and ends in bewilderment and hurt withdrawal with his account of Reagan's victory—the piling of entitlement on entitlement renders government more and more unmanageable. It is not just that taxes rise to unconscionable levels, though surely that contributes to the intelligent citizen's disaffection with government. No, what he senses, and what is most profoundly discomfiting, is a disarticulation between what he perceives as desirable first priorities and what the politicians are squandering money and energy upon.

Most of these truly major issues are nonconfrontational and, being thus essentially undramatizable in media terms, they have been largely ignored over the last decades. It is only recently, as the abstract has become concrete, that is, as these economic issues have translated themselves into pain that the ordinary citizen feels in the region of his wallet, that the feeling of disaffection has been incoherently vocalized. We are talking here about a nation whose per capita income has dropped to ninth in the world, whose real discretionary income has declined some 18 percent in the last decade, whose industrial productivity grows at the slowest pace in the Western world, which has faced years of persistently high inflation and unemployment while watching the government add to the inflationary burden by mindlessly wasting billions on a defense establishment that, paradoxically, grows less and less able to respond effectively to the realistic challenges it faces (if the Vietnam War proved that on a large scale, the attempt to rescue the Iranian hostages proved it on a small one). Finally, between the sacrosanct military budget, service on the national debt, social security, and the rest of the mandates and entitlements already mentioned, at least 57 percent of the annual $600 billion federal budget is literally irreducible—beyond any sort of effective, rational control by our elected representatives.

Meanwhile, irrelevant clamor whether it is raised by advocates of the so-called Right to Life or capital punishment (how curious that the same people often believe in these seemingly antithetical causes) or the school prayer amendment or ERA—all of the many incantatory remedies for our malaise—drowns out even such hesitant discussion of the real issues of governance as takes place. The media is distracted, *we* are distracted, by every bright bit of efflorescence as drifts past the camera eye. While the monster in Washington grows like the Blob. Some of Theodore White's statistics are crushingly relevant in this regard: the social regulatory agencies (as opposed to the older regulatory agencies designed to patrol one or another of the large industries whose activities have major social consequences) grew from twelve in 1970 to eighteen in 1980, and their budgets increased in the process, from $1.4 billion to $7.5 billion as they searched in every nook and cranny of the society for malefactors. Meantime, the Code of Federal Regulations grew from some 54,000 pages, to nearly 100,000 pages. The right, expensive lawyer might be able to guide the questing citizen through this rain forest of regulation, but it requires a rich person, more likely a rich corporation, to make the effort. Here again Ellul's words rise up to haunt us. It indeed requires a supreme leap of faith (or, conversely, extraordinary stupidity) to maintain the illusion that any elected official can take or maintain control over a bureaucracy of this magnitude.

We have, in short, reached a point where we are, in any sense that the framers of the Constitution, or for that matter, Franklin D. Roosevelt, Harry S Truman, or even Lyndon B. Johnson would understand, ungovernable. Which is to say that even the old balancing acts in which the compromised interests of one group could be traded off against the half-interest of another group, with each side emerging manageably dissatisfied, but with an inch-by-inch progress toward a slightly improved social order the result, no longer work. Nor can presidential personality be effectively employed anymore to ease this process. Personality in the age of television can be employed only to defend and enhance itself in a public life that is a riot of personalities trying to stay fresh in a world bent on trying to freeze-dry them, and thus improve their shelf life a bit.

Gore Vidal, raised a populist but pulled up by his own elegant bootstraps to the status of intelligent dilettante, insists this is all the result of a conspiracy. In whose interest is it, at last, that government be unable to govern? In whose interest is it, finally, to convert the political process into a long-running television show, diverting the attention of the electorate from thieving substance to gaudy shadows? The answer is obvious (to him at least)—the bankers, the corporate elite, who profit from a state of affairs that is anarchy by another name. They, after all, are as well organized as the government and the citizenry are disorganized and they are, uniquely, a single-issue constituency in a world where only single-issue constituencies profit from our disarray. Since their single issue is profitability, and since their profits appear to grow in all atmospheres short of world war or worldwide depression, both of which ultimate disasters they seem able to fend off, it is clear that the succession of slightly smaller disasters we have all endured these many years, serves them well—as a cover for their machinations if nothing else.

It may be so. One does not embrace Vidal's thought fully only because it is impossible to believe, given the complexity of the world and the perversity, ennui, and ultimate stupidity of the people who think they are running it, that the corporate world has the wit and the will even to orchestrate chaos so that it is beneficial to it. One imagines it profiting more by happy accident than by dark design.

In this, as in so much that has preceded it politically over the past two decades, it may be that Theodore White again serves as the intelligent liberal's tribune. There was, when he began his chronicles of our electoral process, a hearty certainty about him. He knew how the business worked, how its necessary arrangements were arrived at, in the grungy yet glamorous inner world of electoral politics. But, in 1976, he fell unaccountably silent, later admitting that he had been forced to retreat from the campaign trail in confusion because he "no longer knew how to string the stories together in any way that connected with history," such was the effect of television primarily, the media in general, on our electoral mores. In 1980 he was back at it, but he was a sad heart at the supermarket when the new supermen came calling, and somewhere in the middle of this campaign he retreated again, aware that "I could sit at home and learn as much or more about the frame of the campaign as I could on the road."

The result is a final book suffused with melancholy, a sense that a great tradition—or at least a great hope—was ending, its dying captured in the literally unearthly hues of the cathode tube; a sense that, perhaps, the brave hopes we had entertained such a short time ago had all been imprisoned and disarmed by the illusionists of politics, whose first victims have been themselves, in that even the old actor who now commands the tube no longer knows he is acting. Alas, White, with his intimate knowledge of how the game used to work and how it is working now, knows, and verges on bitterness as he contemplates the practical impotence of the politics of illusion in a world that actually requires statecraft of a high order if we are once again going to be able to manage our lives and our future. From the far coast, Gore Vidal calls for a new constitutional convention and a rewrite that will reflect not only the postcolonial reality but the postmodernist one as well. It is good of him to clothe the proposal in his customarily jaunty prose. But the despair that underlies it is not different from White's. Or mine. Or anyone's who takes a contemplative step backward from chaos only to find himself teetering on the brink of nothingness, voicing black humor at the edge of a black hole.

SIX

Heroic Figures, Heroic Numbers

I am thumbing idly through *People* when suddenly my attention is arrested by a name one does not expect to find there—and not merely because he is an acquaintance. For he is neither movie star nor television personality, neither sports star nor psychotherapist peddling some avocado oil cure to pour on our troubled spirits. No, he is a scholar of impeccable credentials and achievements, the author of studies in poetic meter, eighteenth-century prosody and Augustan rhetoric. And, most significant to me, he is the author of a work about the prose and poetry of World War I that combines brilliant critical analysis, balanced cultural history, and a subtle emotional engagement between author and subject that makes for the rarest of literary enterprises, a book with footnotes and bibliography that can yet move a reader to tears.

But more startling than the name in the headline is the almost unrecognizable face in the portrait beneath it. For it peers out from beneath a soldier's helmet liner that appears to be shellacked like General Patton's was during the second Great War. The mouth is turned down radically in a cartoon scowl, and in the background is a copy of the American revolutionary war flag with the snake and the legend Don't Tread on Me. The accompanying text quotes the author rather churlishly on such subjects as his recent divorce, his experiment with homosexuality, his dismay with the present state of American life and culture. He comes off as several things I am pretty sure he is not: misanthropist and misogynist, bully boy and whiner.

I am at first dismayed by this performance. How can a man who has devoted his life to making fine distinctions now present his views and his experiences so vulgarly? And what can he hope to gain by this public display of his mid-life crisis? To be sure, his next book seems to have somewhat more popular appeal than his previous productions— but not that much more. It hardly seems to have much potential among the mouth breathers. But upon reflection I am less certain of my response. In my few dealings with this man I realize that it has pleased me to play the worldling and that I had some need of my own to see him as a purist, austerely sequestered in his academic grove, safe from the temptations of commerce and self-display. Doubtless when I knew him he still found this role, and the manner of life that both sustained and in some measure dictated it, gratifying—perhaps not least because of the simple (simpleminded?) respect it generated in the likes of me. But as his books show, he is particularly adept at discerning how our inner lives and our behavior are conditioned by shifts in the flow of broad social and intellectual currents. I now speculate that instead of writing one of these insights he was acting it out. Or acting out of it.

We have reached the point—or my subject and I imagine we have reached the point—where the consolation that traditionally sustained the cloistered scholar and the unappreciated artist in their poverty and isolation no longer appears to be operative. Or if still operative in certain tasteful circles, then no longer worth considering in light of the larger and more immediate gratifications one observes others, no more gifted, grabbing. That consolation was the judgment of history, which, until roughly the day before yesterday was commonly understood to right all wrongs by bestowing immortality—or anyway, a decent post-humous regard for a few years—on the artist or the scholar who lived by his own principles and did not truckle to fashion or mammon or the Establishment in his field. Did not—to borrow a phrase virtually unspoken anywhere in my hearing since the fifties—"sell out." Particularly did not sell out simply to get his name in the papers.

This was, I think, the last remaining article of faith among those of us who came of age late in the modernist age, a period that ended, suitably enough, with an unacknowledged whimper. It was replaced by what we are now pleased to think of as the postmodernist age. Among the several blessings of this new epoch is this: it is really impossible to imagine history as a responsible judge, a final arbiter of our efforts, if only because it is difficult to imagine the history of the future being written to traditional standards.

To oversimplify the matter, it is difficult today for any reasonable senescent person to believe he can assert his claims on posterity solely through a combination of decorum and good works. It has been obvious for some time that history's judgments will be heavily influenced by the secondary sources, as it were, by the weight and shrewdness of one's publicity, by one's ability to turn oneself from artist into phenomenon or symbol, from mere intellectual into intellectual force.

The first writer to notice this was, perhaps, George Gissing, that gifted, devoted, and largely unrewarded novelist of the late nineteenth century. His masterpiece, *New Grub Street,* published in 1891, was the most powerful early acknowledgment of the fact that in the new world of the mass audience the qualities he personified carried with them no assurance of success, or even of a decent livelihood. His novel, indeed, has a continuing power to move—and instruct—the modern writer, or, indeed, anyone attempting to survive without subsidy or inheritance as a serious practitioner of any artistic enterprise. Among the inhabitants of *New Grub Street* he numbers one Jasper Milvain, a mildly talented but extremely shrewd journalist, who watches with ironic dismay as more gifted literary purists fail while he goes from strength to strength. His success is based purely on the perception that in an age of mass literacy, literature must become a commodity and must, like any other commodity, be sold through advertising, the most effective form of which is, in the case of artists, personal publicity. As he says: "If I am an unknown man, and publish a wonderful book, it will make its way very slowly, or not at all. If I become a known man, publish that very same book, its praise will echo over both hemispheres. I should be within the truth if I had said 'a vastly inferior book,' but I am in a bland mood at present . . . *You have to become famous before you can secure the attention which would give fame.*"

Perhaps Gissing, perhaps all of us contemplating this subject, ignore isolated earlier phenomena like Lord Byron or, to name a writer with whom he had a particular affinity, Charles Dickens, but in a way that is just the point; they were isolated, no machinery was in place to turn out new sensations on an almost daily basis. In the late nineteenth century, whether we are talking about English writers or French painters, the machinery by which sensation and scandal or just plain interesting reviews could be magnified and broadcast, namely, a greatly expanded and generally apprehensible press, was in place. And a little more than three decades after Gissing wrote, publicity became crucial to success, not only of the immediate variety, but of the long term sort as well.

Think a moment. Think how a distinctly minor writer named F. Scott Fitzgerald has become not only a major academic-critical industry in the relatively few decades since his death—but a major symbol of his age and of the writer's condition in a modern society as well. He did not achieve this exemplary status on the basis of his one elegant novella, one ambitious and strained longer work, a handful of polished short stories, and an unfinished last novel that was silly and poorly observed. He did not, in short, achieve exemplary status hunched over his typewriter, in splendid isolation. One wonders: if the *People* photographer came around, would Scott and Zelda have climbed into a bathtub as big as the Ritz, pulled the bubble bath up over themselves and, looking slightly abashed, damply submit to what has become the magazine's obligatory Fun Couple pose? Or suppose its reporters had stumbled upon Scott a few years later in Hollywood and had decided to work up a few "where are they now?" sniffles over his fallen state. Would Sheilah Graham have then been referred to as the writer's "main squeeze"? Who can say? One would not, however, bet confidently against these possibilities—not at a time when Nobel laureates in literature give their recipes to the New York *Times* Living Section. What one assuredly can say is that, whatever status literary historians of a traditional stripe assign Fitzgerald in the future, the historian of publicity will find in his career (and in those of a handful of his contemporaries on the cultural scene) a pioneering paradigm, the beginnings of a model that now holds controlling sway over the way we apprehend cultural work, which is primarily through cults of personality, through authorial image, and not, primarily, through the work itself, which is also why—putting the matter briefly and brutally—respected and respectable people like my friend appear in public wearing funny hats and telling us more than we need to know about their private lives and thoughts.

But we are, perhaps, getting ahead of ourselves. What we need to study is why serious individuals choose to engage in these strange rites. And that requires still more reference to that heavily discounted subject, history.

"To be modern is to experience personal and social life as a maelstrom, to find one's world and oneself in perpetual disintegration and renewal, trouble and anguish, ambiguity and contradiction: to be part of a universe in which all that is solid melts into air. To be a modern*ist* is to make oneself somehow at home in the maelstrom, to make its rhythms one's own, to move within the currents in search of the forms of reality, of beauty, of freedom, of justice, that its fervid and perilous flow allows."

One could find a similar quotation in any of a dozen—a hundred—sources. But these sentences from Marshall Berman's *All That Is Solid Melts into Air* are recent and felicitous and cover all the necessary ground. One notes an irony: that his long analysis of modernism is for most of its length an exercise in historicism. He does however make one point rather more conclusively than anyone else has until now, and by so doing begins the process of defining postmodernism. For when Berman relates the theories of Karl Marx to Robert Moses' brutal concrete realities, or the poetry of Baudelaire to the destruction —in the name of the public good—of the Bronx neighborhood in which he grew up, he is saying that the modernist sensibility has moved out of the salons and the literary journals and into the streets. That sense of life as a maelstrom, once pretty much the exclusive property of the intelligentsia and the artistic avant-garde and their hangers-on, has become, in some immeasurable degree, part of the common wisdom, the folk sense of the way things are. It has left the realm of ideas and entered the world of things, which we cannot perhaps touch, but which touch us all the time. The ambivalences of the war in Vietnam had something to do with spreading this knowledge of the way things really are. So did the failures of vast, apparently well-reasoned social programs to alleviate the ills they were supposed to cure. So did the assassinations. And Watergate. And the drug traffic. And the divorce rate. And naturally the Bomb and the Pill. The litany of our ailments is so familiar that one's fingers begin to throb in protest as one types it all out again. And it is germane to this discussion only because one wants to make this point: everyone is now, in some sense, a modernist—even those who have not heard the term, or who would not be caught dead using it. Our politics, our social order, our economic structure make it so.

This, of course, is stale news to the artistic and intellectual community, which as early as the turn of the century began predicting, (and practicing) the disintegration of its traditional forms, and with them the disintegration of traditional social forms. But the passage of this information from the category of (literally) privileged information to the status of folk wisdom has, for the serious artist or scholar, the most serious consequences. When the artist held this knowledge close and dear it was the source of his identity and of his power, and his puzzling annunciations and heroic renunciations were the stuff of legends—at least potentially. They set him apart from the mass and assured him (or so he might safely permit himself to imagine) fame everlasting.

A somewhat mythologized history of art—very supportive—was concocted. It showed that all great artists were unappreciated, scorned, and neglected when they first appeared—a condition that might pertain for much if not all of their lifetimes. "That is an absolute rule," wrote Zola, "to which there are no exceptions." But the distinguished art historian Francis Haskell begs leave to "repeat like a litany the names of Giotto and Giorgione, Parmigianino and Caravaggio, Watteau and David"—all of them, he says, throwing Zola's phrases back at him " 'great creators' who did *not* meet with 'strong resistance at the beginning of their career.' " A nice ironic point, that —but one that has never stayed the armies of the avant-garde from their mildly paranoid rounds.

Understandably so. For a life in art, no matter how conducted, is never easy. And there were compensations for the avant-garde in its isolation from the mainstream. In opposition there was identity. A member in good standing knew who he was because he knew what he was not. And a certain, manageable sort of fame often grew up around the leading figures of the leading edge. They had their salons and magazines, their publishers and theater groups. They had their knowing audience, whose members were generally well-heeled, influential socially and in their own professions and, above all, delighted to be permitted intimacy with a creative process grown increasingly, thrillingly, mysterious. That they were drawn largely from the very bourgeoisie to whose values the avant-gardists most loudly and frequently proclaimed their opposition was not an irony anyone chose to linger over for very long. By buying their way in, or if they were critics or publicists, toadying their way into close contact with the modernist creators, these hangers-on constituted themselves an elite. And, at least at the beginning of each new movement in art, a severely limited one, since every modernist development presents itself as an enigma and a controversy—and thus automatically limits its adherents to the self-chosen few.

It is in painting that this pattern presents itself most vividly. The critic and historian Harold Rosenberg was very clear on this point. "The esoteric nature of Cubism," he wrote, "gave rise to the modern art audience, composed of experts, intermediaries (or explainers), and a mass recruited through publicity and art education to react to whatever is presented to it as art. Thus Cubism inaugurated the enfolding of art creation within increasingly numerous layers of auxiliary professions, from showmen-curators to art-movie makers—a process accelerated to the point of near-suffocation by recent museum and foundation programs."

One does not wish to rush past this point quite as quickly as Rosenberg does. It is important to linger for a moment over the benefits the early modernists in all the arts derived from the condition he described, from being, to put the matter bluntly, big frogs in small ponds. One could in these semiprivate accommodations find rich emotional support and even, in many cases, sufficient financial support for a life in which a family might be maintained in respectable poverty while the artist proceeded with his work—without recourse to hack work or other equally debilitating jobs, like school teaching. The later life of James Joyce is exemplary in this regard. Indeed, in his final decade Joyce became well-known for his unknownness. Or should one say his unknowableness? So much so that when *Finnegans Wake* was published in 1939, *Time* made him a cover subject as a kind of reward for being so widely unread, so famously unreadable. One can, of course, think of analogous figures in all the other arts—poets, painters, composers—who came to symbolize for the large public the great offenses against the artistic proprieties, which included tonality in music, rhyme and meter in poetry, moral and narrative in prose, figures in the landscape of a canvas.

This was, one cannot help but think, a very agreeable kind of fame, fame without social responsibility and without obligation to anything but one's own work. In a curious way the life of the avant-gardist in the first half of the twentieth century was an extraordinarily protected one. He could depict the maelstrom without himself becoming involved in it. This is particularly true of the matter which we are here addressing, the matter of public self-presentation. We do not find a Joyce or a Schoenberg, an Eliot or a Miró indulging in the sort of public displays of private matters described at the beginning of this chapter. There were, of course, modernists who almost from the beginning had a taste for that sort of thing—or led lives that provided scandalous copy too good for the popular press to ignore; one thinks of Isadora Duncan, Frank Lloyd Wright, Picasso, Dali, among others. But they were not typical of their kind. It was much more typical to work obsessively at one's art, to present it in relatively obscure forums and leave the matter of explaining it and publicizing it, and oneself, to third parties who were specialists in work of that kind. These explicators could be trusted as intermediaries precisely because they did not function as critics in one important sense, did not, that is, question the underlying philosophy of an artist's work; they were entirely at one with it. These apologist-publicists were, in fact, quite like the artists they puffed, in that they operated with one eye ever cocked in posterity's directions and were not about to enter it as horrid examples— people who shared the earth with great men, shared the historic moment when a great movement began, and missed their importance. Or worse, sneered at it. The faintly comic immortality of a Hanslick linked forever to Wagner because he was the contemporary who not only didn't get it, but most loudly and persistently despised it, was not for them. Meanwhile, the artist could, if he chose (and many did), lead a quiet life, insulated from the hurly-burly by his acolytes and those busy agents of his fame and well-being who, having attached their fates to his, were every bit as eager as he was to see him succeed. The possibilities for corruption in this arrangement are endless and obvious; self-interest on the part of a critic is where conflict of interest begins.

Still, there were many advantages to this system, not the least of which was the way it cushioned the shock of the new. It required a certain amount of time—time measured in years, not months—for word of the latest thing to get around, to percolate through the society; and though there was never any lack of outrage over the latest avant-garde outrage, it tended not to reach the mass media and the mass public—or even the middlebrow public—as a traumatizing blow. There was time to absorb and adjust and generally keep one's wits about one, which is a pleasant way of doing business with the arts— helps to keep them distinct from the fashion industry. Far more important, however, was the fact that the artists themselves did not have to deal with the problems of overnight celebrity, overnight wealth, did not have to redefine themselves in terms more appropriate to movie stardom than to their line of work, which above all requires privacy and a lack of performance pressure for its pursuit.

Indeed, it is the principle argument of this chapter that although the forms of the old avant-garde community persist, especially when it comes to promulgating ideals and perhaps in certain economic arrangements, it no longer can, and no longer wants to, perform its old mediating functions. As a result, it has become the maelstrom of maelstroms. If one is yet uncertain about Vidal's dark belief that big business deliberately encourages political and social anarchy the better to sell products in the resulting vacuum, one has no doubt at all that this small business—the art market—profits mightily by the tactic, and may well be aware of what it is doing. It is clear also that there are consequences to this state of affairs that are both dangerous to our cultural life and, in some tragic instances, literally lethal to the artists themselves. We will come to those matters in a moment. Before we do, however, it is both interesting and profitable to trace the change in the way the avant-garde community has functioned in recent years. It is most clearly visible in the realm of painting. It is about that realm that the most acute commentary on this subject has been written.

Harold Rosenberg's little description of how the modern art audience was formed was accurate enough as far as it went. But it did not go far enough precisely because Rosenberg was perhaps the most prominent "explainer" of American avant-garde activities from the forties to the seventies, and he had a vested interest in pretending that the functioning of that community was essentially unchanged since the days of the Cubists, and also, of course, that he was himself an objective chronicler of its doings, when in fact he was one of the principle theorist-apologists for a particular school of work.

It remained for an outsider to present a more truthful, not to say wicked, portrait of the way things actually worked. This, of course, was Tom Wolfe, and his instrument was that funny and ferocious polemic, *The Painted Word.* In it he argued, with more persuasiveness than the art world could admit, that modern art, particularly after World War II, was created mainly at the inspiration of critical theory, thus reversing the customary order of things in the arts, where theories are supposed to arise in explanation of creativity's spontaneous combustion. Or, as Wolfe italicized it, *"Modern Art has become com-*

pletely literary: the paintings and other works exist only to illustrate the text."

The text, of course, is a critical text, a kind of journalism—thus a kind of publicity—no matter how elevated (and, often, obscure) the prose is. The need for these texts arose, as Rosenberg said, when painting ceased to be realistically representational and the art audience began to require guides to what they were peering at in puzzlement, could not, indeed, begin to understand, let alone appreciate, what they were seeing without these trots. This problem became particularly acute in the years immediately after World War II, when a radical proposition was put forward, namely, that the only worthy subject for painting was painting itself, that whatever drama a picture carried must arise not from observation of the world shared by painter and viewer, but from the confrontation of artist with canvas. One's attention was focused on the picture plane itself, on the tensions and harmonies of the colors one found there, the evidence it presented of how the painter's very brush had moved across the surface, in serenity or anger, let us say, or in conflict between the two moods. Violations of the picture plane, hints of three dimensionality (i.e., references to the way everyone sees nature in nature), were, clearly, violations of the new rules, and no worthwhile careers were made outside the rules. Perhaps the most famous formulation of all this was, again, Rosenberg's: "At a certain moment the canvas began to appear to one American painter after another as an arena in which to act. What was to go on the canvas was not a picture but an event."

The rise of Action Painting, Abstract Expressionism, or the New York School (call it what you will) had two great consequences. The first and most obvious was that as the paintings grew ever more resistant to interpretation, interpretation became ever more important to their success—and to their sales. At a certain moment the critical article began to appear to one American art fancier after another as the arena in which unquestionable values were set. And to one American painter after another as the place in which not just his ultimate standing but his immediate future would be determined. The power of criticism, long on the rise, almost inevitably became, in this new context, a dominant power. Where once an artist hoped to please critics, it now became possible to plan one's works so that it was near-impossible to not please them—so coherent was the critical consensus and, technically speaking, so easy was it to satisfy. In short, something unprecedented had happened, and the traditional order of dependency between prime creator and publicizing mechanism had been reversed. There were other ramifications to the new painting as well—ramifications that were, if anything, even more relevant to our subject. The first is that Abstract Expressionism is obviously the most enigmatically subjective form of painting ever invented. If it may be said to have any subject matter at all, it is the subjective state of the artist as he approaches his canvas, his arena and the "event" he hopes to stage therein. Thus, more than ever, our attention is focused on him, his moods, and his consciousness in general. There is simply nothing else on which we can focus our search for meaning—and despite many variations on the thought that a picture should not mean but be, despite the yards of verbal impasto slathered over the modernist enterprise by the writers for *Art News,* people continued to ask for it. And since they could not find it in the paintings themselves they turned to the only place they could logically turn—to the artists themselves. Meaning would be found in their personalities, in their presence. (In the small world of high art it was possible to be quite literally in touch with them, to visit their studios or to invite them to one's seminars or at the very least to meet them at the openings of their shows.)

This was, for a time, a satisfactory arrangement. As Rosenberg admitted well before Wolfe expanded on the point, "The core of the new-epoch art audience . . . has consisted of individuals who have gained direct understanding of the innovating ideas through personal intimacy with the artist . . ." Worldwide, this crowd consisted of no more than ten thousand people in Wolfe's estimate, and even if he was deliberately underestimating the population of "Cultureburg" it was not by much. Even if, by counting everyone in its "metro area," you came up with a figure of one hundred thousand, it is still clear that, like its paintings themselves, the community was disastrously self-referential. It could not exist as a viable economic entity, consuming enough of its own economic product to sustain its rapidly expanding production capacity. It had to export. But if the cognoscenti themselves required a heavy dose of critical theory before they could understand a work, how could they hope to create an external market for their pictures? If, indeed, Abstract Expressionism itself, for all the ink that had been spilled on and over it, was not moving off the gallery walls into the houses of this small, prime audience, and the museums it patronized (in both senses of the word), how could it expect to create a market outside its tight little island? The answer, of course, was the lower forms of publicity.

On this front, there was good news and bad news. The good news was that the painters were luckier than the avant-gardists of literature and music. To apprehend the latter's work real concentration was required, real effort, even an educated sensibility. That may have been equally true of the Abstract Expressionists too, if you intended to fully engage with their work at the highest level. But the popular culture was becoming increasingly a visual culture, and the means were at hand—on film, in the picture magazines, in book publishing—to spread the (painted) word. Far easier for *Life,* for instance, to devote some bright, eye-catching color pages to Jackson Pollock than it was to devote a similar number of pages to the gnomic poetry of a Wallace Stevens, which would place a real intellectual demand on the reader. To put the matter simply, this art suited the ever-more-sophisticated technology of mass communications very well. As for the readers, they could, literally at a glance, get some kind of message. The worst suspicions of the simple and conservative about the avant-garde were instantly confirmed; the best hopes of the outlying culturati were equally gratified. There was titillation all around. From 1949, when it first noticed Pollock, until its death as a weekly in 1972, *Life*'s pages dripped with what the critic Frank Getlein took to calling *schmeer-kunst.* So did those of all the other magazines this side of the *Reader's Digest* (including not a few that were brought into being to mediate between the high culture and the burgeoning middlebrow culture). In due course the PBS screen would pullulate with the stuff, the museums would abandon historiocity for the blue-chip celebrities, living or dead, often with their exhibitions underwritten by corporate America, which knew a good thing when it saw one. Indeed, modern art was almost as useful to the corporations as ancient art. Time had robbed the latter of any controversial residue, and since there were by design no ideas in the most modern work, there could be nothing in it to outrage a congressman or a customer either. It was, in that sense, an almost perfect product, not different from sausages or I beams in its apparently value-free neutrality. Only poor, dumb Huntington Hartford stood athwart the breech, shaking his wallet as the herd thundered past. The bad news, of course, was that the critical values necessary to appreciate this new work, to apprehend its drama, its story if you will, made up a complex structure—to put the matter charitably. To put it uncharitably, the rationalizations required to defend this work and to create an appreciation of it among those admitted to Cultureburg on green cards, were complicated to the point of self-parody. They were not really reducible to a text block and a set of captions. Again, the obvious solution was to refer the befuddled middlebrow to the artist himself, to create cults of personality around the leaders in the field.

It should have been easy. As noted, there was no tiresome subject matter to get between the artist and his public, no distraction. There was just this paint and this canvas and this artist recording his state of mind, or anyway his state of mind about art (if, indeed, art was truly the subject of art and not, as one suspects, just a sop thrown out to the fogies who kept insisting that pictures had to be about *something*). Here was the kind of pure subjectivity actors like Brando were fighting off the texts of plays and films to try to express, here was the kind of subjectivity that poets and novelists had been for years chipping away at the traditional literary forms in order to release, and these downtown subliterates had in their childish way found it. And made it look easy. It sent a little frisson through the general public when they saw pictures of Pollock or his rival de Kooning heaving paint at their canvases, or spreading them on the floor the better to dribble paint on them right from the tube. No more the mediating influence of even so simple a tool as the brush! No more the artist standing contemplatively, objectively at his easel applying a thoughtful daub here, a musing stroke there. In action, the writers had always said, was character. Now the action was built right into the process of creation. No need, now, to create heroic fictions and then pretend that you were just their humble servant, and the muse's. No, your struggle was now the one and only approved subject of the art. Given this new directness of the relationship between the artist and what he was making, the effort to turn at least some of them into heroic cultural figures need not have been monumental.

Yet that is what it turned out to be. For as Wolfe observed, very few of the artists were amenable to the mythologizing process. They had a model if they cared to study him: Pablo Picasso, the Hemingway of the art world if you will. He was a man who had created a life drama out of his shifts from style to style, medium to medium, who was capable of running up a peace dove for the Communists while the millions added up in his bank account, or permitting photographer David Douglas Duncan the run of his studio, caring not a whit that what was revealed was scarcely romantic self-denial but a sybaritic prosperity that the movie stars and millionaires Duncan snapped on their visits to the painter must have envied. Alas, most of the action painters didn't get it—"Double-Tracking" as Wolfe called it. Products, many of them, of the proletarianized thirties, they clung to their old conception of themselves as bohemians, set in unalterable opposition to the world of consumption, even when it seemed that what that world wanted most to consume was their work. They were often inarticulate, if not downright surly, when the publicists came to call. Up to a point, that was all right; the cognoscenti had been trained to expect a certain peevishness from artists.

But for all the prodigies of publicity, and for all the upward trends on their sales charts, they did not seem to come alive for the general public. They remained, most of the them, as flat, as opaque and enigmatic, as their paintings. Picasso, at least, projected a certain *joie de vivre*, a certain goatish playfulness, that was infectious as well as photogenic. There was something dour about these newer chaps. Even their problems and scandals were rather dreary. It was as if, overall, they were inhibited by their press notices. Never has there been a body of criticism as humorless and ungainly as that which surrounded the Abstract Expressionists. The prose seemed to combine the worst features of the scholarly journal, the papal encyclical, and the lively arts section of *Pravda*. And it sometimes seemed as if the victims of this critical impasto dared not look like they were having any fun, or exercising any wit in their work, lest their membership cards in the modernist movement be lifted.

But another problem, at once paradoxical and unprecedented, pressed down upon them. That was not that they were misunderstood, but that they were understood all too readily and, if not perfectly, then with an eager imperfection that was for many of them far worse to bear than neglect. Understanding that is too quick and too complete, as Denis Donoghue has pointed out in *The Arts Without Mystery*, robs art of the most significant element of its power, that sense of mystery that holds us in thrall by endlessly tantalizing us with the promise of explication, then eluding us just when we think we've got it. As Donoghue says, "The difference between a great painting and the materials from which it is made is finally mysterious; 'finally' in the sense that much can be said about the painting before reaching the point at which you have to leave it in silence." But in silence one must finally leave it, because if a work is great enough whatever "meaning" we impute to it cannot possibly exhaust its mystery.

The trouble is, as Donoghue also points out, mystery both affronts us and frightens us nowadays, in part, I would argue, because the conventions of our journalism, at every level at which it is practiced, imply that an explanation for everything is readily at hand and easy to grasp. The secret, it says, is not to be found in the art itself, but in the lives of the artists, which turn out to be different from ordinary lives but—reassuringly—only a little bit different. At which point the well-publicized artist finds himself in a paradoxical situation. For though the publicizing process gives him a status in the society that he might not have found in other eras, a sort of demi-heroism, it at the same time denies him that larger heroism that a life self-sacrificingly devoted to his calling formerly conferred, especially on creators who were understood to be ahead of their time—a posterity of truly heroic proportions, which proportions can only be shaped out of mystery.

Here indeed is an exquisite torment for the devoted artist, one that might be comical, perhaps, if it did not so often have real and deadly consequences. But, indeed, success was the one thing for which men and women born in the Depression and raised on the tradition that when one embraces art one embraces with it—at least for many years —a life of denial, a renunciation of worldly rewards, were entirely unprepared. Who among this generation of painters (and poets and novelists, dancers and musicians) would have, could have, predicted the postwar American cultural revolution, which was in turn based on an unprecedented prosperity that gave rise to expanded education, expanded leisure that could be devoted to cultural pursuits. Who could have imagined, remembering what ugly controversy the modest WPA arts programs engendered, that within the wink of history's eye, government would be a major patron of the arts, with vulgar American capitalism close behind. Or possibly a half step ahead. It turned out that artists, no matter how radical their art, had a public after all. It was not, to be sure, generally a mass public (though that too was often available on an intermittent basis), but it was one that could afford the artist a respectable livelihood and an all-too respectful hearing, one that softened rather than hardened the recipient of its applause by granting him the sort of misunderstanding that John Updike has so humorously (and finally so touchingly) satirized in his Bech books.

To put the matter simply, an artist's heroism is denied him when the

Pulitzer Prize goes to his off-Broadway play, when the corporation buys his paintings for its permanent collection, when the invitations to read his poetry or his novel or to become the new writer-in-residence arrives from a college, when the State Department sends him on tour to foreign climes as an exemplar of capitalist culture, when the National Endowment for the Arts bestows its whimsical largesse on him. The modern artist in America is cursed not by rejection, but by a disorienting partial acceptance that cannot reasonably be construed as dismissal—except by a deadly, unreasonable stretch of the imagination.

This process begins, as we will shortly see, by inflating slights into grievous affronts, by conjuring up cabals of enemies where there exists only that irreducible minimum of people who, for one reason or another, simply do not respond to a particular artist's work. Out beyond the adepts of modern art, and its good-natured if slightly addled camp followers, a vast indifference does, of course, exist. But the lumpy mass need not concern any serious artist. They cannot be reclaimed from "The Dukes of Hazzard" and gothic romances—except perhaps by Rod McKuen and LeRoy Neiman. What may interest the artist as he contemplates the ways and means of reasserting his claim to heroic status is, perhaps, the children of the mass, and their children's children. Maybe only 50 percent of them will be functionally literate by the time they enter the unselective college of their choice, so if one seeks admission to their remedial reading textbook, it is essential that a certain easily graspable drama adhere to one's name, something that will arrest the none-too-critical attention of people incapable of apprehending the subtleties of elevated expression, something that will make one stand out in the crowd of creators thronging down the corridors of time. There is, in the final analysis, no better method of so doing than to attach oneself to the tragic myth of the misunderstood artist, a myth of such simplicity that people began making movies about it a half century ago and continue to make up-market television specials revolving around it.

Not that one wishes to sound cynical on this subject. There are real people suffering from lack-of-persecution complexes. And they are often enough people of great, even transcendent gifts. It is to some of these lives that I wish to turn now—in part because they form such vivid contrasts to the lives of other artists who have so neatly fitted themselves into the spirit of the age.

If modern painting offers a paradigm of how the relationship between art and culture proceeds in our time, then Mark Rothko's life is
the paradigm's paradigm. In his studio, Rothko was an altogether
admirable figure. He did not, for example, believe that art was the only
valid subject for art. No, it was the "tragic and timeless" that he was
after, and he pursued it with a single-mindedness that can perhaps
legitimately be characterized as heroic. As Robert Hughes put it in his
superb essay on Rothko's life, death, and troubled patrimony, he was
"one of the last artists in America to believe, with his entire being, that
painting could carry the load of major meanings and possess the same
comprehensive seriousness as the Russian novel." Throughout the fifties and sixties the art world took him at *his* word; the words that were
painted around him unquestioningly accepted his own high seriousness about his endeavor and, in its comments upon his accomplishments, implied that he had fully realized his ineffable aim. About no
artist was there, in that time, such unanimity of critical opinion.

Despite that, or perhaps because of it, his life outside the studio was
a mess, "a long, troubled preparation for a failure that eluded him," as
Hughes put it. For his own reasons, Rothko had to maintain a beleaguered posture, had, in fact, to invent enemies when there weren't any
who were significant, had to permit others to handle his increasingly
complex financial affairs and, if you will, his public relations. Such
material considerations, had he permitted himself to become involved
with them, would have diminished the purity of his struggle in his own
eyes. Paradoxically, this, too, commended him to his public; he could
be seen as a kind of holy fool, and his unworldliness seemed to further
guarantee the integrity and profundity of his work.

Eventually, of course, he lost touch with reality, in just the way so
many more conventional celebrities, in all walks of life, now do.
Hughes argues very persuasively that the waste of his estate, after he
died—a matter that became, when the case went to court, one of the
celebrated scandals of the seventies (and in and of itself a media cir-
cus)—had its roots in the artist's almost psychopathic hostility to the
practical when he was alive. While he was alive, however, the failure
of journalism and publicity to engage Rothko's art on any terms other
than those of his announced aspirations, served him at least as ill as
his gallery and financial advisors did. By "burbling its muffled threno-
dies to the ineffable," the higher criticism helped to keep the artist

imprisoned in the moral-aesthetic system he had himself devised, and since his art, essentially that of an exquisite colorist, could not possibly fully realize the sublimely mystical goals he had set for it, he was forced yet further in on himself. If there is any journalism that harms an artist more than uninformed condemnation it is uninformed praise. For if even the people who claim to appreciate what one is doing misunderstand one, it completes one's sense of isolation. In the dark night of his soul Rothko must have known too—as every artist does, better than any critic—how often he fell victim to his own formulas and clichés, how often he merely repeated himself, how often, in short, he fell short of his lofty ideals. If the language of Rothko-speak has about it, as Hughes says, something that is discomfitingly "coercive," how much more so it must have been for the artist himself, a man whose very sense of himself was based on resistance to all coercions. One is led inescapably to the belief that in some immeasurable measure his suicide was related to his celebrity. In effect, in his mind, his fame mocked his achievements as he evaluated them. His efforts to cast himself as the beleaguered artistic radical, the misunderstood and rejected innovator—despite all the evidence to the contrary—suggest that he was trying single-handedly to construct for himself the life he might have led forty or fifty years earlier as a member of the old-style avant-garde actually beleaguered by the uncomprehending bourgeoisie, yet genuinely protected by the fellowship of like-minded souls and content to let history—as opposed to fashion, media attention—be the arbiter of his efforts. There was, here, a killing nostalgia.

If one's art cannot be forced up to the highest mythic plane, if one cannot, through conscious effort, make the connection with the ineffable that ambition and conscience require, then a connection with another kind of mythology becomes highly seductive. We are talking here about the romantic monomyth in which the artist, misunderstood by the world, takes leave of the world. It is more than an act of self-destruction; it is an act of self-denial, in which the self denied is the falsely inflated self of wealth and publicity. It may have seemed to someone like Rothko—or for that matter, Marilyn Monroe—the only way to redeem one's true self, offer an authentic testament to history in which the encrustations of success are, in a stroke, stripped off and the true self stands forth clean and pure again.

It may even be that some artists have come to believe that this self-denial is preordained, that they are, all their lives, heading inevitably toward a rendezvous with a suicidal destiny. This provocative thought was put forward, also by Denis Donoghue, in the course of reviewing a biography of John Berryman, the poet. In his review he speaks of the "extravagantly untidy" lives of those of the poetic "generation" that was roughly contemporaneous with the generation of the Abstract Expressionists. These poets included, among others, Robert Lowell, Randall Jarrell, Theodore Roethke, Elizabeth Bishop, and Delmore Schwartz, all of whom wrote verse as subjective in its way as any action painting, and much more readily apprehensible as "confessional." All of them died prematurely, by suicide, by accident, by illness that could be read as the inevitable consequence of the craziness and strain imposed on lives devoted to art as it is presently defined. This enterprise, because of the near-impossible demands it places on mind, spirit, and gift, is supposed to carry with it little but the promise of obscurity, poverty. Under that definition, failure at the self-imposed task of making meaningfully ordered art out of contemporary chaos must come to seem inevitable, to the artist unarmored by an ironic worldliness.

The poets, like the painters, like nearly everyone engaged in the modernist enterprise, thus required—and easily acquired—a sustaining mythology. Building on the romantic nineteenth-century tradition of the garret-bound artist starving for his art, they invented and promulgated a myth that posited "the continuous possibility of heroism . . . maintained in the face of a public world in nearly every respect corrupt," corrupt at least in comparison to those media of the spirit in which they worked. In a sense, as Donoghue says, theirs was a no-lose mythology, for even if a poet failed, "his failure could readily be construed as a constituent of tragedy, the most exalted and exalting artistic form, according to the Western assessment of art." "To what extent," Hughes asks us, "did Rothko's suicide confer a profundity on the paintings which, had he lived, they might not quite have had?" The question may be asked about any artist assuming the heroic burden of living, and then dying, within the modernist mythology.

Even to entertain such thoughts makes one queasy, and I do not wish to reduce the tragedy of suicide to the level of a publicity stunt, or to make the milder forms of self-destruction into examples of careless self-display. It must be obvious that for the serious modern artist, living in the "maelstrom" is something more than a metaphor. It is the prime condition of his life, one which presents to him an endless and essentially insoluble set of confusions, the resolution of which, through art, is often too intellectually demanding, too spiritually sapping, to sustain for a full lifetime. To a man or woman working at the most intense and problematical levels of expression, pursued by and pursuing demons that always resist simple definitions, death must always seem a temptation, a seductive relief—and perhaps never more so than when one has achieved a certain success. For what now beckons one on, after the first youthful creative flowering, is a confrontation with the literally inexpressible. Many, of course, manage that confrontation without damaging themselves. One thinks of the serene autumnal works of many a revered master. One thinks, too, of other older artists who work splendidly and retire without quite announcing the fact, spending their late years as sages, collecting the honoraria due distinguished age. Yet one understands the temptation of the early and dramatic exit, the gesture of heroic disgust that can be interpreted as heroic despair. The residue of such foreshortened lives, the works themselves, may well take on, as Hughes proposes, a certain patina as a result of this seemingly exemplary gesture. And they may, as a result, more readily disarm the would-be critic in the years to come. No artist can escape knowledge of these posthumous possibilities—not today, not with keening over our sudden losses having become a critical mode, a virtual subgenre, and the manner of the artists' leavetaking being significant linchpins in our continuing concern for those as diverse as Dylan Thomas and Sylvia Plath.

Reluctantly one concludes that there is an unmistakably Wertherian atmosphere surrounding modernist art, something that partakes of an epidemic quality in the way that so many modern artists beat their way toward the calm they seem to feel lies at the maelstrom's center, a rush toward the tragic gesture which, in our age, seems immutable in the ways that a body of work is not. Death seems to resolve everything, including the temptation to "sell out," that most awful of threats to purity. Above all, it links the lonely, suffering, insecure individual to what one is tempted to call the great chain of nonbeing.

Since death is the most intimate act in which a stranger can involve us, it is, seen from a certain angle, the ultimate imposition. Nothing an artist can do more definitively diminishes the distancing effect his necessarily complex art can have on us. Death then comes to seem, sometimes, as if it is the final revision, the last brilliant retouching one can perform on the collected works, a brilliantly clarifying final stroke, cutting through the complexities of the modern artist's difficult modernism, guaranteeing the integrity of his effort and rendering its largest meaning unmistakable—and permanently poignant.

🦋 🦋

We have been treading dark, bloody, supremely discomfiting ground. We can see why those who inhabit it come to believe that only the lightning flash of tragedy can illuminate its contradictions, briefly resolve its ambiguities. Extending the metaphor, we begin to see why publicity—in effect, a thousand flashguns popping in pallid and parodistic imitation of true illumination—can disgust.

And on the other hand . . . ? On the other hand, puzzled from the start by the surfaces of any modernist work, less concerned than the artist is with posterity's view of his work, unable to comprehend the emotional investment that an artist's life inevitably entails, a certain portion of the contemporary public tends to behave around the scene of one of these tragedies rather like the crowd at a street accident. Morbid fascination draws them to it: horror, the inability to comprehend its causes makes them turn quickly aside.

We would, if we could, avoid both enigma and ugliness. We would, if we could, find simpler resolutions to the anguish of art, just as we would to the pain of life. In these circumstances there is a tendency among those who own modern art, as well as those who take merely a spectator's interest in it, to try to find a way of connecting with it in some way that does not strain the intellect or drain the emotions. In our time that connection has come largely to be an economic one, which is surely something a man like Rothko would have perceived, and by which he would have been disgusted. In the end, and this is where Abstract Expressionism predicted the future, this art tended to refer most people conclusively to only one other thing, and that, too, was an abstraction—price. On this level, the level of conspicuous consumption, this work eventually succeeded very well. People who had bought de Koonings and Pollocks and Klines early, when the prices were ridiculously low, tended to be smug about it, like people who had bought Xerox before Xerox became a generic name or Beverly Hills real estate around the time Doug and Mary moved in. People who arrived later, of course, had a means of flaunting their wealth in a socially acceptable manner.

It is as Hughes says in another of his remarkable essays: "No work of art has an intrinsic value, like a brick or a car. Its price cannot be discussed in terms of the labor theory of value. The price of a work of art is an index of pure, irrational desire, and nothing is more manipulable than desire." We are arrived, he suggests, at pure fetishism, and not accidentally so, since the old purposes of art, "the manifestation of myth and the articulation of social meaning, have largely been taken away from painting and sculpture by film, TV, and photography." It then follows that the largest, most apprehensible meaning an abstract work can have for the vast majority is to be found in its market valuation. This is a point that cannot be emphasized too strongly, for price is among other things a statistic, and a statistic is an attempt to quantify complex reality, reduce it to something everyone can comprehend. Particularly in recent years the sale and auction prices of contemporary art have become a large part of the publicity, thus a large part of the legend, surrounding the great figures of the art world. But below a certain level, and beyond the inner circle, publicity, legend, image (call it what you will) did not translate into sales. Abstract Expressionism has, from the start, presented a problem in manipulability to the art world. The dealers, some of the artists, a few critics and curators did well enough with it. They, indeed, achieved the American apotheosis, they made a market where none had existed before. Talk about Xerox! Talk about oil for the lamps of China! But that market, compared to the market they kept catching glimpses of (or thought they did; it might have been a mirage), was small and stubbornly refused to grow beyond a certain boundary. Most people gawped, but they didn't buy. It was pretty much as Tom Wolfe said: "We may state it as a principle . . . that collectors of contemporary art do not want to buy highly abstract art unless it's the only game in town. They will always prefer realistic art instead—as long as someone in authority assures them that it is (a) new and (b) not realistic." We may state as a corollary to that axiom that having done pretty well in the media with abstraction, it came logically upon the art marketeers that they could do still better with artists who were more pliable and who worked in more readily apprehensible forms, something journalism in all its expanded forms could really get behind, something that would amuse and titillate its public.

Enter Pop Art. Essentially what it did was to banish the heroic necessity and to stylize, to reclaim for art if you insist, the machine-made (or anyway machine-disseminated) junk of commercialized culture, by aestheticizing it and sometimes mildly satirizing it. It was a stroke of genius on every level but the artistic.

To begin with, the public, looking at the images offered by Pop Art, found itself in the position of the Bourgeois Gentleman, delighted to discover he had been speaking prose all his life without knowing it. For now the public was informed that all the while their eyes had been sliding across comic books, movie star posters, even the American flag, they had been appreciating art without knowing it. It does not seem entirely coincidental that the popular craze for "collectibles"— objects ranging from tobacco tins to (fortuitously) "pop" bottles— coincided with the rise of an art that took this material for its subject. Beyond that, however, this new art was, in itself, infinitely reproducible in a way that no art prior to it ever had been, since it drew on material that was in itself originally designed to catch the eye with a bold, simple flourish (posters, billboards, etc.) or to be conveniently duplicable by even the crudest technology (the halftone, for example). To be sure, something was lost when one of Jasper John's Flags was reproduced in magazine or coffee table book; you couldn't quite see the choppy little brush strokes that were his personal, *personalizing* contribution to the image. Similarly, the deliberate slips in Andy Warhol's silk screen renditions of movie star imagery didn't always come through on the printed page (though his garish color overlays did). But who cared? The mass public is not so much interested in technique as in knowing "What's the story here?" Pop answered that question in terms as apparently unmistakable as they were obscure in the Action Painters' answer.

Pop Art is all surfaces, which is what allowed it, under a loose construction of the rules, admission to the modernist tradition. But beneath the surface, something very interesting is going on. Walter Benjamin argued that what "withers in the age of mechanical reproduction is the aura of the work of art." By this he meant that the singularity of any given object arises from the fact that it is created at a particular point in time and space, is a response to a peculiar set of circumstances, to history if you will. But "the technique of reproduction detaches the reproduced object from the domain of tradition," pries it from its shell, its frame, thereby depriving it of its "aura." When this happens, the beholder of the reproduced object is moved to incorporate it into his own psychological domain; the old objective relationship between viewer and art (out of which, of course, "mystery" arose) is replaced with a more intimate and subjective one. The difference between seeing a painting in the formal, historically-aware context of the museum and seeing it reproduced on the wall in your living room (or on the magazine page open on your lap) is similar to the difference between hearing a symphony in a concert hall and playing a recording, seeing a film in a theater and watching it on TV. Robbed of proper context, and of a sense of occasion, these secondary images feed, are probably largely responsible for, "the desire of contemporary masses to bring things 'closer' spatially and humanly, which is just as ardent as their bent toward overcoming the uniqueness of every reality," as Benjamin put it.

The forces behind Abstract Expressionism knew (or sensed) what Benjamin had been talking about. They had, given the historical sense and theoretical acumen of its publicists, a firm and sophisticated grasp of art history. They were able to give Abstract Expressionism the air of being well-connected historically, of evolving logically out of the older modernist tradition. But with its obscurantism, its emphasis on "pure" form, its deadly fear of anything that might hint at three-dimensional realism, or some lingering nostalgia for representationalism, they also sought a radical detachment from tradition and history, from being too easily and quickly understood in terms of what we used to quaintly call "art appreciation." Offense, it seemed, was the best defense against the incorporative drive of the mass public that Benjamin had described.

The brilliance of Pop, the reason for its sudden, sweeping popular triumph lay in the way that it seemed to satisfy most of the theoretical dictates that had sustained Abstract Expressionism while at the same time it managed a reversal of Benjamin's thesis. It took as its subject common objects and symbols, material that we have long since internalized (and in the process psychologically neutralized) as part of our everyday visual and psychological landscape. Objects that had lost any such "aura" as they might once have had were invested with a new "aura," the aura of art, of high culture if you will.

It may indeed be that there was more than a mere reversal going on here; we may have been dealing with nothing less than a perversion. Consider Trow's dictum that "The most successful celebrities are products" (he asks if any man is as well loved in America as Coca-Cola). If this be even partly true, then high art—that elitist enterprise, sustained in a mass society largely by various artificial life support systems (otherwise known as subsidies)—by incorporating commercial imagery, may be understood in the case of Pop, to be stealing an aura even as it creates one. Campbell's Soup cans or Brillo boxes may, in themselves, be faintly comic in their invocation of the quotidian. But as presented on a Warhol canvas, their images multiplied or enlarged, they also remind us, if only subconsciously, of where the true power in this country lies—in mass production and in the massive enterprises required to create and sustain such production. Similarly, Warhol's celebrity series—his Elvises, Lizs and Marilyns. It reminds us that celebrity power as we now understand it arises precisely from a similar power—to endlessly replicate a product (in this case, to be sure, a human product) and bombard the public with it until it is accepted.

All of this imparted to Pop an easy command of the media such as no movement in the history of art had ever enjoyed. And that command, in turn, signaled an unprecedented expansion of the art market. By coincidence, Pop Art burst on the world in the bull-market sixties; go-go prosperity meant that the new, media-shilled audience had new money to spend on the stuff. And the more they bought the more prices rose, for even this prolific and essentially untroubled group of artists could not keep up with the new demand. Thus scarcity could be maintained, and with it, ever-increasing valuation. In the sixties and seventies art prices rose faster than inflation, so that even the entirely unaesthetic could be persuaded to buy—as an investment offering a hedge against inflation. This giddiness extended to many a new school of painting, refining still further modernist critical doctrine, with the schools arising and declining in what seemed a matter of months, responding to Warhol's law of acceleration, by which we are allowed, if we are lucky, our fifteen minutes of fame, before the media's kittenish attention span darts elsewhere. For the details on this, see Wolfe; ours is not to reason with the recent history of modern art.

We must, however, pause over a problem. And that is this: if this new painting presents very little in the way of interpretive problems (and it doesn't), if its imagery is painfully obvious to us at a glance (and it is), then what about it is going to catch at our attention and hold it for more than the specified fifteen minutes—if only to keep that inflationary hedge over the dining room table from withering right before someone's dismayed eyes? Normally, the answer would be easy. When the content of the painting is thin or elusive, we can divert ourselves with style or manner, as in the case of Abstract Expressionism. But these offered little to reflect upon in post–post modernism. So much of the new work had a mechanical air about it, hard-edged, deliberately without subtlety in color or form as it sought to divest itself then not just of traditional subject matter, but of the last vestiges of traditional painterly technique as well. The abstractionists of the earlier generations had possessed that technique, had visibly employed it even in their subversions of traditional subject matter. If they had not, their "action" on the canvas could not have sustained the endless analysis that it did. Now, however, technique itself was deemed senti-mental-by-association. It was a last link with art history. Even though it was not being used to realistically represent art's traditional subject matter, it could be: any time a well-trained painter wanted to, he could stop placing color stripes on unprimed canvas, he could theoretically go back to painting water lilies or, for that matter, cuddly puppies.

In short, there was a void here. Though content had been somewhat restored to painting, it was scarcely a profound content, especially since historiocity was still barred from sober consideration. Though stylistics were now more readily apparent to the untutored eye, they were not very interesting either. One might imagine that the lives of the artists could have been employed to fill the gap. In this realm, however, the new artists were something of a disappointment; in their way more so even than the Abstract Expressionists. To be sure, the younger crowd did not see the world in quite the black-and-white terms their predecessors had. Having grown up with the media, in-cluding its latest and most powerful manifestation, television, they were cool and neutral about it, and incorporated its imagery into their work guiltlessly and without moral or political comment. They were just as cool and neutral about allowing the media to incorporate them into its scheme of things. They felt in general (and correctly) that they could get as much use out of the media as it could get out of them. There was in this generational style a certain clarity of vision and a refreshing lack of pretense. Ironically, however, their ease in the new electronic environment worked against them. There was no drama here, no danger, no potential for tragedy. There was nothing contro-versial about the newcomers except that which was inherent in their work, but that moved only a small number of people in the art world.

It was a shame. Art was poised for its great assault on the mass market, it even had a product the mass market could comprehend, by which, at the very least, it did not feel threatened. What it needed was a figure such as all the other arts, and the various branches of the intellectual world, were beginning to produce, an individual who could be made to symbolize, in all the expanding forums of mass communication, the issues, ideas, and styles of advanced thought and creation; someone who had, if not necessarily the right stuff, then the latest stuff, and who had the knack of coming on a TV panel and arguing engagingly with the squares. (David Susskind, in those days, made a career out of being the nation's square, earnestly inquiring, earnestly liberal-minded, disagreeing with all these creatures, his puzzlement and fretfulness mirroring his audience's. His guests didn't have to argue if they didn't want to; it was often enough to just sit there and exude your point through dress and manner and a few catch phrases.)

For the new audience, composed of the New Class, the freshly educated B.A.s and M.B.A.s charged with managing the new service economy, a group that had the time to read, go to galleries and deplore movies that were not subtitled, were randomly, superficially curious about everything: radical priests in peril of defrocking; visionary and apocalyptic intellectuals; pop psychologizers; cult movie directors (and, God help us, cult movie critics); unreadable novelists who had been politically victimized somewhere or other; homosexual aesthetes with an ear for gossip and a gift for put-down and put-on; journalists with a knowing air about the future, or total recall of the scandalous past; anyone else who felt he or she had a grievance that was shared or shareable. These figures dramatized; they concretized; they humanized; above all, they entertained. They were the Henny Youngmans of the New Class, stand-up performers in the expanding intellectual cabaret of public and off-network broadcasting, of trade paperbacks and brightly packaged special interest magazines. In short, the art world needed someone into whom the publicists could sink their teeth, their claws, whatever, if it expected to compete. It would have had to invent Andy Warhol if he had not already invented himself so that he would be ready for this brave new world when it beat a path to his door.

That inventive process begins, if we are to credit the testimony of those who were present at its creation (see *Edie),* with a large and disordered pile of movie magazines. They were a feature of the decor in Warhol's first town house, the one he acquired after he had achieved his first success as a commercial illustrator, which taught him much about the manipulation of the consuming impulse. It appears that, since his childhood in the poverty-level boondocks of Pennsylvania, he had been an ardent reader of the fanzines, and their imagery, of course, would be a source for his art in the years to come, but they were much more obviously a source for his way of presenting his pale, pocked face for the world to see.

A fan magazine is a curious thing. The famous people presented in its pages are always shown in ways that detach them from their work. Oh, the new film may be mentioned in passing, but where journalism on a slightly more elevated level insists on a "hook" or "peg" on which to hang a story about an actor or an actress—some current work or accomplishment that justifies the gush—the fan magazines require nothing of the sort. It is sufficient merely to drop in on the star and update the gawking reader on how life is with him or her at the moment. How are you coping with the divorce? Whom are you dating? How's the new marriage going? The kids? The redecoration of the living room? It is well known, indeed, that an actual interview need not take place, that a press agent will supply all the quotes and pictures anyone needs for a layout, and if he won't, you can count on gossip, rumor, and the paparazzi to provide enough material for a story.

What a wonderful thing this must have seemed to a shy and inarticulate nullity thumbing through these magazines, looking for a little glamorous light to brighten his provincial gloom. No wonder the fan mags accompanied him to New York to serve as material for his art and inspiration for his life. The connections here were quite deep. Robert Hughes in yet another piece identifies Warhol's famous portrait of Marilyn Monroe "as a sly and grotesque parody of the Madonna-Fixations of Warhol's . . . Catholic childhood, of the pretentious enlargement of media stars by a secular culture, and of the similarities between both." There is no evidence, however, that the parodistic element in the work was ever more than semiconscious. No, Warhol's eye was fixed on matters that cannot and should not be understood (as many foreign, leftist critics insist on doing) as cultural or social criticism. How can anyone be expected to criticize a culture he wants to dominate (at least imagistically), a society in which one wants only to rise? In any event, Warhol was honest enough on this point. "If you want to know all about Andy Warhol," he once told an interviewer, "just look at the surface of my paintings and films and me, and there I am. There's nothing behind it."

One is inclined to take him at his word. But if he was patterning his public behavior on the movie star model, it was on a somewhat outdated one. The sixties breed for the most part was relentlessly articulate. They wanted to be taken seriously not only as artists, but as intellectuals and social philosophers. Warhol is not like that. He seems unable to speak a complete sentence in public, and although rumors of meanspiritedness in private abound, he is vaguely, universally, if monosyllabically, approving of almost anything he is asked to publicly comment upon, avoiding all personal or ideological controversy. To put the matter simply, his public manner is as opaque, as witlessly detached, as that of the stars and starlets he so formatively studied in the *Photoplays* of yesteryear. He is, in fact, the dumb blond of Hollywood lore, displaced but distinctly reincarnated.

As Hughes noted, this turned out to be a very good strategy for the sixties. Warhol was "a walking void," and in a period when "craziness was becoming normal, and half America seemed to be immersed in some tedious and noisy form of self-expression . . . Warhol's bland translucency, as of frosted glass, was much more intriguing." But Warhol was not, shall we say, a one-issue personality. Besides his almost childlike desire to display himself, and perhaps as a function of that desire, he wished to redefine the role of the artist, especially in his relationship to work, the actual processes of creation. Here, too, his model was old-fashioned. His studio he called The Factory (though it was, in fact, no more than a loft space with its walls silvered), and he presided over it, in something like the manner of an old-fashioned entrepreneur, cranking out his novelty products and hoping to get rich on one of them (and, indeed, Warhol quickly succeeded as a result of his success with prints and paintings).

There was only this difference: where the old American dreamers had dreamt of devising some machine that the world could not live without, Warhol proclaimed, "I want to *be* a machine" (emphasis added). Actually, however, the distinction was more apparent than real, for Warhol did employ (though not necessarily for wages—more often it was for a share of his chic) all kinds of helpers. The testimony Jean Stein collected for *Edie* strongly indicates that even when The Factory's only products were, as it were, flatware, paintings, and silkscreens, the work and the ideas for them were collaboratively created. In due course, a larger crowd gathered at The Factory, many of whom could not lift a brush larger than one designed for mascara. But that was all right. Andy, the bent Catholic, believed that an idle mind was the devil's workshop. He would find them something to do.

That something, of course, was movies. Scriptless, virtually actionless, crudely improvised by any and all, they were more travesty than parody. As Gerard Malanga, who functioned as a sort of "chief of production," said, "Andy never actually directed a film. He was a sort of catalyst genius who would get people to do things for him in front of the camera." But now, as The Factory turned back into a studio of a different kind—a movie studio of sorts—Warhol altered his entrepreneurial model. Now instead of being a parody of the primitive inventor-entrepreneur, he turned into a parody of the primitive movie tycoon, a sort of demented Louis B. Mayer. He knew even less than the old (or new) studio bosses knew about the technique and technicalities of moviemaking (Malanga: ". . . he never went for anything like rehearsals. All he did was turn on the camera button and turn it off"). It goes without saying that he was even less literate than the old Hollywood chieftains, and, quite unlike them, had no one in his employ who could either make a movie with some degree of artfulness or write one that might be worth shooting. "He wanted everything to be Easyville," as Malanga put it. "He thought of himself as Walt Disney, you know: just put your name on something and it will turn to gold . . . some kind of alchemy."

Yet however childish all this sounds, the fact is that in at least two important respects he was like Hollywood's industrial pioneers. For one thing, he instinctively knew what his audience wanted, or anyway could withstand. To be sure, it was at first a tiny audience, the Manhattan demimonde of the sixties, that fringe where the "interesting" people met to dope and disco and have their pictures taken first by the fashion press, then by the general press. But yet their buzzing and twittering did much to overcome the inherent stupefaction of the movies, and Warhol's films had a certain vogue—enough so that their repute, like that of his painting, added to his general fame. But his real power, like that of his antique role models, lay in the fact that he held absolute sway over his domain. His whim was law and the poor trashed, or soon-to-be trashed, creatures who became his "superstars" knew it as surely as John Gilbert or Joan Crawford knew that Louis B.'s word was law. (It is interesting to think, incidentally, that the one lasting contribution of Warhol's venture into filmmaking may be that now-overworked term, "superstar." One of his associates Chuck Wein claimed with some slight exaggeration that he found it used only once before, in an old movie magazine.) Indeed, considering how weak and vulnerable Warhol's creatures were, how much they needed him emotionally, he had a power to destroy lives far in excess of Mayer's.

Be that as it may, as an "artist"—anyway, a presumptive artist—Warhol accomplished many things for his profession, the most important of which was the demonstration that one no longer had to "profess" anything in order to be taken seriously. Hughes is very good on this point, noting that Warhol's work goes against the most basic assumptions of modernism, in that image was detached from, apparently no longer dictated by, either the artist's unconscious or the race's. Similarly, the variously expressed reformist, utopian, political, transcendental hopes of previous art movements completely disappeared in Popism. The leftist notion that Warhol offered a satirically anti-capitalist message, was and remains pure imputation. And pure nonsense.

What he had actually done was make a kind of television on canvas, painting that was as devoid of the difficult and the discomfiting as anything TV's self-censorship permits to pass. He similarly simplified the problem of understanding the way the creative mind works for people whose minds are not creative. They could see him simply as a pure celebrity, a man who gets his picture in the papers a lot, and appears to work only effortlessly and pleasantly, just enough to give the media some "events" to cover occasionally. Or they could see him as a business man, a little weird in looks and manner, but basically a good old American hustler. If the observer were particularly venturesome, he could see him as an entertaining hy-bred, the star-entrepreneur. In short, instead of making images, he had become an image. Just like those he had "read" as a child, he was an empty vessel, into which the large public could pour its fantasies without fear of contradiction. Come to think of it, how did this star-entrepreneur differ from the Hollywood versions where the actors had just recently begun to form their own companies in order to profit directly from the business of packaging themselves in congenial forms? Warhol's original works sold, and for the plain people there would be posters of his posters, nonbooks under his name, *Interview* magazine, a punk rock group that he would have a piece of. He had what few artists have in their lifetimes, secondary markets for his products, for he was then a brand name no different, really, from the stars he had once used as subjects. As Harold Rosenberg said, he "liquidated the century-old tension between the serious artist and the majority culture."

What was left after the liquidation was a void. Warhol did not melt into air; he has, rather, seemed to hover in it, perhaps the most vivid contemporary representation of someone known for his knownness; a name in the columns—does he ever miss a party or an opening?—a pale, almost ghostly smear in the tabloids' halftones. In the art world proper no one has yet managed to take his place, if only because Post-Pop Art is so fragmented, lacking a dominant school or personalities. Everything is now tolerated, but that which we too easily accept cannot move us very strongly. The "tension" Rosenberg spoke of was more vital to culture's health than we fully understood. If the dialogue it produced never quite turned into a dialectic, moving history along in some direction or other, it yet provided us with metaphors of partial understanding of ourselves, our world; it helped us to make distinctions as we contemplated our experience.

Too bad. Who cares? Dimly aware that this face was fading right before its cameras' eyes, unable to find replacements for it, yet aware that the events of the past two decades had established what appeared to be a permanent public interest in the doings of the art world, aware, too, that the enlargement of the art market (with its constantly spiraling prices and the continuing attention being paid it by socially prominent people and significant elements in corporate America), the media made do with what it had. And what it had was the pure, distilled essence of Warholism, his equivalent of the Cheshire Cat's grin. Namely, his prices, the astonishing prices people were willing to pay for his utterly vacuous art. There was more to mull over, more to conjecture with, in that than in anything else he had accomplished. It irritated. It amused. It flummoxed. And lo, equally amazing—one might say heroic—sums were being ladled over the products of all kinds of artists, the quick and the dead, everywhere one turned: $2.3 million for Rembrandt's *Aristotle Contemplating the Bust of Homer,* $5.5 million for Velázquez's *Juan de Pareja.* And so on.

It began to seem that the heroic price, not the heroic effort to express the inexpressible, was the place to look for art's true meaning. Anyway, that's where the action now was. And, since there appeared to be no necessary correlation between the two, one could not help but wonder if the intertwining of misery and achievement in this realm— the pain, the madness, the deaths that had fertilized the cause of art— were not perhaps, how shall one say it, a bit *de trop?* Andy made it look "Easyville," and he was certainly doing all right. And Rembrandt? Velázquez? One can't quite recall how it went with them. Oh well, no matter. They couldn't have lived to see these prices, anyway, and that's what matters. Value, it turns out, is the ultimate value.

A new and unprecedented form of celebrity had come to the art world, celebrity that was no longer tightly attached to an individual or his work. This was statistical celebrity, an abstraction as pure as a minimalist's white-on-white canvas. And as the numbers soared toward the mathematical stratosphere, they tore the work itself loose from its moorings in history's continuum and, of course, not so subtly changed our relationship to it, thus posing a new problem for us in ascertaining the meaning of a work's meaning. It had been difficult enough separating the value of a work or a body of work from the legend of its creator. But that had been kid stuff compared to the exquisite problems presented by the task of disentangling work from the legend of price and evaluating its import, culturally and subjectively, when this dance of the digits was being performed in the space between it and our wondering eyes. If, as Walter Benjamin proposed, mere reproduction dims a work's aura, then this kind of massive intervention by the numbers radically distorts that aura. Or perhaps substitutes a new and false one for it. Hughes again: Extraordinary price "removes the painting from the flow of discourse about experience that art is meant to sustain . . . makes the price part of the subject of the work, turning it from one painting among others into a dead whale on a flatcar, a curiosity to be gawped at."

Almost incidentally, but presciently considering the primitive state of our interest in the matter when he wrote, Benjamin noted that as reproductive reductionism is to the field of perception "the increasing importance of statistic" is to our sociopolitical life. Both are crucial to the "unlimited" process by which "the adjustment of reality to the masses and of the masses to reality" proceed. It did not occur to Benjamin—why should it have?—that the statistical reduction of experience could be coupled with reproductive reductionism within the realm of art where they might function reciprocally to strike dumb the once-complex, ideally complicated encounter with a work.

Price is the crudest form of numerical quantification. That is one of the reasons I chose to use the art world—where it is the only meaningful statistic—as a metaphor in which to catch the workings of the celebrity system within traditional high culture. But this method of simplifying experience is now at work everywhere. If statistical celebrity is not yet choking off the expression of ideas, then it does inhibit the process of spreading them. It has become a commonplace to complain that in all the arts the almost exclusive emphasis on the relative handful of contemporary artists who can command celebrity prices reverses a long-cherished hope. This hope was that as art expanded into previously undreamed-of forums, meeting the desires of the coincidentally expanding New Class for morally bracing contact with "the finer things" (a lovely antique, that locution), both the loneliness of the serious artist, catering at best to an elitist audience and the "great and terrible barrenness" of our common life as J. Robert Oppenheimer once put it, would be mitigated.

In the fifties and sixties this dream extended to all the traditional arts, and to the popular arts as well—movies, television, the Broadway theater. In this period, when I was newly arrived in New York and beginning to work on magazines, there was a distinct air of idealism about much of what we cultural journalists were attempting, a sense that we were, in a sense, hosts at a grand new party, moving about the room, making introductions from which all would benefit. And we saw signs of progress on every hand whether it was in the reception accorded new voices in literature—Beat, Jewish, extravagantly comic —or in the growth of the audience for the New York City Ballet; whether it was in the birth of regional theater or in the excitement that attended the release of a new film by Truffaut or Bergman or Fellini. Even oft-deplored commercial television continued to preempt its regularly scheduled programming for serious plays and sober documentaries—and find, still, respectable audiences for these offerings.

It seems odd now to reflect on how innocent we were a scant quarter of century ago about the possibilities of the cultural enterprise, the heady directions in which it might go. Looking back on one's own justifications for what one was doing, and thought one might go on doing, it is near-impossible to believe anybody could be that stupid. For what has happened is that the older forms of elitism have been all but entirely replaced by a new and deadlier form, a marketplace elitism in which all success is measured quantitatively rather than qualitatively and critically. The traditional methods of conducting the business of serious art were very simple. Promoters, managers, agents, publishers—the people who tended to the commercial side of things— had been, legend to the contrary, quite open to young talent, taking on gifted if unformed aspirants, taking a modest loss as they managed and promoted their early careers, angling for a break, a lucky accident —often in the form of critical appreciation—that was often not that at all, but the end product of a long, slow research and developmental phase in which interest on the part of the knowledgeable public built slowly until a breakthrough point was reached. Obviously some, perhaps many, did not stay this course; obviously some, perhaps many, reached no more than the journeyman's level, achieving reputations for competence and professionalism and the opportunity for a respectable livelihood. There were, doubtless, unfairnesses in this system. Some people did, in fact, enjoy astonishingly easy arrivals at the star level; others, equally gifted, somehow never quite made it. Yet looking back—and the system is for all practical purposes no more than a memory—one could almost grow nostalgic.

In its whimsicality and capriciousness, in its wild guesswork about what the public might go for, its surprise at its own successes, its puzzlements about its failures, the business of art in some measure reflected the astonishments of art itself. The eccentricity and subjectivity of the manager's judgments, the patience with which they waited for the public to form and express its answering judgments, contained an implicit acknowledgment of the accidental nature of art, and of the transitory, provisional nature of all contemporary judgments about it. The whole idea of running this show was to make it as accident-prone as possible. That was the fun of it, actually. And if, ultimately, the bottom line could not be ignored, it was somehow understood that one must not try to arrive at it too quickly, or to attempt to predict how it would read on the basis of a quick poll or one or two performances.

The movies—the despised movies of the thirties and forties, supposedly so crass and vulgar, so full of Sammys running—offer an excellent example of how this system worked. Gable's ears were too big, Jack Warner said, refusing to sign him, and if they had had public opinion polls in those days, that judgment would probably have been confirmed. Fred Astaire's singing voice—for that matter, his speaking voice, not to mention his cadaverous appearance—would have won him no victories in anyone's sampling of mass taste. Garbo's pictures did not generally return blockbuster grosses, only nice little ones. But someone saw something in them all, called attention to it and called attention to it, until we, the audience, began to see what it was about them that was singular and gifted, and rewarded them with delighted and enduring regard.

No one disposed of this system by fiat. Rather what happened was that slowly, almost unnoticeably, a new and more apparently reasonable system began to grow up beside it, its leaves and branches subtly intertwining with the older one until, in its vigor, it choked off its predecessor and supplanted it without anyone quite being aware of it. So silent was its early growth, so lacking in threat its first products, that it is almost impossible to date its beginnings, though probably its first shy shoots were the public opinion polls of the 1930s, and the extension of their primitive techniques to the determination of which radio shows were the most popular with the audience. When television came in, of course, the samplers switched their attention to the new medium, with results that have been so often, so roundly, so correctly deplored that there is no further need to discuss them. We need only note that when this medium became the dominant one in the fifties and early sixties, it presented the whole cultural-entertainment community with a model of seemingly spectacular efficiency.

In the beginning, before anyone understood just how big the money in television was going to be, the medium operated pretty much as radio had. The ratings, to be sure, were important, but a show's cost was small (one movie studio, Columbia, got into television by appropriating $25,000 to found a TV subsidiary, which in the early fifties was enough to produce two pilots). As with radio, a certain number of marginal shows could be sensibly (and profitably) carried—series that attracted only a small, but a vociferously loyal audience; prestigious specials that Mr. Paley or some significant sponsor just damned well wanted to put on; documentaries, literary adaptations, musical events that attracted favorable critical notice, and the attention of the upscale market and thus prestige to the network.

Slowly, however, it began to dawn on broadcasters that this was a troublesome way to run a business. It would be much easier to do it by the numbers. All you really had to do was renew all the prime-time shows that attracted a 30 share of the audience in their time spots and cancel all that consistently fell below the 25 share. Those in the gray area you could try to save, if you felt up to it, by moving them around in the schedule or by altering their formats slightly. Demographics, always expressed in comforting numbers rather than in slippery words, become the language of the trade, replacing the more ambiguous language of the critics and aesthetes. Its seeming concreteness, and its pseudoscientific resonance, made selling the shows to advertisers, to affiliates, to the public itself, infinitely easier.

As the years went by it began to seem possible—though the going was trickier here—to use numbers predictively (and, in this context, "creatively"). Shows were tested before sample audiences in specially rigged auditoriums where the audience could instantly register whether it liked a scene or, for that matter, a line of dialogue or an actor's expression. Changes—including major cast changes—were made on the basis of this "research" though of course no important

TV role is nowadays cast with an actor whose name and face are not easily recognizable to survey respondents. Indeed, in very recent times, certain situations and character types are either encouraged or discouraged as a result of still other surveys (heroic blue-collar types, not surprisingly, are desired, intellectuals and older men and (especially) women are loathed; scene where characters talk to one another on the telephone are frowned upon, while the appeal of car chases is apparently infinite). Walter Benjamin, thou shouldst be living at this hour!

There is irony in the fact that the ineluctable power of demographics was discovered just as a more sophisticated and possibly more critical understanding of art was actually beginning to inch its way into the hearts and minds of a somewhat larger audience. It is certainly some sort of irony that we journalists were so enthralled by the evidence of this "cultural revolution" (as some among us took to calling it) that we did not observe the statistical revolution quietly proceeding across the street.

But, as it turned out, that was the real story. The numerical infection spread first to popular music. It was logical, given the record companies' close corporate ties with television. The managers of the all-music radio stations looked at their surveys and saw that their core audience was predominantly adolescent. They also observed that the youngsters were taking an increasingly proprietary air about rock and roll, a mildly outlawish sound that, early on, had a surprising capacity to outrage parents. The corporate types decided to program their stations with "your" music, and the record companies, whose sales were closely tied to the number of plays they could get from the disc jockeys, went along and, as journalist Sidney Zion put it, the catalogs of the top pop artists, who worked in a more traditional vein, were inexorably withdrawn from the market. He quotes the singer Tony Bennett, one of the victims of this change, "We're talking about lawyers, accountants and marketing guys . . . imagine an industry run by people who don't know anything about the product."

The predictable end of this trend was the Top 40 station, which every day, week in and week out, programmed only forty songs, the ones its surveys informed it were the ones its listeners most wanted to hear. The predictable nadir was reached, according to Zion, in April 1964, when the top five singles and the top two albums on the charts were all by the Beatles. Sometime later that year it was discovered that 60 percent of the disks played on all the stations in the country were by the Beatles. "Just giving the people what they want," murmured the music managers, aping their brethren in television.

It has become—that phrase—one of the ruling clichés of our time. If its sway were confined only to popular music and to television, one could afford to regard it as an anomaly. But, in fact, the experience of these two enterprises has come to be regarded as exemplary, a model to guide the economic organization of our culture, both popular and high. It is, obviously, a ruthlessly impatient model, in which the drive is always for instant gratification. What we observed in television, we can now observe everywhere. The top of the line, the artists and the works that achieve immediate public acceptance, command the immediate attention of the marketeers. Money and energy are instantly mobilized for prodigies of promotion, maximizing their profitability as quickly as possible. The more difficult artists, the less immediately apprehensible works, needing more time and more care to establish themselves, are, as a direct result, starved of attention. They cannot hope to make it on their own merits, not against competition that is intrinsically strong to begin with and is then given the reinforcing attention of a crudely powerful exploitational machine. And it is not just the commercially marginal that is ignored; it is the commercial middle as well, that once broad and interesting and hopeful place where one might once have hoped to find a career, a livelihood, an audience, and even a staging area for a final assault on the top.

One sees this system—or rather nonsystem—at work everywhere. On Broadway, the shows that do not receive virtually unanimous praise—which praise must include that of the critic from the *Times*— the morning after they open, close by the end of the week. There is no point in making a fight for them. In the movies a new picture's fate is decided on its first weekend of release. If the tally is not promising, no matter what the reviews are, promotional attention is switched from it to one of the studio's other releases. No sense pouring good money after bad. In serious music the major recording companies cut their contract lists to a handful of top stars who record a repertory of familiar favorites. On the concert circuit only the major names are booked with any consistency, and then, generally, only in the very largest halls. The smaller auditoriums, even in the musical capitals, are utilized less and less, because it is pointless to book the aspiring or even the merely solid artist into them; no one will come. In publishing, "midlist" writers, writers who command a small and formerly modestly profitable following, are no longer of interest. They do not command review attention, book club interest, worthwhile advances from the reprinters. Only the big names (or the flukey title that somehow promises self-help, irresistible gossip, or a predictably simple emotional response) are worth marketing as opposed to merely publishing —a feckless and frustrated ritual about as appropriate to late twentieth-century life as holding a rain dance. And about as useful in obtaining the desired result.

The Top 40 mentality has spread, in a very few years, into every corner of the cultural enterprise, distorting values wherever one looks. Gross revenues, in almost all fields, continue to hold their own, depending on the business cycle, but the largest share goes to a smaller and smaller number of people. The successes are fewer, but richer, the failures more abysmal, and the correlation between commercial success and critical success (and their opposites) grows ever more distant. There is no arguing with these whopping successes—or these glum failures. The intervention of criticism (by which I don't mean merely the formal variety, but also the response of the intelligent audience, discoursing among themselves, in the process making a viable and healthy market for an interesting artist or a challenging work) grows increasingly irrelevant. It is, in fact, the business of marketing to subvert this process, to protect the cultural entrepreneur from the unpredictable vagaries of this discourse, to place as many cultural products as possible beyond discussion and thus, in a sense, outside of the historical continuum and in the realm of sensation. This, in turn, suits journalism, which is always in pursuit of sensation at the expense of complexity.

In recent years, dollar figures have become perhaps the most important—or, anyway, the easiest to utilize—factor in the process of trying to lift any given cultural object out of the realm of routine coverage. The cliché "Names make news" must be expanded, for numbers now make news, too. The effect is similar to that which we observed in painting, where the price paid for a work becomes the most significant measure of its interest for the general public. But in the other arts the dance of the digits is more complex. For example, let's follow the commercial course of a book by a well-known author who has broached the bestseller charts before, or even better—since Cinderella stories are so surefire—an unknown author who has somehow come up with the right steaming recipe for popular success. The marketeers, looking at past performance, are quick off the mark. The book club grabs, the reprinters get into a bidding war (the results of which make the papers), the movie companies (or their television branches) join in, and, well before publication, an eminently reportable sum of money has changed hands. And with bucks like that on the table, no one is going to be modest in promoting the book in question. It will get the best display in the stores, the best television spots (and print features) when the author goes on tour. A year later, protecting his investment, the reprinter will repeat this process when he brings out the paperback edition. And a year after that it will be the movie or TV producer's turn. Obviously, such an expensive "property" requires expensive casting, and the search for the right, pricey actors (and, nowadays, the director) becomes public knowledge, too. Thereafter, the cost of the production itself becomes news, especially if temperament on the set or difficulties in realization *(Apocalypse Now, Heaven's Gate, Annie)* send it dramatically over budget, possibly even imperiling the management of the studio backing the enterprise. By the time such films are ready for release an almost irresistible drama has been created around them. A critic cannot dismiss them—as they often should be dismissed—with a few well-turned contemptuous lines. You cannot even bury your review—as you should in many cases—beneath a review of some smaller, but worthier, film. No, the film, like the book, has transcended itself; it is no longer a movie, it is a project celebrity. And a media event.

And not one that is soon over. For by buying the book or attending the film or just reading about its newsy numbers, the public gets involved with the thing, its career if you will. And the press caters to this avidity for inside information. Where once the New York *Times Book Review* published but one bestseller list, it now offers four, plus a column of commentary on what is moving up and down the lists. No metropolitan newspaper fails to list in the Sunday book section not only the national bestsellers but the leaders in its region. And now, each week, the general press publishes the previous week's television ratings, news that was once thought to be of exclusive interest to the trade press. Each week, as well, the wire services move a story about the previous week's motion picture grosses, indicating which films are succeeding, which failing, at the nation's box offices. Again, this is information that was formerly privileged. But prominent appearance on one of these lists is vital to the perpetuation of a work's success. It is the only way to get producer or publisher or network to keep promoting the work at hand. Equally important, it makes ordinary people

—"the civilians" to borrow the show biz term for the audience—want to get with it, if only for fear of being left out of the excitement.

🙢 🙢

What we are witnessing now in the arts is nothing less than a rage for quantification. And immediately a new analogy occurs. It is, of course, to sports, where the passion for compiling and studying increasingly sophisticated statistics has accompanied the growth, in this century, of games to their present place as a central—indeed, domineering—metaphor in American life. They suit the national spirit somehow, perhaps because their salient feature is the rapid (briefly suspenseful, occasionally exciting) plunge toward the bottom line, the score, which resolves all ambiguity, determines with brutal simplicity how we are supposed to feel about what we just witnessed. We may, on state occasions, when we are hanging a medal on some distinguished old party, some philosopher or artist or activist in a worthy cause, enjoy assuring ourselves and the world that we have other, more spiritual values, that we know there is more to life than winning and losing. But mostly what we think about is winning and losing, and it has heretofore been a defect of art that it was impossible to say how the game was coming out. It was up to history to make that decision, history that took its good-natured time making up its mind, and then was always changing its mind. Who could wait around for that? And who could get really interested in something that operated that way? These charts and lists, these movements of price in the marketplace— they solve that problem. They reduce art to a product, functioning in a marketplace, just like everything else. Suddenly, it is all very simple. Creation, like everything else in America, becomes a problem in advertising, in public relations and, finally, at its delicious best, a matter for the tax attorney.

The reader who follows sports will perceive here a delicious irony, which is that sport itself is now threatened by the numbers in a way that is not so very different from the way that art is threatened. For something like a decade the sports pages have been full of discussions about how our games have been distorted by the influx of big money, stemming originally from television's avid interest in sports and the ever-mounting fees it was willing to pay for the right to broadcast our most popular pastimes. Exposure on the tube led, naturally enough, to the creation of a favored new class of athletic superstars, men and women who transcended mere stardom based on excellence in their specialties to become "personalities" recognized even by people who did not follow their game. Again there were precedents: Babe Ruth, Red Grange, Joe Louis, Bobby Jones, Don Budge, et al. were scarcely unknown figures in the old days. But, for the most part, great wealth did not follow in the train of their endeavors, and neither were they frequently invited to play touch football with the power elite, or to offer their opinions on how things were going in our society. These people led, in fact, rather cloistered lives; reports of their doings were rigidly segregated in the sports pages. But television and the big bucks have changed all that, if only because it was impossible for the owners and promoters to keep all the TV money for themselves and not share it with the men and women whose presence on the field was a requisite for ratings. All this, of course, has changed our perspective on sport.

It was never as pure an enterprise as its apologists and promoters said it was (certainly violations of the amateur code were rife everywhere), but, on the other hand, there was no cocaine problem in the NFL, either. And no appearance guarantees for tennis tournaments, which turn the question of whether someone wins or loses into an irrelevancy. On every hand the jocks now justify themselves by saying that what they do is just after all, a branch of show business, which is the kind of remark you pick up around your agent's office, and is both a truism and an invitation to travesty.

It is sufficient, perhaps, to note that the long-standing addiction to statistics in sports has been no more proof against the power of more vulgar economic quantifications than the art world's relative innocence of the statistical passion has been. When the news of a multimillion-dollar pact for some baseball or football player rates headlines, when earnings on various sporting tours and circuits are published weekly on the same page with the team standings and the batting averages, then we witness in the sports world what we are witnessing in the art world—the degradation of the true measure of a man or woman's worth, the de-aestheticizing of their endeavor, the vulgarization of something that was, within living memory, both elegant and complex and like art not to be understood too readily or without trained (or anyway well-versed) intelligence.

We can put the matter simply: art is, in part, a game *(homo ludens* and all that) and games, at their best, partake of some of the aspects of art, but when success in either is defined largely in dollar terms, both endeavors are opened up to control by a new kind of player, the marketing expert. These people, with no more sensibility than a kumquat, are permitted to play in both as influentially—sometimes more so—as the prime creators. In art, in particular, they rush to transcend their original roles. They are no longer passive salesmen doing their best to flog what their sullen suppliers have sent them to sell on a take-it-or-leave-it, consignment basis. Nor do they function as the traditional art dealer or publishing house editor has, offering welcome advice and support. No, these new people, operating on the show biz model, have "input," which input is designed to rig the market or, if you will, fix the game, an activity that is against the law in sports but can win you the Irving Thalberg Award on Academy Award night.

Art—certainly the high arts, and to a surprising degree, even the movie business as it once operated (which was on the basis of whether or not Harry Cohn's ass started to twitch while the rough cut was being screened)—was a classically free market until recently. It was, indeed, one of the last such in our corporate economy. Now, however, with the intervention of marketing as a pseudoscience, it becomes a market organized as a series of self-fulfilling prophecies. A couple of common phrases sum it up: "Them that has, gets" and "If you're hot you're hot, if you're not you're not." Or as Michael Bennett, the choreographer and director *(A Chorus Line, Dreamgirls),* succinctly put it, "Unfortunately in America today, either you're a star or you're nobody." That is to say, by extension for this discussion, your work is either a hit or a flop; there is no viable middle ground. And that status is decided beforehand in the marketing meetings, which may well precede production, assuredly do precede distribution.

The chances of the market reacting unpredictably, resisting the massive interventions of promotion and publicity, of consumers revolting against the prophecy that is really a fix, is minimal. Obviously it does happen. Sometimes the books pile up in the stores unsold. Sometimes the movie dies, or is the victim of its self-dramatizing process, wherein the costs mount so high that their recoupment is impossible even with huge grosses. Sometimes, too, the orphan work, the one the marketing experts despise (usually because they cannot sum it up in a catchy slogan for the ads), gets adopted by the public despite its muttish qualities. Sometimes, for some unpredictable reason, an accidental concatenation of critical attention makes up for the lack of enthusiasm in marketing, helping a wandering work to find a place for itself in the world. This is the way new life is introduced into the system—just enough to keep it alive. Or perhaps one should say, just enough to keep alive one of its sustaining myths, which is that discovery, overnight success, the descent of stardom on the unlikely, is possible.

Be that as it may, we are approaching now, in all the arts, a point where the circle of possibilities tightens to noose-like proportions. One need but consult the model—television—to see that point. The number of consumer-proved genres has narrowed to a handful, and the same tired faces, or clone faces—the pollster's faces—turn up on these shows; the known cashing in on their knownness. This, inevitably, is what you get when a system is based on statistical models that can cope only with very large, very simple numbers. It can translate them —package and promote and distribute them—only into a limited number of very limited products. Popular culture—and now high culture—becomes more and more analogous to popular democracy, where there is no longer any point in counting the write-in votes or paying attention to third party candidates or grass roots rebellions. They are no more than quixotic and romantic gestures—good for a light spot on the evening news, but not to be confused with the serious business at hand, which can only be defined as big business.

The machinery cannot accommodate anything else, even if it wanted to. But of course it does not want to. If your game is lightning calculation, quick quantification, then that which cannot be speedily and meaningfully quantified—that is, turned into an efficient market— tends to make you edgy. It tends to send you back into the gray area of aesthetics, which is precisely what the lawyers and accountants and marketing M.B.A.s sought to avoid when they chose their professions in the first place.

It might be argued, of course, that the real challenge of marketing lies in devising ways of winning the large public over to things that initially seem strange and difficult. But that requires wit, patience, cunning, a capacity for risk and, above all, a commitment to a standard of values (or, at least, personal taste)—the qualities that artists possess and that people whose business is counting things and predicting things, do not, in their natures, possess. Moreover, it is hard to justify such efforts—more romanticism, more quixotism—to top management, boards of directors, stockholders. That is especially the case when it is so easy to work within the comfortable limits of well-tested numerical patterns, to hire a star who has succeeded before, to do the kind of show or album that has worked before (and we have the figures to prove it). Finally, efforts in this direction challenge the happy democratic assumptions that support the "we're just giving them what they want" argument. If, indeed, "they" went for a whole new thing, some radically different kind of music or programming, might not that imply that the whole mighty media enterprise was a fraud? Better not to tempt fate—especially as long as there is nothing like a real consumer revolt going on out there any more than there was ever a real political revolt going on out there either.

There is a basic law of mass communication that holds that what the audience does not see, has never seen, it cannot possibly miss. It may feel vaguely restive, it may be tuning in only because your program is the least offensive item in its time slot, it may, therefore, be somewhat cranky in its passivity, a little puzzled at its lack of perfect contentment, but it is present and maybe even fairly alert as it tries to get all the nourishment it can out of a skimpy meal. Besides, you can't measure such vagrant moods, only overt concrete behavior.

What we arrive at, finally, is a triumph of reciprocity—between celebrity and demography, stardom and statistics, names and numbers, put it as you will. Each has a magical force in today's world, and when they are combined their marketing power is, or can be, greater than the sum of their parts. And when the guide to the future is, predominantly, the records of past performance by genre piece or star or star in genre piece then—putting the matter mildly!—our culture will have about it a certain lack of venturesomeness. Then Gresham's law acts with a terrible vengeance.

In this context it becomes more and more difficult to assert one's singularity through one's art. When the numbers attached to it acquire heroic proportions, then the need for heroic assertion in the practice of one's craft begins to seem counterproductive. We have no Barrymores before us now, and no young Brandos, either. And it is hard to think of writers, poets, painters, composers either who are, at present, greatly at risk in their art. Or, for that matter, in our public forums. Our stars now trail behind them not clouds of glory, but clouds of grosses. They are in danger of being known not so much for their knownness as for their wealth. If they use their power it is not in pursuit of dream or ideal, but in self-defense. Or, at most, to stick it to somebody—an old enemy, perhaps, or (if they are in show biz) to the studio they darkly (and probably correctly) believe is stealing part of their percentage. There is a joylessness in this materialism that makes one yearn for the giddiness of days gone by. And the earnestness of aspiration that often accompanied it. The stars of today are guarded and careful and muted—like democratized royalty self-conscious about not offending, too aware of what they have to lose. They have become the sum not of their strivings but of their successes. There is no magic about them, no danger in them. They seem as abstract as an accountant's statement or a filled-in tax form. Or, shall we say, a painting of the old New York school? Reflecting upon their own prosperous reflections, they only rarely reflect something of ourselves and our world back on us through their work—and then, it seems, only when they are very young, and trying, or very old, and don't give a damn.

So much of art having failed us, we the audience engage ourselves now in acts of do-it-yourself transcendence. There being few worthwhile myths to refer to, we seek to become, in our loneliness, our own myths—and manage only to imitate Narcissus, which does little to ward off the chill in the melting air.

SEVEN

Coherent Lives

Finally, there is this question: How do we apprehend celebrity? I am not now talking about our individual celebrity dreams, our furtive lusts and fugitive longings, our fantasy relationships, whatever their emotional tone, with this or that famous person. No, we must at last move beyond the kind of largely unacknowledged social and media transactions that have up to now preoccupied this inquiry. We must consider the larger dream scheme that has evolved out of this century's countless billions of fantastical encounters between the celebrity elite and the anonymous mass. We must, if we can, consider what celebrity as an idea consists of, how, in its light, we generally perceive the entire celebrity enterprise, how that perception, in turn, affects the quality and nature of our public life and how, in the end, all these factors affect the private man's sense of himself and his place in our peculiar historical moment.

A question posing itself in such complex terms requires a complex response. Broadly speaking, it consists of two partially contradictory parts, for celebrity appears to the noncelebrity to fulfill both a dream of autonomy and, at the same time, a dream of intimate, almost familial connection among figures of glamour and authority. Both are thus, at bottom, dreams of power inevitably tinged by envy and resentment.

Of the two, the dream of autonomy is the easiest to describe. Very simply, in their highly visible passages through life, the famous, without any conscious exertion on their parts, convey to the drudging world an impression of near-perfect freedom. The reason for this lies partly in the nature of the work they do. Actors, performers of every sort, politicians, corporate leaders, even writers, of necessity lead far-flung existences. Their work continually takes them to and fro, hither and yon and, very often, this habit of movement carries over into their personal lives. The backyard vacation does not have much appeal in this set. Nor does a house an hour away at the lake. Not when they can as well afford Gstaadt. Indeed, nowadays it is a mark of distinction to make your principal residence at some inconvenient distance from your principal place of work. But no matter, whether they are en route to work or play or merely "skying in for confabs" or to "ink a pact" (to borrow *Variety*'s ineffable jargon), the fact remains that it is when they are out and about on their travels that they are least well protected, thus most vulnerable to the prying lenses of the paparazzi. That, of course, enhances the public's impression that they are constantly on the go, which is the one thing that most people are not— tied as they are to the obligations of office, family, community—and set free only for limited periods—at best on the fringe of those venues where the moveable feast of the famous seems most often to come to rest.

But enviable as the right of free passage is in and of itself, it is symbolic of a still more admirable autonomy. For it is clear that, almost uniquely these days, the celebrity is his own boss, that he is, in fact, one of the last among us still enjoying the blessing of that most profound of American dreams, private entrepreneurship. The celebrity's enterprise is, of course, only himself, which makes him a very small businessman indeed, if often a very rich one. Yet pleasant as our imaginings of the tax advantages of the personal corporation are, an indication that besides having shaken free of the time clock and the Monday morning staff conference, the favored few have also shrugged off the binding chains of payroll deduction as well, this is by no means the end of our awe.

What is finally so splendid about these lives as we imagine them from the outside is that in the corporate age they appear to have no permanent institutional allegiances. All such are temporary, the length of the film they are making, for example, or the television contract under which they are laboring. And the more successful they become, the less dependent they are on the corporations that order the lives of the rest of us. (In this sense there is an analogy between show business figures and the politicians whose cults of personality render them im-

pervious to calls for party loyalty or threats of party discipline.) Indeed, for a few it becomes entirely possible to reverse—at least for a
time—the usual order of things. They achieve what most of their
fellow citizens can only fantasize, the ability to make the corporations
wait on them.

In this respect, as in so many others, Johnny Carson has been a
paradigm. How many hundreds of jokes has he told at the expense of
his ostensible superiors, the NBC executives? How often has the simple business of holding up a can or box of one of his sponsor's products been turned into a little comedy of errors, the result either of a
casual carelessness that would be the cause of a reprimand for us if we
tried it at work or of a deliberate attempt at sabotage that would be a
firing offense for anyone else. But Johnny, with his boyish grin, his
class cutup's insinuating cheekiness, gets away with it. Just as he gets
away with political jokes that might, in mixed ideological company,
cause us social embarrassment. At these moments he speaks our secret
thoughts, is our surrogate rebel without a cause. He is not, of course,
Lenny Bruce, or even Mort Sahl, but neither are most of us. He is
merely the symbol of a not unnatural national desire to give occasional
razzberryish tongue to our unspoken (and distinctly nonrevolution-
ary) thoughts about the institutions that rule our lives and impose
upon us, in their corporate wisdom, a delicate insistence on gentility
and decorum that is somewhat at odds, shall we say, with their own
ability to transcend such niceties when it suits their interests to do so.

Some kind of apotheosis in this regard was achieved by Carson in
1980. He had been increasingly on vacation in that year as he sought
to renegotiate his contract. He would, he let it be known, agree to
appear more regularly on the show only if its running time were cut by
a third—from ninety minutes to an hour. It was not something NBC
wanted to do, especially considering its troubles everywhere else on its
schedule. But, after protracted unpleasantness he prevailed, and actually ended up with more money for less work. And was there anyone
in his regular audience, or in the still larger audience that attended
this dispute, who was on the network's side?

This was the dream of autonomy acted out on a grand scale, an
exhibition of the raw power of celebrity that is rarely witnessed by the
public. But it is often, of course, witnessed by studio and network
executives. The stars of long-running TV shows, aware that their continued presence is essential to the profitable life of the enterprise, are
wondrous to behold when they decide that $50,000 or $100,000 or

whatever per week is insufficient recompense for their toil. Health suddenly deteriorates, requiring sudden recuperative absences or imposing small but costly delays in reporting to the set. Of course, in these circumstances, the size of the dressing room, or the color of its walls, becomes a depressant too oppressive to bear. And as for the scripts—approval of them will be a necessity in the future if the star is not to be irreparably injured in the image. Tantrums on the set, requiring the replacement of the director, naturally become epidemic. At the feature film level the details differ, but the result is the same. Established stars have their prices, and everyone knows what they are—unless he or she is just coming off a big, surprise hit and a raise is in order, or the inevitable decline has set in and a cut must be accepted. Ordinarily, however, negotiations focus on the fringes—per diem expenses, the number of first-class airfares to and from location for family and entourage, limousine service, the hairdresser, all the various perquisites of stardom, failure to provide which so often results in delays more costly than any frill.

This is not all idle ego- or power-tripping. Many TV leads have been around the business for a long time as supporting players and have suffered their share of humiliation and insecurity at the hands of the studios and the networks. The same is true of many movie stars. When power is belatedly thrust on them, they have the opportunity for revenge, and they would be less than human if they did not take advantage of it. They also know that their time at the top is likely to be brief. Five or six years is the most that you count on for even a very hot show to keep running high in the ratings; a decade or so may be all the room a movie star finds at the top, with the rest of his time being devoted to his rise and fall—all dog food commercials and dinner theaters.

But these conditioning realities need not detain us here any longer than they do in life. We know all about them thanks to all the self-referential (not to say self-reverential) material show business cranks out about itself. While our favorite stars have it in their power to exert power, we are all for them, unless they are peculiarly unpleasant about it when they discuss their latest labor-management crisis (on Carson's show, naturally). The fantasy they are living out for us is much more valuable to us than a detailed moral analysis of the rights and wrongs of any specific situation laid before us. To everyone reporting to his or her desk on time, world without end, a little thrill is felt whenever one of these show people puts it to a producer. It may contain, this thrill, an admixture of envy, but the immediate impulse is toward the silent cheer. And if the upshot is nothing more elevating than some minor increment to the good life invisible to the naked and distant eye of the fan, who cares?

For added to his traditional duties the modern celebrity, with his freedom of movement, his occasional imperiousness, the impression he conveys of being the master of his own fate, keeps alive a dream of individuality that, like the pioneers of American industrial capitalism a century ago, verges always on the socially irresponsible. And, indeed, often falls over that line (especially when they presume to inform us on current political and social issues). In effect, they are supposed to run the risks and reap the rewards that are systematically denied corporate man and woman. More than that—they may even be said to be charged with getting even for the rest of us poor saps, who suspect, in the dark nights of our souls, that we have bargained away freedom too easily for a security that is perhaps not worth our acquiescence. And may be illusory, since we can never be sure that our corporate masters will stick to the (mostly implicit) deals they make with us. We all know too many people who clapped hands and believed—right up until they were asked to accept early retirement. Celebrities seem somehow to avoid all that—even their falls often have about them a certain melodramatic interest, a tragic beauty. Meantime, they've ridden Lear jets all the way.

Among the most visible perquisites of celebrity is access to one's fellow celebrities. All the imagery reinforces this impression as powerfully as it does the belief that the famous are in constant, exciting motion. As a result, we hold this fancy to be self-evident: That there is a small and seemingly cohesive group of well-known individuals of both sexes, of all ages, of several pleasant, profitable, and (obviously) highly public occupations who as a result of success—or anyway notoriety—in their fields share close communal ties with one another at the high center of our public life—ties that are enhanced by the fact that they share the pleasures and problems inherent in their celebrity status, no matter how disparate their routes to that status.

This sense of the way things are when you are rich and famous has some basis in reality. "In the aristocracy of success there are no strangers," S. J. Perelman once wrote, and he was not being funny. Richard Stern, the very fine—and, alas, insufficiently celebrated—novelist wrote: "There was no greater star-lovers than stars. This fellowship of celebrity was more than expert appraisal of expertise: it was the sediment of the old need for authentic power and grace." If the point needs to be proved any further, we can take the testimony of Gay Talese, whose explorations of tasty subject matter (a Mafia family, the sexual revolution) in the novelistic manner of the new journalism have brought him the kind of publicizable riches (an alleged advance of $4 million from all sources for one of his books) that, as we have noticed earlier, in and of themselves make one a celebrity, which Talese surely is. "To me," he once said, "parties are diverting and celebrities are often more exciting to be around. They are people who like being public performers, and there is a romantic vibrance about them, something sensual, sexual, an electricity."

But if being curious about their peers from other realms, and having as a result of their own fame ready access to them, makes it easy for celebrity to speak to celebrity, if there is a need among these people for the security against the gawking and often importunate mob which can best be obtained by gathering with one's equals in venues that guarantee the exclusion of people clad in polyesters and thrusting out bits of paper for autographing, if finally, one of the ways for a celebrity to test the potency of his own celebrity is to see how it shines when placed in close proximity with that of others, that still does not mean that there is anything like a cohesive celebrity community. Or that the well-known have any great family feeling for each other. Access is not intimacy. It is, in fact, nothing more than an essentially empty perquisite, like the limousines and the private jets that are, as Stern writes, "regal hangovers."

But if the notion of a celebrity community is largely a fiction or anyway a fictive convention, it is still one that is worth the trouble to which its ostensible members go to maintain it, for it is also a highly visible manifestation of their mysterious otherness, and of their essential, exclusionary power.

An anecdote demonstrates the point. A writer I know was indulging in that peculiar rite known as the "author tour," designed to promote his latest book. He arrived in Los Angeles more than a little bent from several dozen television, radio, and "print" interviews in cities the order of whose appearance on his itinerary was already blurring in his mind. There the high point of his schedule was an appearance on "The Merv Griffin Show"—nationally syndicated, and thus one of his two or three best bookings. In the green room he encountered an actress he knew very slightly—they had a mutual friend and the three of them had killed time together at a film festival many years before. They chatted pleasantly, and then the actress departed for hairdressing and makeup, from which she went directly to the stage, for she was to precede the writer on the air. In due course, he found himself waiting sweatily behind a curtain, cringing as he listened to Merv's introduction of him, which seemed to him too fulsome by half. There was at last a burst of applause and in response he burst through the curtain. Abandoning his customary shambling pace, he bustled across the stage in the eager manner he had seen people practiced in the art of public appearance employ on such occasions. There was a warm handclasp from the host—just as if they were old pals. He turned to take his seat and there was his actress friend standing in greeting. He suddenly remembered that in similar circumstances he had observed that guests on these shows often kissed, though he was also perfectly aware that a handshake, perhaps a touch on the arm, was all this particular relationship permitted. He also knew that he dared not dither over protocol in front of the watching millions, and he was, as well, eager to appear before them as a man at ease in the world of the celebrated. And so he kissed the woman, who was a good sport about it, pro that she was. Being, however, a literary fellow, the incident sent him into a near-Jamesian tizzy of self-examination over his manners and their meanings. Later he would feel that his confusion and embarrassment over that moment, his sense that he had violated his own standards of decorum in the attempt to satisfy those the occasion seemed to require, prevented him from effectively selling his book. On the other hand, he would later reflect, he deplored appearing thus, tooting his own horn, in a context unlikely to prove hospitable to the serious issues he believed he had taken up in his writing, so perhaps he was justified in trying to brazen out a discomfiting social situation as best he could. And so on—to no firm conclusion, except that he had made a damn fool of himself.

One does not wish to dwell overlong on his seriocomic self-abasement. The point is only that the ritual in which he found himself participating was essentially an exclusionary one, designed to subtly reinforce the separation from and superiority of the people seated on Merv's stage over those seated in his audience in the studio and at home. We have become, all of us, adepts at reading the status signals implicit in these appearances. Is the singer or the stand-up comic invited to join the host and the other guests for a bit of chat after they have completed their speciality? If they are not, we understand that they have not yet arrived at a significant level in the show biz hierarchy. And what about those who are seated on the host's right hand in the conventionalized desk chair and sofa set? How may segments of his valuable time does each of them command? And in what order do they appear? First is not great, for that one will be, obviously, the first to be shunted aside and the one who has to longest suffer attention being directed elsewhere. The last spot is even worse. For the chances are that time will be eaten away in tiny increments in the preenings that precede it, leaving the poor soul in the closing spot trying to cram his or her message into a couple of hasty moments. Often this spot is reserved for authors; and authors with wit, clout, and powerful press agents will not accept it, knowing not only that it won't do the book much good, but that this visible statement of exactly how the writer and his work are valued by the powers that be, may actually work against him and send a sign of insignificance to the viewer.

But yet, few will turn down any opportunity to appear in this context of false intimacy with the celebrated. And not just because of the practical effect that even a brief talk show appearance can sometimes have on a book, film, play, or plastic novelty. There is also in it a gratifying enhancement of self-esteem, even if not a single unit of one's current product is moved off the shelves. Even those of us who are amateurs and supernumeraries in this little world come quickly to understand that. All of us who write for a living are occasionally asked to turn up for this or that televised discussion of this or that topic to add the minor authority of the authorial to the revels. And all of us, in the aftermath of such an appearance, have felt ourselves rise in our mothers' estimations—especially if the show was national. Mothers do not read *The New York Review of Books,* nor even the New York *Times Book Review.* But, of course, they watch television. And, better still, Edna and Madge down the block watch it. When they are impressed, Mom is impressed and then, in turn, you are self-impressed, even against your better judgment.

But why? Partly for the most obvious reason. Because you have been seen publicly rubbing shoulders with the famous, which must mean that you have some celebrity of your own. But there is, I think, a subtler force at work here, an unspoken and only partially formed idea. "America," as opposed to that geographical and political entity best identified by its full title, "The United States of America," has traditionally been understood as an idea (sometimes, especially on

gaseous state occasions, as an ideal), and that, in turn, has traditionally been understood to be as multifarious and as fluid as the number
of people—mainly literary—who have attempted to define it. Indeed,
part of the idea consists of an implicit acknowledgment that no one
ever has, and no one ever will, successfully encompass it in words, just
as no one ever managed to write The Great American Novel back in
the days when earnest people cried out for it. But that sweet vagueness, that attractive ambiguity, that tantalizing elusiveness that used
to attend our ruminations on the subject of "America" are all now
vastly reduced.

Television now provides us our only meaningful context for that
speculative enterprise, the only external reality that matters. It is
often, to be sure, a surreality in the original sense of that term, that is
to say, a super-reality, one that overwhelms all other realities. And it
is often to be apprehended as many objects of surrealistic art are, that
is, as a radical and discomfiting rearrangement of a familiar scene,
often with some dislocating symbol inserted willy-nilly into it. But if
classical surrealism had the effect, at its best, of transforming reality,
expanding its parameters as we perceived it, television, like any other
mass medium, shrinks it. Which at the moment is of no matter. What
matters is that if we do not somehow manage to insert ourselves into
this reality, we run the danger of being, in our own eyes, unpersons.

It was the novelist Walker Percy who began the process of clearing
the path to this point. His first novel, *The Moviegoer,* was published in
1961, when the movies were still (just barely) the movies as they had
been for some forty years. That is to say, they had not yet been entirely elbowed from their former position at the center of mass consciousness—though, of course, people had been observing the bullying
power of television for over a decade at that point. Still he could
accurately observe, in a passage that has since become quite famous
(in its modest, literary way) that: "Nowadays when a person lives
somewhere, in a neighborhood, the place is not certified for him. More
than likely he will live there sadly and the emptiness which is inside
him will expand until it evacuates the entire neighborhood. But if he
sees a movie which shows his very neighborhood, it becomes possible
for him to live, for a time at least, as a person who is Somewhere and
not Anywhere."

This was good, this dictum, as far as it went. But in 1961, despite
the new power of television, a power that had, of course, vastly diminished that of the movies already, and was day by day vitiating it still

further, Percy could not go further. Rereading him now, in fact, one is struck anew at how simply the movies tend to work on us, how complicated, by contrast, are the metaphors we require to apprehend television's effects on us, if only because the normal language of criticism is entirely unavailable to us as we consider its workings. This is because criticism requires the discrete object or event as a precondition of its employment. But television is not what it pretends to be, a neutral medium purveying a sequence of individual programs. That is doubtless what its developers intended it to be, and that is surely what it suits people who write about it to pretend that it is. But after living with it for almost four decades we know (even if we do not acknowledge) that at least in this basic respect Marshall McLuhan was right; it is an environment. We know this from our own behavior in relationship to it. Which is to say that generally we decide to "watch television" before we consult TV Guide to find out what is going on in that environment at the moment we make that basic decision, before we decide whether or not to slip into this ever-ready, ever-tepid electronic bath. It is difficult to write critically, or for that matter to think critically about an environment. It simply is. And all you can do is to decide to exist in it or not.

It is apparent then, that television has, to a degree, taken over the old "certifying" function of the movies (most particularly on the local news shows), but it is also obvious that this is one of its lesser functions and that the movies, which retain a greater aura of old-fashioned glamour (if only because of the trouble and expense they require to mount, and because we continue to think of them as "events"), still outstrip TV in this one regard. But that is a matter of only minor consequence in comparison with the power of television to reverse Walker Percy's dictum, the power of this environment, this neighborhood, to certify *us.* Which is why it means so much to our mothers when we appear to be at home in it, comfy and cozy, confident and confidential.

This reality is so attractive because so many of the conventional realities have either diminished in their power to sustain and nurture us psychologically, or are in a state of transition with their future directions unpredictable when they are not downright discouraging. For a long time—for much of this century, in fact—social commentators have been decrying the steady erosion of our old sense of community, the decline, as it were, of our psychic neighborhoods. The diaspora of small-town America is actually a reality that is older than our century. The decline of a sense of neighborhood in the cities that have been absorbing wave on wave of both external and internal migration since before the turn of the century has become vividly marked in the last twenty or thirty years. And, since the end of World War II, the mobility of Americans, who in larger and larger numbers have given their primary allegiance to our corporate states-within-the-state, who are moved hither and thither at the whim of the managers—who *are* the managers or the managers manqué—has commanded much sociological attention. Of late, the dissatisfaction of corporate communal life—or rather the spurious nature of the surrogate communality offered there—has commanded similar attention. Given the disruptions of the century, given the sheer amount of to-and-froing that we do (even if our careers are relatively stable geographically, the jet plane and the interstates give us unprecedented ability to move about voluntarily), it is no wonder that we have a need to believe in a relatively stable celebrity community, one which, in effect, stays put while we hop around.

In addition, everyone these days mourns the demise of the extended family. Justifiably so. Not only is the family smaller, not only are the generations within it increasingly segregated from each other, but whatever its size, it is increasingly seen as a fragile institution. The divorce rate, the numbers of children who run away, the other fragmenting forces—ranging from the sexual revolution to the increasing number of married women who stay in or reenter the work force—all combine to increase destabilization.

In this context, the celebrity community, which has about it—as small-town life once did—aspects of the extended family, offers a kind of compensation. Yes, its membership does change—though mostly through expansion rather than contraction. Yes, relationships within it are constantly being redefined as accomplishment (or merely publicity) changes an individual's status or as feuds develop, often in public view as a result of some remark on a talk show or in an interview. But the community abides, no matter what.

In the dimmest motel room in the farthest reaches of the nation, we can always find that community, or it can reach out and touch us—whichever locution suits your fancy. And when we come down in the morning, there on the newsstand, on the way to the coffee shop, are *People* and *Us* and, if we are really without amour propre that day,

The National Enquirer and *The Star,* eager to put us in touch with our friends. Indeed, the morning paper will be glad to do so, for every one of them, from the New York *Times* on down, carries what amounts to a gossip column, though it is less blatantly that than the old Winchell and Hedda Hopper classics, calling itself by some bland title like "Names in the News."

And there are other sources of information as well. The magazine shows on television, from the august *60 Minutes* to its less secure imitators, nearly always feature a celebrity profile of some sort, and then, of course, there are the romans à clef which proliferate on the paperback racks, with their feebly imagined incursions into the bedrooms of characters clearly modeled on famous people. Since the external details of the celebrity lives thus presented include facts generally known to be true, the naïve reader assumes (or is meant to assume) that the novelist has inside information about more intimate behavior as well, that the whole package is titillatingly "realistic" in tone.

Still, all this printed matter amounts to is a kind of surrogate television, material that attempts to offer what might at best be thought of as a dietary supplement to our main meal, which is served to us electronically and is as conveniently available to us as Chicken McNuggets. But even if one resists the notion of television as a moveable junk food feast, it is, without question, a moveable neighborhood, since our TV friends are ever with us, no matter how remote our motel room, no matter how deep in the woods we have built our Thoreauvian cabin. At the flick of a switch we can summon up our crowd, share a warm, warming moment or two with them.

Still, I would argue there is more to the matter than that. I would argue that in this realm a large number of us have very nearly transcended technology, that many of us—in a kind of parody of that transcendence of corporality that George Bernard Shaw so entrancingly toyed with in plays like *Back to Methuselah* (and so many fans of the spiritual life today embrace)—are in daily spiritual communion with our celebrity favorites. At a certain point of overexposure to the endlessly transmitted, symbolically weighted images of famous people, these figures take up permanent residence in many inner lives as well, become, in fact, omnipresent functionaries in their reveries and fantasies, guides to action, to sexuality, to ambition. Technology may be essential to keeping these characters lively by almost daily recounting their adventures, but what I really meant when I said earlier that the celebrity community stays put, is that it is now permanently insinuated in a substantial number of sensibilities, and that they carry its major characters around with them wherever they go as part of their mental luggage. Like the rest of us, they may enjoy catching up with the latest on one of their favorites via television or a magazine piece, but somewhere along the way constant exposure becomes superfluous. They know all they need to know about these characters—may even, in fact, resist finding out information that would blur their sharp, clear images with ambiguities.

I do not claim that this is yet the norm. All of us are not yet arrived at that dismal point. But this internalization, this incorporation, this near-spiritual communion that many of us hold with starry favorites is no longer the exclusive prerogative of dreamy adolescence. It is the logical extreme toward which we are heading, and at which the psychopaths among us have indeed arrived.

But forget the psychopaths for a minute. Let's talk about ourselves, our dear, normal selves. We are not goners; the reality principle does from time to time assert itself in our inner lives. But even so, it is painfully obvious to us that our communications with our celebrated favorites is all one-way. They send (and send and send) while all we do is receive (and receive and receive). They do not know we exist as individuals; they see us only as the components of the mass, the audience. And that is frustrating. In the dark night of our souls it makes us feel bad. (If we are John Hinckley, Jr., it makes us feel very bad indeed.) It makes us feel bad because these people run the most desirable neighborhood in the Global Village. They are—let's face it—the bullies on the block, however pleasantly they play the role. Or maybe one should say they are the gang that sets the standards and the social tone, they have it within their power to "certify" us—or deny certification. And they behave in that way that used to drive us crazy in high school—cliquishly. Or to return to the word with which this discussion began, in an exclusionary manner. Thus when they let us in, permit us to sit down in earnest confabulation with the host, to banter with his other guests, it matters to us in ways that are far more significant than whatever immeasurable amount it contributes to the prosperity of our current enterprise. There is no one among us who emerges from these close encounters of a strange kind refusing to refer to the host on a first-name basis. And who does not sow at least a few seeds of envy among his acquaintances, most especially the ones he left back home in the boondocks of childhood. And everyone who emerges

unscathed from this experience inevitably begins to harbor the fantasy
that he, too, could run permanently with this crowd. Barbara Walters
made the transition, didn't she? And Gene Shalit? And others no more
obviously to the manner born. Oh to be exclusionary! Oh to be at the
center of the gang, ruling the roost! It is, for some, for many, the
heart's desire that dare not speak its name.

Sometimes, superficially, the celebrity world quite self-consciously
presents itself in terms that fit our old-fashioned, neighborly, communal sense of the way things work. Or ought to work. It has the capacity to delude onlookers by showing itself especially—and ironically—
on its large state occasions in carefully leveling terms. I am referring
to premieres, opening nights, publication parties, and prizegivings as,
perhaps, forms of the higher Rotarianism, glamorized, often nationally reported variants, say, on the small town's high school sports
nights, where the mayor and the principal and the other local dignitar-
ies gather, under some civic club's sponsorship, to award letter sweaters and trophies to the kids on the teams. This being America, where
the superficial forms of democratic behavior are followed at every level
of social congress, this is perhaps inevitable, possibly even endearing
in its way.

But, of course, there is this fundamental difference between those
sweetly modest functions of years gone by and a public gathering well-
populated by famous people. The former is designed to reinforce a
sense of communality; the latter (whatever else it pretends to be) is
designed to do the opposite, is thus anxiety producing to the anonymous onlooker. The photographers and newsmen kept at bay, either
outside the entrance to the hall or segregated in a special section inside
where they may watch but not intrude; the general public kept out on
the sidewalk, generally under the eye of the police—this spoils the
analogy with more ordinary social forms. So does the fact, alluded to
by Talese, that celebrities are always aware that people are looking at
them, that they are therefore at all times "on"—a condition that does
not apply, let us say, to a gathering of hardware salesmen, who may be
"up" for the occasion, but are not necessarily "on."

The difference is subtle. If, as private citizens, we attend a public
function, any attention paid to us is by chance. It behooves us to be on
our best, that is to say, our most winning behavior in these circumstances. We can never tell what good—or ill—we will do ourselves if

we are caught in the glance of a wandering eye. But the well-known person, attending the same function, carries within himself the utter certainty that he will be watched, that he must therefore, to a degree, perform. Indeed, for him to behave "naturally" in these circumstances requires a degree of conscious performance that most of us would find burdensome, at least until we had acquired the technique for so doing. And, in fact, once one gets used to carrying oneself in this manner, the absence of the need to do so can be disconcerting. There is an odd emptiness about, let us say, a Hollywood production executive—or a Washington politician—used to a certain attention on his home turf, robbed of the deference—and the curious sidelong glances—he is used to at home when he is making his way through a New York restaurant or a foreign vacation spot. As for a faded star, ignored by the paparazzi in favor of the latest television cutie as they both make their entrance to the same party at a Beverly Hills restaurant, the experience can be most disconcerting. After years of complaining about the scavenger attentions of these creatures, the star finds he or she actually misses them. The star's entrance is not quite an entrance without the flashing of their lights, and so the occasion becomes not quite what it might have been.

Be that as it may, it is this sense of always being under observation, of therefore having to perform, that accounts for the "vibrance," the sensual and sexual "electricity" of which Talese speaks. And it is one of the spoilers in our fantasies of celebrity communality. For people who are consciously performing do not, cannot, relate to one another in the same way that the rest of us do. The theatrical element militates against that possibility, precisely because it raises one's levels of self-awareness at the expense of one's awareness of others. And so the stars —many of them—playact trust, responsibility, friendship itself. The showy gesture replaces the thoughtful act, sentimentality replaces sensibility, the main chance blots out such memories as acquaintances in this realm may share.

And then there is the problem of stupidity. That is to say, there is always a handful of celebrities who believe their own publicity, insist against all the evidence to the contrary—their clothes, cars, companions, houses—that they are just ordinary guys and gals, a little luckier than most, but fundamentally unchanged by their good fortune. These are, of course, the most dangerous kind of celebrities, for to affect a lack of self-consciousness in a trade that is based on that quality, is to involve oneself in an inner contradiction of devastating proportions.

These people will eventually do harm to all who must treat with them, for they cannot be trusted since, quite literally, they do not know who they are. Or, perhaps more accurately, what they have become.

Taking all this into account, what a gathering of well-known people reminds one most of is a business convention, an occasion of the wary gregariousness, the strained (not to say false) bonhomie of people who, having been thrust together for a time, strive to maintain civility, despite the fact that they spend the rest of the year competing for shares of the same market. At these events one may offer the odd tip or two about how different firms have approached similar problems, but one is also on guard against spilling a trade secret, and one is always acutely aware of where the greatest prestige rests, how the power arrangements are worked out. You can have a good time at a convention, but it is primarily an occasion for using—and avoiding being used. It offers the illusion of fellowship, but one mistakes it for the real thing at one's peril.

I raise this point because it is of paramount importance for the rest of us to observe the distinction between the celebrity world and the ordinary world, to insist on the otherness of the public world of public figures and to maintain, nowadays, intellectual and psychological barriers against the confusion of their realm and our private realms. It is the only kind of segregation that is worth fighting *for*. (And is it not paradoxical that the greatest of the desegregationists, Dr. King, was among the most adept of our public figures at maintaining this socially useful form of segregation?)

It may make a difference morally whether a public figure is deliberately participating in the effort to tear down the barriers between the public and the private realms or whether, like the rest of us, he is the plaything of forces he does not entirely comprehend and cannot fully control. But it makes no difference practically speaking. The effect on our minds is the same, and the effect on the quality of our public life is the same whether he is an innocent victim or a guilty party in this sowing of confusion. What we need to do, is to try to break away from all metaphors, to see our subject steadily and whole—if only because there are now moving among us a number of rather dangerous people who have succeeded in doing just that, breaking away from (and breaking through) the comfortable evasions of metaphor the better to act on an uncomplicated and deadly understanding of our contemporary reality.

But before getting to them and to the reality they define so starkly for us, I must rid myself of two metaphors that have from the beginning of this enterprise haunted its pages—the theatrical and the novelistic.

First, the theatrical. It would be foolish to deny that celebrity life is assuredly, and in large measure, a public performance by people acting roles, whether or not they are fully conscious of that fact. But except for state occasions of the celebrity world—the Academy Awards, for example—we do not perceive this kind of performance as drama. A play is a much more tightly structured form, full of carefully prepared climaxes and resolutions designed to lead us to a conclusion more or less well thought out by its author and further refined through much conscious effort by director and actors in rehearsal. In fact, the players will have—at least in the ideal—suppressed some part of their personalities in order to sustain the playwright's vision, may perhaps even have disguised or distorted themselves physically in order to better serve the writer's purpose. In the event, we, the audience, happily and fairly consciously surrender to this manipulation. And, however caught up we are in the drama, we never entirely erase our consciousness of the invisible fourth wall that separates us from the players on stage. No matter how artfully they are arranged, the visible presence of theatrical conventions—the working of lights, the movement of scenery, the intermission between acts—all serve to remind us that this is not life we are witnessing, but a representation of life. If it is good enough the play may, of course, take up permanent residence in our sensibilities, and certainly a fine performance will become part of our theatrical memories. But we remain, in the theater, in what might be termed a passive-objective state. That is to say, we enter the playhouse consciously willing to surrender ourselves to the author and actors, passively receptive to whatever delights are about to unfold, while at the same time retaining our consciousness of the formality of the setting. Above all, we will be under no illusion that we are, or could be, participants in the drama, that we have anything at stake in the proceedings other than enjoyment and, possibly, edification.

I am well aware that the spirit of modernism and/or postmodernism is upon the theater as it is upon all the arts, that in recent times there has been a strenuous and concerted effort on the part of the theatrical avant-garde to break through the proscenium stage's fourth wall. Thrust and arena staging, entrances through the aisles, direct address of the audience—all of these are but the most modest manifestations of this spirit. Street and guerrilla theater represent far more radical efforts in the same direction. This revolution in stagecraft, stage aesthetics, may be seen as a practical recognition of what theater people see as a defect in their art, an inability to directly appeal to the audience's subconscious, to get in there and mess with it directly as they see film, television, publicity in its many forms, doing.

To greater or lesser degree all artistic conventions objectify and distance, and the drive of contemporary, popular art, of our public life in general, is to subjectify and render immediate all experience. Contemplative rationality does not move products off the shelves, or make anyone a star. Nor, by this time, does it suit the way most people want to live, which is to have their needs gratified immediately, their wants as soon thereafter as possible. A public figure must, therefore, make his impression on us as quickly and firmly as possible, and the best way to do that is not to brook the delays of art, if that is your field, or the delays inherent in carefully developing a complex position, if politics is your game. Indeed, the more unstudied one's image appears to be, the more naturally it appears to fit one of the several highly stylized roles that are always open in our public life, roles which the great audience never seems to get too much of.

The kind of celebrity performances we are talking about are not performances in the classical sense of the term. But they are not reality either. They are obviously, however, some kind of fiction in that they blend a sense of felt reality with the invented—not to say fantastical. It is therefore easy, and tempting, to think of the celebrity drama of our times not as playacting but as a new fictional form, in its essence— since it deals with a kind of community—a descendant, perhaps, of *Winesburg, Ohio* or maybe even *Peyton Place*. Or, if it is not a new version of the old small-town saga, then perhaps it is a sort of family saga—something like one of R. F. Delderfield's fictions, which one cannot appreciate without resort to the genealogical table the publisher kindly provides on the endpapers to help us keep the relationship straight. Certainly it seems sometimes that what Madame Bovary, Raskolnikov, Stephen Dedalus are to the cultivated imagination —archetypal representations of certain familiar, endlessly recurring responses to the human condition—celebrity figures have become to the popular imagination. No need, actually, to be snobbish on this point. These new archetypes are as much a part of the educated and finely tuned sensibility as they are figures in the daydreams of the less favored—as the amount of interpretive writing about celebrities and their images in the intellectual journals attests.

But like the analogy with drama, the analogy with any formal fictional form—even a very crude and popular one—is restricting. For the differences between this new novel, if we can call it that, and the traditional one to which it may be kin, are obvious. Clearly, these celebrated people whose doings we so closely attend are, in the beginning, self-created. Thereafter, however, our understanding of them is not the work of a single authorial hand, but of many journalistic craftsmen. Beyond that, the intricate yet sprawling plot in which they function is too multitudinous, too multifarious, to be confined between a single set of boards, however many pages they might encompass. The story is formless—without beginning, middle, or end—and in some respects it is far richer than any literary fiction we are likely to encounter. Its characters are sexier, more adventurous, less predictable than any novelist would dare to place before us, and the amount of melodramatic coincidence the unfolding tale offers is larger than even the rankest popularizer would dare to soberly present—which is one reason why the works of the Jacqueline Susanns and the Harold Robbinses—which pretend to deal with behind-the-scenes celebrity life—disappoint the imaginative reader. The story his busy brain has already concocted is much better, far loonier than these foot soldiers of fantasy can present within the conventions of popularly debased realism, can possibly offer.

It may be that if we seek a useful historical mode for this collective fiction of ours we need to look back far beyond the tradition of the modern novel, which not coincidentally had its beginnings in the eighteenth century, the Age of Reason, to something more primitive, something along the lines of the bardic, for instance. A case could be made that the professional gossipists, upon whom we are dependent for the latest word on the only mythic beings we believe in, are rather like the wandering poets of the deep past, spinning their yarns by the campfire—and, one imagines, no less than the media merchant of today, closely attending the listeners' psychic needs, adjusting tales to those needs as they went along, since the quality of the storyteller's welcome would depend, as it were, on his ratings. In this connection one thinks of E. M. Forster: "Neanderthal man listened to stories, if one may judge by the shape of his skull. The primitive audience was an audience of shock-heads, gaping around the campfire, fatigued with contending against the mammoth or the woolly rhinoceros, and only kept awake by suspense. What would happen next? The novelist droned on, and as soon as the audience guessed what happened next, they either fell asleep or killed him."

In this passage from *Aspects of the Novel,* Forster also invokes the figure of Scheherazade in aid of his point that suspense—that crude and simple thing—is essential to the success of a novel, keeping the reader interested at the most basic level, keeping him open (and awake) for the writer's larger purposes. And here we come still closer to a useful analogy with modern celebrity story forms. For the essence of the appeal of a long-running star's serial tale lies in our identification of unresolved themes running through the life, our curiosity about how they are going to come out. Will Liz find permanent happiness with some husband or other? Will X win his fight against booze? Will Y get off drugs for good? Will Z avoid madness and/or self-destruction? We are not kept in daily contact with these stories, for our media Scheherazades drop them at crucial points, then return just when we're dying to find out what happened next. This policy is not consciously designed to enhance the development of suspense. Journalism—even at this vulgar level—must, after all, await events, but it works out neatly all the same.

Yet tempting as this metaphor is, I don't want to make too much of it, to impute to Barbara Walters, let us say, the qualities of a modern Scheherazade. Certainly I do not want to make the mistake that defenders of popular culture made in generations past, suggesting that something like the pure spirit that animates folk art is to be found in movies and comic strips and pop music. Generally speaking, too much highly rational commercial calculation goes into the creation of these works, although, of course—and herein lies their fascination—something authentic often does get through, or can at least be perceived by the knowledgeable to be lurking, let us say, beneath the surface of a film's generic conventions. Indeed, it is probably fair to say that there is no such thing as a pure folk culture in any industrialized society, so inescapable are the media and their messages. We seek to satisfy primitive needs at these technologically sophisticated altars because there is no place else we can go.

But—and I cannot emphasize this too strongly—we are not talking here about works—discrete individual artistic and intellectual achievements. We are talking about public lives seen in their entirety as works, acts of self-creation amplified and distorted by publicity. And if those lives partake of the drama, the novel, the ancient saga as we stand back and look at them, none of those forms quite seems to fit the cases under consideration. Perhaps, considering that we are dealing essentially with a twentieth-century phenomenon, we should look to what is widely regarded as the great twentieth-century art form, the movies. Perhaps what celebrated lives come to, as they play in our minds, are something like the biopics of yore, technicolored, melodramatized versions of personal history, vaguely factual, but essentially mythic in character. But there is something wrong with that analogy, too, namely, that we do not attend these lives one at a time, but rather follow dozens, hundreds, of them more or less simultaneously, switching channels as it were, dropping in and dropping out.

Individually—unless we are one of those unfortunates who is obsessively focused on a single celebrated individual, a fan who is actually, as the derivation of the work implies, a fanatic, and therefore potentially a deadly danger—none of these lives is of great moment to us. But taken together the lives of the celebrities create a sort of psychic energy field that surrounds us and penetrates us, binding our universe together.

Does that last sentence ring vaguely familiar? It should, for it is a close paraphrase of the definition of the Force offered by Alec Guinness as Obi-Wan Kenobi in *Star Wars.* Socially and psychologically celebrity power has come more and more to function in our real world as the Force does in the mythic world of George Lucas's invention. It is everywhere, we do internalize it in ways that are not entirely explicable through rational means, and it does bind our universe together, offering some sense of community—common idols, if not common ideals—in a world where the traditional communitarian forms have lost much of their hold on many of us, are honored more in the nostalgic breach than in living lives. Above all, more and more of us seek to join the sacred circle of the adepts, to be, in effect, the Luke Skywalkers of this brave new universe of ours.

That our celebrity Jedi hold no coherent set of values, ideological or spiritual, we may count as a blessing. If they ever got together on a program and started trying to put it over on us, their combined power would be awesome. One can scarcely imagine the consequences if they elected Jane Fonda or Ed Asner El Supremo. Or declared Warren Beatty and Shirley MacLaine their First Family. We may thank whatever god controls the performing ego that this cannot occur.

No, the clear and present danger is not from these Darth Vaders in designer clothes. It arises, obviously, from our Luke Skywalkers, those who seek the secrets of the elect, and entrance to their circle. And here, at last, we return to something like our starting point.

For it is my contention that there is a small but growing number of people among us who require no metaphors whatever to apprehend the meaning of celebrity in today's world, who understand the demands of that role and, more important, the demands of winning it in open audition, with deadly directness. After which they are prepared to live within it, comfortable and unperplexed, for the rest of their notorious lives. These, of course, are the psychopaths who come to our horrified attention when one of them strikes out against a celebrated individual in order to link himself immortally to that person's fame, or, with growing frequency, in recent years, commits a succession of capital crimes that rivet the attention of the media and the public. By so doing the criminal of this type creates for himself a kind of perverse celebrity that can be used, in his warped subjectivity, as a way to rationalize his antisocial behavior.

And why not? On every hand they see that in the less deadly realms of criminality every kind of immorality will be excused if its perpetrator is sufficiently celebrated. From that insight it must seem to follow, if one's mind is twisted in a certain direction, that murder itself is but a hop and a skip, a hoot and a holler, from "certification" by the media, may even achieve it if the circumstances are properly orchestrated.

We have not yet arrived at that pass, and doubtless never will in the sense that we will find the editorial page of any responsible newspaper endorsing assassination. On the other hand, media attention of the most gratifying kind will be paid the murderer or would-be murderer if he strikes boldly enough. To him, manifestly, this attention can be equated with approval. And that says nothing about immortality, the permanent linkage history will make between the famous victim and his victimizer. The assassins are, it would seem, aware of this. They keep diaries for the record, and both Lee Harvey Oswald and John

Hinckley, Jr., carefully labeled these effusions *"Historic* Diary" (emphasis added).

But before we get more deeply into what might be termed The Subculture of Assassination, let us briefly study the context in which it operates. It took root, obviously, in the aftermath of the Kennedy assassination, took shape during and just after the Nixon years. Some years ago, Alexander Walker, the English critic, identified a new type of hero, whom he dubbed "the benign betrayer," described as "men, and women too, who see no prospects of promotion or ways of changing the satisfactions of the job and have therefore every incentive to seize the hour and means to create change in the institution that employs them." This they do by the simple act of betraying that institution's secrets. It is Walker's belief that one's reputation and bank account can profit from such a sellout if one fulfills two simple requirements: you must be sure to indict yourself while indicting others, which allows you to play the gratifying role of the repentant sinner, and you must be sure to demonstrate that only the call of the higher good (and nothing as mean as the possibility of criminal indictment) caused you to rat on friends and colleagues. With fine impartiality Walker names two pioneers of this new path to success: one was Daniel Ellsberg, he of the Pentagon papers and the psychiatrist's report that deemed him full of aggressive tendencies and a "need for recognition" which was not forthcoming as he labored in a back room at the Rand Corporation concocting harebrained schemes for winning the war in Vietnam; the other was John Dean, he of *Blind Ambition* and other profitable mea culpas about the Watergate affair. Being English, Walker cannot resist the contrast between these two and the likes of Burgess, Maclean, and Philby, the defected Soviet spies of a few years earlier, who "suffered the fate of most pioneers, which is to see latecomers reap the benefits of their betrayal. Nowadays they wouldn't have to leave the country in haste: They wouldn't even have to leave the stage. They'd be on *Panorama* and write 'instant books' bearing the Old Bailey's imprimatur, where it would no doubt be hard to find juries to convict."

Walker wrote before all the returns on the Watergate scam were in, but a more recent commentator, Barbara Goldsmith, has estimated that there have been 169 books about that unpleasantness in a little more than a decade, generating more than $100 million in profits, most of them going to the very people who perpetrated this set of crimes against the state. And that doesn't count their lecture fees, their TV fees, or Sam Ervin's ten grand for testifying in commercials that he does not leave home without his American Express card. It says nothing about the responsible and respectable jobs most of them have found. And it says nothing about Richard Nixon's latest appearance as a phoenix with a five o'clock shadow, as an elder statesman writing earnest books about the conduct of foreign policy, the area of his governance untainted by scandal and therefore left to him as safe province in which to disport himself. An elder statesman for hire, he is a convenience to the media (being ever available for a quote) and no burden to the society whose best traditions he was prepared to traduce.

It is really incredible, this. But America is now the land of multiple opportunity—and infinite forgiveness. One need only remain interesting to retain the prerequisites of celebrity. And the model established by Nixon and his cronies is now virtually a tradition. Goldsmith is good on this point: caught embezzling, film executive David Begelman is ordered by the court to keep seeing his shrink and to make a film about the dangers of angel dust. Producer Robert Evans, busted on a cocaine possession charge, is forced to make TV spots warning youngsters about the dangers of drugs, though his scotfree example actually sends an opposite message. Art dealer Frank Lloyd, convicted of bilking Rothko's estate out of a few million by cooking his books, is ordered by the court to donate $100,000 to a fund to educate children about art. Goldsmith contrasts this with a life sentence handed out to an anonymous criminal for three nonviolent crimes that brought him $230.11, to the life sentence meted out to another man for writing a bad check for $100.

It may, of course, be argued that essentially unpunished crimes of the sort just described threaten no lives, that they are committed by the sort of privileged people who have traditionally been treated with great leniency by our courts, that we are even witnessing here a kind of enlightened jurisprudence that at least relieves the pressure on our overcrowded prisons while moving us away from the notion that stark vengeance is a necessary component of punishment. Yet we are always in this realm dealing with the law of unintended consequences. And a certain percentage of the population is bound to see that fame, like certain deodorants, forms an invisible protective shield, preventing a lucky few from offending unforgivably.

Nor is it always necessary to calculate this effect in advance of a crime. It is frequently possible, after the fact, no matter how heinous that fact, to fabricate an image that will appeal to influential people, who will, in turn, appeal for you in the courts of public opinion as well as in the courts of law. Even a figure like William Buckley, scarcely a bleeding heart, was moved to take up the case of Edgar Smith, a convicted murderer who discovered in jail a gift for both literary expression and the law, persuading Buckley that he had been wrongfully accused. Despite this august sponsorship, it developed after Smith had been freed that he was not only guilty (by his own admission) of his previous crime, but that he was capable of a new one. More usually, though, the jailhouse lawyer-litterateur works on the sentiments of a literary-intellectual community that leans naturally to the left, and is thus inclined to believe that a capitalist state is bound to be particularly error-prone when it comes to sentencing individuals who give evidence of having rebellious natures. This community is also predisposed to a belief in the perfectibility of man. Or anyway his capacity for reformation—even in such unpromising venues as a state pen. It is necessary only to give evidence that both processes have been at work on the unfortunate prisoner, especially if that evidence is presented in a succession of well-turned phrases.

Hence the much-discussed case of Jack ("America is worse than the Soviet Union") Abbott, who wrote his way into the heart of Norman Mailer, who then helped him to shape his prison letters into a book, and with his literary friends sponsored his parole, which was brought up short in a matter of weeks when Abbott knifed and killed a man in the course of an inconsequential dispute. Mailer compounded what seemed to many his own complicity in this act by defending the principle on which he had acted thus: "Culture is worth a little risk."

Romantic outlawry from François Villon onward has had an indisputable appeal to the literary man. And perhaps we can see how it works more clearly in the exemplary case of Roger Knobelspiess. His crimes were of a genial sort; he robbed banks, an activity that has never greatly exorcised anyone, unless some bystander gets rubbed out in the process. From Jesse James to Willie Sutton we have tended to take this class of criminals affectionately to heart. In any case, Knobelspiess, a Frenchman doing time for a 1977 heist, whiled away his hours in durance vile by writing a couple of volumes critical of French penal procedures. These found their way to the likes of historians such as Michel Foucault and Claude Manceron, who were soon enough joined by Yves Montand and Simone Signoret, among others congenitally eager to take up leftist and humanitarian causes, all of whom took up the cry for pardon. "France must not deprive itself of this national treasure," said Manceron. "We want to have him at our table, to walk with him in the fields, to advise him and receive his advice." Predictably, when Francois Mitterrand's socialist government came to power in 1981 Knobelspiess got his pardon. Equally predictably, the police found themselves, less than two years later, picking up for armed robbery the man who had once proclaimed himself "the legitimacy of the left." When they surrounded him he cried the words that should become the emblem of our age, "Don't shoot . . . take pictures."

"Don't shoot . . . take pictures." Yes. The man surely has a gift for the apt, summarizing phrase, and no need to reach for obfuscating metaphorical complexity of rich philosophical allusion when, finally, he is caught between the rock and the hard place. None of his ilk do. The criminal lunatics know, with breathtaking simplicity, with what might be termed deadly accuracy, where to find, and act upon, the bottom line of our infatuation with celebrity.

In a seminal article (in *The New Republic)* about the subculture of assassination, Priscilla Johnson McMillan has drawn the portrait of what she says is becoming an American type, the lone assassin, one "who, lacking a sense of who he is, shops among artifacts of our culture—books, movies, TV programs, song lyrics, newspaper clippings—to fashion a character." There are gruesome congruences between these loners. For example, John Hinckley, Jr., included in his small, portable library a copy of *The Catcher in the Rye,* as did Mark David Chapman, who killed John Lennon. (Could they really believe their disaffections were similar to Holden Caulfield's?) And Hinckley's reading included books about his predecessors in the grisly calling (the word is carefully chosen) to which he aspired: *The Boston Strangler,* for an interesting instance to which we will return; *RFK Must Die, Marina and Lee* (which is by Ms. McMillan), Arthur Bremmer's *An Assassin's Diary,* from which, it would seem, Hinckley picked up practical tips about modus operandi. And, of course, the world knows about his obsession with *Taxi Driver,* said to have been seen by him fifteen times, an audio tape of which was found among his possessions. Just as he had bought a duplicate of the gun that had killed John Kennedy, it seems that Hinckley's arsenal also included precisely the number of weapons that Travis Bickle, hero of Martin Scorsese's film, had. But perhaps the most interesting of McMillan's insights is that after Chapman killed Lennon, Hinckley himself discerned from the journalism accreting around the singer's murderer, that they had much in common. Both since early adolescence had admired the Beatles, had grown up in the South dreaming of careers in pop music, had feared insanity and attempted suicide. "And so Hinckley now carried a highly charged burden of associations to which was added a feeling of rivalry with Chapman. Along with sorrow and shock, Hinckley may very well have felt envy at the news of Lennon's assassination. Why hadn't he thought of doing it himself?" (McMillan points out that when James Earle Ray heard of John Kennedy's death he went into a rage. He could have done the job as easily as Lee Harvey Oswald. It was near to that moment that he resolved to kill Martin Luther King, Jr. (In contemplating this information we come close to parody of American competitiveness.)

From all this we may reasonably reason that assassination lies in the realm of what the police in recent years have called "copycat crimes," that innocent grade-schooler's word sending a slight chill through one. It is really a very simple phenomenon. If a crime has about it a certain news value, either because of the prominence of the victim, or the novelty of the act itself, then for a time people will be drawn to emulate it. It was a phenomenon first noticed in the 1960s when an early airplane hijacking set off a wave of imitations not yet dissipated. It surfaced again after the so-called Tylenol murders of 1982, when others either imitated or threatened to imitate the Chicago husband and wife who introduced poison into bottles of the painkiller as they rested on drugstore shelves, then sat back to await a wave of mysterious, well-reported deaths. It was, for the crazies, a rich situation. Not only was the publicity terrific, but there was the sense of oneself moving through the world in a mysterious, godlike way, sowing general terror, and a specific horror that settled on its victims through cruel chance. "The aggression is not the only thing seen as primary. A sense of powerfulness also strikes a chord," said psychiatrist William James, who works at a correctional institution for the criminally insane. "The perpetrator can't wait to look in the newspaper to see it. There's a tremendous amount of power and grandiosity in that."

Nor did one always have to come up with an amazingly novel crime to catch the world's attention. There has been, according to press reports (and the subjective impressions of criminologists), a steady increase, in recent years, of criminals who seek power of this sort—and the fame that inevitably accompanies unmasking—simply through the quantity of their vicious acts. Albert DeSalvo, the Boston

Strangler who caught John Hinckley, Jr.'s eager attention, was such a one, being a mass rapist who had escaped apprehension for years before he embarked on his long career as a mass murderer. All over the country now, the police say, similar criminals are operating, moving from place to place in their vans, rootless, motiveless in the conventional sense, reading about their depredations in the paper before they move on down the interstate to their next chance victim, heading toward their apotheoses, when after they are caught they lead the police to one unmarked grave after another, "showing no remorse" as the press reports of these ghastly tours always have it.

A typical, yet almost parodistical example of what we are talking about here, a case on which all the strains of this type of criminality— the stalking of publicity through the stalking of prominent people, and through the commission of multiple crimes—was provided by a man named David Burnette, of Omaha, Nebraska. A dull-witted but (according to psychiatrists) not psychopathic creature, his attention was caught by a feature in *Omaha Magazine,* which offered pictures and short profiles of ten women it termed the city's "Most Eligible Women." By his provincial standards they were celebrities, and he determined, in the spring of 1982, to attempt to rape all ten of them. He succeeded with two of them, was frightened off by a third, and was apprehended while trying to force himself on the fourth—"maybe because they were successful, you know," as Teresa Carpenter reported him saying in her article on the case in *The Village Voice.*

Dim like Burnette or acute like Knobelspiess, a deadly animal like Jack Abbott (his prose style was brilliantly described by Lance Morrow as being like a Doberman, "all speed and teeth"), or rather jackal-like, as one thinks of Hinckley, this disparate group is bound together by this: they have the capacity, which the rest of us do not share, to follow to its end the inherent logic of our age, the terrible logic that dares not speak its name, seeking fame as other criminals seek money, outside the law.

In an article about serial killers, one psychiatrist observes that many of them show signs of narcissistic disturbance, seeing others as mannequins to be moved about at their whim, "props for their pleasure." Another says that the serial murderer is closest in criminal typology to the rapist—which is why I have treated them almost interchangeably in these pages—deriving his pleasure from the power he exercises over his victims—which is why abduction, torture, and rape so often play a part in these murders, and why murder becomes, for him, but the final act of dominance. Yet a third psychiatrist observes that often the serial murderer "seems to get pleasure out of confounding authority . . . There is power in having his little personal secret." A fourth expert makes the point that very few of them appear to acquaintances as raving maniacs. On the contrary, as Ted Bundy demonstrated, they can appear to be utterly charming. And even when they are not, they are often highly intelligent, seemingly well integrated socially, and sometimes quite successful in their trades or professions, which provide them ample means to carry out their complex and costly crimes.

These words and phrases—narcissistic, possessed of a will to dominance, taking pleasure in confounding authority, being physically attractive and economically well favored—to what other group in our society do we frequently apply them? Why to stars of course, to celebrities. It is so simple, really: in our time stardom is dominance, the opportunity to exercise the untrammeled will in its purest and most visible form. And some among us, lacking the luck and the talent, to assert the need for this dominance in socially acceptable ways, have found this other, darker path to the same end.

John Hinckley was outraged that he was declared innocent of his crime by reason of insanity. He believed himself to be entirely sane, and several steps ahead of a psychiatry whose definitions of that condition were formed before the media reshaped our reality. The majority of his countrymen, if the polls are to be believed, shared the criminal's outrage, though for reasons of frustrated morality, a sense that once again a criminal was escaping his just deserts in a society they have come to believe "coddles" criminals.

Be that as it may, one cannot escape the study of celebrity without at least entertaining the possibility that Hinckley had, at least in some respects, a better grip on reality than most of the rest of us have. If his actions were mad, the social observations that conditioned them were rather better than most of those cranked out by professionals in the field. When it was all over—the shock, the outrage, the fumbling attempts of the law and medicine to come to terms with the criminal and his works at his trial—and he was safely incarcerated in St. Elizabeth's Hospital, where once Ezra Pound was permitted to live out his life on his own weird terms (an early example of the public figure whose gifts seem to excuse his offenses), Hinckley addressed a letter, one of several he has sent to the press, to Stuart Taylor, Jr., a reporter for the New York *Times*. In it he reproduced what he said would have been the substance of the speech he would have made in court had he been sentenced as a criminal. It contained his familiar complaints about the way Jodie Foster had ignored him. But then he passed on to these remarkable statements:

"Jodie Foster may continue to outwardly ignore me for the rest of my life but I have made an impression on that young lady that will never fade from her mind. I am with Jodie spiritually every day and every night. I have made her one of the most famous actresses in the world. Everybody but everybody knows about John and Jodie. We are a historical couple whether Jodie likes it or not.

"At one time Miss Foster was a star and I was an insignificant fan. Now everything is changed. I am Napoléon and she is Josephine. I am Romeo and she is Juliet. I am John Hinckley Jr. and she is Jodie Foster. The world can't touch us. Society can't bring us down . . .

"She will never escape me. I may be in prison and she may be making a movie in Paris or Hollywood, but Jodie and I will always be together, in life and in death . . ."

Mad ramblings? No. Not at all. What we study here is a shrewdly intelligent analysis of the (selected) consequences of Hinckley's act. It ignores, of course, the pain he caused, the lives he permanently damaged. It ignores, as well, the fact that, in the short term, he tainted his beloved's life and career by the forced association of her image with his. But what does the short term mean to a man like Hinckley, with his eye fixed at last on that ultimate celebrity, immortality? And who can doubt that the gift of his twisted love was the elevation of his beloved's fame to a level she probably could not have attained on the basis of her own talent and ambition, even if they were very great? Who can doubt that the gift he forced upon her was nothing less than a transcendence that lifted her up out of the entertainment pages and thrust her into history? What deeper devotion can a man demonstrate? One misses among his historical and literary allusions only one name, that of John Wilkes Booth, who had to do for himself what John Hinckley, Jr., so gladly did for the performer he loved.

One feels a despairing gloom to admit that a madman can have, in some measure, a firmer grasp on certain aspects of our reality than the reasonable man has. One thinks of Michelangelo Antonioni's movie *Investigation of a Woman* in which one of the characters pauses to envy the lot of professional political terrorists "because they lead coherent lives." The thought applies to all the mad existences we have been turning over in these pages. For it is the essence of their madness that the single issue that rules these lives, whether or not it is slipcovered with ideological principle or not, the need to grasp fame by any means, at any cost, does, indeed, confer coherence on lives that are otherwise a shambles. As if by magic all ambiguity, all doubts and hesitations, all the softening and civilizing impulses that arise out of the normal person's sympathetic understanding of others is dissolved by the imperatives of dark fame's dark needs and deeds.

Looking at these lives from the outside we see only incoherences. But we are wrong. Obsession is coherence. Next to it all other metaphors of understanding pale. Next to it, all minor incoherences fade to the level of inconvenience. Next to it, all our carefully nurtured sense of modern life's fragility, the debilitations inherent in our delicately nuanced, morally relative, psychologically informed sense of how it should be conducted, seem impotent and futile, weaknesses masquerading as strengths. We are as prey to those who can cut through all that with a knife. Or more properly, coherence's weapon of choice, the Saturday night special.

We dare not turn too quickly away from these creatures. For we must recognize that the forces that move them also move within ourselves in some much milder measure, that we suffer to some degree from the same confusion of realms that brings them, finally, to tragedy. It is no longer melodramatic to suggest that we must learn to resist, even in mild fantasy forms, that impulse to the cheap coherences which moves them. We must learn, or relearn, if not the art of fine distinction, then the craft of simple distinction. Of mature reflection. Of critical nuance. If we can. If it is not too late.

EIGHT

The New Tyranny

It is customary at the end of a volume of social criticism for the author to pull himself up tall and grave and offer some prescriptions (and proscriptions) to alleviate the ills he has diagnosed.

I am not going to indulge that convention at any length. If I am anywhere near right in my analysis of the befuddling power of celebrity and the extension of its reach in recent decades, there is nothing programmatic to be done about it. It is not strictly speaking a social problem, susceptible to a rational redeployment of energies and resources, like, say, poverty or air pollution or even racism, which presents such a clear-cut moral issue. It is true, of course, that the institutions that provide us with information and entertainment could practice some modest self-censorship, and one might here issue a ringing call to their managers urging restraint in the use of individuals to symbolize complex positions on complex issues, or in the constant imputation to the famous of virtues worthy of emulation. Surely one could sensibly ask them to play down the play of personality in their reports of the news and in their evaluations of the arts and entertainment. One might also ask celebrities themselves to exercise a certain modesty in their self-display. They might, the lot of them, profitably pin up on the frames of their dressing room mirrors copies of George Eliot's remark that "the merely egotistical satisfactions of fame are easily nullified by a toothache." And one might also spend some time whistling down the wind, for, in fact, the issues presented by celebrity power finally merge with still larger cultural issues and cannot be isolated from them.

According to a recent survey, we have broken through an historic ceiling; for years we have been shaking our heads over the fact that the average American spends upwards of six hours a day watching TV. Now, at last it seems we spend more than seven hours each day in front of the television set (seven hours and two minutes to be precise). Another recent study points out that two thirds of the nation is now regarded as functionally illiterate. Taken together, these two sets of figures would seem to indicate that the market for fine distinctions is dwindling to uneconomic proportions (though, subjectively this is, of course, old news). Or, to put the matter as bluntly as possible, we have arrived at a point where any hope of conveying the subtle realities of existence, private or social, to a large number of people must be abandoned as feckless, an example of innocent and very old-fashioned idealism spinning its wheels. The reason is simple: there is no substantial number of people in the society capable of comprehending, much less writing, the language required for such an understanding. As a result, there is a large, felt need for the simple, simplifying symbolic figure.

It is, I keep assuring myself, only happenstance that this conclusion forces itself on one in 1984, when the coincidence of calendar and a famous novel title have so well served emblematic journalism's needs. One might note that this attention has succeeded in turning Orwell's book into a celebrity product of precisely the kind George Trow described. What is significant is that a version of Orwell's most profound (and profoundly felt) novelistic invention has indeed arrived, though not in the form he predicted.

I am referring, of course, to "Newspeak." Orwell imagined it to be a systematically simplified form of language, a language robbed of all metaphor, all resonance, thus a language that denied its speaker all subjective possibilities; poetry, of course, but also the critical and fictive ones as well, since they also require a supple, nuanced vocabulary and syntax. Beyond that, Newspeak denies one all the humble, everyday subjective modes—daydreams, fantasies, word play and association, not to mention, finally, the night's ration of dreams. Next to its torture chambers, Newspeak is in 1984 the state's most powerful weapon of tyrannical coercion, a bludgeon designed to beat all human experience into a pulp of slogans.

Now, as George Steiner has observed, our official language has not developed in quite that way; we are typically addressed by our ruling bureaucracies, state and corporate, in a language that obfuscates through inflation, which replaces one precise word with a half-dozen vaguer ones. This does not at all square with Orwell's definition of his invented language which foresaw that "with the passage of time the distinguishing characteristics of Newspeak would become more and more pronounced—its words growing fewer and fewer, their meanings more and more rigid, and the chance of putting them to improper use always diminishing." But that does not mean we have escaped the fate Orwell foresaw. Far from it. Not only do we have this "Corpspeak" to contend with when we try to get our masters to put something in writing, but we have a version of what Orwell predicted existing side by side with it, and working pretty much as he said it would. The reason we have not had much critical comment on this arrival at the worst of all possible linguistic worlds is that most of the writers capable of commenting on the phenomenon remain word-bound.

Were they to look up from their texts they would see that we have actually evolved a form of Newspeak that quite precisely fits Orwell's original definition. It is, however, not a written language, except insofar as advertising copy, headlines, and picture captions partake of its qualities. Nor is it primarily a spoken language, though it is used for lead-ins, lead-outs, and voice-overs on television—both for commercial messages and for descriptions of the news—and on the radio. Indeed, there is a school of thought that holds that this language is becoming the language of the young, a sort of living Fortran. A man who makes his living by employing a computer to concoct catchy trade names for new products says: "People under the age of 30 have watched TV for an average of six hours a day and only spoken with people for 20 minutes a day since they were two years olds. Now they speak something called Youth language, which is a condensed, simplified form of language driven by television." This fellow is, of course, entirely bland, entirely unmoved morally by the creation—actually re-creation, since Orwell's inspiration was a simplified English developed by the BBC for overseas broadcasts in World War II—of a realistic correlative for Orwell's conceit. And indeed, why should he care? He makes his living from this development.

But he makes a point of prime importance for us, namely, that this "television-driven" language, language which evolved as a kind of support system for an imagistic means of communication and has now taken on a life of its own in the culture, aspires to no more than a pallid imitation of Newspeak. We speak now of what is almost entirely a visual language, based on an I-Can-Read vocabulary of bold, blunt images, that, contrary to all the McLuhanesque nonsense about it, are very sharply defined, carry almost no possibility of misunderstanding because of their ambiguity, no possibility of expansion through resort to the subtext, since they carry none, beyond, conceivably, "buy me" or "love me." These messages are sometimes cute and cuddly and even humorously self-deprecating; sometimes they are earnest and pay pious homage to the "intelligence" with which the viewer makes "choices." But none, obviously, represents discourse in any sense that a truly literate person understands the term. It is all reductive in precisely the sense that Orwell suggested.

Lest there be any misunderstanding: I am not here issuing a new denunciation of advertising. It is a familiar nuisance and it has been more than adequately chastened these many years. I am simply reiterating what we all sense, which is that its techniques have been adapted to every subject that we might conceivably want to bring under public discussion—and many that, a very few years ago, we could not have imagined bringing up outside the privacy of our homes or our doctor's consulting room. And it is visual imagery—simplifying, familiarizing, relentless imagery of the crude, commercial kind—that subsumes, masks, and ultimately destroys the capacity for subtler, more reflective, therefore more dangerous confrontations with these issues, indeed with the infinite variety and complexity of our fellow human beings. Without imagery of the kind I am talking about—seemingly concrete, seemingly three-dimensional, seemingly close enough to touch—most of our population cannot apparently imagine in the traditional sense of the word. That is to say, they cannot get hold of abstract concepts—ideas—unless they are in some manner personified (the spokesperson as human diagram). They cannot, it would seem, fill in the blanks that literate culture has traditionally asked its audience to conjure up out of its own memory and experience when it is presented with fictions that have as their purpose the illumination of some truth more curious than the purely documentary, some subtlety that does not lie entirely in what is said, but in the manner of its saying. From this simplification other simplifications follow. We are the prisoners now of crude—if, in the case of the celebrity lives we so eagerly attend, lingeringly serialized—narrative. It had better be fast-moving, action-packed, suspenseful and full of instantly apprehensible sensation. Above all it must be peopled with characters we understand as quickly and as fully as we understand the full meaning of a nice frosty bottle of Coke, and can drain to their dregs as sweetly and as refreshingly as we can suck up eight ounces of empty calories.

The total effect is as Orwell predicted. Most people's supply of words, when they are asked to respond to these images, is diminished radically. And with that diminution has come a corresponding shrinkage in the ability to respond authentically to a complicated play of ideas or to the subtle play of emotions or a complex human relationship. It is uncanny, nowadays, to listen to television or radio interviews with witnesses to any event. The language they throw back at their interlocutor precisely imitates the shorthand clichés, the emblematic words and phrases, that they have learned at television's knee or read in the morning paper. They are like mirrors in that they can only reflect the images that pass briefly before them. They seem unable to bring anything from their past or their communal history to the task. And, as any critic who has written about popular culture will testify, they resent the suggestion that there might be more here than meets the eye. Their occasional expressions of distrust or disgust with the media mirror are nothing compared with their capacity—their will —to believe what they are told. Fretfulness arises only when a disturbing new concept challenges a better-established one. The press, for example, cannot for years puff itself on its capacity to keep military secrets when asked to, and then, seeing a chance to have some Waugh-like fun with the tinpot invasion of Grenada, piously invoke the public's right to know. There must, after all, be a bright bird colonel in the Pentagon who read *Scoop* for extra credit at West Point. And be clever enough to invoke, in his turn, the press's past performance against its transparent—and contradictory—new intentions.

Nor can we ignore, in this connection, the media's prophylactic function. The dimmest among us now senses that the issues confronting us, the pullulating reality spread out enigmatically, incomprehensibly before us, grow daily more complex and less susceptible to simple interpretation, let alone simple resolution. And so most of us gratefully receive a Newspeak version of those issues, that reality, while rejecting interpretations that are more knowledgeable or eccentric, quirky, or individualistic—that attempt, in short, to answer complexity with complexity. We want the simple, spurious order newspeople impose upon events, just as we want the spurious order that a celebrity's beauty and apparent savoir faire seem to impose on human realities. The brutal reductionism of the thirty-second television or radio news item or the punchy who-what-why-when lead is strangely calming. We understand almost nothing, but we can proudly claim to be "well-informed." Indeed, as Ellul observed, the well-informed man is to our secular, democratic age what the pious man was to more religious eras. He is our ideal, the exemplar of the highest virtues to which the ordinary individual may aspire—though to just what practical use he may put all this information it is hard to say.

But, of course, in the age of the image the true function of journalism is not to inform; its function is to bombard. The result of too much information, presented without critical or historical perspective, is to level everything out, including the mood of the listener-reader-viewer. A multiplicity of voices-words-images has the same numbing effect as a single set of them emanating from a central source à la Orwell. Both effectively keep the average citizen in the dark without leaving him totally bereft of the consolations false knowledge brings. Mostly he is comforted by his condition, believes himself connected with the world outside himself, but in a very simple way. Were he given better information, it would only increase his anxious sense that events are not only out of his control, but out of anyone's control, that incoherence and even anarchy are loose upon his world.

To understand this point in concrete terms we need only look at an institution that almost parodistically summarizes what we are talking about. It is, to be sure, an institution that deals in words, not pictures, but that is less important than the fact that it performs the churchly functions of the news media, giving the "well-informed" man or woman a place to worship, in the purest imaginable terms. It is called News Radio. "You give us twenty-two minutes and we'll give you the world," its announcer intones, as a priest about to celebrate the mass might once have murmured, "You give me twenty-two minutes and I'll give you another world." There is no attempt at interpretation and, curiously, very little attempt to freshen the essentially liturgical product as the day wears on.

As a concept, news radio feeds a fantasy, which holds that news is a fast-breaking, ever-changing drama, requiring nimble journalists to keep abreast of it, requiring our constant attention if we are to keep abreast of them. This notion apparently descends from the glamorizing myth of the news hawk propagated by the old Hollywood newspaper melodramas, though by and large nothing could be further from reality. Almost nothing happens outside our own lives that requires our immediate attention—not in a week or a month, let alone in an hour or a day. But a sense of democratic duty, an imperative to be well-informed—an idea endlessly drummed into us, naturally, by the news media—requires that we honor the fantasy.

As a reality, news radio has almost nothing to do with its concept. What it essentially does, all day long, is recycle the same stories over and over again. All are handled with equal brevity and emphasis—a local sewer bond referendum and an attack on an American embassy somewhere, the weather report and the performance of the Dow-Jones industrials, sports scores and a tenement fire. All are spoken of in the same tones by an announcer who has trained all trace of singularity out of his voice. If you stay tuned in longer than the allotted twenty-two minutes, he begins all over again with the same stories, slightly rewritten, perhaps with a new feature piece (household hints, a movie review, something about managing your money) as relief. And so it will go, throughout the day and night, tiny increments of change being added to a story (reactions from officials, for example, or an eye-witness interview with some participant). The total effect of this wormlike crawl through the day's events is the opposite of alarming; it is soothing. Dropping in and out on a news radio station one gains the (correct) impression, most days, that nothing much is happening and that one is reassuringly on top of what little is going on. But, of course, one is only half listening, for this really is a mass being cele-brated—propitiatory to the secular god of information, and a low-key, low-definition way for the worshipper to signify his respectful connec-tion with another world, a world of events that is as much a fantasy as conventional religious visions ever were.

The language of this rite is, of course, Newspeak. And appropriately so, given its historic origins in the radio service where George Orwell worked. It is severely limited in its expressive range. It is without allusion either to history (there is generally no attempt to link today's story with even yesterday's, let alone with the larger movement of events) or to more personal concerns. There is naturally no attempt at even simple enrichments, a modest simile or metaphor, for instance, a catchy phrase or a touch of humor—Orwell's "improper use." In short, something that purports to represent reality to us has, as its actual function, the distortion of reality. Something that purports to inform actually further stupefies the already stunned.

And, at this point we must see that an unholy alliance is formed. Or, Mr. Orwell, shake hands with Professor McLuhan. For it was always the unannounced intention of the latter's theories to under-mine rationalism and individualism as surely as it was the announced intention of Orwell's fictional tyranny to do the same. Implicitly McLuhan's work endorsed mass communication as ritual, suggesting that all attempts to grapple with it in conventional critical terms were foredoomed, the death throes of hopelessly outdated devotees of hopelessly outdated print—that ultimate expression of the singular consciousness. He saw the book as the serpent (of dragonlike proportions) that destroyed the Edenic preliterate community and the values it shared without resort to intellectual activity as we understand it, or the higher cultural forms as we understand them. He proposed—in something less than forthright terms, it must be said—a connection between the audience and the vague, semiconscious, semireligious values inherent in his version of the racial unconscious, with the media acting as intermediary. That is to say, functioning as the universal Church that Catholicism (to which McLuhan was a convert) had never quite become. Whether he saw the media as a replacement for the Church or as an instrument preparing for its triumph, or perhaps as its ally in some ultimate tyranny that would embrace body, mind, and spirit was never quite clear. All one can say is that he was entirely unappalled by his vision—as unappalled by it as Orwell was appalled by his.

But whether one approaches our Newspeak in Orwellian or McLuhanesque terms, the end result is the same—a diminution of our capacity to conceive our world in humanistic and liberal terms, a diminished capacity to fully conceive even ourselves and our roles in that world (hence the much-discussed narcissism of our society). Most important to this concluding argument, the dominance of Newspeak at every level of discourse places an end to a century and more of hope for redemption through mass education and mass communication. In fact, both have become the instruments of a soft tyranny (more like that of McLuhan's church, than that of Orwell's novel) that has succeeded—far more than the most dire elitist theory ever dared to propose—in subjugating the majority, keeping them endlessly prisoners of those illusions on which their own most precious delusions batten.

It is distressing to entertain such thoughts, let alone commit them to print, for the hope that is thus banished has been the underpinning of the liberal and humane faith that has sustained most intelligent people from the Enlightenment onward. It has surely sustained this writer over the course of a lifetime devoted to journalism, which depends on a belief in the ability of some of the audience to appreciate at least moderately fine distinctions, and on the educability of the rest of that audience. But yet, one must finally admit that the hope of raising up large numbers of people to a condition where they might participate in a rational politics and a rich cultural life, or even a popular culture where a certain wit, style, and grace are in good supply has visibly receded in the course of that lifetime. Indeed, one begins to feel that if a bill of goods has been sold, its chief purchasers were those of us who went into journalism and the other fields of popular culture with some ideals larger than making a living.

Thomas Berger, the novelist, recently permitted publication of a selection of letters to a friend, and among them we find this statement: *"Hoi polloi* are never affected one way or the other intellectually. Peasants have precisely the same quality of mind as those of the Middle Ages; and the sensibility of workingmen has not changed since the beginning of the Industrial Revolution; laboring fewer hours and earning greater wages has had its physical effects, of course, but worked no change on the brain. The middle classes too are frozen in time and only feint toward degeneration . . ." In short, he seems to argue that the whole grand, uplifting enterprise was foredoomed from the start, and that it has produced an unintended consequence of the most dismaying sort. In the same passage he writes, "A century of mass education has brought about the triumph of illiteracy—the most sinister and subtle kind, affecting the intelligentsia." The members of this class, he notes, are "thoroughly polluted and faithlessly go through their impotent rituals, the eunuchs of sociology and psychiatry, slaves to spite and envy." He may overstate the case somewhat, but as a novelist of enormous distinction who has been not merely critically undervalued, but underdiscussed, he is entitled to his exaggerations.

One must pause here to make clear that Berger is not talking about politics at all. And neither am I. No intelligent individual is going to back himself into the elitist corner, no matter how despairing his view of recent cultural history and the human possibilities arising out of it. Elites based on birth, race, wealth, worldly accomplishment, even (or should one say especially?) intellectual attainment all run counter to humane impulse and to such political idealism as I once held dear and continue to honor, if only out of nostalgia for a youth not entirely despised. And—it cannot be repeated too often—these elites are always finally based on self-interest and self-righteousness of the most deplorable kind. As a matter of fact, given the crudeness and irrele-

vancy of the choices nowadays laid before the electorate—choices that
always in the end must be between a pair of celebrities mouthing
slogans at one another—it can well be argued that it is a miracle that
most people remain sufficiently intelligent to carry out their modest
duties under the rudimentary and largely symbolic form of self-gov-
ernment we practice.

Still, what Berger is saying and what I am saying is that there is,
there must be, in any society with even a pretense to greatness, an elite
of some sort, and that this elite is vital to its healthy functioning, as
the knowing repository of its highest intellectual and artistic attain-
ments, as the caring (if sometimes misled) sensors of what, in contemporary culture, may be worthy of that great tradition. It is difficult to
define the nature of this aristocracy, though perhaps E. M. Forster did
it as well as anyone when he called it an "aristocracy of the sensitive,
the considerate and the plucky." It is not difficult, however, to define
the sources of the decline that Berger directs us to in all those qualities, to see that the elite he—and I—would defend is scarcely an oppressive elite, but rather the opposite. It is an increasingly oppressed—
and dwindling—one.

These sources are, naturally, to be found in the workings of the
mass culture that we have observed in this book. Combined with the
long-term historical developments we have also traced, they have had
a profoundly debilitating effect on this group. When its members are
not oppressed with a sense of inappropriateness and irrelevancy, a
feeling of weariness and corruption nags at them. And all around
them they see former friends and colleagues succumbing to the blandishments of publicity, turning themselves into symbolic images,
crudely readable distortions of their formerly complex selves. And
even if they do not submit to or conspire in this process, they will see
their ideas journalistically vulgarized in simpleminded volumes of social commentary or in the self-help books now dominating the bestseller charts. For the scholar or artist who resists this process the
withdrawal into more and more arcane subject matter in the case of
the former, the resort to art itself for the subject of art, or to his own
subjective state for it, is an almost irresistible temptation. It may not
be very plucky of them, and little sensitivity to or consideration of
society's needs is implied by this course. But who dares criticize them
in their peaceful and productive avoidance of engagement in this society of ours.

And yet . . . of this "artistocracy" Forster went on to write,

"They represent the true human tradition, the one permanent victory of our queer race over cruelty and chaos." If they desert formerly closed ranks to endorse the baseness of our culture, or fail to resist it, or withdraw into privacy and silence, then that victory, partial as it is, would seem to have been claimed too soon. Forster did not live to see how cruelly the electronically magnified and multiplied image could tyrannize our cultural life, did not see the chaos its wild oversimplifications would sow. But we can see them. Perhaps. If we will.

In praising Diana Trilling's *Mrs. Harris,* a carefully discerning account of a trial that made a celebrity of the woman who murdered her celebrity-lover, Anatole Broyard wrote how impressed he was by the insatiability and ferocity of the author's curiosity, "by her quality of close and sustained attention in our abstracted and inattentive age. It seemed to me that she rescued the esthetic, the moral and the passionate from the trash basket of the legal." He went on to propose, with what degree of irony it is hard to say, "a government of literary critics because I think we no longer know how to read the text of our lives." He ended with agreeable wit by imagining the presidential campaign speech of a critic-candidate: "The unexamined life is not worth living . . . and if I am elected, you will take that examination. You will scrutinize your life and your world until they reveal themselves as pleasure, boredom, rage, and the thousand other shocks that flesh is heir to. You will put on record the vocabulary of your aspirations, the syntax of your sensibility, the metrics of your emotions, the good, bad, or indifferent novel or poem of self. And then we will set to work to revise. And revise. And revise."

We are not meant to take Broyard literally. One cannot imagine a mass movement toward the examined life. And, in any case, the world has ever been unsalvageable. It will go on, or not, full of miracles and injustices and fatuities no matter what we, as individuals, do or do not do. But the serious person who counts himself a member of the sensitive, considerate, and plucky minority—the world's first oppressed elite—will—must—behave as if there is some kind of future for humankind. And that within that larger future there is a future for *his* kind. He has, therefore, a duty not merely to himself but to his particular posterity to offer what resistance he can to the cruelty and chaos fostered by the tyranny of the image. That resistance must begin with a permanent critical posture, an endless series of critical gestures.

The form these acts take must combine some measure of withdrawal with some well-chosen acts of engagement. Withdrawal, as we have seen, is natural for many artists. And no small number of them continue to resist the blandishments of the celebrity life. On receiving the news that he had won the Nobel Prize in 1976, Saul Bellow worried publicly about what would become of him when that emblematic phrase, "Nobel Prize winning author," was hung around his neck along with his medallion. He feared the distracting weight of public responsibilities. "Being a writer," he mused, "is a rather dreamy thing. And nobody likes to have the diaphanous tissue torn. One has to preserve his dream space." Sometime later John Updike expressed a similar feeling in a self-interview: "as a practitioner trying to keep practicing in an age of publicity, I can only decry the drain on the brain, the assumption that a writer is a mass of opinions to be trucked in and carted off for his annual six minutes on the pan-American talk show. He is not; he is a secreter of images . . . as a secreter he must be at heart secret, patient, wicked even. His duty is, in a sense, to turn his back. This is not easy to understand in an era when everybody says 'Have a nice day' and even two o'clock in the morning is lit up by a phosphorescent glow of money going rotten."

May his tribe increase. And may the example of Updike and Bellow extend beyond the scriveners' ranks. We all need "dreaming space." We all need to secrete images of our own devising. And not just of our private and personal concerns. We need to reimagine the world in images that owe nothing to those which are imposed on us by media, which break free of tyrannical limits and conventions of the ready-to-wear metaphors we buy, as it were, off the peg. Human possibility, we must remind ourselves, extends far beyond those that the celebrated faces imply by their presence, sell more openly with their endorsements, commercial and political.

Imagination of the kind I'm suggesting partakes of many modes, but among them, surely, is the one that Broyard proposed—the critical. If we wish to take our place among a worthwhile elite we must blend our passive, probably instinctive impulse to withdraw, with the more active and rational refusals that criticism often (but not exclusively) entails. We must, for example, penetrate the convention of reportorial objectivity with which the already distorted imagery, celebrity and otherwise, is blandly presented. We must learn anew to read everything critically—the printed page, of course, but also the ideograms of television and film. And we must not confine this effort merely to criticism's traditional realm, which is art. We need to read the front page and the sports page, the editorial page, the style page and (above all) the TV listings with similarly wary alertness.

I am not calling for cynicism. Work of quality proceeds in the popular arts as well as in the higher ones. It cannot be otherwise, given the energy and resources our society pours into the former. And it is essential that one be on the lookout for the good thing that grows on tainted ground. Nor am I calling for puritanical naysaying. "Pleasure," as W. H. Auden once remarked, "is by no means an infallible critical guide, but it is the least fallible." We must give in to it, and we can, with a greater sense of its worth (and our own), when we look at everything with a cocked critical eye, with a spirit that is wry and civilized and slow to anger, but is finally, fully capable of anger—the latter quality being especially necessary nowadays, when we are in constant danger of being stepped all over by our bullying public life, with its endless and neurotic need for our acquiescence in its many mad schemes.

We have spoken of many strange and disparate things in this book, but in the end, and most basically, what we are talking about is language—the way it has been corrupted and, now, what we might do to defend it. Thomas Berger: "Mass communications are the killers of eloquent speech—as mass religions are deicides." W. H. Auden: "There is one evil that concerns literature which should never be passed over in silence but be continually publicly attacked, and that is corruption of the language, for writers cannot invent their own language and are dependent upon the language they inherit so that, if it be corrupt, they must be corrupted. But the critic who concerns himself with this evil must attack it at its source, which is not in works of literature, but in the misuse of language by the man-in-the-street, journalists, politicians, etc. Futhermore, he must be able to practice what he preaches."

What I have been trying to do in this book is to extend that thought, to suggest that in our time the definition of language must be stretched to include visual as well as verbal symbolizations of thought. And to suggest that this development has given to those forces that traditionally have an interest in corrupting us by corrupting language, new and astonishingly powerful weapons with which to coercively diminish our capacity for making fine distinctions. In this situation the defenders of our language need reinforcement, the professional critics can no longer do the job alone.

I do not believe the forces of corruption can be turned back, I do not believe the mass of men can be reclaimed from them. But I do believe in resistance to them, partly because resistance is exemplary, and may, therefore, comfort some lonely and afflicted soul, stiffen his spine in some trial of the spirit; partly because it may bring in a surprise recruit here and there; partly because it is morally bracing and therefore pleasurable to the degree that it makes one feel good about oneself. But mostly I believe in resistance because I think the very plucky can continue to hold out now as they always have, preserving in their secret encampments the essence of a decent civilization, the unrealized, doubtless unrealizable (because it is entirely imaginary), ideal of a good society which is, finally, the last, the best defense not only against impositions and exactions of tyranny as it has been traditionally defined, but against our new tyranny of the image. We cannot redeem the world. But we can, we unhappy few, redeem ourselves. If we cannot say no in thunder we can at least whisper subversion among ourselves.